ETHICS AND SOCIETY

ETHICS AND
SOCIETY

AN APPRAISAL OF SOCIAL IDEALS

MELVIN RADER

Professor of Philosophy, University of Washington

GREENWOOD PRESS, PUBLISHERS
NEW YORK   1968

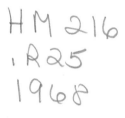

First Greenwood Reprinting, 1968

LIBRARY OF CONGRESS catalogue card number: 68-56040

Printed in the United States of America

TO VIRGINIA

PREFACE

THIS BOOK is a discussion of the meaning of a good society. It considers the nature of social well-being and well-doing, and critically examines such rival social ideals as liberalism and communism. It is written, not for the recondite scholar but for the student and the general reader. The specialists supply us with indispensable knowledge, but unless our ideals are sound, this knowledge will be misapplied.

Science and technology may be either blessings or abominations: they may be used either for good or ill. Knowledge of drugs may be used to heal the sick or to poison one's enemies; military art may be used for legitimate defense or ruthless conquest; economics can be used to swindle or to aid; education may inculcate base ideals or true wisdom. Hence, it is very important to choose the proper goal. As Francis Bacon remarked: "The lame man who keeps the right road outstrips the runner who takes the wrong one. Nay, it is obvious that when a man runs the wrong way, the more active and swift he is the further he will go astray."[1] A society, like a runner headed in the wrong direction, may be efficient and yet damned. Hitler provided the most vivid illustration of this contention. With the technical resources of a highly civilized ruler but with the moral impulses of a barbarian, he was able to wreak havoc beyond the wildest ambi-

[1] *Novum Organum*, in *Works*, Houghton, Mifflin, Boston, no date, p. 89.

vii

tions of an Attila. Hell may be paved with good intentions, but it is also paved with science and techniques. Was it not to *know* more that Faust answered the devil's call?

I do not decry knowledge, but only the absence of valid purpose. Knowledge without purpose is not sufficient. If we are to live good lives in a good social order, we must go back to fundamental ethical questions. What is the essential value of human life? What is the nature of the good society? What is right social action? What is the essence of civilization? Unless we can find reasonable answers to these questions, we shall fritter away our energies in senseless, inconsistent, whimsical strivings until disaster overtakes us. This book tries to answer these questions and, by so doing, to clarify the ideals that can guide us in an uncertain world.

I have written in the conviction that the world has great need of the philosophical spirit—of the will to see things whole, critically and dispassionately, and to act accordingly. If there is nothing but revolutionary fervor or reactionary opposition without broad vision, the future will be quite needlessly cruel. The philosophical consideration of social ideals should, therefore, contribute to a more humane and rational world.

This book is a study of the ethics of social reconstruction As such, it is part fulfillment of a grant-in-aid from the Rockefeller Foundation for work on the subject of "Crisis and Reconstruction." I hope eventually to publish a sequel on the meaning of social crisis and the ideal of community as the basis of reconstruction. I am deeply grateful to the Foundation for funds which permitted months of concentrated work without the necessity of teaching.

It would be impossible to make the many acknowledgments to the men and books that have inspired me. I am especially indebted to my former teacher and colleague, the late William Savery, whose course in Social Ethics, which I took as a freshman, moved and excited me as no other course has ever done. My friends and colleagues, Arthur Smullyan, A. I. Melden, and

PREFACE   ix

Brents Stirling, and my wife, Virginia Rader, have made very
helpful criticisms. The editors of the *Journal of Philosophy*,
the *Antioch Review*, the *Kenyon Review*, and *Interim* have
kindly given me permission to reprint portions of articles
which I have contributed. Helen Lea and Dorothy Smullyan
have capably typed the manuscript. I heartily thank all who
have aided.

Seattle, Washington   M. R.
February 15, 1950

CONTENTS

Conclusion

ETHICS AND SOCIETY

Part One

THE ETHICS OF LAWS

INTRODUCTION TO PART ONE

IN THIS BOOK, we shall try to answer two great questions: What is right social action? and What is a good social order? These are questions of social ethics. By ethics I mean the theory of good and bad, right and wrong; and by social ethics, I mean this theory applied to any group or society.

Ethics, whether individual or social, may be divided in terms of the *standard* for the evaluation of action. The two main standards are ideal and law. According to the first standard, an action is right if it promotes an ideal; according to the second, an action is right if it conforms to a law. I am using *law* in a broad sense to include rule, prescription, or command.

The ethics of ideals maintains that an action is right if it brings about the ideal; and the ideal is that which is ultimately good. Thus right action is the useful in the sense of causing good. Professor George E. Moore states the point of view of this type of ethics very clearly:

To ask what kind of action we ought to perform, or what kind of conduct is right, is to ask what kind of effects such action and conduct will produce. . . . What I wish first to point out is that "right" does and can mean nothing but "cause of a good result," and is thus always identical with "useful." . . . Our "duty," therefore, can only be defined as that action, which will cause more good to exist in the Universe than any possible alternative.[1]

[1] *Principia Ethica*, Cambridge University Press, Cambridge, 1922, pp. 146-148.

3

According to this point of view, morality is the effectuating of purposes—it is action to realize an end—and the ethical problem is to find out the nature of ultimate goodness and the means of its attainment. Well-doing is the promotion of well-being.

Such an ethics will be subdivided in accordance with various conceptions of well-being. Hedonistic ethics maintains that good is pleasure; voluntaristic ethics maintains that the good is the satisfaction of desire; intellectualistic ethics maintains that the good is wisdom; etc. But all of these varieties agree that right action promotes goodness or diminishes evil. This type of ethics we shall call "teleological" or, in the wide sense of the word, *utilitarian*.

The second main type of ethics accepts moral law as its standard. It maintains that the nature of right is set forth in a law or rule or decree. The law is supposedly self-evident or derived from some authoritative and unchallengeable source. It is accepted as ultimate; there is no attempt to penetrate behind it to determine whether it is useful or conducive to welfare. The law declares what is right, and one ought to do what is right irrespective of consequences. The essence of this point of view is stated by Immanuel Kant (1724-1804) as follows:

Duty is the obligation to act from reverence for law. . . . The supreme good which we call moral can therefore be nothing but the idea of the law in itself, in so far as it is this idea which determines the will, and not any consequences that are expected to follow.[2]

Ethics of this type can be subdivided according to the supposed source of moral laws. Customary or legalistic ethics is based upon the laws of society; theological ethics is based upon the laws of God; naturalistic ethics is based upon the laws of nature; intuitional or rationalistic ethics is based

[2] *Fundamental Principles of the Metaphysics of Morals*, translated by John Watson, in Gordon H. Clark and T. V. Smith, *Readings in Ethics*, Crofts, New York, 1935, pp. 260-261.

upon the laws of the mind. Ethics of this general type, including all these varieties, I shall call "nonteleological" or "formalistic."

I am using the term *formalistic* in a wider sense than ordinary. Most writers on ethics confine it to the type of rationalistic ethics that we find in the philosophy of Kant: an ethics based upon universal rules supposedly validated by pure reason. According to my terminology, this type is only one of the varieties of "formalistic ethics." As I am employing the term, *formalism* is the doctrine that the moral quality of acts depends upon conformity to laws or rules of action; and the varieties of formalism are distinguished from one another in accordance with the varying sources of these moral rules. Theories of this type are "nonteleological"; but this is merely a negative denomination, whereas the term *formalistic* serves to indicate the positive characteristic of these theories, namely, their strict adherence to or observance of prescribed "forms"—the forms being, in this case, moral laws or rules.

These two main types, the teleological and the formalistic, mingle in the minds of most people. Even those who cling most tenaciously to moral law probably permit themselves, in a hesitating, uncertain, guilty way, some small infractions to secure philanthropic or expedient results. Likewise even those who are most intent upon the realization of an ideal lapse at times into conformity, accepting without question some moral rule or law.

In Part One we shall expound and criticize formalistic ethics and contrast it with teleological ethics. In so doing, we shall gain insight into both types. Our discussion will stress the *social* implications of these rival ethical views.

Chapter One

THE LAWS OF SOCIETY

1. *The Morality of Custom*

IN THIS CHAPTER we shall consider the doctrine that moral standards consist of authoritative prescriptions, in the form either of custom or positive law, imposed by society upon the individual. According to this doctrine, a man's duty is not to decide for himself what is right but to obey the rules laid down by society.

The initial expression of this point of view is to be found in the morality of custom. A custom is a long-continued usage that has become established by social habit and tradition and has acquired the force of law. Customary morality results whenever moral judgments are based on customs. Such morality is strictly formalistic in so far as the customs are accepted unreflectively and unconditionally.

The absolute, formal character of customs or folkways is made clear in the classic account by William Graham Sumner of primitive life:

> The folkways are the "right" ways to satisfy all interests, because they are traditional, and exist in fact. They extend over the whole of life. There is the right way to catch game, to win a wife, to make one's self appear, to cure disease, to honor ghosts, to treat comrades or strangers, to behave when a child is born, on the warpath, in council, and so on in all cases which can arise. The ways are defined on the negative side, that is, by taboos. The "right" way is the way which the ancestors used and which has been handed down. The tradition is its own warrant. It is not held subject to verification by experience. The notion of right is

in the folkways. It is not outside of them, of independent origin
and brought to them to test them. In the folkways, whatever is,
is right. This is because they are traditional. When we come to
the folkways we are at the end of our analysis.[1]

We might raise the question whether morality ever does
function at this level of quite unreflective acceptance of custom.
Franz Boas, Bronislaw Malinowski, and other anthropologists
have demonstrated that primitive people often reflect and
deviate from custom, but a relative distinction between customary and reflective morality still holds. Among reflective
persons, moral choice is determined with considerable fre-
quency by independent critical judgment. But among those
who are dominated by custom, there is comparatively little
reflection. Agreement is sound and respectable; dissent is considered a fault or even a kind of depravity.

In this relative sense, customary morality exists to a certain extent in all periods and in all countries. We merely
have to open our eyes to discover individuals who are moving
in grooves that they have done nothing to fashion. No doubt
these people if pressed will supply reasons for their beliefs;
but in this very act their thinking will be controlled by
habitual prejudices or uncriticized assumptions.

In its more naïve forms, the morality of custom is easy to
criticize. Almost no one today would maintain that custom
should *always* be followed or that it should be regarded as
moral merely because it is custom. Few people are prepared
to admit that "cannibalism is moral in a cannibal country."[2]
In primitive cultures, there are examples of shocking customs, such as refraining from washing, burning widows, eating one's parents, and sacrificing one's first-born. In modern
civilized countries, there are sometimes very harmful customs,
such as the retributive practices of warfare, the cruel subjection of women to men, the maltreatment of Negroes, and the

---

1 *Folkways*, Ginn, Boston, 1906, p. 28.
2 *The Notebooks of Samuel Butler*, Dutton, New York, 1907, p. 29.

cruel acquisitiveness of capitalism in its more predatory aspects. If custom is always right, none of these abuses, so long as it is customary, can be challenged. We need scarcely refute so naïve a view.

What must give us pause, however, is that men of sophistication and genius sometimes defend the morality of custom. Such men as Hegel and Savigny in Germany, Taine and Renan in France, and Burke and Maine in England have been deeply impressed by the values of custom. To see what can be said in its defense, we cannot do better than to turn to the eloquent pages of Burke.

2. Burke's Defense of Custom and Tradition

EDMUND BURKE (1729-1797), political theorist and a leader of the Whig party in the British Parliament, is famous not only for his valiant support of the cause of freedom in Ireland, India, and America but for his passionate defense of tradition against the terrific onslaught of the French Revolution. His *Reflections on the Revolution in France* (1790) and his later writings on the same subject constitute some of the most powerful and influential pamphlets ever composed.

Just as the specter of Communist Revolution has haunted our generation, so the specter of the French Revolution haunted his. From the beginning, he sensed in this Revolution something far more significant than a mere fracas in French internal affairs. He saw it as a great crisis not only in the life and culture of all Europe but of civilization itself. He believed that all traditional values were jeopardized by "this strange chaos of levity and ferocity."[3] With all the stunning power of his eloquence, he depicted the horrors and terrors of the Revolution in words that strongly remind

[3] Edmund Burke, *Reflections on the French Revolution and Other Essays*, Dutton, New York, 1910, p. 98.

us of the outcries of Winston Churchill and other conservatives in our own age of crisis.

Like so many of our leaders today, Burke sought protection
in the traditional values of his nation and his class. Amid the
tide of change, he wished to tie the British nation to the
secure anchorage of immemorial customs and prescriptive
rights. He maintained that custom and tradition represent the
accumulated, tested experience of many generations, the fundamental heritage of a people. Because of the continuity of
customary ways and institutions, as embodied in the state,
society "becomes a partnership not only between those who
are living, but between those who are living, those who are
dead, and those who are to be born."[4] This binding nexus of
use and wont, the creation of many minds in many ages, is a
safer repository of wisdom than the giddy, inconstant, un-
guided thoughts of isolated individuals. It is safer not only
for morality but for political choice and governmental policy.

It is a presumption in favor of any settled scheme of government against any untried project, that a nation has long existed
and flourished under it. It is a better presumption even of the
choice of a nation,—far better than any sudden and temporary
arrangement by actual election. Because a nation is not an idea
only of local extent, and individual momentary aggregation, but
it is an idea of continuity, which extends in time as well as in
numbers and in space. And this is a choice not of one day, or
one set of people, not a tumultuary and giddy choice; it is a
deliberate election of ages and of generations; it is a constitution made by what is ten thousand times better than choice,
it is made by the peculiar circumstances, occasions, tempers, dispositions, and moral, civil, and social habitudes of the people,
which disclose themselves only in a long space of time. . . . The
individual is foolish; the multitude, for the moment, is foolish,
when they act without deliberation; but the species is wise, and,
when time is given to it, as a species, it almost always acts right.[5]

4 *Ibid.*, p. 93.
5 Speech in the House of Commons, May 7, 1782, in *Works*, Little, Brown,
Boston, 1894, VII, pp. 94-95.

Hasty, ill-considered action, Burke believed, is less frequent in a society where custom and tradition hold sway. The patterns of personality are more tightly woven and do not readily disintegrate into immorality. Crime and foolish experiment are prevented by even, uniform, and consistent public opinion, the pressure of which is multiplied by an endless number of intimate contacts. It is much safer to trust to the institutions of our forefathers than to rely upon a revolutionary passion for innovation.

By this unprincipled facility of changing the state as often, and as much, and in as many ways, as there are floating fancies or fashions, the whole chain and continuity of the commonwealth would be broken. No one generation could link with the other. Men would be little better than the flies of a summer.[6]

The value of the individual human life, Burke contended, depends upon identification with the wider life of the community as embodied in its customs and traditions. Each individual thereby unites his mind with the minds of his fellows and in doing so gains a precious bounty of sympathy and support. He thinks in terms of "We," not in terms of "I," and thus escapes from the pettiness of his own nature. His mind becomes enriched by a continuing tradition of sentiments, associations, and loyal attachments; his whole being becomes permeated with the organic life of the neighborhood, the province, and the nation. Doubts and uncertainties are cleared away by the unison of many minds. Without this social consensus, the individual is but a frail reed.

We are afraid to put men to live and trade each on his own private stock of reason; because we suspect that this stock in each man is small, and that the individuals would do better to avail themselves of the general bank and capital of nations and of ages.[7]

Such, in brief summary, was the tenor of Burke's defense

6 Burke, *Reflections on the French Revolution, op. cit.,* p. 92.
7 *Ibid.,* p. 84.

of customary ways and institutions, and such likewise, to some extent, is the mood of conservatives in our own age.

3. *The Dangers of Custom in an Age of Rapid Transition*

THE OPPOSING MOOD is best expressed in Thomas Paine's fiery pamphlet, *The Rights of Man,* which was written as an answer to Burke. It is not to the immemorial past that Paine appeals but to the burning needs and exigencies of the present.

Every generation must be free to act for itself *in all cases* as the ages and generations which preceded it. The vanity and presumption of governing beyond the grave is the most ridiculous and insolent of all tyrannies. . . . Every generation is, and must be, competent to all the purposes which its occasions require. It is the living, and not the dead, that are to be accommodated.[8]

Each new generation has its own problems, its own resources, its own unprecedented crises. If custom that arose on other occasions and fitted other conditions persists despite these changes, the result is what sociologists call "cultural lag." This lag may become extremely serious if the society in certain respects changes both rapidly and fundamentally. The circumstances of life in the last seventy-five years, for example, have changed stupendously. It has been said "that there has been a greater spiritual change between the world of 1870 and the world of today than between the Middle Ages and the Mid-Victorianism of that date."[9] The rapidity of change seems to be increasing in a geometric ratio, especially in our new "Atomic Age," and traditional forms of thought have not been able to adapt themselves to these radical transforma-

8 In *Writings,* edited by Moncure D. Conway, Putnam's, New York, 1894-1896, p. 278.
9 John H. Muirhead, "Why Everybody Needs a Philosophy," in *The New World,* edited by Harold Bruce and Guy Montgomery, Macmillan, New York, 1927, p. 548.

tions. The consequence is that moral custom has not been exerted against the really telling sins of modern society, such as the overcapitalization of industry, the renting of unhygienic tenements, the sweating of labor, the maintenance of factory conditions injurious to health, the manufacture and sale of fraudulent patent medicines, the incitement to war by a jingoistic press. Customary morality is decisive when it condemns petty personal crimes of a traditional sort, but when crime is novel in form and social in character it is unprepared and undecisive. It is even less prepared to work out the reconstruction so loudly demanded by present maladjustments. We can look only to reflection, and to bold social initiative, for example, to bring the rampant forces of science and technology under responsible international control.

The plain fact is that we are living amid a vast tide of change, and there is a very urgent need to adjust certain of our traditional institutions such as the absolute nation-state to the swift dynamic growth of modern technology. Despite his conservatism, Burke realized that there are periods in human history when such fundamental alteration is a necessity. He pointed out that it is folly in these circumstances to oppose it.

If a great change is to be made in human affairs, the minds of men will be fitted to it, the general opinions and feelings will draw that way. Every fear, every hope, will forward it; and then they who persist in opposing this mighty current in human affairs will appear rather to resist the decrees of Providence itself than the mere designs of men. They will not be resolute and firm, but perverse and obstinate.[10]

Blind to the imperatives of their age, the men who made "peace" after World War I failed to heed the wisdom of these profound remarks. Their slogan was "Back to Normalcy." Overinfatuated with the past, they did not comprehend that great new forces had been loosed upon the world. The best

10 "Thoughts on French Affairs," in *Reflections on the French Revolution and Other Essays, op. cit.,* p. 330.

comment upon both their opportunity and their failure is to be found in T. E. Lawrence's account of the intense idealism of youth during World War I and the bitter disappointment of its aftermath.

The morning freshness of the world-to-be intoxicated us. We were wrought up with ideas inexpressible and vaporous, but to be fought for. We lived many lives in those whirling campaigns, never sparing ourselves: yet when we achieved and the new world dawned, the old men came out again and took from us our victory, and remade it in the likeness of the former world they knew. Youth could win, but had not learned to keep: and was pitiably weak against age. We stammered that we had worked for a new heaven and a new earth, and they thanked us kindly and made their peace.[11]

These blind old men, in making their "peace," could not hold back the tide of change, but they made the transition vastly more bloody and wasteful than it would otherwise have been. Because of their failure mankind had to endure the awful ordeals of economic collapse, fascism, and a second world war. It is more imperative than ever that the old men should not once again take over and try vainly, but with terrible cost, to restore the world to the old forms. Now as never before we need the courage of the morning. Mindful of the great traditions of the past, but never enslaved to them, we must renew the world from its foundations, so that "nation shall not lift up a sword against nation."[12]

4. The Limitations of Custom in Normal Times

EVEN WHEN critical reflection is less essential than at present, men should be aware of the necessity of it and the disadvantages of customary morality. What is needed, even in quite normal times, is not the rigidity of undeviating adher-

11 *Oriental Assembly,* Dutton, New York, 1940, pp. 142-143.
12 Isaiah 2:4 (King James' translation) .

ence to custom but a dynamic adaptation of the individual to his environment. When two individuals differ greatly in personality the same adaptation will not serve for both. As the poet Blake said, "One law for the lion and the ox is oppression."[13] A single invariant code for the weak and the strong, the healthy and the neurotic, the practical man and the artist, the introvert and the extrovert, the emotionalist and the intellectualist, the mystic and the man about town, is not well designed to secure the happy release of energies and the accommodation to basic differences. We cannot reduce everybody to a least common denominator without violating the sanctity of personality. In a primitive culture, where thought and action remain very homogeneous, the violence dealt to individuality by custom may not be very serious; in an advanced culture, where a great deal of differentiation has emerged, the harm of an inflexible code is extreme—as it was for example in the case of Jude the Obscure and Tess of the D'Urbervilles in Thomas Hardy's novels.

The "cake of custom" must be broken if a society is to be progressive. It is only when individuals diverge from a single peremptory pattern of custom that they can critically reflect upon their differences. If my friend Jones is different from me I am impelled to ask, is he better or worse? If he is exactly like me I ask nothing, I remain thoughtless. In case he is superior, he will tend to display his pre-eminence and thus to establish a model to pattern after. But others need not necessarily choose between him and me—they may combine our values and thus achieve a synthesis that will include what is good in both of our lives. Difference between personalities is the indispensable precondition of such a synthesis. When a great many people are originative, there is a wealth of material to be fused and organized into new and more adequate patterns. In so far as custom represses the rich ferment of contrasting individualities, it makes impossible

[13] "The Marriage of Heaven and Hell," in *Poetry and Prose of William Blake*, Random House, New York, 1927, p. 203

the open, spontaneous society that has a real capacity for growth and improvement. While admitting many of the values of tradition that Burke emphasizes, we must insist that the interaction of diverse, creative individuals is the prime condition of any higher culture. Without it, the artist dies, the thinker is shackled, and all that makes for greatness shrivels in the level desert of mediocrity.

The strong emotional re-enforcement, such as the feeling of "taboo," that backs up customary morality is frequently an obstacle to scientific or critical reflection. The traditional attitudes toward sex and religion, for example, have been intensely emotionalized; consequently a great deal of prejudice and irrationalism have characterized thought about these matters. I would not for a moment suggest that we can dispense with feeling in the moral life, but it should be feeling that harmonizes with intelligence. Feeling that is customary is often a dangerous hurdle in the way of a reasonable solution of life's problems.

Morality must grow if it is to keep pace with the advances in knowledge, but it cannot grow if it is forever constricted to the narrow limits of the past, if it is not adventurous, pliable, keenly aware of new horizons.

5. *The Ethical Basis of Positive Law*

IF WE TURN from custom to positive law, similar considerations of human welfare apply. By *positive law*, as opposed to mere custom, we mean a body of rules, drawn either from precedent or statute, according to which courts or magistrates as judicial organs decide cases.

We can distinguish between a formalistic and a teleological interpretation of law. On the whole, the more formalistic point of view tends to prevail. Judges and lawyers rarely acknowledge that social expediency or welfare is the proper ground for law. The "legalistic" type of mind is retrospective in habit; it looks to the past rather than to the future; it depends upon laws made, precedents set, legitimacies established. It seldom admits that the law should be remolded or set aside in the interests of social well-being.

Almost every conceivable interpretation of law has been advanced at some time or other, and most of these interpretations try to explain and justify law in some formalistic manner. Among these interpretations are the following: that law is a gift of God and is sanctioned by His divine decree; that it is the teaching of ancient wise men whose authority is not to be challenged; that it is a reflection of natural laws which provide the norms for all legislation and judicial interpretation; that it is the result of a social contract to which all citizens at some time have agreed and which is therefore binding with all the sanctity of a formal promise; that it is the embodiment of immemorial custom or the expression of the spirit of a people or of an age; that it is an instrument of social solidarity whereby a society achieves cohesion; that it is a means of social domination whereby a ruling class legalizes and perpetuates its power; that it is the embodiment of the intuitive truths of conscience; that it is the affirmation of the immutable principles of abstract deductive reason; that it is a self-contained, self-justifying body of statutes and precedents to be tested and interpreted exclusively in terms of juristic premises and inner logical consistency.

Most of these interpretations are more or less valid as *descriptions* of the law. It is true, for example, that law is sometimes the result of deliberate contractual agreement; that it may embody custom or express the spirit of a people or of an age; that it usually intensifies social solidarity; that it very frequently expresses the interests of a dominant economic class; that it may be influenced by intuitive ethics or abstract deductive reasoning; and that it tends to become a separate, independent discipline governed by its own internal rules. But these interpretations are invalid if they are intended not as partial descriptions of what law is but as standards of what law ought to be. The only valid standard of law is its success in promoting the good life.

This fact is widely acknowledged when law is being enacted. "Nearly all legislation," Mr. Justice Brandeis has declared, "involves a weighing of public needs as against private desires; and likewise a weighing of relative social values."[14] Most people would grant that when private desires triumph over public needs which represent the greater good, there has been an abuse of legislative power. But the attitude toward the judicial interpretation of the law is different. Rarely do writers on jurisprudence explicitly acknowledge that the only real justification of law is its efficacy in promoting human welfare.

Felix S. Cohen, who is both a philosopher and an attorney-at-law, has ably advanced this latter view.

Ethics is the study of the meaning and application of judgments of *good, bad, right, wrong,* etc., and every final valuation of law involves an ethical judgment. When we say, for instance, that a given law is bad, that one judicial decision is better than another, that the American constitution ought to be revised, or that laws ought to be obeyed, we are passing judgments whose truth or falsity cannot be established without a consideration of ethics. There is no way of avoiding this ultimate responsibility of law to ethics. . . . Every final determination of the general end of law . . . must reduce to the general form, "The law ought to bring about as much good as it can."[15]

It is impossible to deny the cogency of these remarks. The law is made for man, not man for the law. There are good laws and bad laws, wise laws and foolish laws; and it makes a great deal of difference what kind of laws we have. Whenever the general welfare can be advanced by altering or abolishing the law, it should be altered or abolished. The Declaration of Independence, in ringing sentences, affirms this great truth.

14 The Opinion of Mr. Justice Brandeis in the case of Truax *v.* Corrigan before the United States Supreme Court (1921), 257 U. S. 312, p. 357.
15 *Ethical Systems and Legal Ideals,* Falcon Press, New York, 1933, p. 7.

I would not deny for a moment that there are generally excellent reasons for respecting and maintaining the law. The rule of law is necessary, especially in a complex society, if criminals are to be restrained and anarchy is to be avoided. Legal order is the only substitute for private war, and even irrational rules are ordinarily better than no rules at all. Law also provides a necessary protection against the fallibility and abuse of power among the rulers of the state. Even the judicial following of precedent is a reasonable safeguard against individual whimsy and unpredictable miscarriages of justice. As Aristotle points out, law is a necessary safeguard against the subjectivism and irrationalism that eschews fixed precedents and depends upon the momentary decree.

He who bids the law rule, may be deemed to bid God and reason alone rule, but he who bids man rule adds an element of the beast; for desire is a wild beast, and passion perverts the minds of rulers, even when they are the best of men. The law is reason unaffected by desire.[16]

Nevertheless, law is to be tested in terms of its benefits and to be respected only when it is, on the whole, good in its effects. Precedents should not be followed nor statutes maintained if the total effect is to injure the public weal or the parties involved. Clear recognition of this fact, not only by the public but by lawyers and judges, would avoid a great deal of legalistic obscurantism and lend a progressive spirit to the law.

The effect of such recognition is illustrated by the famous Nuremberg trials of Nazi war criminals. The defense pleaded, in the traditional manner, that the charges were not based upon legal precedents and were therefore not valid; but the judges decided that welfare, not legal precedent, should be the paramount consideration. Mr. Justice Jackson, who acted as chief prosecutor, pointed out that the only hope of the accused was "that International Law will lag so far behind the moral sense of mankind that conduct which is crime in

16 *Politics,* Jowett's translation, Clarendon Press, Oxford, 1921, 1287, a.

the moral sense must be regarded as innocent in law." Against
this position, he argued that law must be remolded when it
fails to correspond to the best moral insight of society.

I cannot subscribe to the perverted reasoning that society may
advance and strengthen the rule of law by the expenditure of
morally innocent lives but that progress in the law may never be
made at the price of morally guilty lives. . . . It grows, as did the
Common Law, through decisions reached from time to time in
adapting settled principles to new situations. . . . It advances at
the expense of those who wrongly guessed the law and learned
too late their error.[17]

The concern for human welfare that inspires these utterances is essentially sound. Custom for the sake of custom, or
law for the sake of law, is never an adequate basis for social
policy. Each is to be justified or condemned by its fruits; each
must meet the test of critical reflection.

Long before the birth of Christ, the Buddha indicated the
nature of such reflection. He rejected the appeal to custom,
authority, superficial sense impressions, and abstract deductive reasoning and insisted instead upon careful observation
and reflection with a view to weal and woe:

It is proper and very natural that doubts should arise in you;
blind belief is to be rejected. Do not judge by hearsay, nor by
tradition, nor on mere assertion, nor on the authority of so-called
sacred writings, nor by logical deductions, nor by methodological
derivation, nor by the mere evidence of the senses, nor by long-
accustomed opinions and conceptions; do not judge according to
appearances, nor believe anything because an ascetic or teacher
has said it. But when you yourselves perceive: "these things are
wrong, these things are objectionable, these things when done
produce woe and suffering for us and others," then reject them.
But when you perceive: "these things are right, these things are
unobjectionable, these things when done produce weal and happiness for us and others," then adopt them and act accordingly.[18]

17 Quoted by T. V. Smith, *Constructive Ethics*, Appleton-Century-Crofts,
New York, 1948, p. 11.
18 C. T. Strauss, *The Buddha and His Doctrine*, Rider, London, 1923, p. 101.

Chapter Two

THE LAWS OF GOD

1. *God as Moral Lawgiver*

IN THE SPONTANEOUS EFFORT to invest moral customs and laws with an awesome authority, ancient civilizations have conceived these customs and laws as godgiven and enforced by a divine concern. It will be instructive to glance at a few examples.

The oldest written code of law known to historians until recently is that promulgated by Hammurabi, King of Babylon, in 1955-1913 B.C. On a great pillar of black diorite, almost eight feet high, a code setting forth the moral and legal concepts of Babylon is inscribed. Carved into the same rock is a representation of the king receiving his laws from the seated figure of Shamas, the sun god, "the judge of heaven and earth."

Similar representations are to be found in other ancient civilizations. In the Old Testament, for example, we have the stories of God's command to Adam, his covenant with Abraham, and his dictation to Moses of the Ten Commandments. The Book of Manu (*circa* 250 B.C.), an authoritative source of moral law for Hindus, is declared to be an emanation from the Supreme God. The moral teachings of Islam are likewise represented as a direct revelation from God, communicated word for word to Mohammed by the Angel Gabriel. The opening passage of Plato's dialogue, *The Laws,* reads as follows:

Athenian Stranger. Tell me, Strangers, is a God or some man supposed to be the author of your laws?

Cleinias. A God, Stranger; in very truth a God: among us Cretans he is said to have been Zeus, but in Lacedaemon, whence our friend here comes, I believe they would say that Apollo is their lawgiver: would they not, Megillus?

Megillus. Certainly.[1]

Such illustrations could be multiplied.

The laws or commandments thus "God-given" are held to be sacred and enforced by divine decree. According to the purely formalistic interpretation, these divine laws are right simply because God commands them. The opposing point of view is that the right is not established by God's arbitrary decree and that it has an independent nature.

The issue involved in this clash of opinion is set forth clearly in Plato's *Euthyphro*. As portrayed in this dialogue, a soothsayer named Euthyphro, impelled by his sense of religious duty, has come to the Athenian hall of justice to file a charge of murder against his father who through cruel negligence has caused the death of a slave. He happens to meet Socrates, who has come to the hall to respond to the charge of "introducing false divinities and corrupting the youth," for which "crime" he will ultimately be sentenced to drink the hemlock.

Socrates, as is his habit, soon draws Euthyphro into philosophical conversation. Upon being questioned, the latter explains that he considers the killing of the slave a religious offense, and that he is actuated by piety in bringing the charge of murder against his father. He is asked to explain what he means by piety, and very soon as a result of Socrates' searching questions, a basic issue is formulated: Is an act right because it is commanded by the gods, or is it commanded by the gods because it is right? The former alternative is embraced by Euthyphro, who asserts that "piety is that which is dear to the gods, and impiety is that which is not dear to them."[2] Throughout the entire discussion, Eu-

[1] In *The Dialogues of Plato,* translated by Benjamin Jowett, Oxford University Press, London, 1924, V, p. 1.

[2] *Ibid.,* II, p. 80.

thyphro never argues on the ground of humanitarianism or utility. His position is that certain acts, being disapproved by the gods, are sacrilegious, and certain other acts, being approved by the gods, are holy. Although he later modifies this position, he is unable to advance clearly and unequivocally beyond a formalistic conception of religious ethics.

The criticism of Socrates calls into question this entire approach. He points out that Euthyphro's definition of the pious act as an act approved by the gods is a purely externalistic characterization. It tells us nothing about the *essence* of the act—the quality that excites the gods' approval. Socrates implies that there must be something about the act itself that makes it right—that the gods are on the side of the right because it *is* right, not that it is right because they are on that side.

In the centuries that have elapsed since this dialogue was written, a great many people have in effect agreed with Euthyphro that right depends upon arbitrary divine will. So influential was this theory in the Middle Ages that St. Thomas Aquinas took especial care to combat it; and yet it bobbed up again after the death of Aquinas in a number of late medieval philosophers. Many subsequent thinkers maintain that right depends upon the arbitrary will of God, that obedience to God's law is a virtue and disobedience a vice, and that morality is enforced by divine rewards and punishments, either on this earth or in heaven and hell.

One of the simplest and clearest statements of such a formalistic theory is to be found in the *Principles of Moral and Political Philosophy* by William Paley, an eighteenth-century English divine, whose ideas were immensely popular. "Right," he declares, "means no more than conformity to the rule we go by, whatever that rule be." He then goes on to state that God's will must be our rule, and that "right therefore signifies consistency with the will of God," which can be discovered either through God's revelation, the Holy

Scriptures, or by "the light of nature."[3] The latter consists in inferring God's will from an examination of his "works," namely, the created world including man and other animals. Paley believes that it is possible to show by such inferences that God intends the happiness of mankind and that therefore action that promotes this happiness is in accordance with God's will. At this point in his argument an ambiguity creeps in. His definition of right as that which agrees with God's will is purely formalistic; but there is at least the suggestion that happiness is intrinsically good, and that an act may be right because it promotes this good. The moral law, it is stated, is of divine origin; but this law, it is implied, may not be entirely arbitrary and purposeless and contrary to human nature.

The political and social applications of religious formalism are illustrated by the ideas and practices of John Calvin (1509-1564), a French Protestant, who in time became the political and religious dictator of the city of Geneva and a very powerful influence in the development of modern thought. According to his point of view, any good government is a theocracy; God is the personal, omnipotent, arbitrary ruler of the world; the civil magistrates are His ministers on earth; and the Bible is the sole source of law. Moreover, Calvin's God resumes the anthropomorphic form of the Jehovah of the Old Testament except that He is inscrutable, His will is absolute, He is a God of wrath rather than of love; and He predestines part of mankind to salvation but the larger part to eternal damnation "by a just and irreprehensible but incomprehensible judgment." God's rule, so interpreted, is exceedingly stern. In Geneva, under Calvin's control, men's lives were minutely regulated; drunkenness was severely punished; dancing and other harmless pleasures were forbidden; heretics were burned; and prostitutes were thrown into the Rhone. Calvin's ideas spread in Europe, be-

---

3 William Paley, *Principles of Moral and Political Philosophy*, Boston, 1811, pp. 61, 65ff.

came deeply rooted in Scotland, and flourished in the New England colonies, where they became the basis of the Puritan tradition in American life.

Not only in Protestant but in Catholic literature, there are many traces of theocratic concepts. For example, the Papal encyclical *Diuturnum* (1881) contain these statements:

> If one wishes to determine from what source is derived the power of the State, the Church teaches, with reason, that it must be looked for in God. This is what she has found expressly set forth in the Holy Scriptures and in the monuments of Christian antiquity. . . . Modern theories of political power have already been the cause of great evils, and it is to be feared lest in the future these evils should reach the worst extremes. For indeed, to refuse to refer to God, as to its source, the right to rule men, is in effect to deprive public power of all its dignity and all its vigour. To make it depend upon the will of the people is, first, to commit an error of principle; and, further, to set authority upon a foundation both fragile and inconsistent. Such opinions are a perpetual irritant to popular passions, which will be seen daily growing in boldness, and preparing the public ruin by fraying a way for secret conspiracies or overt sedition.[4]

Theocratic doctrines such as this do not necessarily imply a strictly formalistic theological ethics but are often combined with such an ethics.

2. *Criticism of Formalistic Theological Ethics*

IF WE EXAMINE the formalistic view in its purity, we are confronted by a theory that few reflective people today would espouse. The theory asserts that moral distinctions depend solely upon the decree of God. Cannibalism, for example, would be right if God so willed; it is wrong merely because God prohibits it. Such views make God's power and not his goodness basic to his essence; but if God is to be regarded as

---

[4] Leo XIII, *Diuturnum*, in Michael Oakeshott, *The Social and Political Doctrines of Contemporary Europe,* Cambridge University Press, Cambridge, 1939, pp. 52-53.

merely the most powerful being in the universe, there would seem to be no valid *moral* reason for obeying Him. Promethean defiance, if that were possible without too much sacrifice, would be quite as justifiable and much more heroic. If the reply be made that "morality" simply *means* obedience to supreme power, we can object that this does violence to our moral sense. The worship of power *merely* because it is power is incompatible with ethical and religious maturity. Although religion may begin with fear, it rises to a reverence for goodness and wisdom, which Bertrand Russell has described as the essence of "the free man's worship."

If it be maintained that God is not only powerful but also good, the formalistic interpretation of ethics is no longer tenable. On this view, since God is good and goodness has a certain actual character, the good is not determined by some extrinsic factor, such as an arbitrary command. In reply, one might argue that right is entirely independent of goodness, and that right, if not goodness, is determined by mere decree. If God is good, however, his decrees are surely not wholly arbitrary; they must reflect and express his goodness, and therefore right as formulated in these decrees is not independent of goodness. We are told in the First Epistle of John that God is good will, is love. If so, the right as embodied in His aims must be directed to the good. Moreover, since good has a character of its own, God by His mere will could not make that good which is not good, any more than He could make that round which is not round. Even God cannot do that which is contradictory: even He cannot make a round square or a good evil.

In addition to pointing out such difficulties, we can criticize formalistic religious ethics for its naïveté. It depends upon a highly anthropomorphic conception of the Deity. God is thought of as a sort of king or lawmaker, handing down arbitrary decrees from on high. As Walter Lippmann has pointed out in his *Preface to Morals,* it is difficult for modern educated men to take such views seriously. Gone are the old certainty and vivid imagery that once made "God and His Plan seem as real as the lamp-post." We can no longer picture Him: "his throne, his crown, his scepter, his seraphic retinue, his laws, rewards, and punishments."[5] This concrete visualization was always poetry in a measure, but it made the scheme very much more vivid and therefore far more profound in its influence. The modern tendency is to banish all this vivid spectacle: God is thoroughly abstract; hell is unreal; heaven is inconceivable. The prevailing mood is conveyed by the English poet Edith Sitwell when she declares:

> This modern world is but a thin match-board flooring spread over a shallow hell. For Dante's hell has faded, is dead. Hell is no vastness; there are no more devils who laugh or who weep—only the maimed dwarfs of this life, terrible straining mechanisms, crouching on trivial sands, and laughing at the giants' crumbling.[6]

It may be that the mood of disillusionment typified by this quotation has gone too far, although I, for one, am quite willing to omit any hell, even Dante's, from among the more permanent furniture of the universe.

This change in men's outlook, in any event, is an inevitable accompaniment of the growth of science and knowledge. Modern man has become aware of many religions each claiming authoritativeness and of many ways of reading and interpreting the Bible. He thus has discovered that much is conjectural that once was regarded as certain, that the so-called "revealed" ethics of his own religion is paralleled by other "revealed" ethical systems, and that basic moral concepts such as the "Golden Rule" are to be found in these other religions. The development of modern science, moreover, has dispelled many supernaturalistic beliefs and has instilled a spirit of tentativity opposed to religious dogma. Also modern critical philosophy, represented, for example, by the writings of Hume, Kant, and McTaggart, has very effectively questioned the arguments for traditional theism. Responding to these

5 *Preface to Morals*, Macmillan, New York, 1929, p. 22.
6 *Bucolic Comedies*, Duckworth, London, 1928, p. 51.

various influences, modern man finds it impossible to believe that God, acting like a despotic king, has imposed a
specific code of morals by arbitrary external fiat. However
much fundamentalists may lament this change in sentiment,
they must recognize it as a fact.

If we are to have a world order, we cannot build it upon
the basis of attitudes that have so largely crumbled or that
represent only a small minority of mankind. We must not
make the mistake of Tom Jones' narrow-minded tutor,
Thwackum, in Henry Fielding's novel, who pontifically an-
nounces: "When I mention religion I mean the Christian religion; and not only the Christian religion, but the Protestant religion; and not only the Protestant religion, but the
Church of England."[7] As soon as we escape from such narrow
bounds, we leave the confines of an exclusive, authoritarian,
and formalistic religious ethics and either flounder in moral
anarchy or achieve a more liberal, flexible, humanistic, and
purposive moral outlook.

3. *A Historical Example of the Transition to a Teleological Religious Morality*

THE BIBLE ITSELF is the record of such a transition from a
formalistic to a relatively teleological conception of morality.
In the parts of the Old Testament that are most primitive,
the lawgiver to the Jewish people is conceived to be Yahweh
(translated Jehovah in the King James' version), a tribal god,
jealous and revengeful, whose power, according to Abraham,
is greater than the combined strength of all the other gods.
The doctrine is not monotheism but henotheism, devotion to
one god while recognizing others. This view is implied by
such admonitions as "Thou shalt not revile the gods" and
"Thou shalt have no other gods before me."[8]

7 *Tom Jones*, Modern Library, New York, no date, p. 82.
8 Exodus 22:28 and 20:3 (King James' translation).

Yahweh lays down a commandment code, in which rituals and taboos are prescribed along with moral customs.

> Never carve yourselves any metal gods. Hold the festival of unleavened cakes. . . . All the first-born belong to me, with the firstlings of your cattle, both oxen and sheep; you may buy back a firstling ass with a lamb or a kid; but if you do not choose to buy it back, you must break its neck. Any first-born boy you must buy back. . . . For six days you shall labour, but on the seventh day you shall desist from work. . . . You must hold the festival of Weeks . . . and the festival of ingathering. . . . You must never present the blood of any sacrifice with leavened cakes, and no part of the sacrifice at the passover festival must be left over all night. . . . You must not boil a kid in its mother's milk.[9]

If a man is moral, he follows the law as thus prescribed; if he is immoral, he violates the law. Yahweh, who enforces these decrees, is relentless against his enemies, merciless against the unrepentant sinner, exacting an eye for an eye, a tooth for a tooth.

Yet very early in the religious development of the Jews, other conceptions crept in. God was sometimes conceived as kind and forgiving, slow to anger, rich in love. Tribal rituals and taboos were supplemented by the admonition of Leviticus, "Love thy neighbor as thyself."[10] Morality, moreover, was broadened: it transcended the tribe and embraced the stranger: "The alien who settles beside you shall be treated like a native, and you must love him as you love yourself; for you were aliens yourselves in the land of Egypt."[11] A similar statement is to be found in the twenty-third chapter of Exodus, which dates from the ninth century B.C. and perhaps is retained from a much earlier period. Gradually primitive polytheism, with its tribal exclusiveness, passed over into monotheism. The doctrine that the Jews are a "chosen people" was retained, but this particularistic emphasis was para-

---

9 Exodus 34:18-27. From *The Bible: A New Translation*, by James Moffatt, copyrighted in 1935 by Harper & Brothers, used by permission. I have used whichever version seems to be better for the specific passage.

10 Leviticus 19:18 (King James).

11 Leviticus 19:34 (Moffat).

doxically combined with a universal trend. The chosen
people, according to this new and sublime interpretation,
would prepare the way for a realm of true brotherhood
among all human beings, a united humanity under a universal God.

Two types of religious leaders, the priests and the prophets,
sprang up among the Jewish people. The priests were the
formalists, generally insisting upon the ritual observance and
the letter of the law, such as circumcision, the dietary taboos,
the keeping of the Sabbath, and the observance of religious
ceremonies. They became scribes and scholars of the Torah,
codifying, interpreting, and sanctifying the law. The prophets
were the seers and the idealists, sitting loose from the traditional rules and laws, not for the sake of being above moral
law but for the sake of better principles and laws. Criticizing
the past and anticipating the future, they insisted upon the
active pursuit of ideals—righteousness and justice, loving
kindness and mercy. In the great prophets, such as Amos,
Hosea, Micah, Isaiah, and Jeremiah, we find utterances with
revolutionary social implications—the condemnation of the
rich, the praise of the poor, and the vision of peace and justice:

And He shall judge among many people, and rebuke strong
nations afar off; and they shall beat their swords into plough-
shares, and their spears into pruning-hooks: nation shall not lift
up a sword against nation, neither shall they learn war any
more.[12]

God is no longer a tribal deity enforcing ritual law or demanding sacrifice, but a universal loving Father-God:

He hath showed thee, O man, what is good; and what doth the
Lord require of thee, but to do justly, and to love mercy, and to
walk humbly with thy God.[13]

In the time of Jesus, the intense vision of the prophets had
somewhat faded, and there was considerable moral backslid-
ing. The Jewish people, by that time in subjection to Rome,

12 Micah 4:3 (King James).
13 Ibid., 6·8

could not sustain the lofty idealism of the prophets. Their lives were dominated by the traditional Jewish law, conceived largely in terms of strict ritual, dietary taboos, and other petty or repressive regulations. Fanatical sects, such as the Zealots and the Pharisees, insisted upon the literal observance of the law. A priestly class, jealous and intolerant, imposed itself upon the masses. At the same time, the old Messianic hope of the people—the doctrine that a God-given leader would eventually deliver the Jews from bondage—was being widely agitated. It was a time of transition; the culture of Greece and Rome was declining; the old Jewish culture was decaying; it was high time for a beginning of the new.

The attitude of Jesus was creative and open-minded. He insisted upon the spirit rather than the letter, the purpose rather than the formula, the inner value rather than the outer circumstance. His nonformalistic, liberal attitude is most clearly illustrated in his remarks about the Sabbath. The law that the Sabbath must be kept—one of the Ten Commandments—was perhaps the most strictly guarded of all the traditional religious rules. In Exodus 31:12-17, God is represented as declaring to Moses that the Sabbath "is a sacred day for you, and anyone who desecrates it shall be put to death. For whoever does any business on the Sabbath, that man shall be outlawed."[14] Many of the acts prohibited on the Sabbath were entirely harmless, such as lighting a fire, sewing two stitches, or tying and untying a knot. Reaping was also forbidden, and even the gathering of a few heads of grain was classified as reaping. One Sabbath when Jesus and his disciples were passing through a field of grain a number of Pharisees rebuked them for pulling some heads of grain. Jesus replied: "The Sabbath was made for man, and not man for the Sabbath."[15] If we generalize this remark, it means that the law is made for man, not man for the law. This is a central thesis of teleological ethics.

Jesus was thoroughly familiar with the Jewish moral and

14 Exodus 31:12-17 (Moffat).
15 Mark 2:27 (Moffat).

religious law, and he did not intend to overthrow it. "Never imagine I have come to destroy the law or the prophets," he said; "I have not come to destroy, but to fulfill."[16] Yet he interpreted the old law with a new flexibility. Again and again he used the phraseology: "You have heard it said of old. . . . But I say to you. . . ." He insisted not upon a moral code but upon a spiritual community, the brotherhood of man under the fatherhood of God. When he was asked the question: "What is the greatest commandment?" he replied:

> You must love the Lord your God with your whole heart, with your whole soul, and with your whole mind. This is the greatest and chief command. There is a second like it: you must love your neighbor as yourself. The whole Law and the prophets hang upon these two commands.[17]

As we can judge from the story of the Good Samaritan, moreover, one's "neighbor" is every man. His basic injunction was kindness to all, without restriction of sex, nation, race, class, or creed. Indeed, his special concern was for those "beyond the pale": the poor, the lowly, the stranger, the outcast, the prostitute, the prodigal son. In essence he was saying that the whole moral law is the law of love. Though he spoke of the coming of the Kingdom of God, he visualized it as an inward state—the widest possible community realized through kindness. "The Kingdom of God," he said, "is within you."[18] Like the prophets of the Old Testament, he enunciated a great moral ideal and not a set of formal rules.

4. Conclusion

WHEN religion reaches maturity, it no longer conceives morality as imposed arbitrarily from on high but as immanent in men's purposes and deeds. It emphasizes not the

16 Matthew 5:17 (King James).
17 Matthew 22:36-40 (Moffat).
18 Luke 17:21 (King James).

letter of the law but the inner spirit and the consequences of action. In some of its modern forms, it is essentially humanistic: a consecration to life-enriching ideals, a very present bond among living men, a sense of the universal human community. If it speaks of God, it interprets Him naturalistically as the society of all the forces pushing on toward the good in this world. It does not confine men's gaze to heaven but leads them to see more clearly what is to be done here on earth while they are still living. It seeks to realize the ideal and not merely to idealize the real. If its mood is optimistic, its optimism is qualified by the realization that

> The very source and fount of day
> Is dash'd with wandering isles of night.[19]

A religion of mere acquiescence is, in spirit, not purposive, because it does not recognize that there are genuine evils to be combated. A religion that glosses over the injustices and suffering in the world can do little to realize the old, old ideal of human brotherhood that so many great religions and moral systems have advocated.

[19] Alfred Lord Tennyson, "In Memoriam," XXIV, 3.

Chapter Three

THE LAWS OF NATURE

1. *The Ambiguous Meaning of Naturalistic Ethics*

BOTH THE FORMALISTIC ethics of custom or positive law and the formalistic ethics of religion insist that morality is imposed upon the individual from without. In the one case, the source is society; in the other case, God. In both, morality is thought to consist in obedience to rule or law.

Another variation of the theory that morality is imposed or derives from without can be found in certain types of naturalistic ethics. These maintain that morality is rooted in the structure of nature rather than immanent in the distinctive character and needs of man. Morality consists in being in harmony with nature. Nature supplies models, rules, or laws which man should follow. Such a view, for example, was expressed by John Gay, the poet, when he wrote:

> He who studies nature's laws
> From certain truth his maxim draws.[1]

One difficulty with this view is that there are many conceptions of nature and a different set of "natural laws" corresponding to each conception. "She's a rum 'un is Natur'," said Mr. Squeers in Dickens' *Nicholas Nickleby*. "Natur' is more easily conceived than described."[2] It is more easily conceived because the mind in its speculative flights is less

[1] Quoted by William A. Robson, *Civilization and the Growth of Law*, Macmillan, New York, 1935, p. 234.
[2] Quoted by C. D. Broad, *The Mind and Its Place in Nature*, Kegan Paul, Trench, Trübner, London, 1925, p. 1.

weighted down by a sober sense of fact. In view of this diversity of interpretation, we must turn to a number of alternative viewpoints and consider each in turn. I shall review two historical examples—Stoicism and Evolutionary Ethics—and shall more briefly consider a number of additional interpretations. Thereby I shall indicate something of the variety and range of naturalistic ethics.

2. *Stoicism as a Type of Naturalistic Ethics*

STOICISM is a good example of naturalistic ethics not only because of its intrinsic characteristics but also because it has been immensely influential. It had a profound influence upon such outstanding Roman philosophers as Cicero and Seneca and greatly affected more modern conceptions of natural rights and natural law.

It sprang up in a time of troubles, the period of latter-day Hellenic civilization. After the Peloponnesian War, Greece was so rent by internal strife and bitterness, and so seriously drained and weakened, that it fell an easy prey to the imperialistic designs of Macedonia and Rome. It lost its freedom, its political confidence, and its creative verve. The political scene exhibited only despotic monarchies and warring city states. By conquest Rome eventually achieved peace and a wide dominion, but its cultural achievements, especially in the field of philosophy, were no match for its political dominance.

Originating in Athens and spreading to Rome, Stoicism reflected this "time of troubles." It was essentially a philosophy of refuge, finding a limited salvation not in vigorous political and social reconstruction, which men no longer had the courage or vision to undertake, but in individual self-management—the deliberate cultivation of mental tranquillity raised above the storms and vicissitudes of life. In its cosmopolitanism, it reflected the age of imperialism, an age of the uprooting and migration and mixture of peoples, in which the little city-state was dissolving and the great empires of Macedonia and Rome were demanding new concepts of universal citizenship. Stoicism became strong and flourished because it marched with the times, in pace with the mood of an expansive but declining civilization.

Its leadership indicates something of its cosmopolitan and varied character. Its founder was Zeno (*circa* 336-264 B.C.), a Phoenician from Cyprus, who lived in Athens as a resident alien, giving lectures in a building known as the Stoa Poikile, or Painted Porch, whence the name Stoic is derived. The early Stoics were recruited from many places, especially from Syria; the later Stoics were mostly Romans. Their leaders came from high and low station; for example, Epictetus was a penniless slave and Marcus Aurelius a mighty emperor. Its doctrines varied, modern scholars distinguish between an early, middle, and late period of Stoicism. In this brief summary, however, I shall take no account of such variations but emphasize particularly the views of Marcus Aurelius and Epictetus, whose writings we fortunately possess whereas the writings of most of the other Stoics were lost.

The Stoics were interested in two questions: what to believe, and how to live. Some of them exhibited a real and independent interest in the first question, but most of them were mainly interested in the second. They believed, however, that the second question could be answered only if the first could be resolved. We must know what is real, they contended, before we can judge what we ought to do.

In giving an account of reality, Stoicism, as Zeno formulated it, started with what appears to be an uncompromising materialism. Everything is material; even God and the soul are bodies; the Divine Reason is a kind of fire. No doubt this is a bit hard to make sense of; it is difficult to see the consistency of a doctrine which identifies reason with a material substance. The Stoics, however, were hylozoists: they believed that all matter is endowed with life. If we grant this premise, it no longer seems so strange to say that the material universe is a living being and that matter is shot through with reason. Just as a soul or life force animates the human body, so a spiritual force rolls through all things. This soul or life force can be called God, Nature, Reason— synonyms for the inner essence and animating principle of the world. It is the productive, formative power, the natural spontaneity, the force that makes for movement and growth. It is divine reason, all-pervasive and all-powerful; hence there is no sheer evil in the world, and nothing is left to chance. From this standpoint, it is also Fate—not a blind mechanical necessity but a purposive, providential force, the living activity of the whole expressing itself through every natural event.

The divine fire is in every man: reason is his governing principle, the core and center of his being. What corresponds to his reason and expresses his nature also corresponds to the world soul and expresses the universal nature. To "live according to nature" is to express our rational nature and, at the same time, to be in harmony with the rational order of the world. This means that one should not merely submit to fate but approve and welcome it.

At this point, however, we meet a serious difficulty. If nature is fate, it seems that we have no choice—it is not that we had "better" accept it; we *must* accept it. The Stoics met this difficulty by making an exception. They said that all *outward* occurrences, all matters of fortune, are fated, but in his inner attitudes man is free. He cannot thwart nature, but he is free to accept nature wisely or rebel foolishly. He cannot determine his role in life, but he can play it well or ill: silly rebellion or dull submission may be left behind, and a mood of cheerful serenity, or at least equanimity, can take its place. Epictetus writes:

Remember that you are an actor in a play, and the Playwright chooses the manner of it: if he wants it short, it is short; if long, it is long. If he wants you to act a poor man you must act the part with all your powers; and so if your part be a cripple or a magistrate or a plain man. For your business is to act the character that is given you and act it well; the choice of the cast is Another's.[3]

To live wisely, a person must know what he is free to do and what he is not. He must be simultaneously aware of external fate and inner freedom, he must realize that reason is impotent in altering the outward stream of events but has immense power over the inner life. Again to quote Epictetus:

Of all existing things, some are in our power, and others are not in our power. In our power are thought, impulse, will to get and will to avoid, and, in a word, everything which is our own doing. Things not in our power include the body, property, reputation, office, and, in a word, everything which is not our own doing.[4]

The essence of morality is to make the "things in our power" —our inner attitudes—harmonize with the "things not in our power"—the outward course of events. "Ask not that events should happen as you will," admonishes Epictetus, "but let your will be that events should happen as they do, and you shall have peace."[5] The logic here is rather simple: if you want what you get, you will get what you want.

What *really* matters is one's attitude. External "goods" of property, physical "goods" of the body, are not truly good. Only goodness is good, and it is a state of mind. If a man loses health or wealth, this should be a matter of complete indifference to him; if he is laid upon the rack, this too should be indifferent. In the face of every vicissitude, he should preserve an unchanging inner tranquillity. "Remember . . . on every occasion which leads thee to vexation to apply this principle," admonishes Marcus Aurelius: "not that this is a misfortune, but that to bear it nobly is good

---

[3] *The Manual of Epictetus*, in Whitney J. Oates, *The Stoic and Epicurean Philosophers,* Random House, New York, 1940, p. 472.
[4] *Ibid.,* p. 468.
[5] *Ibid.,* p. 470.

fortune."[6] In practice, this means to live a simple, austere, meditative life, concentrating upon the inner man rather than upon outward endowments. The following advice of Epictetus is typical:

> Be silent for the most part. . . . Do not laugh much, nor at many things, nor without restraint. . . . For your body take just so much as your bare need requires, such as food, drink, clothing, house, servants, but cut down all that tends to luxury and outward show. . . . It is a sign of a dull mind to dwell upon the cares of the body, to prolong exercise, eating, drinking, and other bodily functions. These things are to be done by the way; all your attention must be given to the mind.[7]

The ethical and social implications of this philosophy are, on the whole, quietistic. If external events are rational, providential, and fated, and if the inner life is alone good, the only wise attitude is to look upon external "evils" such as poverty with perfect equanimity. One result is a deliberate checking of the impulse to love or pity, so that you may remain detached and self-sufficient. Epictetus advises:

If you kiss your child, or brother, or friend, never allow your imagination to range at large, nor allow your exultation to go as far as it will. You must remind yourself that you love a mortal, and that nothing that you love is your very own; it is given you for the moment, not for ever nor inseparably, but like a fig or a bunch of grapes at the appointed season of the year, and if you long for it in winter you are a fool. . . . And therefore in the very moment that you take pleasure in a thing, set before your mind the opposite impressions. What harm is there in whispering to yourself as you kiss your child, "Tomorrow you will die," and to your friend in like manner, "Tomorrow you or I shall go away, and we shall see one another no more"?[8]

In other words, one must not love too much but preserve a detachment even in the most intimate concerns of life. Instead of becoming deeply involved with love or pity, instead

---

6 Marcus Aurelius, *Meditations*, in *ibid.*, p. 516.
7 *The Manual of Epictetus*, in *ibid.*, pp. 478, 480.
8 *The Discourses of Epictetus*, in *ibid.*, pp. 397-398.

of being indignant at the injustices of the world, the Stoic sage accepts his station and its duties: "It is sufficient if each man fulfills his own function."[9] Individual self-management not social action, resignation not vigorous social reconstruction, aloofness not love freely given, are dominant notes of Stoic ethics.

The conservative and individualistic implications of this philosophy are somewhat counterbalanced by the Stoic doctrine of universal human fellowship. All men, they taught, are parts of the whole: they are all bound together by "the natural law of fellowship," the kinship of all men as children of nature and citizens of the universe, that "highest city of which all other cities are like families."[10] Marcus Aurelius declared:

If our intellectual part is common, the reason also, in respect of which we are rational beings, is common; if this is so, common also is the reason which commands us what to do, and what not to do; if this is so, there is a common law also; if this is so, we are fellow-citizens; if this is so, we are members of some political community; if this is so, the world is in a manner a state.[11]

This doctrine, that the whole world is a state or city or political community, is stressed, for example, by Cicero, who was profoundly influenced by Stoic doctrine. He asserts that we must conceive "this whole universe as one commonwealth of which both gods and men are members," that "no single thing is so like another, so exactly its counterpart, as all of us are to one another."[12] Reasoning similarly, Epictetus points out the ethical implications.

Every matter has two handles, one of which will bear taking hold of, the other not. If thy brother sin against thee, lay not hold of the matter by this, that he sins against thee; for by this handle the matter will not bear taking hold of. But rather lay hold of it

9 *The Manual of Epictetus*, in *ibid.*, p. 474.
10 Marcus Aurelius, *Meditations*, in *ibid.*, p. 506.
11 *Ibid.*, p. 509.
12 *Republic*, in Michael B. Foster, *Masters of Political Thought*, Houghton Mifflin, Boston, 1941, pp. 185-186.

by this, that he is thy brother, thy born mate; and thou wilt take hold of it by what will bear handling.[13]

This noble profession of human brotherhood differs from Christianity mainly in its coolness, its intellectual detachment. The Stoic is restrained by his aloofness from any passionate commitment. He must retain, at all costs, an unruffled inner composure.

The Stoic doctrine of human brotherhood is closely connected with the doctrine of natural law. If "the whole universe is one commonwealth," then there is a common law, the law of nature, which as fellow citizens and brothers we are all bound to observe. Again Cicero's words will serve as illustration.

Law is the distinction between things just and unjust, made in agreement with that primal and most ancient of all things, Nature; and in conformity to Nature's standards are framed those human laws which inflict punishment upon the wicked but defend and protect the good.[14]

Whereas human law is relative to time and place, the law of a specific state, enacted at one time and repealed at another, natural law is of universal application, unchanging and everlasting. Cicero continues:

We cannot be freed from its obligations by senate or people, and we need not look outside ourselves for an expounder or interpreter of it. And there will not be different laws at Rome and at Athens, or different laws now and in the future, but one eternal and unchangeable law will be valid for all nations and all times, and there will be one master and ruler, that is, God, over us all, for he is the author of this law, its promulgator, and its enforcing judge.[15]

No man, we are told, is morally obliged to obey human law unless it conforms to the law of nature, for the natural law

---

[13] Quoted by Matthew Arnold, "An Essay on Marcus Aurelius," in Oates, *op. cit.*, p. 594.
[14] Cicero, *op. cit.*, p. 183.
[15] *Ibid.*, p. 188.

represents absolute and immutable principles and should be followed whenever it conflicts with human law.

Unlike purely physical laws such as "the law of gravitation," natural laws, in the Stoic meaning of the term, can be violated. They represent not what men *must* do but what they *should* do in order to be in harmony with nature. They represent the rational order that governs the whole universe rather than the brute physical necessity. In the immensity of the universe there is only a tiny plot, the human soul, in which freedom is to be found; here at least in an indefeasible area of choice. It is here, within the recesses of one's own soul, that one can choose to accept or reject the common laws of all humanity as citizens of the universe. Here one may freely embrace the laws of reason, equity, justice, and inborn natural rights.

This conception of natural law not only deeply affected Roman lawmakers and jurists but persisted, with various transmutations, throughout the Dark Ages and the Middle Ages into modern times. For example, St. Thomas Aquinas, the greatest of medieval philosophers, was restating this doctrine when he wrote:

> Every law framed by man bears the character of a law exactly to that extent to which it is derived from the Law of Nature. But if on any point it is in conflict with the Law of Nature, it at once ceases to be a law; it is a mere perversion of a law.[16]

Such ideas played a great role in the development of liberal philosophy and in the great transformations of the English, American, and French Revolutions; and even in recent decades men have talked similarly about natural laws.

Professor Gilbert Murray has called Stoicism "the greatest system of organized thought which the mind of man had built up for itself in the Graeco-Roman world before the coming of Christianity."[17] I would not praise it so highly

---

16 *Summa Theologica*, Part II, 1 Q. 95, art. 2; quoted in Robson, *op. cit.*, p. 221.

17 *The Stoic Philosophy*, George Allen and Unwin, London, 1921, p. 12.

since I believe that the earlier philosophies of Plato and
Aristotle represent the high mark of classical thought. Yet
there is much to admire in Stoicism: the courage, the tranquillity, the cosmopolitanism, the sense of universal fellowship, the attempt to see the rational connections and necessity of things, the poise and magnanimity of outlook that
result from identifying oneself with the whole frame of
nature. Even a pessimist such as A. E. Housman catches
something of the Stoic mood when he writes:

> The troubles of our proud and angry dust
> Are from eternity and shall not fail.
> Bear them we can, and if we can we must.
> Shoulder the sky, my lad, and drink your ale.[18]

In so far as trouble is unavoidable, it is well to bear as
pluckily as we can every turning of the screw.

Yet there are many difficulties in the Stoic system. The
central doctrine—that nature is divine, rational, and fated,
and that all man's external behavior is necessitated—under-
mines the basis of moral choice. If the ideal is the actual,
and the actual is the necessary, there is obviously no reason
to bestir ourselves to improve the world. The exception made
by the Stoics, that man is free to accept or reject fate, leaves
far too little room for choice: the implications are still very
quietistic. Moreover, there seems to be no good reason for
saying that man in his inner life is independent of fate. If
he is a part of nature, as the Stoics allege, why is he not
subject to the fate that governs nature? The Stoic interpretation of the world tends to be inconsistent, with its paradoxical combination of fate and free will, cosmopolitanism
and self-sufficiency, tacit admission that certain things are
preferable, and yet explicit teaching that all happens for the
best.

One of the basic errors is the underestimation of our
power over external events and the exaggerated estimation

18 *Last Poems,* Holt, New York, 1922, p. 25.

of our power over the "inner man." The Stoics maintain
that health, sickness, wealth, poverty, high or low social
status, even pleasure and pain, are determined by inexorable
necessity. We now know, on the contrary, that the great positive evils of the world—war, disease, poverty, ignorance—are
not eternally fixed. In a thousand ways men have demonstrated their power to alter their environment and to improve their lot. Especially in this age of science and technology, the human power to change life, either for good or
ill, is an immensely impressive fact. On the other hand, the
Stoics exaggerated the extent to which reason controls the
mind. They insisted that the essence of the human soul is
reason, and that if a man makes rational judgments, he can
control every part of his soul. We now know that reason plays
a less absolute part in man's life, that feeling, desire, and
instinct are fundamental, and that subconscious promptings
often determine the content of our conscious mental life.
Some modern psychologists such as Freud insist that the
mainsprings of personality are to be found in this subconscious realm, and that conscious processes represent very
largely the disguised or sublimated expression of subconscious urges and conflicts. It may be that Freud goes much
too far; but the resolute Stoic assertion that "I am the captain
of my soul" has to be interpreted and modified.

Stoicism is the prototype of all the theories that put extreme or exclusive emphasis upon changing the "inner man"
as distinct from environmental factors. Far more realistic is
the view that we must change both minds and institutions,
thoughts and things, agents and circumstances. We change
men's minds *by* changing their environments; we change
their environments *by* changing their minds. The two factors—the individual personality and the environmental situation—are in continuous interaction, each being conditioned
by the other, each altering the other. This alone is the
realistic basis of social and ethical action: psychological and

social, mental and physical, inward and outward at the same time.

3. Evolutionary Ethics

ANOTHER very influential type of naturalistic ethics has been based upon the theory of evolution and, in particular, upon the doctrines of Charles Darwin. These doctrines, which are familiar to all educated men, are the concepts of struggle for existence, variation, natural selection, and survival of the fittest.

The possibility of explaining evolution in terms of these factors struck Darwin with a sudden flash of insight when, by chance, he was reading an *Essay on Population* by Robert Malthus, an English parson, who published his famous "essay" in 1798. In this work, Malthus contended that the human race tends to increase much more rapidly than the means of subsistence, and that consequently a great many human beings cannot survive. The weaker ones, he argued, are eliminated by such "natural checks" as famine and pestilence. Darwin explains:

> In October 1838, I happened to read for amusement Malthus on Population, and being well prepared to appreciate the struggle for existence which everywhere goes on from long continued observation of the habits of animals and plants, it at once struck me that under these circumstances favorable variations would tend to be preserved, and unfavorable ones to be destroyed. The result would be the formation of new species. Here then I had a theory by which to work.[19]

Work he did, and it was not until after many years of laborious research that he amassed a body of evidence great enough, in his opinion, to sustain his interpretation of evolution.

[19] Quoted in William Cecil Dampier, *A History of Science*, Macmillan, New York, 1949, p. 276.

His theory is as follows. All animals and plants multiply more rapidly than the means of subsistence, and therefore many perish before they can reproduce themselves. Some survive by mere luck, but most of those that survive are in some sense better adapted to their environments than their fellows. Just as there are no two fingerprints exactly alike, so plants and animals always vary, if ever so slightly. Fortunate variations give their possessors an improved chance of surviving and passing on their characteristics, in accordance with the laws of heredity, to their offspring. Accumulation of these variations over the course of many generations gradually produces a change in type. Given long enough time, this process can account for the evolution of life from protozoa to man.

This theory was supplemented by some additional notions which enthusiastic disciples of Darwin were quick to provide. First, evolution was equated with progress, and the "survival of the fit" was interpreted as the survival of the best. Second, the struggle for existence was depicted as a ruthless competitive affair, and nature was described as "red in tooth and claw."[20] Third, man was interpreted as a part of nature and as properly subject to natural selection. There was a very marked tendency to conceive of capitalistic economic competition and even war as extensions into human life of the Darwinian "struggle for existence."

A host of writers seized upon these ideas as a basis for reinterpreting man's moral life. For example, Herbert Spencer (1820-1903), a most influential English philosopher, contended that man is an animal subject to the general laws of evolution and that human progress results from the stern discipline of nature which eliminates the unfit.[21] The rigors of the human struggle for survival are therefore blessings in disguise. Spencer went so far as to declare:

20 Tennyson, "In Memoriam," LVI.
21 Cf., Herbert Spencer, Social Statics, Appleton, New York, 1888, pp. 352-357, 412-413.

The poverty of the incapable, the distresses that come upon the imprudent, the starvation of the idle, and those shoulderings aside of the weak by the strong, which leave so many "in shallows and in miseries," are the decrees of a large, far-seeing benevolence.[22]

All of these apparent evils are blessings, Spencer argued, because they eliminate the unfit; therefore no regulation of industry, no poor relief, no program of public sanitation or health care, no social legislation to soften the human struggle for survival, should be permitted. Economic and social *laissez faire* involves the least interference with the "laws of evolution" and is therefore the ideal state of society for the improvement of man. In such a society, human beings can rapidly progress to the evolutionary goal, namely, the perfect adaptation of man, the individual organism, to his surroundings. This state of perfect equilibrium, when fully realized, will permit an abolition of all government, a utopian anarchy in which human happiness will be realized to the full. Even before all government is abolished, it can be greatly minimized; and Spencer believed that we should immediately abolish such governmental functions as postal service, public coinage of money, and state education.

Others sought to make use of evolutionary theory to justify racial and class conflict. For example, the Austrian sociologist, Ludwig Gumplowicz, viewed history as a succession of tribal, racial, nationalistic, and class struggles, in which the fittest individuals and groups survive. In Germany, militarists such as Marshal von Moltke and General von Bernhardi exalted war as a means of "natural selection" and therefore as one of the prime conditions of human progress. Oswald Spengler, the famous German historian, insisted that "man is a beast of prey," and denounced as unnatural "the toothless feeling of sympathy and reconciliation."[23] Mussolini, Hitler, and the Nazi philosopher Alfred Rosenberg similarly argued

22 *Ibid.,* p. 354.
23 *Cf.,* Oswald Spengler, *The Hour of Decision,* Knopf, New York, 1934, p. 21; and *Man and Technics,* Knopf, New York, 1932, p. 43.

that throughout nature there is a ceaseless struggle for survival and that the strong and fit survive. Man, they said, is also a fighting animal; in strife, mankind has become great. The nation, or the race, is the natural fighting unit; and its combative force depends upon its rejection of humanitarian and democratic principles as unnatural.

The giant among all these proponents of evolutionary ethics was Friedrich Nietzsche (1844-1900). His philosophy, being remarkably varied and ambivalent, is very hard to classify or to summarize. "I know both sides, for I am both sides," he said.[24] At times he shocked and swaggered like a moral desperado; at other times he was a model of subtle refinement. He taught, among other doctrines, that life, in its very essence, is a will to power; that evolution results from the triumph of strength over weakness; that the kind, democratic type of person is decadent; that a warlike aristocratic élite, a proud master class, is the highest instrument of evolutionary advancement; and that the ruthless domination of the "masters" over their "slaves" will prepare the way for a higher evolutionary type, the Superman.

Unlike Herbert Spencer, Nietzsche believed that natural processes should not be left to themselves but should be actively aided and abetted. In his conception of evolution, he resembled Darwin less than he resembled Lamarck, who maintained that organisms adapt themselves to new environments by struggling to overcome handicaps and that these adaptations are transmitted to their offspring. Like Lamarck, he maintained that man's advance will not take place as the result of a haphazard struggle for existence but as a result of deliberate effort. The main agents in bringing about the evolutionary upsurge will be a new class of masters, who will throw off the shackles of conventional morality and will live by the subjection of an immense class of slaves. These

24 Quoted by Harry Slochower, *No Voice Is Wholly Lost*, Creative Age Press, New York, 1945, p. 1.

new masters will be the counterparts of the barbarian over-lords who, in the dawn of civilization, installed themselves as victors over weaker populations which they reduced to slavery. Deliberately rejecting the values of Christianity, democracy, and socialism, the future masters will revive the ancient values of aristocracy, pride, strength, hardness, and contempt for all that is common. As a result of their heroism and creative *élan*, Western culture will be renewed and the way prepared for the Superman. Nietzsche's imaginary prophet, Zarathustra, proclaims:

> I teach you the Superman. Man is something to be surpassed. What have ye done to surpass man? All beings hitherto have created something beyond themselves: and ye want to be the ebb of that great tide, and would rather go back to the beast than surpass man? What is the ape to man? A laughing-stock, a thing of shame. And just the same shall man be to the Superman: a laughing-stock, a thing of shame. . . . The Superman is the mean-ing of the earth. Let your will say: The Superman *shall be* the meaning of the earth.[25]

All ethics must be transvaluated so that, by forging a new moral code, we may express the drive of men now toward the Superman that is to be.

Nietzsche's philosophy is far from a justification of the *status quo;* but the evolutionary theory has often been used as a prop to the existing order, especially to an economy of "rugged individualism." For example, William Graham Sumner, an immensely influential American sociologist, was lecturing as follows during the general economic depression of 1879:

> If we do not like the survival of the fittest, we have only one possible alternative, and that is the survival of the unfittest. The former is the law of civilization; the latter is the law of anticivil-ization. We have our choice between the two, but a third plan—

25 *Nietzsche, Thus Spake Zarathustra,* Modern Library, New York, no date, pp. 27-28.

the socialist desideratum—a plan for nourishing the unfittest and yet advancing in civilization, no man will ever find.[26]

Such views are still common in America, as Robert and Helen Lynd point out in their famous study of "Middletown," the representative American city which they chose to study. "You can't make the world all planned and soft," says the typical businessman of Middletown. "The strongest and best survive—that's the law of nature after all—always has been and always will be."[27]

There are a number of fallacies and difficulties in Evolutionary Ethics. Most of its proponents, with the exception of Nietzsche, have committed the genetic fallacy, the fallacy of identifying something in its developed form with its origins. They have argued that since man's moral life flows out of nature, it must exhibit the same characteristics as the nature out of which it flows. Since man evolved from the lower animals, he must exhibit in his moral life the same characteristics as these animals, and abide by the same "law" of survival of the fittest that holds for ape and tiger. But development or evolution, if it means anything, must mean change. Various characteristics must exist at the end of the process that were not present at the beginning. An oak tree grows out of an acorn, but it is not an acorn. Man evolves out of apelike ancestors, but he is not an ape. Human beings alone have the capacity to think out a plan of life and to live according to the plan. They alone have the capacity to substitute rational persuasion in place of force. For man to live as a wolf, therefore, is folly, because this is to live at the subhuman level. In *genesis,* man may be akin to the wolf; in his *developed character,* he is very different.

Most of the proponents of Evolutionary Ethics have also committed the "fallacy of factualism." This consists in supposing that *what is,* is synonymous with *what ought to be.*

26 *Essays,* Yale University Press, New Haven, 1934, II, p. 56.
27 *Middletown in Transition,* Harcourt, Brace, New York, 1937, p. 500.

Given the factual proposition, *x is the case,* we are asked to infer the normative proposition, *x is good* or *x ought to be.* We cannot thus leap from a factual proposition to a normative proposition unless we assume that whatever exists is good, which is surely a dubious assumption. The fact that this fallacy is involved in Ethical Darwinism tends to be concealed by the equivocal meaning of the word *fittest.* If we fail to distinguish between the biological and the ethical meaning of *fittest,* it is easy to commit this fallacy: we will assume that the biologically fit are the ethically fit; that what survives *ought* to survive. But the fittest, from the standpoint of biological survival, may be merely the cunning or the cruel or a combination of the weak. What is fittest, moreover, depends upon the environmental conditions and is wholly relative to them. If the earth were to cool again in a new ice age, for example, the "survival of the fittest" might bring about more and more stunted and humbler organisms, such as lichens. Within a gang of human cutthroats, perhaps only the most ruthless cutthroat could survive. There is nothing in mere survival, therefore, that attests to a high ethical character or goodness of any kind.

Even if, waiving all these objections, we were to assume that the fittest are always the best and the more evolved are always the better, we would have no right to conclude that the natural *means* to the natural *end* are best. Nature may be enormously wasteful and cruel in arriving at its goals. There may be a blind proliferating and a vast eliminating process in nature that brings about real progress but at terrible cost. Perhaps man, with his power of reason, cooperation, sympathy, foresight, and scientific control, can achieve the end of evolutionary advance by far more economical means than nature ordinarily employs. Perhaps the proper role of man is to improve upon nature rather than to imitate it. As Tennyson said of nature, "Of fifty seeds she often brings but one to bear."[28] Why should man be so spendthrift merely because nature is?

Moreover, we can no longer accept as adequate the account of evolution given by Spencer, Nietzsche, and the Ethical Darwinists. This account, as we have said, depicts nature as a war of each against all, with the fittest animals living to fight another day and to breed warrior victors like themselves. However, Darwin, in a number of interesting passages, pointed out that cooperation often helps animals to survive; and since his death, a vast amount of evidence has accumulated to show that mutual aid is a powerful factor in evolution. Kropotkin, Geddes, Conklin, and many other biologists have discovered innumerable cooperative traits among animals. After surveying the evidence in great detail, Dr. W. C. Allee, distinguished American biologist, has said:

> There are both egoistic and altruistic forces in nature, and both are important. The question arises insistently as to which of these is the more fundamental and potent. . . . After much consideration, it is my mature opinion, contrary to Herbert Spencer, that the cooperative forces are biologically the more important and vital. . . . Under many conditions, the cooperative forces lose. In the long run, however, the group-centered, more altruistic drives are slightly stronger. If cooperation had not been the stronger force, the more complicated animals, whether arthopods or vertebrates, could not have evolved from the simpler ones, and there would have been no men to worry each other with their distressing and biologically foolish wars.[29]

This opinion has been endorsed by some of the world's leading scientists. Moreover, many biologists have pointed out that natural selection is not a creative factor, that it merely conserves what is otherwise created, and that we must take account of other factors such as mutation if we are to explain evolution. In view of these opinions, we can confidently declare that the "struggle for existence" with consequent natural selection is not the whole story and that a cooperative

28 Tennyson, "In Memoriam," LV.
29 "Where Angels Fear to Tread," *Science,* Vol. 97, 1943, p. 521.

way of life is no less "natural" than a competitive or aggressive way.

Aggression, in the form of modern warfare, is indeed unjustified biologically. It is absurd to argue that the next great war will weed out the unfit. In its use of the draft, modern war is counterselective: it selects the fit for the battlefront and leaves the unfit behind. Among those exposed to combat, the most intelligent and healthy are selected for the most dangerous forms of service, for example, to man the airplanes and the submarines, and to serve in the signal corps or as paratroopers. In so far as modern war is not counterselective, it is indiscriminate. When an atomic bomb, for example, falls upon a great city, it exterminates fit and unfit alike. War is as foolish biologically as it is catastrophic ethically.

I have been dealing with a particular interpretation of Evolutionary Ethics as advanced by such thinkers as Herbert Spencer and William Graham Sumner. Others such as John Dewey, Henri Bergson, and Samuel Alexander have been encouraged by the theory of evolution to enunciate a liberal and humanitarian creed. Evolution, they have said, indicates that the universe is constituted so as to permit novelty, growth, the development of richer capabilities, the upsurge from protozoa to the high level of humanity exhibited in its heroes, artists, thinkers, and saints. They have argued that nature, in producing man, has at last created an animal that has the power to create himself. Hence they have emphasized the value of an open-minded and adventurous morality, not imitating the lower animals but pushing forward to new horizons.

Evolution can be variously interpreted and its ethical implications are ambiguous. It has not solved our ethical riddles or provided us with a model of conduct. In the light of biological science, we are inclined to interpret man naturalistically rather than supernaturalistically; and we are more aware of the immense past of the human race and the im-

mense promise of its future. If man looks to nature as a
model to imitate, however, he fails to use his greatest natural
gift—his free intelligence.

4. *A General Criticism of Naturalistic Ethics*

NATURE has meant many things to many people, but in most
of its meanings, it supplies no adequate norm for individual
or social action. Perhaps all that is valuable is natural, but
not all that is natural is valuable. Only in so far as the natural
coincides with the valuable can it be the valid basis of ethical
choice.

Let us consider some of the meanings of *nature*. First, the
term can be used to denote *all that is*—the entire system of
things. So construed, it provides no basis for selection. Anything and everything is natural; hence the injunction, "Follow nature," is meaningless, since one could never do anything else.

Second, *nature* is sometimes used to mean the typical,
common, or usual. Nature, so understood, is not necessarily
good or right. We have no duty to be typical if the type is
mediocre or bad. The advice "When in Rome do as the
Romans do" is a counsel of prudence and not of morality.
It is not always our duty to be on the winning side. Even
the majority may be wrong. High attainment, by virtue of
its height, is bound to be unusual. As Spinoza says in the
concluding sentence of his *Ethics:* "All excellent things are
as difficult as they are rare."[30] There is a touch of exaggeration in this statement, but at least a great many excellent
things are rare.

Third, *nature* may mean the primitive. For example,
Rousseau in his early writings used the word in this sense.
Here, too, there is no reliable basis for ethical choice. The
primitive may have a pristine vitality or unspoiled simplicity

---

[30] *Ethics*, Dutton, New York, 1910, p. 224.

that we rightly admire, but it may also be "poor, nasty, brutish, and short." The mere fact that something occurs early in a developmental process does not make it good.

Fourth, *nature* may mean the innate rather than the acquired, as when we contrast it with *nurture*. But unless we are to abandon all education, all training and cultivation, we cannot assert that nature is always to be preferred to nurture. Practically the whole business of civilization consists in the improvement of what is innate.

Fifth, *nature* may mean that which exists apart from human control or contrivance, as when we speak of nature as wild and untended and spontaneous. Here, again, we have no basis for an ethical norm, because all of man's arts and sciences consist in interfering with nature, so understood. Without such an interference, human life would be impossible. There can be no sound reason for excluding it on the ground that it is "unnatural."

If we are asked to live according to *nature* in any of these five meanings of the word, we are being asked to commit the fallacy of factualism. We are being asked to take some merely factual characteristic—all-inclusiveness or typicality or primitiveness or innateness or lack of cultivation—and to turn it into a norm for conduct. But the factual is not the ideal: physics and ethics are distinct. "What is" is not identical with "what ought to be." Ideals, of course, sometimes come true: the good and the actual overlap, yet they do not coincide. The whole tragedy of existence consists in this fact.

If by *nature* we do not mean the actual but the ideal, it may indeed serve as a basis for conduct. Sometimes the word is used in this sense, as when we speak of "natural" as the fully realized, the ideal fulfillment of the type. An ethics based upon such a concept, however, is essentially purposive: it does not ask us to imitate a given pattern; it is forward looking, end seeking, open-minded, and adventurous. Ethics of this type—the ethics of ideals—we shall study in Part Two of this book.

Such an ethics need not be indifferent to, or independent of, fact. It can and should recognize that actuality—the factually real world—supplies us with the materials with which we must work and sets limits upon what we can do. Moreover, we can determine what is ideal only in the light of actual needs and tendencies, but we cannot identify fact with norm, actual with ideal. If nature means goodness, we should embrace it; if it means anything else, it is not a valid object of ethical aspiration.

Chapter Four

THE LAWS OF THE MIND

1. *The Ethics of Conscience*

IN TWO WAYS men have sought to find moral law: by looking beyond themselves or by looking within. Seeking an authority external to the individual mind, they have looked to society or God or nature; seeking the direct witness of their own minds, they have looked to some inner faculty, such as conscience or reason.

In the preceding chapters, we have examined customary, theological, and naturalistic ethics, each of which, in its own way, seeks moral laws from a source outside the individual mind. In this chapter, we shall examine theories which seek moral guidance, whether with respect to individual or social action, from an inner faculty whose function is to distinguish between right and wrong.

That faculty may be conceived variously and may receive various names. The term most often employed in everyday usage is *conscience*. I wish first to consider a particular interpretation of conscience, namely, that it distinguishes the rightness or wrongness of acts or motives without consideration of the value of their consequences. According to this view, conscience is a kind of innate, primeval, intuitive faculty that prompts us to certain moral beliefs and attitudes, and it does so in an immediate, unreasoned manner without considering the ulterior effects of our actions. In the final section of this chapter, I shall consider another interpretation of conscience—the conception of a teleological and non-authoritarian "inner voice," recalling each man to his true self. In this first section, however, we shall be dealing with nonteleological conceptions of conscience.

Some people—usually the least philosophically-minded— think of conscience as providing a ready-made decision for each moral occasion. It operates almost instantaneously like one of the sense organs or in the form of a particularized instinctive prompting without regard to rules or principles.

Such an interpretation scarcely requires an extended discussion. It supposes that the injunctions of conscience are so unrational and capricious that they are based upon no principles whatever. This view would leave us with nothing but a chaos of emotional attitudes; all idea of objective morality would be lost. If we are to have moral objectivity rather than whimsy we must take the view that similar cases should be treated similarly and identical cases treated identically. As Hastings Rashdall, in *The Theory of Good and Evil*, points out:

> We do not say to a child who asks whether he may pick a flower in somebody else's garden, "My good child, that depends entirely upon the circumstances of the particular case: to lay down any general rule on the subject would be a piece of unwarrantable dogmatism on my part: consult your own conscience, as each case arises, and all will be well." On the contrary, we say at once: "You must not pick the flower: *because* that would be stealing, and stealing is wrong." Make any reserves you please as to the inadequacy of the rule, its want of definiteness, its inability to meet many problems of life, the necessity for exceptions and the like; yet it must be admitted that if there be any one point about morality as to which there is a consensus alike among all plain men and nearly all philosophers it is surely this—that general rules of conduct do exist.[1]

Even a moral iconoclast like Nietzsche has certain ideals and principles. To discard all such guiding considerations and to allow subrational impulses dubbed "conscience" to determine action in the light of the moment only, is to rely so completely upon caprice as to destroy morality entirely.

[1] *The Theory of Good and Evil*, Oxford University Press, 1907, I, pp. 82-83.

By *conscience,* however, one may mean something different, namely, the immediate insight that certain *kinds* of acts are right or wrong. According to this point of view, there are self-evident rules for determining right action in the different departments of conduct. Certain classes of acts, such as theft or murder, are to be disapproved upon the basis of rules intuited by conscience; and certain other classes of acts, such as truth-telling or the keeping of promises, are to be approved upon the same basis. This doctrine has had such a wide acceptance that Henry Sidgwick, writing at the end of the nineteenth century, called it the point of view of "common sense morality."[2] His criticism of this theory in his *Methods of Ethics* is a classic of reasoning. Except that my remarks are much briefer, part of what I have to say differs but little from the considerations that he advances.

First, the rules enjoined by *conscience* are not really self-evident. What is meant by self-evidence is clearly stated by Thomas Reid (1710-1796), a proponent of the view that we are now criticizing. Self-evident propositions, he declares are those "which are no sooner understood than they are believed. . . . There is no searching for evidence, no weighing of arguments: the proposition is not deduced or inferred from another; it has the light of truth in itself, and has no occasion to borrow it from another."[3] The simple propositions of mathematics or logic may be said to have this character. That "two and two make four," for example, will be assented to by anyone who understands the proposition: its denial would be logically contradictory. Or to take another illustration, we know independently of observation or proof that "if x implies y, and if x is true, y is true" (where x and y symbolize propositions). To say that the proposition y is false when it is implied by a true proposition (namely x) is clearly contradictory. On the other hand, the denial of an ethical

2 *Cf.,* Henry Sidgwick, *The Methods of Ethics,* Macmillan, London, 1922, Book III, Chapter XI.

3 *Essays on the Intellectual Powers of Man,* Macmillan, London, 1941, Essay VI, Ch. IV.

rule, for example that "a person ought not to steal," is not logically contradictory; and indeed the rule has not always been maintained. The children of ancient Sparta, for example, were taught to steal; and Polish or French children, during World War II, were taught that stealing from the Nazis was a meritorious, although dangerous, act.

Second, the supposedly self-evident moral rule turns out upon examination to be ambiguous. Let us consider, for example, the rule that one should not murder. What is murder? The Quakers have condemned war and capital punishment as forms of murder. Most people have disagreed, but we can scarcely decide such a question by merely counting the number of proponents or opponents of the belief. In practice, murder is hard to define; it is often difficult to distinguish between justifiable homicide, manslaughter, and murder; juries have deliberated such questions for many hours. Or consider the rule that one should not lie. Is the literal truth, if its effect is to deceive, a lie? Is deceit by look, gesture, or silence a lie? Is it a lie when one tells a falsehood to a child if he cannot understand the real truth or if the truth would hurt his feelings? Every such moral rule is ambiguous when applied to certain borderline cases.

Third, the moral rules may conflict. One rule, for example, may say, "Do not lie," but another rule may say, "Do not inflict suffering"; and the two rules, as applied to a given situation, may be in conflict. When the duty of veracity conflicts with the duty of benevolence, which should take precedence? The old question, "Should a physician ever lie to the sick?" involves this moral dilemma. Or again, suppose at a dinner party someone deliberately slanders a friend of yours. Should you act on the injunction, "Be loyal to your host and do not make a scene by challenging or denouncing the slanderer"? Or should you act on the principle, "Be loyal to your friend and defend him even at the cost of precipitating an embarrassing argument"? The moral perplexities of life arise precisely in this way: one principle impels us to act contrary to another principle. When we are confronted by these perplexities, the apparent self-evidence of the moral rule disappears, and in practice we cannot decide what to do without a consideration of the consequences of our actions.

Fourth, the injunctions of conscience vary from time to time and from place to place, and this fact implies that they are not really infallible or self-evident. For example, the ancient Greeks believed that the exposure and fatal abandonment of unwanted infants was morally permissible. Even Plato, a morally conscientious man, believed in such exposure when it would serve a eugenic purpose. Homosexuality was likewise approved among many Greeks. Or to cite another period in history, very strait-laced and conscientious Christians engaged in slave traffic, and there seemed nothing morally reprehensible to them in the terrible suffering and huge death ˙toll among the Negroes they transported from Africa. The burning of "witches" was also engaged in by Christian communities. Indeed, this practice was carried to fantastic extremes; altogether, many hundreds of women were burned, and in some towns and villages nearly all women over forty were exterminated. Almost invariably they confessed to being witches when tortured and retortured; and the good Christians of the community thereupon burned them with the most conscientious of scruples. It is difficult to find any practice, however cruel or reprehensible, that has not been accounted virtuous in some time or place. Almost everything morally condemned by any one community has been morally approved by some other.

In view of such differences, it is impossible to regard the "intuitive" promptings of conscience, which usually coincide with the mores of the given society, as genuinely objective and universal. Modern psychologists, such as Freud, have explained conscience as the "internalization" of the commands of the external authorities within the individual's environment, especially his childhood environment. Erich Fromm, a contemporary psychologist, explains the authoritarian type of conscience in this way:

> In the formation of conscience . . . such authorities as the parents, the church, the state, public opinion are either consciously or unconsciously accepted as ethical and moral legislators whose laws and sanctions one adopts, thus internalizing them. The laws and sanctions of external authority become part of oneself, as it were, and instead of feeling responsible to something outside oneself, one feels responsible to something inside, to one's conscience. Conscience is a more effective regulator of conduct than fear of external authorities; for, while one can run away from the latter, one can not escape from oneself nor, therefore, from the internalized authority which has become part of oneself.[4]

The prescriptions of nonreflective, authoritarian conscience are the voice of custom or traditional authority, so deeply ingrained in the human mind as to appear self-evident.

I do not mean to imply that a man should never seek the answer to moral questions in the quiet of his own conscience. Every person should act conscientiously in the sense of being true to his best ethical insights. Indeed, I shall contend in the final section of the present chapter that the rehabilitation of conscience is one of the necessities of our age.

2. *The Ethics of A Priori Reason*

WE have been criticizing the kind of intuitional ethics that maintains that conscience is an infallible inner voice judging right and wrong action in terms of a considerable number of independent self-evident rules. These rules condemn as wrong certain kinds of acts, such as lying or murder, and prescribe as right certain other kinds of acts, such as the keeping of promises or the preservation of chastity. Another form of intuitional ethics holds that all rules of this type can

4 *Man for Himself,* Rinehart, New York, 1947, p. 144.

be subsumed under one or a few supreme general laws which are intuitively certain.

The most impressive of all such attempts to derive specific moral rules from a few general principles is to be found in the ethical treatises of Kant. He believed that the rightness of single acts must always be judged by their relation to rules, and that the many ethical rules advocated by "common sense morality" could ultimately be reduced to a very few general principles or laws apprehended by a priori reason.

His ethical philosophy is best expounded in his *Fundamental Principles of the Metaphysics of Ethics.* A reader of this book will find within it a brief and seemingly clear statement of Kant's ethical philosophy, but the argument has been frequently misunderstood. One reason for the misunderstanding is that Kant has been traditionally depicted as some sort of intellectual machine, without spontaneity or emotional resilience. Heinrich Heine's witty characterization is famous:

The history of the life of Immanuel Kant is hard to write, inasmuch as he had neither life nor history, for he lived a mechanically ordered, and abstract old bachelor life in a quite retired street in Könisberg, an old town on the northeast border of Germany. I do not believe that the great clock of the cathedral there did its daily work more dispassionately and regularly than its compatriot Immanuel Kant. Rising, coffee drinking, writing, reading, college lectures, eating, walking, all had their fixed time, and the neighbors knew that it was exactly half past three when Immanuel Kant in his grey coat, with his Manila cane in his hand, left his house door and went to the Lime tree avenue, which is still called, in memory of him, the Philosopher's Walk.[5]

Unquestionably there is some basis for this characterization, but it is a caricature that leaves out the more human side of Kant's nature. He was, for example, fond of and remarkably good at cards, though often impatient at the slowness of his partner's playing. He loved good company, especially at dinner, and never thought of dining without guests. As a teacher at the university, he was popular with his stu-

5 "Germany," in his *Works,* Heinemann, London, 1891-1905, V, p. 136.

dents and had the power to excite them both to laughter and
to tears. "Even when he was old and withered," according to
H. J. Paton, "he did not lose his simple and kindly and cour-
teous character. When he was so weak that he fell in the street
and could not rise till two unknown ladies helped him up,
he presented one of them with the rose which he happened
to be carrying."[6] Despite his addiction to routine and system-
building, there was a touch of the true romantic in him and
a great deal of emotional warmth. Those who overlook this
side of his nature are inclined to interpret his ethics as coldly
formalistic and purely intellectual; but such an interpretation is one sided.

In terms of the historical background of his thought, Kant
was a child of the Protestant Reformation and of the American and French Revolutions. Reared in a pious family, he
was deeply imbued with the spirit of Protestant ethics and
religion. One of his main ambitions as a philosopher was to
vindicate the belief in God, freedom, and immortality, not
as the dogmas of an authoritarian Church but as the articles
of a reasonable moral faith. In his insistence that every human
being is an end in himself, he expressed in philosophical
terms the Christian doctrine of the infinite intrinsic worth of
the individual human soul and also the new revolutionary
doctrine of the Rights of Man. He sympathized with the
French Revolution until the Reign of Terror and admired
the new American republic; and he believed that freedom
is basic to all morality and all social progress. He was also
greatly influenced by the Enlightenment, the great critical
movement in European thought that led up to the French
and American Revolutions. Like many of the apostles of this
movement, he had a strong confidence in reason, but, like
Rousseau, he wished to vindicate the "heart" as well as the
"head." It must be admitted, however, that he lent some support to a subordination of the individual to the edicts of an
authoritarian state. In a complex way, he combined rigor

[6] *The Categorical Imperative,* Hutchinson, London, 1947, p. 198.

and kindness, reason and faith, belief in freedom and respect for authority.

After a short introduction in which he insists that ethics must be based upon a priori rather than empirical principles, Kant begins his ethical argument by maintaining that nothing is unconditionally and unqualifiedly good except a good will. Knowledge, wealth, health, or any talent of mind or body is not good if employed for villainous ends. Even pleasure is bad if malicious. For example, the pleasure that a sadist might obtain in torturing an innocent child is thoroughly bad. Good will is the sole exception: it is good intrinsically and absolutely. Like a jewel, it shines by its own light.

This doctrine does not mean that good will is the whole good or the only noninstrumental good. For Kant there are two goods: the good will, which is unconditionally good, and happiness, which is good for its own sake only when combined with good will. He believes that virtue merits reward, that good will should be crowned with happiness. By happiness he frequently means a maximum of pleasure, but sometimes he uses the term more broadly to denote the maximum satisfaction of a man's needs and inclinations.

To realize one's own happiness, he believes, is the principal aim of prudence. Every man has the right to pursue his own happiness in his own way so long as the effort does not conflict with the moral law. In certain circumstances, it may even be one's indirect duty to pursue one's own happiness, since an unhappy man is so fettered by his misery that he finds it difficult to fulfill his duty, whereas a happy man may find it relatively easy. Nevertheless, Kant feels that there is a fundamental difference between a life of prudence and one of moral goodness, and that love for oneself, or striving for one's own happiness, is not directly virtuous.

Since a virtuous will is absolutely and unconditionally good, it must have its full worth in itself, apart from any consequences that may ensue. In holding this doctrine, Kant

rejects all forms of utilitarianism—the theory that the right
is the useful in promoting welfare. This does not mean that
a good man ignores consequences; to act intelligently he must
have in mind the intended effects of his actions. He will aim
at certain consequences because it is his duty to do so, but
his duty is determined by universal moral law rather than by
the specific consequences of an act.

Inclination is likewise not the determining ground of a
moral act. The good man acts upon the maxim, "I will do
my duty, whatever my inclination may be." He does not say,
"I will do my duty if I happen to be so inclined." This does
not mean that the good man must always act *contrary* to his
inclination. Kant has often been criticized for holding that
duty must always be disagreeable, but this objection is based
upon a misunderstanding. It is no sign of moral imperfection
to do one's duty with a cheerful heart. Indeed, Kant believes
that the highest type of will is the "holy will," in which duty
and inclination perfectly agree. Such a will, unfortunately,
is superhuman, and the call of duty for human beings is not
only distinguishable from inclination but often contrary to it.

If the criterion of rightness of motive is neither consequences nor inclination, what is it? The answer is that a right
motive is based upon moral principle, the principle of "the
categorical imperative."

An imperative is an injunction or command: it says that
a person ought to do so and so. There are two kinds of imperatives: hypothetical and categorical. A hypothetical imperative always takes the form, "*If* you wish to achieve *x*, then
you ought to do *y*." It is based upon the fact that "whoever
wills the end, wills also (so far as reason decides his conduct)
the means in his power which are indispensably necessary
thereto."[7] Ordinary rules of skill and counsels of prudence
are hypothetical imperatives: they tell us what we ought to

---

[7] *Fundamental Principles of the Metaphysics of Ethics,* Longmans, Green,
London, 1916, p. 41.

do—"ought" in the sense of what we would be well advised to do—*if* we desire certain ends. They may be entirely legitimate but they are not moral. A categorical imperative, on the other hand, asserts simply and unconditionally, "You ought to act thus and thus." There is no "if" in front of the "ought." Obligation is not determined by wish or expediency but by objective moral necessity, which can be stated in a universal rule. When I say, for example, that a man ought to respect the rights of others, or that he ought not to murder, I do not mean that the "ought" is conditional upon the man's wish or is merely a matter of prudence. Such an "ought"— objective, necessary, unconditional, absolute—is a categorical imperative; and every such imperative and no other kind of imperative is moral.

The kind of necessity and universality involved in a moral imperative is explained by Kant as follows:

> Everyone must admit that if a law is to have moral force, *i.e.* to be the basis of an obligation, it must carry with it absolute necessity; that, for example, the precept, "Thou shalt not lie," is not valid for men alone, as if other rational beings had no need to observe it; and so with all the other moral laws properly so called; that, therefore, the basis of obligation must not be sought in the nature of man, or in the circumstances in the world in which he is placed, but *a priori* simply in the conceptions of pure reason; and although any other precept which is founded on principles of mere experience may be in certain respects universal, yet, in as far as it rests even in the least degree on an empirical basis, perhaps only as to a motive, such a precept, while it may be a practical rule, can never be called a moral law.[8]

Kant is here stating the position of ethical absolutism: that moral laws admit of no exceptions and hold universally without regard to differing circumstances or inclinations. He is not even willing to base morality upon human nature or apply it specifically to man. It must rest upon abstract reason and apply uniformly to all rational creatures—even to angels,

8 *Ibid.*, p. 4.

if they exist and are rational. The categorical imperative is necessary in the sense of being morally obligatory upon all rational beings.

This kind of necessity is quite different from physical necessity. It means strict obligation: it does not mean any kind of physical compulsion. Indeed, when I am compelled to do something, there is no sense in saying that I ought to do it; I can only say that I *must* do it. Empirical science, in describing or causally explaining a succession of events is simply concerned with what is, not with what ought to be; whereas ethics expresses the ideal rather than the factual. Since moral judgments are not judgments of fact, since they are not empirical generalizations, they must be derived a priori—that is, independently of experience.

They can be so derived and will exhibit a kind of necessity if they are akin to mathematical propositions. There is an absolute, unconditional necessity about the proposition that 2 and 3 equal 5. We do not mean that 2 and 3 sometimes or usually equal 5 but that they always and necessarily do. It is contradictory and therefore impossible for the sum of 2 and 3 to be anything but 5. We can know this by pure reason without considering any particular case. According to Kant, the moral law is likewise necessary and universal because its denial involves a contradiction. A moral principle is consistent, and an immoral principle is inconsistent.

When we are considering some type of action, such as telling a lie, we should formulate the principle manifested in it and see if we can consistently will it as a universal principle. If not, it is inconsistent and immoral. In this way, Kant derives his first formula for the categorical imperative: "Act only on that maxim through which you can at the same time will that it should become a universal law."[9] This formula expresses the very conception of the categorical imperative,

9 H. J. Paton, *The Moral Law* (a translation of Kant's *Groundwork of the Metaphysic of Morals*), Hutchinson, London, 1947, p. 88.

namely, that it be independent of empirical and hypothetical grounds—that is, strictly universal and formal.

Consider, as an example of how the formula is applied, the above-mentioned case of lying. To will that lying should be universally practiced would be self-contradictory, for if everybody lied the liar would not be believed. Lying tends to undermine itself; it tends to its own defeat. It is parasitic upon truth-telling; if it were universalized, there would not be any truth to lie about. Or suppose that you are thinking of making a promise that you do not intend to keep. It is clear that the maxim of your action could not be universalized.

For supposing it to be a universal law that everyone when he thinks himself in a difficulty should be able to promise whatever he pleases, with the purpose of not keeping his promise, the promise itself would become impossible, as well as the end that one might have in view in it, since no one would consider that anything was promised to him, but would ridicule all such statements as vain pretences.[10]

The principle that one should lie, or that one should make promises with the intention of breaking them, cannot be *thought* as holding universally. It is somewhat different with certain other types of immorality, which can be *conceived* as holding universally but cannot be *willed* as universal. Take for example the refusal to help others in need of aid.

Now no doubt if such a mode of thinking were a universal law, the human race might very well subsist. . . . But although it is possible that a universal law of nature might exist in accordance with that maxim, it is impossible to will that such a principle should have the universal validity of a law of nature. For a will which resolved this would contradict itself, inasmuch as many cases might occur in which one would have need of the love and sympathy of others, and in which, by such a law of nature, sprung from his own will, he would deprive himself of all hope of the aid he desires.[11]

10 Kant, *Fundamental Principles, op. cit.,* p. 48.
11 *Ibid.,* p. 49.

One reason, therefore, that we cannot universalize the principle of immoral acts is that every man wants to be treated with respect; he does not want to be a victim of wrong action, and therefore he cannot consistently will that this sort of action be universalized.

The ultimate reason for this fact is that every man is an end in himself and wants to be so regarded. A personality is precious; it is a center and focus of value; and in so far as it is free and rational, it recognizes this fact. Therefore Kant is led to his second formulation of the principle of the categorical imperative: "Act in such a way that you always treat humanity, whether in your own person or in the person of any other, never simply as a means, but always at the same time as an end."[12] In other words, treat everyone as a spiritual being having intrinsic value, never as merely a means, a tool, as a thing with only instrumental value. This principle follows from the fact that man as rational and moral, and as capable of happiness, possesses dignity and inner worth. When applied to conduct, it rules out all forms of selfishness, for the essence of selfishness is the employment of someone as a mere tool without proper respect for him as a person. Every sort of vengeance, exploitation, aggression, or gratification of sadistic impulses must be considered immoral, because it involves the use of someone as a mere means.

The characteristic that makes man an end in himself is above all his autonomy. Only a free agent can be actuated by good will, which is the sole unconditional and absolute good, the supreme jewel of life. Without freedom there is no meaning in moral obligation: "I ought" implies "I can." Hence Kant is led to a third statement of the principle of the categorical imperative, namely, insistence that every man should act as a free moral agent, himself willing the moral law and willingly submitting himself to it. This formula is expressed in a number of ways, but Kant's thought can be briefly epitomized as follows: "Always act as a member of a

12 Paton, *The Moral Law, op. cit.,* p. 96.

kingdom of ends."[13] This means that every man should unite with others in a society in which each freely realizes his own good in promoting that of others, and in which he is both subject and sovereign. As sovereign, he should exercise his freedom; he should will the right; he should develop and exercise his capacity for rational choice. As member, he should exhibit moral responsibility, willing his own obedience to moral law. The result of thus exercising both freedom and responsibility is to unite with others in a self-governing society of rational agents, each one of whom is an end in himself and a means to the ends of others:

> For all rational beings come under the law that each of them must treat itself and all others *never merely as means,* but in every case *at the same time as ends in themselves.* Hence results a systematic union of rational beings by common objective laws, i.e., a kingdom which may be called a kingdom of ends, since what these laws have in view is just the relation of these beings to one another as ends and means. . . . A rational being belongs as a *member* to the kingdom of ends when, although giving universal laws in it, he is also himself subject to these laws. He belongs to it *as sovereign* when, while giving laws, he is not subject to the will of another.[14]

Kant explains that this "kingdom"—which might better be called a "republic of ends"—is "certainly only an ideal," but it is none the less a valid norm for human conduct.

In his political writings, Kant applies these moral principles to society. Especially important, in this connection, is his emphasis upon the a priori universal character of morality, his conception of the human being as an end in himself, and his conviction that freedom is indispensable to the good life.

The ideal of the political state, he believes, is to embody universal moral law. The moral law that should serve as the basis of the state is determined by the categorical imperative rather than by utilitarian considerations. Although Kant

13 *Cf.,* Kant, *Fundamental Principles, op. cit.,* pp. 61-62.
14 *Ibid.,* p. 62.

recognizes that a good government promotes the welfare of the people, he insists that "by this is not to be understood the individual well-being and happiness of the citizens of the state. . . . The welfare of the state as its own highest good signifies that condition in which the greatest harmony is attained between the constitution and the principle of right."[15] Law should be essentially an application of the categorical imperative, and as such it should be obligatory upon all rational beings, irrespective of their class, sex, race, nationality, or personal peculiarities. With this conception of universal law, he is impelled to reject the ideal of separate states, since these represent only a halfway stage in the realization of the universality of law and morality. Only a universal state can embody the idea of universal law, and hence Kant is an ardent advocate of an international confederation or world state, capable of expressing universal laws and securing eternal peace. All history, be believes, is the checkered story of human progress, and progress is essentially the movement of humanity toward this ultimate ideal.

Kant's conception of the human being as an end in himself underlies his democratic convictions. The democratic idea that all men are created equal implies that all men have the same basic right to be considered as ends in themselves and not as mere means. If no man is a mere tool, to be exploited for the benefit of others, it is immoral for any class to live off the sweat of another, or for any individual to rule over others for the sake of his personal aggrandizement. The state, likewise, is not entitled to use its citizens as mere tools. Hence the state is made for man, not man for the state. A human being, in other words, is not a mere ant in a social ant heap: he is an end and is entitled to be treated as such. To deny this is to blaspheme against the essential dignity of man and to degrade him to the status of a machine or a slave. Kant is here expressing the fundamental moral basis of democracy.

15 *Philosophy of Law*, Clark, Edinburgh, 1887, p. 173.

Kant's emphasis upon freedom underlies his liberalism. Man as free should be subject and sovereign in both the moral and the political sphere. As subject, he must freely accept the law of the state if it truly embodies moral principles; a social return is to be demanded of all; there are to be no parasites. Freedom entails responsibility, and duties are correlative with rights. As sovereign, man is free; he has the right to legislate over himself; he has the right to participate in the decisions of the community; he cannot legitimately be the pawn of any dictatorship. Kant is here expressing the essence of the liberal ideal.

3. A Criticism of Kant's Ethics and Politics

IT IS TIME to turn from an exposition to a critical evaluation of Kant's ethical principles and political ideals. The criticism of Kant opens a vast field for discussion, and what I shall say merely touches upon the many controversial questions involved.

First of all, we must grant that there is much in his thought that is extremely valuable. No one can read him understandingly without being impressed by his high seriousness and deep insight. Whatever may be his mistakes, he has performed a great service in formulating his basic principles, such as the central importance of good will, the impartiality and universality of duty, the clear-cut distinction between a hypothetical and a categorical imperative, the recognition that "I ought" implies "I can," and the insistence that everyone should be treated as an end in himself. In applying his principles to society, Kant provides a strong moral foundation for democracy, liberalism, and internationalism. No doubt there is much to quarrel with here, and some of his more valuable principles, such as the concept of a categorical imperative, need to be fundamentally reinterpreted; but as C. D. Broad remarks, "Kant's failures are more important than most men's successes."[16] Nevertheless, it is worth while to see in what respects he does fail.

The principal weakness of his moral philosophy is its excessive abstractness and formalism. He declares that morality can be determined only by universal moral rule irrespective of inclinations and consequences. It is immoral, he believes, to violate a universal rule even for the sake of very good consequences. It is this view that I wish to challenge.

Let us consider his first formula of the categorical imperative: "Act only on that maxim through which you can at the same time will that it should become a universal law." Now in practice we often apply this type of formula. For example, in reference to a certain election I may ask myself, "Should I vote?" I may reason that my vote is insignificant in comparison with the many votes cast, and that in all probability it will decide nothing. But then I think to myself, "What if all people should think similarly and abstain from voting?" I cannot *will* that this should be so: if nonvoting were universalized the effect would be disastrous; indeed there would not even be any elections and so no chance to refrain from voting; and the realization that this would be the case helps to make clear to me that I have a real obligation as a citizen to vote.

Yet this mode of reasoning involves a tacit appeal to consequences. Why *not* will that nobody should vote? Similarly, why not will that every man should break his promises, steal his neighbor's goods, commit adultery with his neighbors' wives, or murder his friends and associates? It is because we value human life that we would not care to have it thus completely undermined. To a complete amoralist or cynic or pessimist, who puts no value at all upon life, there would be nothing repugnant to reason in the universalization of some or all of these forms of wrong-doing. Some anarchists have advocated the view that nobody should ever vote; and if we

16 *Five Types of Ethical Theory,* Harcourt, Brace, New York, 1930, p. 11.

disagree, it is surely because we think that voting does some good.

Without such an appeal to consequences, there is nothing plausible about Kant's formula. His attempt to derive his rules upon the basis of pure logical consistency is specious. We can no more derive moral truth from a formal logical law than we can derive scientific truth from such a law. No juggling of the principle of contradiction will ever give us a particular law of nature, such as Boyle's law of the behavior of gases. Similarly no manipulation of the principle of contradiction can ever yield a particular moral truth, such as that we ought to vote.

Let us assume, however, that the rule that one should vote is morally justified. Should it ever admit of exceptions? Kant would apparently have to say no, because he insists in the very strongest language that moral rules do not permit exceptions. Yet I might have a very weighty reason for not voting. I might be ill, or I might be needed to tend someone who is ill, or there might be some other special circumstance that would justify my decision not to vote. To say that no consideration of welfare, no view of consequences, could possibly justify my failure to vote would be fanatical. In opposition to Kant, any reasonable person is prepared to admit some philanthropic exceptions.

In Kant's defense it might be argued that one maxim of duty must be limited by another maxim of duty: the duty to vote, for example, must sometimes be limited by the duty to tend someone in distress. If duties conflict with and limit one another, however, they must necessarily have a relative and tentative character, and not the absolute, unconditional, a priori character which Kant ascribes to them. Moreover, when duty conflicts with duty, it is difficult to see how Kant could decide which duty takes precedence. Unlike a utilitarian, he could not say that we have the stronger obligation to perform the act that would bring about the greater welfare.

Despite the fact that in real life duties often do conflict, he apparently sticks to the position that morality should be utterly uncompromising and that a certain kind of action such as truth-telling is right in all circumstances. At least he is almost always so interpreted, and it is difficult to see how some of his statements could mean anything else. But if so, it is hard to see how this position is consistent with his second formula of the categorical imperative, "Always treat every rational being as an end, never as a means merely." This second formula, if it signifies anything, surely signifies a respect for the intrinsic value of personality, but such respect is inconsistent with a willingness to sacrifice human life and its values for the sake of abstract moral law. A story has been told about the philosopher Fichte which illustrates the point I am making. He was once asked the question, "What would you do if your wife were very ill and to tell the truth to her, when the truth is very shocking, would kill her?" Now like Kant, Fichte would not admit that a person is ever justified in saying to himself: "It is almost always better to tell the truth, but in this case I shall do much more good by telling a lie; and therefore I had better lie." Instead he is said to have replied, "If my wife must die by the truth, let her die."[17] Surely in so responding Fichte was not treating his wife as intrinsically precious, as an end in herself. Kant's formula that we should never treat anyone as a mere means implies, among other things, that a person is not to be used as a mere means for the carrying into effect of an abstract moral code: that morality is made for man, not man for morality.

The inconsistency within Kant's ethics is primarily a conflict between the abstractness and absolutism of his ethical formalism, expressed most clearly in his first formula of the categorical imperative, and the concreteness and humanitarianism implied by his second and third formulas of the categorical imperative. Despite the fact that Kant feels that the first formula implies the other two, there is a real conflict

17 Cf., Wilbur Marshall Urban, *Fundamentals of Ethics*, Holt, New York, 1930, p. 40.

between them. The first formula insists upon strict moral universality, admitting of no exceptions. This insistence is not consistent with the second formula, that every person is to be treated as an end in himself; because every person is a concrete individual, and he must be dealt with individually if he is to be treated as an end. As Master Eckhart, the German mystic has said:

That I am a man, this I share with other men. That I see and hear and that I eat and drink is what all animals do likewise. But that I am I is only mine and belongs to me and to nobody else; to no other man nor to an angel nor to God—except inasmuch as I am one with Him.[18]

Every man is an individual: he is "man" in the singular: he is not the abstraction "mankind." He shares many characteristics with other animals and with other men; but there is always a peculiar temperament, a unique blend of talents, a separate and distinctive consciousness. Just as there are no two fingerprints exactly alike, so there are no two personalities exactly alike. There is always something about me that is never common to you and me. Respect for a person includes respect for this core of individuality. It means appreciation of the real man of flesh and blood—the individual and human *me*—not just a grammatical abstraction. Kant never sufficiently appreciated this fact.

If he had put more emphasis upon the value of love and less emphasis upon abstract duty, he would not be so open to the criticism that I have been urging. Despite some implications to the contrary, there is scant recognition in his ethics of the importance of love toward the individual human being. He talks about duty far more than he speaks of love. But unless reverence for duty is touched by love, it will be too cold to possess much driving force and to do justice to the individual. Although the sense of duty is necessary to put iron in the human constitution, love is the more creative and elemental force. It is not just an additional value, on a par

18 *Fragments*. Quoted by Erich Fromm, *op. cit.*, p. 38.

with the others: it transforms other values, lending them its own beauty and warmth. Many psychologists maintain that love is the root impulse and primary motivation of life. In its wide meaning, moreover, it stands not only for the sexual bond between man and woman but for the diverse and innumerable ties of affection without which life is a sad affair.

Kant was a man of kindly feelings, but the abstractness and rigor of his ethical formalism prevented him from putting enough emphasis upon the ethical importance of love, especially love toward concrete human beings. In his first formula of the categorical imperative, he based morality entirely upon universal rule, with no regard for the distinctive human personality. In his second formula, on the other hand, he declared that every human being must be treated as an end in himself, thus implying respect and affection for every person as distinct from other persons. Thus he was inconsistent.

His third formula, that one should join others in a "kingdom" of free and responsible moral agents, likewise implies an individuation of morality. There can be no real freedom except in so far as the individual expresses himself. Freedom surely does not mean reducing all human beings to a common denominator: it means releasing and asserting the individuality in every man. Freedom without self-realization is impossible. Self-realization, of course, is not selfish realization, and individuality is not the same as individualism. Perhaps maximum freedom for the individual can be realized in a cooperative or socialist society. Freedom necessarily involves, however, the autonomy and expression of the real concrete individual.

Kant did not perceive the implications of his own doctrines. He did not clearly realize that only an individual, expressing his individuality, can be free and an end in himself. He supposed that a man is free only when he is following the dictates of universal abstract reason, and that a man is being treated as an end in himself whenever his "good will," as the embodiment of abstract moral law, is exalted as the highest of values. In maintaining that morality is exclusively obedience to universal law, without regard to the individual and his peculiar circumstances, Kant dissolves the individual personality in an ocean of ethical abstraction, like an individual grain of sand dissolved in a vast sea.

The recent philosophical movement called Existentialism, which has had a current great vogue, is in great measure a protest against such an abstract and inadequate view of man and of human values. Such Existentialists as Sören Kierkegaard and Jean Paul Sartre have insisted upon the reality of the individual, the particularity of his plight, and the impossibility of expressing the concrete truth of existence in abstract, universal terms. Some members of this school, unfortunately, have gone to the opposite extreme from Kant's and have denied to the individual any significance beyond the momentary state. Man is both individual and universal—an individual being with universal qualities—and the whole truth about him emphasizes both aspects of his nature.

The insistence upon the reality of the individual is one of the main tenets of liberalism. It is because Kant slights this side of the truth that he is not always a liberal. Unlike ordinary liberals, he does not emphasize the importance of protecting the individual from the encroachment of state power. Good government for him means the application of a rational system of law, which must, in turn, rest upon the universal rules of morality rather than upon the interests or rights of individuals. The essential question is whether the law does or does not agree with a priori principles of right; the question whether it serves the public interest or corresponds to the wishes of the people or protects the civil rights of individuals is not paramount. Slighting in this way the consideration of welfare and of individual rights, Kant denies to the individual the right to rebel even under the most tyrannical of governments. He goes so far as to declare:

Resistance on the part of the people to the supreme legislative power of the state is in no case legitimate. . . . There is no right

of sedition and still less of rebellion belonging to the people. . . .
It is the duty of the people to bear any abuse of the supreme
power, even though it should be considered unbearable.[19]

The weakest part of Kant's ethical and political philosophy
is his formalism. This leads him to neglect considerations of
welfare and the rights of the individual. It is ultimately inconsistent with his belief in freedom and in man as an end
in himself.

4. *Prima-facie Duties*

SINCE THE TIME of Kant, a new influential school of intuitionists has arisen in England. Its most prominent representatives
have been Professors H. A. Prichard and William D. Ross.
I shall briefly discuss the ideas of Ross, the Provost of Oriel
College, Oxford, as an example of this new intuitionism.

Ross rejects the doctrine of Kant that there are duties
which admit of no exceptions. He believes, as almost everyone does, that we are justified in telling an untruth or breaking a promise when the benefit in doing so is very great. A
person is justified, for example, in telling a lie to save a life.
Ross agrees with Kant, however, in maintaining that we must
have some principle of obligation other than benefit. He
thus admits a duality of moral standards: first, production
of welfare and, second, intuited obligation independent of
the welfare or harm produced.

He introduces the conception of "prima-facie duties" to
explain his view that there are conditional yet nonteleological obligations. A prima-facie duty is an obligation which
holds in the absence of a stronger obligation. Other things
being equal, we have, for example, a duty to keep a promise;
but it may be that a stronger and conflicting obligation
should have the right of way. Sometimes the duty of keeping
a promise, however, is stronger than any conflicting duty,

19 *Philosophy of Law, op. cit.,* pp. 176-177.

even the duty of maximizing the good. The duty of producing the greatest good, in fact, is only one duty among a number, and it has no necessary priority over other duties.

Ross believes that we intuitively recognize that something is a prima-facie duty, and that we also intuitively estimate which duty is the stronger when there is a conflict of duties. We intuitively sense the importance, for example, of such duties as telling the truth, fulfilling our promises, returning services rendered, repairing wrongs done, giving to each according to his merits, and showing gratitude to our benefactors. "For the estimation of the comparative stringency of these *prima facie* obligations," Ross declares, "no general rules can, so far as I can see, be laid down."[20] We can only say that there are obligations to perform certain acts irrespective of their consequences, and that the decision what to do in the event of a conflict of obligations ultimately rests with intuition.

Since Ross thus makes intuition the final court of appeal, it is appropriate to reply that I do not find his "intuitions" at all self-evident. Unlike Ross, I find it very difficult to suppose that it is ever my duty deliberately to realize a lesser good when I might realize a greater. I find it difficult, for example, to believe that I ought to keep a promise if to do so will bring about less good than evil—as in the case of a promise that turns out to be hurtful to the parties involved. Similarly, in the case of social policy, I believe that the promises made by one state to another should, in general, be kept; but I believe a treaty should be broken if it becomes quite clear that the welfare of mankind is best served by breaking the treaty. It seems to me self-evident that good, being good, ought to be maximized and that evil, being evil, ought to be minimized, and that we therefore ought to act in such a way as to achieve the maximum surplus of intrinsic good over intrinsic evil. None of Ross' nonteleological principles seems to me so evidently true as this principle.

[20] *The Right and the Good*, Clarendon Press, Oxford, 1930, p. 41.

I grant that we should reject the sort of utilitarianism that takes account only of consequences and leaves out of account the immediate values and disvalues of the act itself. Certainly we must consider the intrinsic nature of an action before we can rightly decide whether to do it or not. We are not justified in doing evil so that good may come, if the evil outweighs the good or if the good could be achieved at less cost.

When you break a promise, for example, there are certain immediate disvalues that should not be overlooked. You may be motivated by selfishness or hatred; and there is almost always injury to your self-respect and injury to the other person's respect for you. On his part, there is usually a sense of unmerited wrong. All of these disvalues, and any other immediate evils, must be weighed against future advantages that might accrue. Injustice, ingratitude, and infidelity are real evils, and a moralist should, in general, disapprove of acts involving them. This is not to say, however, that a right-for-right's-sake theory is valid. You may still believe that the best act is the one most conducive to welfare; but in judging welfare you will not arbitrarily exclude the values and disvalues of the act itself and of the immediate situation which it creates.

Moreover, there is a strong utilitarian reason for disapproving such acts as breaking promises or telling lies even when the consequences to the persons immediately involved are quite good. Considered as an individual act, a lie might be justified, yet it might be better to tell the truth for the sake of maintaining the general rule of truth-telling. It is better for mankind in general to follow the well-established rule that one should tell the truth, even if in specific instances truth-telling imposes penalties, than to allow individual taste and judgment to decide in each particular instance what ought to be done and thus to weaken and undermine the rule.

The question whether the law of the state should be obeyed is similar. The law may specify that an automobile driver should not cross a street intersection if the traffic signal light is red. Yet it may seem desirable to the driver in certain circumstances to cross despite the red signal. But he might validly reason that the law in general should be obeyed, and obeyed in this instance, even though in the specific case a substantial advantage is to be gained by breaking it. The law should be obeyed because it is important that laws be maintained and because there should be a general respect for law. It is better to have traffic regulations, even though they are often inconvenient, than to have no regulations; and it is better *in general* to obey the regulations even when it is quite inconvenient to do so. The advantage in maintaining the general rule is greater than the advantage to be gained from particular infractions. This is not to deny that there are unusual situations when we would be justified in breaking the law or a moral rule.

Moreover, we can judge the value of moral rules only if we appraise them from a social and not merely individual standpoint. Arthur Koestler, in his *Insight and Outlook,* cites an instructive example. During World War II, there was a very serious fuel shortage in England, and to save fuel the government imposed regulations upon the use of hot water. One rule was that bathtubs should be filled to a maximum limit of five inches. As Koestler points out, "the temptation on a cold winter morning, particularly after a night spent at an air-raid post, to add two more inches was strong." From the standpoint of enlightened self-interest, there would seem to be no reason to resist the temptation.

Behind the locked door of one's bathroom the contravention would remain undetected; the quantity of water used was so negligible that in itself it could not harm the community; it could only do so if others were encouraged by the bad example to act in the same way; but as nobody would know, there was no question of giving a bad example.[21]

Yet as Koestler says, the welfare of the people of England

---

21 *Insight and Outlook,* pp. 230-231. Copyright 1949 by Arthur Koestler and used with the permission of The Macmillan Company.

depended upon the "self-imposed observation of the law by millions of individuals in the privacy of their bathrooms." He cites this example to show the "fallacy of utilitarian ethics," but the illustration merely shows the fallacy of a particular kind of utilitarianism. A narrow, individualistic utilitarian standard would excuse the infraction of the rule, but a broad, social utilitarianism would recognize that a rule that is of great benefit to society should be maintained, even though individuals, taken severally, find it to their advantage to break it. An ethics of welfare, therefore, cannot validly be based merely upon the individual decisions of separate persons, each acting in his own special interest.

It is sometimes supposed that what is a good rule for individuals taken severally is a good rule for society. But to leap to this conclusion is as illogical as to suppose that, since all the notes in a symphony are short in duration, the symphony must be short in duration. Reasoning of this type commits what logicians call "the fallacy of composition"—namely, the fallacy of supposing that what is true of the parts of a whole must be true of the whole. To return to our earlier example of voting, it scarcely pays for individuals, as mere individuals, to take the trouble to cast their ballots in a national election, since the voting of any single individual in such an election is very unlikely to affect the outcome; but it is nevertheless very important for a democratic society that its members vote, and the members therefore have a real obligation to vote. Consequently, we cannot judge what is our duty simply by calculating the utility of our acts taken separately and severally. We have many duties to society that are based upon social welfare, and that cannot be determined upon the basis of merely individual welfare. It is true that social welfare is realized in the lives of individuals; but the individuals function within a social whole that has its own distinct characteristics, and these characteristics must be taken into account in judging the duties of individuals. This is one of the reasons why *social* ethics is not identical with *individual* ethics.

I have pointed out that an act, in view of its intrinsic character, may be wrong even if its future consequences are good; that we must consider not simply the value of the individual act but the value of the rule which commands or forbids it; and that we may, for social reasons, have a duty to perform an act even when we, as individuals, find it not beneficial to do so. All of these considerations are quite consistent with a nonformalistic, teleological ethics—an ethics of purpose.

When these considerations are given proper weight, the contention of Ross that there are prima-facie duties irrespective of welfare is no longer plausible. We can explain the force of our obligation to keep a promise or to tell the truth, for example, without invoking his "intuitions." We need not employ, as Ross does, both the teleological standard of welfare and the nonteleological standard of intuited rightness; we can thus avoid the duality of two kinds of moral criteria, with the inevitable conflicts between the two standards. We do not need to fall back upon our subjective "intuitions" when judging the relative strength of conflicting obligations, but can employ the more objective method of investigating the actual needs of human beings and the consequences of their actions.

5. *The Rehabilitation of Conscience*

WE have now reviewed several attempts to base action upon the laws or dictates of the mind. First, we have briefly considered the doctrine that conscience provides a decision for each new occasion, commanding or forbidding a specific act without regard to rules or principles; and we have concluded that conscience thus described is so unprincipled, so without guiding ideas, that it cannot serve as a basis for individual or social morality. Second, we have pondered the doctrine that conscience supplies us with immediate unreasoned knowledge of many independent ethical rules, for example, that one ought to keep promises, or that one ought not to murder; and we have seen that conscience so interpreted cannot be justified rationally and is not an adequate guide to individual or social action. Third, we have discussed the doctrine of Kant that ethical rules can be reduced to a few universal a priori principles which duty unconditionally prescribes; and we have seen that his theory, in so far as it is formalistic and nonempirical, fails to meet the demands of liberalism and humanitarianism. Fourth, we have examined the conception of intuited prima-facie duties as advanced by Ross, and we have concluded that the force of obligation can be explained without his questionable assumptions.

Nevertheless, it would be a great mistake to conclude that the concepts of *conscience* and *duty* are illegitimate. A man's proudest boast is that "I have been true to my own conscience." In the name of conscience Socrates drank the hemlock, Joan of Arc burned at the stake, and many a nameless hero braved the worst tortures that the Nazis could devise. Conscience has inspired the best in human conduct; without it, man is no better than a beast.

Conscience involves a combination of several factors: first, convictions about right and wrong; second, emotional attitudes of approval or disapproval; and third, a sense of duty or obligation. If the convictions are irrational, then conscience is irrational. If they are authoritarian, then conscience is authoritarian. But if they are reasonable and sound, the fact that they are reinforced by emotions and a sense of obligation is all to the good. The business of ethics is not to supplant emotion by intelligence. As Francis Bacon has said, ethics should so compose the passions that they fight on the side of intelligence rather than against it.

So many people associate *conscience* and *duty* with a puritanical, authoritarian, or superstitious ethics ·that the liberal meaning of these terms is obscured. But we must distinguish between the authoritarian and reflective level of conscience. Authoritarian conscience seems to involve immediate unreasoned knowledge of ethical truths, but actually these "self-evident truths," as we have said, are the mandates of custom or traditional authority which have become so much a part of oneself that they seem self-evident. Quite different is the reflective level of conscience, present for example in a person like Socrates. Although he often spoke of his "inner voice," he insisted that "the unexamined life is not worth living." He realized that the conscience of every individual must be deeply informed by the norms of cultural tradition, but he subjected these norms to the habit of reflection and unfettered discussion. In fulfilling the philosopher's mission, he strengthened rather than weakened the force of his own conscience.

Today we are in great need of such a reflective yet forceful conscience. The ethics of formal rules and authority seem rapidly to be crumbling. We have become aware of many conflicting traditions and many "moral worlds," and we are aware of too many contrasting standards to rest comfortably in the illusion that our own are necessarily the right ones. To many people there no longer seems to be any reasonable course of action; there is merely a babble of voices, each calling without justification to some divergent path. Amid all this confusion, we need something more than the internalized voice of authority, however self-evident its dictates may appear.

Reflection is especially necessary in respect to social ethics in our modern age. Authoritarian conscience is quick to condemn the old familiar personal crimes, such as undisguised murder or theft; but it is not nearly so quick to condemn the new *social* forms of wrong-doing. Deliberate overcapitalization of an industry is a form of theft, but it is very likely to be accepted as shrewd business practice. Misleading advertising or "slanted" newspaper reporting are forms of lying, but they have become so common as to be downright respectable. Employment of workers under unsafe or unhealthful conditions may be a form of murder, but since the effects are not immediate, violent, or obvious, it usually escapes without punishment. As Edward Alsworth Ross, the American sociologist, has warned:

> Today the villain most in need of curbing is the respectable, exemplary, trusted personage who, strategically placed at the focus of a spider-web of fiduciary relations, is able from his office-chair to pick a thousand pockets, poison a thousand sick, pollute a thousand minds, or imperil a thousand lives. It is the great-scale, high-voltage sinner that needs the shackle. To strike harder at the petty pickpocket than at the prominent and unabashed person who in a large, impressive way sells out his constituents, his followers, his depositors, or his customers, is to "strain at a gnat and swallow a camel."[22]

The type of ethics that can be depended upon to condemn such social malefactors is not an unreflective "intuitional" ethics, intent upon "right for right's sake," but an informed, reflective ethics, intent upon right for the sake of maximum welfare and keenly aware of the modern and subtle forms of crime.

The quotation that I have cited from Professor Ross was written at the beginning of this century. Since that time social problems have become immensely more complex and urgent. The world has rocked on from crisis to crisis—from war to depression to war and to the threat of a new depression and a new war far more terrible than the last. Strange forms of tyranny and diabolical types of cruelty have decimated mankind. Science and technology have so prodigiously increased human power, both for good and for ill, that the issue "What shall we do?" has acquired a terrible urgency. The problems of our Atomic Age are too acute and unprecedented to be resolved in terms of the old static formal rules. No authoritarian standards, whether based upon custom, nature, God, or mind, will any longer suffice. We must seek a rehabilitation of conscience upon a reflective, empirical, teleological basis.

22 *Sin and Society,* Houghton Mifflin, Boston, 1907, pp. 29-30.

REVIEW OF PART ONE

WE HAVE BEEN seeking an answer to the question: What is right social action? Formalistic theories assert that it means obedience to law; teleological theories aver that it means promotion of welfare. Part One has been devoted to a critical discussion of formalistic theories.

These vary in accordance with the real or supposed sources of law. We have distinguished the following:

1. The laws of society, in the form either of customs or positive laws,
2. The laws of God,
3. The laws of nature,
4. The laws of mind, as derived from conscience, a priori reason, or intuition.

I have devoted a chapter to each of these four types.

In Chapter One, I have maintained that the laws of society, either customary or positive, cannot serve as a substitute for moral reflection. No sophisticated person would argue that *every* customary practice is right, or that it is right *merely* because it is customary. One custom can be morally better than another; some customs are irrational; when customs conflict, or when novel problems arise, reflection is necessary.

Nevertheless, a number of sophisticated thinkers, such as Edmund Burke, have maintained that custom represents the funded wisdom of a nation, providing security against the precipitate, self-willed actions of individuals and the dis-

tempers of a revolutionary age. Although Burke's social philosophy contains some deep insights, it is inadequate to cope
with unprecedented crises. In the twentieth century, for
example, the swift and stupendous development of technology, including atomic warfare, has made critical reflection
and bold social reconstruction the mandates of human survival. Even in less crucial periods, an unreflective morality
of custom tends to crush individuality, to discourage origi-
nality, to retard progress, and to limit scientific thought.

Similar considerations apply to a formalistic interpretation of positive laws, whether in the form of legislative en-
actments or judicial precedents. Although there have been
many attempts to base law upon formalistic doctrines, what
ultimately counts are human weal and woe; and every final
evaluation of law requires a reflective teleological judgment.
I have concluded that wise social policy cannot be based
upon mere obedience to the customs or positive laws of
society.

In Chapter Two, I have examined the doctrine that right
social action consists in conformity to the laws of God, a view
widely current in both ancient and modern civilizations. In
evaluating this doctrine, we must face the great question that
Socrates directed at Euthyphro: "Is an act right because it is
divinely commanded, or is it divinely commanded because
it is right?" Calvin and Paley and other formalistic theolo-
gians favor the first alternative; right *means* commanded by
God. This interpretation would give us a God of power rather
than of righteousness and would deny that moral goodness
has an independent validity. It would imply, for example,
that murder would be right if God should happen to command it, and that there is nothing in the nature of murder or
its consequences that makes it wrong. This view is naïve,
depending upon an anthropomorphic conception of the Di-
vinity and a literal acceptance of an authoritarian decalogue.
Such a view is too narrow and dogmatic to be the basis of a
world order.

When properly understood, the Bible lends no support to a formalistic creed. Although its narrative begins with Yaweh, the stern lawgiver, it eventuates in the intense, forward-looking idealism of the prophets and the purposive, humanistic teachings of Jesus. Religion's coming of age involves this kind of transition from a formalistic to a teleological ethics. Our conclusion to Chapter Two, therefore, is that a mature religious ethics consists in the pursuit of life-affirming ideals rather than conformity to an authoritarian code.

In Chapter Three, I have examined several attempts to base ethics and social policy upon the injunction: "Obey the laws of nature." Among the more important proponents of naturalistic ethics were the Stoics, who conceived of nature as divine, providential, rational, and fated. The ideal, they said, is the actual, and the actual is the necessary; but they admitted a little plot of freedom, the interior of a man's soul. The Stoic sage, in exercising this freedom, renounced a craving for external goods and harmonized his will with nature. He conceived the whole of nature as a great "republic," governed by natural laws to which every rational being is morally bound. All men as citizens of this republic are by nature equal and free. Here is a doctrine that influenced innumerable later thinkers, including Thomas Jefferson in penning the Declaration of Independence.

Although there is a touch of revolutionary verve in this Stoic doctrine, it exaggerates the extent to which the real is the rational, and hence ultimately makes for social conformity; and it underestimates man's power over external events and overestimates his power over his own mind.

Very different is the conception of nature that sprang up among evolutionists in the age of Darwin. They maintained that competitive struggle, natural selection, and survival of the fittest are the great "laws of nature"; and that if human beings break with nature, nature will break with them. Such is the view variously expressed by Spencer, Nietzsche, Sumner, and a host of other writers and still widely current as part of the "folklore" of our competitive business civilization.

But this theory is a nest of fallacies: it identifies human life with its animal origins; it fails to distinguish between the biological and the ethical meaning of *fittest;* and it assumes that the *natural* means to the evolutionary end are the best means. Moreover, it is based upon an inaccurate account of evolution and a superficial interpretation of the values of human life.

If we consider other meanings of *nature*—for example, that it means the all-inclusive, or the typical, or the primitive, or the innate, or the uncultivated—we likewise find no adequate basis for ethics. All these interpretations commit the fundamental fallacy of naturalistic ethics: the assumption that *what is* coincides with *what ought to be.* Only if nature is conceived to be the ideal, and the ideal is distinguished from the actual, can the natural be the basis of a valid ethics. But this implies that we must reject the doctrine that right action, whether individual or social, means mere conformity to nature's laws.

In Chapter Four I have discussed the theory that morality consists in obedience to the laws of the human mind. I first considered the naïve doctrine that conscience is an intuitive faculty which commands or forbids *particular* actions without regard to rules or principles; and I concluded that such a view would surrender life to caprice. A more plausible interpretation is that conscience forbids or commands *types* of action in accordance with self-evident rules. But the rules thus supposedly enjoined by conscience are not really self-evident; they turn out to be ambiguous; they often conflict with one another; and they are not objective, varying from time to time and place to place.

More sophisticated is the theory of Kant that the essence of morality is "good will" determined neither by inclination nor utility but by a principle of formal consistency, "the categorical imperative." Kant gives us three formulations of this imperative: (1) act only on the basis of those maxims that are capable of being universalized; (2) treat every human being as an end and never as a means only; and (3) join with others in a "kingdom" of free and responsible moral agents. These ethical principles impel him to adopt, within limits, a liberal and democratic social philosophy, and to advocate a world government.

Although some of his insights are admirable, the weakness of his ethical and social philosophy is its abstract formalism, which leads him to neglect the consequences of acts and to slight human individuality. Moreover, his second and third formulations of the categorical imperative are much less purely formal than his first formulation, and hence there is a serious inconsistency in his philosophy.

In an effort to find a more satisfactory theory than Kant's, Professor W. D. Ross has maintained that we should combine the teleological standard of welfare and the nonteleological standard of intuited rightness. But I do not find that his intuitions of "prima-facie rightness" are self-evident or that his nonteleological standard is necessary. Moreover, his use of two opposed standards is logically incoherent.

I have concluded that conscience, a priori reason, or intuition, is no satisfactory substitute for reflective purpose. This does not mean that we can dispense with conscience. In our age of atomic power, when science and technology have developed far more rapidly than moral insight and social control, the world desperately needs a mighty reaffirmation and rehabilitation of conscience, provided that it is critical and purposive rather than authoritarian and nonreflective.

We have thus completed our survey of formalistic ethics and have rejected the doctrine that right action is mere obedience to law in any of its forms. Law is made for man, not man for law. We must therefore turn to a consideration of human ideals—to a teleological rather than a formalistic basis for social action.

Part Two

THE ETHICS OF IDEALS

INTRODUCTION TO PART TWO

WE HAVE NOW completed our survey of the ethics of laws or formalistic ethics, and we are beginning our account of the ethics of ideals or teleological ethics.

Since teleological ethics is an ethics of goals, we shall try to discover what is good as an end—good for its own sake—ultimately and intrinsically good. Then we shall try to determine what is good as a means to this end—good instrumentally.

At the beginning of Book II of Plato's *Republic* there is a brief classification of goods in accordance with their intrinsic and instrumental values. Glaucon speaks and Socrates responds:

Let me ask you now:—How would you arrange goods—are there not some which we welcome for their own sakes, and independently of their consequences, as, for example, harmless pleasures and enjoyments, which delight us at the time, although nothing follows from them?

I agree in thinking that there is such a class, I replied.

Is there not also a second class of goods, such as knowledge, sight, health, which are desirable not only in themselves, but also for their results?

Certainly, I said.

And would you not recognize a third class, such as gymnastic, and the care of the sick, and the physician's art; also the various ways of money-making—these do us good but we regard them as disagreeable; and no one would choose them for their own sakes,

but only for the sake of some reward or result which flows from
them?

There is, I said, this third class also.[1]

The three classes of goods here enumerated are, first, the
intrinsically good but instrumentally indifferent, second, the
intrinsically and instrumentally good, and third, the intrinsically bad but instrumentally good. We can add six other
classes to these three, and the list would then be as follows:

Intrinsic value	Instrumental value
1. Good	Good
2. Good	Bad
3. Good	Indifferent
4. Bad	Good
5. Bad	Bad
6. Bad	Indifferent
7. Indifferent	Good
8. Indifferent	Bad
9. Indifferent	Indifferent

In assessing the worth of any act or state, it would be necessary to judge to which class it belongs and what are its values
both intrinsically and instrumentally. Sometimes the intrinsic
goodness is outweighed by the instrumental badness, or the
instrumental goodness is outweighed by the intrinsic badness.
Anything is instrumentally good or bad only because it produces or helps to produce what is intrinsically good or bad.

Now the term *intrinsic goodness* can be understood more
or less strictly. For example, one can speak of a vacation as
intrinsically good, meaning that the vacation is worth having
for its own sake—in other words, that it is good even if the
consequences are indifferent or even if it is considered quite
apart from any consequences. But many aspects or incidents
of the vacation are intrinsically bad or indifferent, hence we
cannot say that the vacation is intrinsically good throughout.

[1] In *The Dialogues of Plato*, translated by Benjamin Jowett, Oxford University Press, London, 1924, III, p. 36.

We can use the term *intrinsic good* more strictly. We can mean by it, for example, that ingredient in the vacation which *makes* it worth having for its own sake, namely, that ultimate goodness which is good through and through, so that no part of it is bad or indifferent. A hedonist, for example, would maintain that the vacation is intrinsically good (in the less strict sense of the term) because it contains pleasure, and that, in the last analysis, it is pleasure and pleasure alone that is good for its own sake—ultimately good, or good throughout, or intrinsically good in the strict sense of the term. As G. E. Moore declares:

> We may, in short, divide intrinsically good things into two classes: namely (1) those which, while as wholes they are intrinsically good, nevertheless contain some parts which are not intrinsically good; and (2) those which either have no parts at all, or, if they have any, have none but what are themselves intrinsically good.[2]

He uses the term *ultimately good* to denote the second of these classes.

In the chapters in Part Two, we shall try to discover the meaning of intrinsic good in this sense of ultimate good; and when we employ the term *intrinsic good,* this will be its meaning. We shall also try to determine what is good as a *means* to such ultimate goodness—what is good instrumentally. Without so doing, we cannot judge what is right or wrong, because, according to teleological ethics, the rightness or wrongness of an act cannot be estimated apart from its usefulness. Our main interest is to find out what is ultimately good and what is right. Construed in terms of social ethics, our two great questions are these: What is a good society? and What is right social action?

Among the theories of ultimate goodness that we shall consider are these: relativism, the doctrine that there is no valid universal ideal; extreme individualism, the doctrine that the self-enclosed individual is the locus of goodness;

2 *Ethics,* Oxford University Press, New York, 1912, p. 75.

extreme collectivism, the doctrine that society is the locus of goodness; intellectualism, the doctrine that the good is reason; hedonism, the doctrine that the good is pleasure; voluntarism, the doctrine that the good is the satisfaction of desire; and the interest theory, the doctrine that the good is the cultivation and fulfillment of interests. In the light of this survey of human ideals, we shall seek to describe the nature of a good social order.

We shall then consider the meaning of right social action, discussing the basis and nature of social obligation and distinguishing between valid and invalid theories of right. Adopting a universalist standard—the maximum good rather than the good of any single individual or restricted group— we shall consider the criteria whereby choice can be made among numerous and competing goods.

Chapter Five

RELATIVISM—THE DENIAL OF
ANY UNIVERSAL IDEAL

1. *The Meaning of Ethical Relativism*

AT THE OUTSET of our search for the ideal of a good society we must consider the view that there is *no* universal ideal, that only local, ephemeral, and variable ideals exist. Each individual, each group, or each age can lay claim to its own virtue and its own standard. There is no single objective universal standard. What is one man's meat is another man's poison.

Relativism can best be defined in terms of its opposite— absolutism. An absolutist maintains that certain ideals are unconditionally valid, good in any time and any place, eternal and immutable. This view is most frequently associated with the doctrine that there is one God ruling over the entire universe and determining, by an unvarying will and wisdom, what is valid for all peoples in all ages. It may also be associated with other philosophical theories, such as the view that all reality is one—a single unity—or that ideals are abstract universals, like Plato's "ideas" or forms, existing independently of any exemplification. Whatever may be its religious or philosophical basis, absolutism insists that ethical standards are unconditional and invariable, whereas relativism denies that there are any such unconditional, universal, and objective standards of right and good.

In his pungent style, Pascal expresses (although he goes on to reject) the relativist position.

We see neither justice nor injustice which does not change its nature with change in climate. Three degrees of latitude reverse all jurisprudence; a meridian decides the truth. Fundamental laws change after a few years of possession; right has its epochs; the entry of Saturn into the lion marks to us the origin of such and such a crime. A strange justice that is bounded by a river! Truth on this side of the Pyrenees, error on the other side.[1]

Both the relativist and the absolutist may admit this diversity in moral customs, but the absolutist points to a higher immutable standard whereas the relativist finds nothing but subjective feelings and variable ideals. The real question at issue is not whether moral ideals differ but whether they ought to differ. It is perfectly possible that an ideal, such as happiness, is valid for all peoples even though, because of ignorance, barbarism, or perversion, certain individuals or groups do not accept this ideal. Just as Einstein's theory of gravitation may be objectively true although many people do not understand or believe it, so a certain ideal may be objectively true or valid even though many people do not grasp or accept it. Moral ideas vary—this fact cannot be denied. The absolutist says that the variation is to be explained by the failure of many human beings to grasp the absolute moral standard or ideal. The relativist says that the variation is to be explained by the absence of any valid universal ideal or moral standard.

We may distinguish between two aspects of relativism. First, relativism insists that standards necessarily vary *from place to place*. Each individual or group has its own ethical standards, and there is no possibility of finding any ideal that is common and valid among all individuals or all groups. At any one time, there is an irreducible variety of ideals. Second, relativism insists that standards necessarily vary *from time to time*. Each age has its own standards, and there are no enduring ethical principles which transcend these temporal limitations. According to the relativist, therefore, the irreducible

1 *Thoughts,* Collier, New York, 1910, p. 105.

variety of ethical norms may exhibit itself either simultaneously or consecutively.

2. Some Ancient and Modern Representatives of Relativism

THE REVOLT of the relativists against absolutism tends to occur in every revolutionary age. It occurred, for example, in the "age of the Sophists" in ancient Greece, a period when the traditional Hellenic culture was being rent by class struggle and war. The effects of the economic revolution, which began in the age of Solon (*circa* 639-559 B.C.), were profoundly disturbing to the structure of Greek life. The early basis of Greek economic life had been primarily subsistence farming; but, in a manner analogous to our modern "industrial revolution," it changed to a more advanced type of cash-crop farming and to commerce and industry. In a little more than a century, this great economic transformation brought into existence a commercial and industrial middle class and a new "proletarian" class of industrial and maritime workers. It destroyed the old isolation of the traditional Greek city-states, drew the cities into commercial and imperialistic conflict with one another, and sharpened the clash between the Greek states and surrounding empires such as the Persian. As a result, Greek culture was churned to its depths, and a series of wars and revolutions ensued. The climax of these developments has never been narrated more vividly than by the Greek historian, Thucydides, who described not only the great catastrophe of the Peloponnesian War but the class conflicts that preceded and accompanied it.

Revolution thus ran its course from city to city and the places which it arrived at last, from having heard what had been done before, carried to a still greater excess the refinements of their inventions, as manifested in the cunning of their enterprises and the atrocity of their reprisals. . . . Thus every form of iniquity took root in the Hellenic countries by reason of the troubles. The ancient simplicity into which honor so largely entered was laughed down and disappeared; and society became divided into camps in which no man trusted his fellow.[2]

The Sophists were philosophic representatives of this age of unrest. They belonged to a generation which had seen a great many laws in the making, revolutions, and counterrevolutions, and they reflected the disillusionment and uncertainty of a period when traditions and customs were being frequently violated. As wandering teachers, traveling from city to city, they were acutely conscious of both the variety and the instability of moral codes. With a skeptical and predominantly practical attitude, they were also reacting against abstract science and philosophy. It seemed to them very plain that the answers to philosophical problems varied from thinker to thinker, from city to city, and that no universal truth could be established. In these circumstances, it was natural for them to conclude that truth and value are relative.

The most famous of the Sophists was Protagoras (481?-411 B.C.), who was an old man when Socrates was young and who died in the early years of the Peloponnesian War. Except for a few brief fragments, his own words have perished, but we can determine his teaching by what Plato and others have said about him. His essential doctrine was that "man is the measure of all things." By this he did not mean that universal humanity is the standard whereby truth and goodness can be judged. According to Plato's dialogue, the *Theaetetus,* he meant by "man" the individual man. Things are to me as they appear to me and to you as they appear to you. There is no *common* real world that can be known by two or more percipients. Every object is relative to the point of view in perception, to a momentary, fleeting act of sensation. The man who is color blind, or who differs otherwise in his perceptions or beliefs, can never be proved wrong.

Protagoras maintained that relativity applies also in the

2 *The Peloponnesian War,* Modern Library, New York, 1934, pp. 189, 191.

sphere of morals and politics. He represented himself as a "physician of the soul": he could not induce truer beliefs about virtue or vice, since no belief is any more objective or "true" than any other, but he could implant healthier and more useful beliefs. In place of judgments of truth he wished to substitute judgments of worth; but here too a relativistic interpretation entered, although not of a purely individualistic sort. He took the view that moral and political values vary from city to city, that these values are embodied in the local customs and traditions, and that the wise and morally healthy man acquiesces in the prevailing standards. His view is stated in the *Theaetetus:* "Whatever appears to a state to be just and fair, so long as it is regarded as such, is just and fair to it."[3]

In Plato's dialogue, the *Protagoras,* he is represented as telling a myth which expresses his fundamental relativism: When the world was very young, Prometheus stole the secret of fire and of the mechanical arts from the gods and bestowed them upon mankind; but men were still unable successfully to cope with other animals and with the rigors of nature, for they lacked political cohesion and the strength that comes from unity. Zeus, fearing that the entire human race would be exterminated, sent Hermes to bestow upon all men the sense of right and justice, necessary if they were to combine for mutual defense. Thenceforward all men, possessing this knowledge, were teachers of virtue to each new generation. According to this interpretation, goodness is to be identified with the mores and conventions of the given community, and the child merely picks up from his elders whatever familiarity with "virtue" he may need. Thus morality is entirely relative, since there is no moral standard more ultimate than whatever is current in a given society.

In comparison with some of the younger sophists, Protagoras was a conservative. The more radical Sophist point of

[3] Plato, *Theaetetus,* in *The Dialogues of Plato,* translated by Benjamin Jowett, Oxford University Press, London, 1924, IV, p. 224.

view is expressed by Thrasymachus, a character in Book I of
Plato's *Republic*. His theory is that right is determined by
the laws and conventions of each society, and that these in
turn are determined by the ruling class. The group that domi-
nates every state acts in its own interests. As the strongest
party in the state, it ordains the ruling ideas of the society,
and these ideas determine what is right and just for that
society. Hence might is right, and "justice" (a term used in
the wide sense of moral goodness) is determined only by force
and self-interest. "Justice," Thrasymachus said, "is the interest of the stronger."

We are living in a period analogous to "the age of the
Sophists," except that now the forces arrayed against one another are of vastly greater scope and power. In our time, also,
relativism has been a reflection of widespread uncertainties.
When we no longer listen to the oracles of the past, and when
we hear so many new and contradictory voices, we are inclined to suppose that there is no way of discovering any
common and objective standard. The causes of the resur-
gence of ethical relativism are numerous and complicated,
but I think that the major causes are the conflicts, confusions,
and revolutionary tendencies of our era.

The more crass and blatant forms of relativism, as we shall
see in a later chapter, have been expressed by fascist spokesmen, but more sophisticated types of relativism have become
characteristic of the thinking of many European and American intelligentsia. Historians and anthropologists have
pointed to the "irreducible" diversity of human societies,
each with its unique "configuration" or "cultural pattern,"
each with its own kind of religion, science, art, and morality,
all in constant flux. The pragmatists, who have made such a
deep impression upon the American educational system, have
tended to reject all concepts which transcend the fluidities
of an ever-changing organism interacting with an ever-changing environment. Various philosophers, especially among the
"radical empiricists" and "logical positivists," have denied

any scientific standing to ethics and any objective import to ethical concepts such as the "ought." Some of the issues raised by these thinkers, including the meaning of "ought," will be touched upon in later chapters, but it will be worth while here to cite some recent advocates of relativism.

Among such advocates, for example, has been Vilfredo Pareto, a famous Italian economist and sociologist, whose *Trattato di Sociologia generale* (translated into English under the title *The Mind and Society*) has been widely hailed as one of the most important works of the twentieth century. This is not primarily an ethical treatise, but relativism is one of its fundamental premises and is expressed implicity or explicitly a great many times in the course of the argument. Pareto asserts that "the concepts various individuals have of what is good for them and good for others are essentially heterogeneous, and there is no way of reducing them to unity."[4] All that the various definitions of "good" have in common is that each definition is "agreeable" to its proponents. Ultimately ideals rest simply upon sentiment, not upon reason or science; and sentiments differ from person to person and from group to group. Therefore any attempt to discover the goals of life is bound to be nonlogical. We may be logical in finding *ways* to realize goals, but the goals themselves, being determined simply by variable sentiments, are beyond the pale of reason.

A similar point of view has been urged by Edward Westermarck, at one time Professor of Philosophy in a Finnish Academy and later Professor of Sociology in the University of London. His works, *The Origin and Development of The Moral Ideas* and *Ethical Relativity*, are among the most famous of modern ethical treatises. Much of his argument is concerned with pointing out the diversity of moral customs throughout the world, but the mainstay of his position is the contention that morality is based upon emotions. "All moral judgments, all moral concepts," he argues, "are ultimately

4 *The Mind and Society*, Harcourt, Brace, New York, 1935, IV, p. 1476.

based on emotions,"[5] and since emotions are notoriously variable and subjective, no objective system of morality can rest upon this foundation. It is meaningless to say that an emotion can be true or false; hence if morality, in essence, is emotional, it cannot be true or false. There are no moral truths; there are only moral emotions; and hence there is no moral objectivity. So runs his argument.

Yet his position becomes rather equivocal. He considers the problem of the difference between moral and nonmoral emotions and finally decides that the distinguishing mark of moral emotions is their impartiality, real or apparent. Moral approval, he argues, is based upon kindly feeling that is or seems impartial; and moral disapproval is likewise based upon resentment that is or seems impartial. Moreover, he directly traces the development of impartiality to the growth and continuous widening of "altruistic sentiment." He declares:

> It is obvious that the expansion of the moral rules has been a consequence of the expansion of the social unit and of increased intercourse between different societies, and if, as I maintain, the range of the moral emotions varies with the range of the altruistic sentiment, there is every reason to assume that an immediate cause of the greater comprehensiveness of the moral rules has been a corresponding widening of that sentiment.[6]

But if Westermarck is correct in these contentions, there are, despite his denial, universal elements in all morality, namely, altruism and impartiality. Many writers, such as David Hume and Adam Smith, have maintained that the very mainspring of morality is altruism (or sympathy) combined with impartiality; hence Westermarck is, tacitly, recognizing the universality of what many would term the heart and core of morality. It is impossible to understand, moreover, how impartiality could occur without an element of thoughtful evaluation or judgment. If we are impartial, we control our

5 *Ethical Relativity,* Harcourt, Brace, New York, 1932, p. 60.
6 *Ibid.,* p. 200.

prejudices, we escape from whims and biases, and we achieve some measure of objectivity. It is true that the impartiality may, as Westermarck insists, be only apparent, but even then, we at least *strive* to avoid favoritism and to be more objective. In thus admitting an element of critical judgment in the moral life, Westermarck in effect is denying his own thesis that morality is purely emotional. I cite these inconsistencies in his argument as an indication of what often occurs in treatises favoring ethical relativism. Few people consistently deny *all* objectivity or universality in the sphere of morality or human values.

3. The Unsatisfactory Character of Both Relativism and Absolutism

THE STRENGTH of relativism rests mainly in its firm stand against absolutism. In the name of absolutism, a great deal of superstition and "thought control" has been foisted upon the world, and the relativists, in opposing this sort of thing, have seemed to belong to the party of freedom and scientific enlightenment.

Ethical absolutism, as we have said, is the theory that ideals are unconditional and invariable, valid independently of time or space, valid independently of the nature or needs of human beings or their historical circumstances, somehow rooted in the will of God or the eternal structure of the universe or a Platonic "heaven above the heavens" or the immutable principles of a priori reason.

I believe that the relativists are quite right in rejecting such absolutism with all its nonempirical implications. The whole spirit of science is opposed to the belief in transcendent "absolutes." What is the scientific spirit? The suspension of belief until the evidence has massively accumulated; the recognition that every theory must be socially verified and that its formulation is therefore provisional and may be dis-

solved by the further progress of research; the unwillingness
to assume imperceivable entities unless one has strong cir-
cumstantial evidence; the attempt to solve the problem with
what is already known and to assume no more entities than
are absolutely necessary for explanation—these are the marks
of the scientific spirit. The assumption of fixed immutable
principles in the mind of a supernatural god or in a realm
of ghostly essences runs counter to this spirit, which has given
us the only relatively secure foundation of belief.

The very "laws" of science, moreover, have become far
more tentative and statistical. At the beginning of the modern scientific era, Leonardo da Vinci could write confidently
of "necessity" as "the eternal bond and rule of nature."
Science was conceived as a system of truths possessing complete certitude and finality. This attempt to attain complete
certainty is the theme of science down to comparatively recent
times. George Santayana relates the change that has occurred
within his own lifetime:

> When I was younger, what was pompously called Science wore
> an imposing aspect. There was a well-dressed Royal Family in the
> intellectual world, expected to rule indefinitely: sovereign axioms,
> immutable laws, and regent hypotheses. . . . Now there is a de-
> mocracy of theories elected for short terms of office, speaking shop-
> dialects, and hardly presented or presentable to the public eye.[7]

Scientific theories can best be regarded as closer and closer
approximations to the truth, but not as absolute and immutable. Indeed, the very structure of nature eludes any
exhaustive final formulations, since the contemporary physics
of quanta indicates "uncertainty" at the very foundation of
the physical order. Variability, far from being a mere appearance due to our incomplete knowledge, has been confirmed
by the most exact observation and experiment. Aristotle long
ago pointed out that there is nothing utterly unchanging in
either the data or the conclusions of the biological and social

---

7 Quoted by Harry Slochower, *No Voice Is Wholly Lost,* Creative Age
Press, New York, 1945, p. xvi.

sciences, but in the last half century this variability has been shown to hold for the physical sciences as well. Therefore, if absolutism is to be maintained it must be upon some basis other than science, and most of us find no such certain basis. Art gives a kind of "insight" or "significance" that may be extraordinarily rich and valuable, but the "truth" of art is more subjectivistic than that of science and provides no foundation for absolutism. The only serious rival of science is religion; those who embrace a religious supernaturalism do have a foundation for absolutism. Since supernatural entities are not subject to the canons of precise verification, however, there are many who will remain skeptical.

The strength of relativism, I have said, is that it is opposed to absolutism. Its strength is not in what it asserts but in what it denies. It is attractive to people in a scientific and skeptical age because it denies unempirical concepts of the good life and the good society. To deny what cannot be empirically substantiated is a virtue, but a purely negative virtue. The weakness of relativism is that it leaves us with mere negativism. It denies that there is any universal objective standard of values and admits only local or ephemeral subjective standards. This leaves us without any objective moral standard, and in so doing it cuts the heart out of morality, whether individual or social. Relativism means that whenever people assert, "Our side is right," they are merely asserting their own subjective preferences. No one moral aim is really any better or truer than any other. Each group is right according to its own standards and that is the end of the matter.

Consider what this means. The British, French, Russian, Chinese, and American people spent untold treasures in blood and wealth defeating the fascist-nazi social system in World War II. Most of these people certainly believed that they were fighting for a just cause. They certainly believed that "our side is right." The relativist in effect tells them that this belief is sheer illusion; that there is no objectively valid ideal; that there are only contradictory voices, each one equally "right," each one right according to its own point of view. In the future, men will be called upon to make many fresh efforts in the interests of a better life. Again the relativist in effect will say that the effort can only be based upon sheer illusion. There is no objective meaning in saying that one goal is better than another; hence there is no reason to try to improve one's moral ideals or to strive to realize one ideal rather than another. Such a view destroys the essential meaning of morality. It amounts to immoralism or nihilism.

The relativist may deny that we have correctly stated the implications of his position, but it is difficult to see on what ground he can deny this. A thoroughgoing relativist, to repeat, finds no common standard to compare and judge ideals; hence he provides no objective basis for declaring, "This is really and truly good. This is really and truly right." To deny that one can ever so speak is to oppose the deepest moral convictions of mankind.

The weakness of absolutism is that it means the abandonment of an empirical attitude in the sphere of values. The weakness of relativism is that it denies all objective basis for regarding one moral idea as better than another. Somehow we must find an alternative to both absolutism and relativism.

4. *An Intermediate Position—Theme and Variations*

WE have pointed out that there are two kinds of relativism, and, by implication, two kinds of contrasting absolutism. First, there is the relativism of the historical moment as contrasted with the absolutism of the timeless creed. Second, there is the relativism of group particularism as contrasted with the absolutism of a single universal code. I shall discuss each of these in turn, and indicate an alternative to each kind of relativism.

In its more exclusive and extreme form, temporal relativism denies enduring moral standards or ideals. Extreme temporal absolutism not only asserts such standards and ideals but denies any change in respect to them. The fallacy, in each case, lies in the extremism and the exclusiveness. The realistic alternative both to a static absolutism and a mercurial relativism is to shun these extremes, to avoid the conception of relativism and absolutism as indissoluble opposites and to recognize *both* the old and the new, the tradition and the innovation. As Whitehead points out:

There are two principles inherent in the very nature of things, recurring in some particular embodiments in whatever field we explore—the spirit of change, and the spirit of conservation. There can be nothing real without both. Mere change without conservation is a passage from nothing to nothing. Its final integration yields mere transient nonentity. Mere conservation without change cannot conserve. For after all, there is a flux of circumstance, and the freshness of being evaporates under mere repetition. . . . A static value, however serious and important, becomes unendurable by its appalling monotony of endurance. The soul cries aloud for release into change. It suffers the agonies of claustrophobia.[8]

If we endeavor, in the spirit of Whitehead, to unite conservatism and innovation, we can find instruction in ancient Chinese civilization. As William Ernest Hocking has pointed out, Chinese sages such as Lao-tse and Confucius realized that we must push thought and action above and beyond existing formulas, not to escape the rules but to revise them. There is no such thing as being above reason and order, nor even above conceptions, ideas, principles, laws, but every wise man sits loose from his definitions for the sake of better principles and laws. Out of respect for "the latent lawfulness of the future," the sage criticizes "the sufficiency of the lawfulness of the past. . . . The way out of a misfit formula is not a policy of no formula, but one of better formula."[9] Such

8 Alfred North Whitehead, *Science and the Modern World,* Macmillan, New York, 1925, pp. 289-290.
9 "A New East in a New World," *Fortune,* August 1942, pp. 124-126.

readiness to find a superior lawfulness in the new and experimental, an attitude which Confucius called "mental hospitality," is quite different from the hostility to lawfulness per se. This combination of adaptability and respect for principle is needed in a disturbed and transitional age such as the present.

If we are to escape moral chaos and anarchy, we must realize that life is more than "a bagatelle of transient experience." We must recognize that the essential values of civilization, such as truth, beauty, courage, and love, are as valid as ever they were. We must sense the continuity in history and establish contact with the best minds of the past. Thus only can we rise above the shifting multiplicity of standards and find a binding power more rational than prejudice and less brutal than force. Yet we must also recognize that enduring values are, like the themes of music, endlessly varied. We must resist the reactionary demand to return to the "eternal verities" and "absolutes" of medievalism or any other vanishing or vanished social system. We must recognize that an "Atomic Age" requires fresh solutions and insights, not an abandonment of ancient ideals but an ever-new embodiment. We must recognize that imagination and foresight no less than memory is a condition of wise choice in the present. To fix our minds upon the past alone, to seek only to repeat or prolong the past, is to stunt our creative energy. It is the way of death rather than of life.

5. The Particular and the Universal

JUST AS we must avoid the extremes of both a temporal relativism and a temporal absolutism, so we must avoid the extremes of group particularism and universalism. Our society is divided into warring gangs of many types: nation is pitted against nation, class against class, creed against creed. Each group claims to possess its own truth, law, and virtue. The universe of moral principles has been split into a chaotic multiverse. Unless we can find certain universal principles which transcend these conflicting particularisms, there would seem to be no chance to avert the violent death of many millions of human beings and the total destruction of civilization in the atomic wars of the future. Yet an overweening universalism, with its ugly implications of intolerance and authoritarianism, is perhaps more to be feared than the rich ferment of conflicting particularisms. The ideal of a universal uniformity is one of the most debased ideals ever concocted by the human mind.

The best solution is to combine the valid insights of both particularism and universalism. As opposed to relativism, we must uphold the ideal of universality. The very possibility of an enduring peace depends upon the organization of an international community upon the basis of a common humanity and a common justice. Such universalism, however, must avoid the rigid and unempirical doctrines of absolutism.

Absolutism is generally based upon unscientific concepts. It is almost always founded on supernaturalism or authoritarianism. In its insistence upon the unconditionality of values, it fails to study the actual conditions of human life. It refuses to recognize that human ideals should be based upon human needs, or if it recognizes needs, it does not seek to determine them in an empirical manner.

It is possible, however, to study human needs empirically and to use the conclusions thus reached as a basis for universal ideals. The fundamental material needs of human beings are universal, or nearly so. If there is anyone so odd that he prefers to starve when he might have a full stomach, to shiver in the cold when he might be sheltered, to be ravaged with disease when he might be healthy, to be overworked and insecure when he might have work that is neither overanxious nor overwearisome, he is at least so rare a "bird" that he can be left out of account in the building of a world order. Not only are the necessities of life—food, shelter, clothing, health, and economic security—basic and universal goals, but they can be carefully studied by well-established scientific techniques that have already been employed by many agencies, such as the United States Department of Agriculture.

Likewise we need not throw up our hands in despair when we consider the subtler, psychological values. Health and disease in the personality are quite as amenable to study and control as health and disease in the human body. We can discover, for example, what human needs are so basic that their repression leads to mental and social breakdown: to neurosis, insanity, and suicide in the individual personality; to crime, depression, war, and revolution in the society. A good beginning of such research has already been made. The well-known sociologists W. I. Thomas and Florian Znaniecki, through a detailed study of social disorganization, have worked out a list of the basic human wants.[10] A reputable psychiatrist, Gilbert V. T. Hamilton, has likewise sought to discover the fundamental drives by examining numerous cases of mental breakdown.[11] These two research studies, each worked out independently and each using different techniques, the one sociological and the other psychological, reach almost identical conclusions. The fundamental human needs as thus defined are first, the need for security (like Franklin D. Roosevelt's "freedom from want" and "freedom from fear"); second, the need for love and companionship; third, the need for constructive expression of one's talents, with the resultant status and self-respect; and fourth, the need for adventure, variety, freedom of expression. It will be noted that the second need—for love and social response—is emphasized by Freud and many other modern psychologists.

I do not mean to suggest that this is a fixed and canonical list of human needs. Others, such as Murray and Tolman,

10 *Cf.*, W. I. Thomas and Florian Znaniecki, *The Polish Peasant in Europe and America*, Knopf, New York, 1927.
11 *Cf., Introduction to Objective Psychopathology*, Mosby, St. Louis, 1925.

have given us alternative statements;[12] and the insights thus supplied valuably supplement the studies of Thomas, Znani-ecki, and Hamilton.

Some of these needs are so universal that they can be considered the proper basis of a world order. Human nature is no merely nominal essence, and universal values can be based upon the needs of human beings as opposed to some unverifiable set of supernatural absolutes. No one would deny that the human body has a basic structure—that Chinamen have hearts and livers as well as Americans—and that therefore the science of medicine, the science of physical health and well-being, is applicable to all men. Similarly, the human mind is not an utterly amorphous thing: it too has its structure of thought, passion, appetite, emotion, and sensation; its laws of operation, its conscious and subconscious levels, common to all men. If it were not so there could be no science of psychology, no science of *mental* health such as psychiatry. No doubt the mind is more profoundly conditioned and modified by varying cultural environments than is the body, yet there is no good evidence that either the mind or the body is absolutely characterless or infinitely plastic. As Professor Dennes has well said:

> We know man only as we find him, and we have found him nowhere, and in no epoch, in which he has not manifested cravings to explore, to understand, to affiliate, to cooperate, to be loyal, to play, to imagine, to sing, to dance, to produce and enjoy various rhythms, as well as cravings for air, food, drink, rest, shelter, sex, child nurturance and tendance, sleep, and pain avoidance. The needs for knowledge, beauty, and cooperation are as basal as those for air, food, and sex.[13]

These are basal, Professor Dennes goes on to say, not only

12 *Cf.*, E. C. Tolman, "Psychological Man," *Journal of Social Psychology*, XIII, February 1941; and H. A. Murray and others, *Explorations of Personality*, Oxford University Press, New York, 1938.

13 William R. Dennes and others, *Civilization*, University of California Press, Berkeley, 1942, pp. 179-180.

because they are widespread, but because their denial ultimately leads to derangement and death—to crime, aggression, suicide, social hysteria, mental breakdown, and war.

The relativist, we may safely conclude, exaggerates the diversity of human societies. Every society, at the very least, *is* a society. Within it, human beings meet together, live together, and are faced with the need of getting along together. The essential maxims of morality—be kind, be considerate, be fair—are the necessary human responses to this universal need. So long as human beings are human, and so long as they live together in societies, there will be certain universal elements in morality. There will be the ideal of satisfying their common human nature and the moral imperative to avoid a suicidal war of each against all. Morality enjoins men to live with that degree of wisdom and justice and kindliness without which life, in any age or in any society, is intolerable.

Admittedly, there will always be a certain diversity as to the means men employ in realizing the good life. This does not, in itself, imply that there is no universal ideal. Let us suppose, for a moment and for the sake of illustration, that the ideal of happiness is universally valid. It might still be the case that one man, or one group, attains happiness in quite a different way from another. One man might become happy by becoming an artist, another by becoming a scientist. Or again, the general happiness might be better served in America by capitalism and in Russia by socialism. If so, this diversity as to means is in no way inconsistent with the universality of happiness as an end. Moreover, it is illogical to suppose that happiness might be intrinsically good for me and yet not intrinsically good for others. If happiness is intrinsically valuable when it occurs in my mind, it surely does not become valueless when it happens to occur in someone else's mind. Happiness is happiness, wherever it occurs; it has the same quality in your experience and in mine; and if it *is* intrinsically good, it must be good in itself, and therefore good wherever it is found. Surely happiness is good the world over.

The recognition of some such universal value is the more necessary in view of the new technological basis of a global economy. Because we are now living in "one world," because the various nations and cultures are now articulated and enmeshed within a world pattern, it is anachronistic and suicidal to live in terms of exclusive particularisms. Not only do our technical instruments for the conquest of space and time create an interdependent world, but these same instruments, combined with the world-wide ramifications of industrialism, add a common human nurture to the factor of a common human nature. The environmental factors, the types of stimuli, are becoming more and more alike the world over. Almost everywhere human beings must adjust themselves to the modern instruments of production, transport, communication, to modern administrative techniques, to modern types of social organization, to the promise and the threat of atomic power. As these factors in man's environment become increasingly widespread, there is an ever-more-imperative need of a moral universality to match a technological universality. It has become tragically clear that if well-intentioned men fail to grasp this moral imperative, evil-minded men will employ these technical instruments of universality to heighten the destructiveness of warring particularisms. What will then be universalized is death and anarchy. A thousand writers have warned us of the disasters that impend if we do not embrace the moral imperatives of our world, but so long as we continue to tremble on the verge of the abyss, the warning must be repeated again and again.

We do not need to rely on vague intuitions in meeting this challenge. We can proceed empirically in working out our plans for a world-wide community. We can define a good civilization as one in which the basic wants of human nature are most fully satisfied, and by studying man and society, we

can find out the nature of those wants. We can then make a
scientific inventory of available resources for meeting fundamental human needs, and, finally, by means of social science
and engineering, we can achieve a planned use of these resources on a world-wide basis.

The world must be unified if we are to avoid terrible
catastrophe, but it should be a unity in variety and not a
monotonous uniformity. Americans are all too prone to think
of world unification as the Americanization of the world, just
as every nation tends to consider its own norms absolute and
universal. World unification based upon ethnocentrism—
upon the cultural standards of a single nation or race—is but
a form of totalitarian domination. It means the ruthless
stamping out of many rich cultural traditions in favor of a
single peremptory pattern of life.

A world government, or a world culture of whatever sort,
should not take the place of restricted loyalties and regional
differentiations. A world state is too colossal, remote, impersonal—too monotonous in its universal sway—for the innumerable human beings on this planet by its means to
achieve social unity in ways that are intimate, spontaneous,
homelike. To do justice to human nature, we must recognize
both the universal and the particular, the parochial and the
catholic, the local community and the world state.

Human beings are alike, but they are also different. They
are alike in requiring food, but they differ in their tastes.
They are alike in needing clothing, but they want individuality in their costumes. They are alike in demanding
shelter, but they do not wish to live in identical houses. They
are alike in needing love and sexual expression, but they love
different objects and in different ways. They are alike in en-
joying beauty and the play of the imagination, but they differ
in their arts. They are alike in needing some creative expression of their talents, but they do not have the same'
talents. They are alike in possessing some religious impulse,
but they satisfy that impulse through different symbols. They

are alike in their need to reason and understand nature, but
they differ in their thoughts and beliefs. Only a stupid and
debased totalitarianism would try to suppress these differences. A society of identical twins, whether in mind or body,
is not the *summum bonum,* and a world-wide uniformity is
but a nightmare.

Anthropologists have called attention to the variety of human cultures. What unites a people above all is their culture,
and this culture always has its unique configuration. The
culture of the Pueblos or the Dobus or the Kwakiutl or the
Bushmen has its idiosyncratic pattern and details. Likewise
the culture of less primitive peoples—the Chinese, the East
Indians, the Latin Americans, the Russians—has its characteristic values and institutions. A knowledge of these varying cultural forms is necessary for realistic social thought. A
tolerance of and a sympathy for the different values which
develop in different cultures is the mark of a wise and catholic
mind. Cosmopolitanism may be carried to an extreme: in
being equally hospitable toward all cultures, one may be un-
attached to any. Nevertheless, a mature mind escapes from
the "illusion of position"—the tendency to judge all human
cultures in terms of one's own cultural heritage and to condemn all variations from the norms of one's own group.

In thinking out the moral basis of world peace, therefore,
we need to appreciate both the universal and the particular
elements in culture. In the first place, we must recognize
that, at a certain level, all the peoples in the world have much
in common. As the ancient Chinese sage Mencius declared:
"The heart of mercy is in all men; the sense of shame is in all
men; the sense of courtesy and respect is in all men; the sense
of right and wrong is in all men."[14] If human beings at times
become so unnatural and dehumanized that they lack these
things, it is necessary to restore them by proper education. In
the second place, we should recognize that cultures, societies,

[14] Lin Yutang, *The Wisdom of India and China,* Random House, New
York, 1942, p. 774.

communities, and individuals differ in their emphases, cherish certain values more than others, enjoy values that others lack. Men must learn to understand and respect these fluctuations. Tolerance is one of the great qualities of civilization; and if we are ever to achieve a lasting peace, we must learn to believe less in self-assertion or group righteousness and more in tolerance.

Universalism and particularism, local and general culture, so far from being in conflict, are truly necessary to each other. A general culture, without local differentiations, soon becomes stale and dies, because it lacks any vital interplay among its parts, and hence any creative ferment and spontaneity. On the other hand, a self-sufficient parochialism is too smug, starved, and constricted to achieve a rich cultural life. Therefore, the ideal of complete local autarchy and the ideal of an undifferentiated universalism must be abandoned in favor of an interpenetration of "opposites": the universal lending breadth to the particular and the particular lending concreteness to the universal. The valid solution is to unite the wider with the narrower loyalties, to encourage a varied and decentralized articulation of group interests but to eliminate the injustices and predatory biases that interfere with the more universal loyalty. We cannot otherwise peacefully enclose within a single world framework national cultures so diverse as the Chinese, the Russian, the German, and the American; nor can we do justice to the rich local variations within each of these cultures.

To conclude, neither relativism nor absolutism, as an extreme or exclusive theory, meets the world's needs. We need ideals flexibly applied yet all-embracing. We need to combine the universal and the particular, the changeless and the changing.

Chapter Six

THE GROUP AND THE INDIVIDUAL

1. The Locus of Intrinsic Goodness

Since we have rejected ethical relativism, we are committed to the theory that goodness has some objective and general import. Although the sources of goodness may vary, goodness itself, in some sense or other, must be common to many lives, groups, or objects. In this chapter, we shall begin to answer the question, "What is the nature of goodness?" By goodness, in this connection, we mean that which is good as an end, good for its own sake, intrinsically and not merely instrumentally. An indication of *where* goodness is found will provide us with a first approximation to an answer. Where does it occur? What is its locus?

The locus of goodness cannot be a completely lifeless world. Value is nonindifference. There can be no intrinsic value, no goodness or badness, if the world is utterly neutral, so that nothing makes *any* difference. Now the world, it would seem to me, *would* be absolutely neutral if it never aroused the slightest glimmer of liking or disliking in any creature whatsoever, beast or man or god. Whenever I imagine that every sentient being in the universe has been completely annihilated or has been turned into an unconscious automaton, so that there is not the slightest spark of feeling or emotion or desire or curiosity at *any* time and *any* place, I find that all value whatsoever is, in my imaginary world, destroyed. The least quiver of interest in any sentient creature is worth more than an irretrievably dead universe, because the interest is value or is an indispensable component or accompaniment of value, and the dead universe has no value.

The term *interest* is here used in an inclusive sense to mean any attitude of liking or disliking, of prizing or disprizing, of preference, selection, appreciation, or appraisal. It involves feeling, emotion, desire, will, or some similar attitude. I am asserting that nothing can possess intrinsic value entirely apart from interest as thus inclusively defined. For the present, I shall not seek to answer exactly where the value lies: whether in the interest or in the object of interest or in a relation between the two. I am simply asserting that intrinsic value requires interest, in some sense or other.

It is true that *extrinsic* or *instrumental* value—the value of a means to an end—may exist without any creature being directly interested. Vitamins were useful before they were "discovered," and hence before anyone was interested in them. Their usefulness, however, depends upon their means relation to intrinsic values, so that even instrumental values *indirectly* or *ultimately* depend upon interest. If no creature ever experienced anything "interest-wise"—that is to say, in terms of some preference—vitamins would be of no use, because there would be none of the zest of health, and all things would be perfectly neutral.

It is also true that *potential* value might exist in a universe without a spark of life. Thus the world might be of such a sort that it would be very enjoyable—for example, delightfully beautiful—*if* human beings, or some creatures that could appreciate beauty, were to be born into it. But the value could not be *actualized* until some animate being is born into the hitherto lifeless universe. A universe everywhere and forever frozen in lifelessness could have no actual value. Admittedly, these assertions of mine cannot be proved; but they seem to me self-evident.

I must confess that some others do not share this belief. Professor G. E. Moore, for example, has maintained that beauty may exist independently of any interest whatever, and that it is intrinsically good when it does so exist. He asks us to consider two alternatives:

Let us imagine one world exceedingly beautiful. Imagine it as beautiful as you can; put into it whatever on this earth you most admire—mountains, rivers, the sea; trees and sunsets, stars and moon. Imagine these all combined in the most exquisite proportions, so that no one thing jars against another, but each contributes to the beauty of the whole. And then imagine the ugliest world you can possibly conceive. Imagine it simply one heap of filth, containing everything that is most disgusting to us, for whatever reason, and the whole, as far as may be, without one redeeming feature.[1]

He maintains that it would be better for the beautiful world to exist rather than the one which is ugly, *even though no one should ever contemplate either.* I would challenge this belief, and also the assumption that beauty could so exist.

It seems to me that beauty cannot exist apart from interest: for the beauty is not in the object alone nor in the mind alone but in the accord between the two. For example, a beautiful sunset, as the slang phrase goes, is "easy to look at"; it is, so to speak, *fitted* to be perceived and appreciated; there is a felt harmony between its appearance and *our* faculties, and if there were no such harmony we would not judge it beautiful. It is true that when we appreciate beauty our attention is focused upon the object, and our enjoyment, as a psychological state, is in the background or margin of consciousness, so that we are not explicitly aware of the subjective pole of the relationship. Hence we impute the value to the object as seemingly independent rather than to the object *in relation* to the attitude of appreciation; and, for this reason, the beauty *seems* to exist entirely apart from us. Yet when we take care to analyze the nature of beauty, we find that it involves a relation between an object appreciated and an organism that appreciates, and that it cannot exist divorced from all interest or appreciation.

1 *Principia Ethica,* Cambridge University Press, Cambridge, 1922, pp. 83-84.

Even if it somehow could so exist, it would *then* be a neutral quality and not an actual value. What difference would it make, what value could it have, if it never aroused the slightest interest? Professor Moore revolts from the image of ugliness and delights in the thought of beauty, and perhaps he neglects explicitly to discount the fact that he is "interested" throughout his mental experiment of imagining a beautiful but lifeless universe. There is value, of course, *in* his experience, and it is easy to suppose that the value remains *apart* from the experience. Value would indeed remain if the universe should include organisms appreciative of external beauty, but I cannot see that it would remain if all such organisms were to disappear.

In any event, value has no relevance for *us* unless we have some interest in it. What matters to us is what falls within the human ken. We are concerned with values seized in the moment of living, not with alleged values that exist apart from all life. For us, the locus of intrinsic value is life, and the life that matters most is human life.

What kind of human life? Does goodness occur in the individual or in the group? This is a question of very great moment. We shall begin by examining two answers that are poles apart: the one can be called the ethics of extreme individualism, the other the ethics of extreme collectivism. We shall thereafter consider whether our choice is restricted to "either/or," or whether we can choose a third alternative.

It might be supposed that what we have already said disposes of the matter. We have said that value is nonindifference, and that without interest, nothing ever makes any difference. It can be argued that this necessarily means that the locus of value is the individual, since only the individual and not the group can possess an interest. Indeed, it is just this position that Ralph Barton Perry takes.

If "good" were a simple adjective connoting an unanalyzable quality or character, it would have no essential connection with individuals or with anything else. It would be impossible to know to what it attached except   contemplating objects and seeing that they were in fact good—or indifferent, or bad. As opposed to views of this intuitive type, there stands the view, here taken, that the goodness of anything consists in its relation to feeling, desire, emotion, will, or some similar attitude. . . . This much having been assumed, there would then remain the further question as to where such attitudes of favor and disfavor are to be found. The answer of social democracy is that they are found, and found only, in individuals; that is, in one or more of those beings enclosed within a skin, born of woman, subject to natural death after a period approximating three-score and ten years, denominated by a proper name, and numerable in the census.[2]

We might unhesitatingly agree with Perry if it were not for the opposite contention that a group may have an interest that is quite different from the sum of the interests of its individual members. Rousseau expresses this latter point of view in his famous doctrine of "the general will." He points out that "the body politic," like the individual human body, has a kind of internal coherence and organic interrelatedness of all its parts, and he concludes that it therefore has a self and is a moral being with a will of its own.

The body politic, taken individually, may be considered as an organized, living body, resembling that of man. . . . The life of both bodies is the self common to the whole, the reciprocal sensibility and internal correspondence of all the parts. . . . The body politic, therefore, is also a moral being possessed of a will; and this general will, which tends always to the preservation and welfare of the whole and of every part, and is the source of the laws, constitutes for all the members of the State, in their relations to one another, and to it, the rule of what is just or unjust.[3]

Rousseau clearly and emphatically distinguishes between the general will and the sum of particular wills:

There is often a great deal of difference between the *will of all* and the *general will;* the latter considers only the common interest, while the former takes private interest into account, and is no more than a sum of particular wills.[4]

[2] *Puritanism and Democracy,* Vanguard Press, New York, 1944, pp. 440-441.
[3] *A Discourse on Political Economy,* in *Social Contract and Discourses,* Dutton, New York, 1913, p. 253.
[4] *Social Contract,* in *ibid.,* p. 25.

Thus is the issue joined. On the one hand, we have the theory that the locus of goodness is always the individual, and that the good of the group or society is never more than the sum of the individual goods. My good is one thing, your good is another, and there is never a common good that fuses them into a single whole or that exists in addition to the separate goods of you and me and of other individuals. On the other hand, we have the theory that there is a general or common interest of the group, and that the fulfillment of this interest constitutes a distinct good that is not the sum of the goods of individuals.

Let us now consider each of these views in turn. We shall discover, I believe, that Perry's view is essentially correct; but we shall find enough truth in Rousseau's point of view to warrant a rejection of extreme individualism.

2. *The Individual as the Locus of Value*

THE ETHICS of extreme individualism can perhaps best be illustrated by expounding the relevant theories of one of its principal representatives, Thomas Hobbes (1588-1679). It is easier to understand Hobbes if we know something about his personality and his times. "Fear and I were twins," he declared, blaming his abnormal fearfulness upon the coincidence that his birth occurred when the Spanish Armada threatened England with disaster. Although it is very unlikely that this is a correct explanation, fear was one of the strongest motives of his life. This temperamental tendency was reinforced by the character of his age, a time of civil war when Charles I lost his head and the nation was thrown into a panic. In his *Behemoth*, Hobbes depicted the civil war as a terrible state of lawlessness, disorder, and anarchy; in his more famous book, *Leviathan*, he described the extreme measures necessary to quell anarchy, fend off disaster, and guarantee security to each individual.

Equal to fear as a motive in his life was Hobbes' determination to discover the real facts about existence. He was resolved to be utterly unsentimental, to let not feelings but only reason and evidence determine his beliefs. As a friend of Francis Bacon, as a contemporary and acquaintance of Descartes, as an admirer of Kepler, Galileo, and Harvey, he was naturally impelled to study the new developments of natural science and to import its methods into the philosophical and political spheres.

It was a very common view among scientists that any material whole is an aggregate of atoms, each one of which, as Newton later expressed it, is a "solid, massy, hard, impenetrable, movable particle."[5] There was also a very widespread tendency exhibited by both scientists and philosophers to think of the world as a mechanism or as made up of mechanisms. Now a mechanism is put together out of separate parts, and those parts, although perhaps geared together, always retain their separate identity. For example, a tire can be taken off an automobile, and it still remains a tire; but a heart cannot be plucked out of a biological organism without ceasing to be a real heart and, indeed, without soon decaying. A part of a mechanism, therefore, is much more of an "individual" than is a part of an organism. Influenced by the science of his day, Hobbes was prone to think of any whole as made of atomic isolates, or of individual parts like those of a mechanism; and he proceeded to describe man and society after this manner.

The economic forces of the time reinforced these ideas. It was the age of early capitalism when "individual enterprise" was being defended against feudal collectivism and monarchical absolutism. The businessmen wished to substitute a relationship of free contract in place of a relationship of enforced status. They insisted upon the right of the enterprising individual, conceived as separate and self-seeking, to carve out his own economic destiny. These capitalistic de-

[5] Isaac Newton, *Opticks*, 2d ed., W. and J. Innys, London, 1717, p. 375.

velopments were just beginning in the lifetime of Hobbes, but they no doubt influenced him to some degree.

Upon these foundations Hobbes reared a materialistic and mechanistic theory of reality and an individualistic theory of man and society. I shall mention only those parts of his philosophy that throw light upon his ethical individualism.

The general foundation of his individualistic doctrines is the view that a whole is simply the additive sum of distinct parts, a theory implied, as we have seen, by his atomism and mechanism. He believed that all reasoning is a kind of addition and subtraction of discrete elements.

When a man *reasoneth,* he does nothing else but conceive a sum total, from *addition* of parcels; or conceive a remainder, from *subtraction* of one sum from another. . . . These operations are not incident to numbers only, but to all manner of things that can be added together, and taken one out of another. . . . In sum, in what matter soever there is place for *addition* and *subtraction,* there also is place for *reason;* and where these have no place, there *reason* has nothing at all to do.[6]

This view of the reasoning process implies that a whole made up of parts is not an organic unity but an aggregate of discrete elements which can be freely added and subtracted. It was a short step from this reasoning to the conception of society as merely an aggregate of egoistic individuals.

This atomistic point of view was reinforced by Hobbes' denial of the validity of universal ideas. He believed that the particular, not the universal, is real. The so-called universal is simply a name to refer to many individuals: thus "man" has no meaning except as a name—the reality is always the particular man. From this position, Hobbes worked out a nominalistic interpretation of groups and organizations including the state. He called them "artificial bodies"—fictions of a sort—and thought of them as mechanisms to serve individuals, in whom reality ultimately dwells.

6 *Leviathan,* in *The English Works of Thomas Hobbes,* Bohn, London, 1839, III, pp. 29-30.

The world, he believed, consists of extended bodies in motion, and a human being is a material body—a kind of elaborate machine, separate and distinct from other machines. When acted upon by other bodies, this machine responds with a motion of its own, which takes the form of sensation. A sensation is a vibratory motion of particles— "only a motion in the organs of sense." "Imagination is decaying sense," and "memory" is another form of the same. "Endeavor," "will," and "desire" are just motions within the nervous system. A man calls a thing "good" when it is an object of desire or motion toward; and "evil" when it is an object of aversion or motion away from. Good and evil are always relative to the motions or volitions of the individual, and there is no suggestion of any objective social good.

According to this point of view, every person is motivated solely by egoistic drives. In a characteristic passage, Hobbes compares life to a race.

This *race* we must suppose to have no other *goal,* nor other *garland,* but being foremost, and in it: To endeavour, is *appetite.* To be remiss, is *sensuality.* To consider them behind, is *glory.* To consider them before, is *humility.* . . . To fall on the sudden, is disposition to *weep.* To see another fall, is disposition to *laugh.* To see one out-gone whom we would not, is *pity.* To see one out-go whom we would not, is *indignation.* To hold fast by another, is to *love.* To carry him on that so holdeth, is *charity.* To hurt one's-self for haste, is *shame.* Continually to be out-gone, is *misery.* Continually to out-go the next before, is *felicity.* And to forsake the course, is to *die.*[7]

Each person, motivated by self-interest, comes into conflict with every other. "If any two men desire the same thing, which nevertheless they cannot both enjoy," declares Hobbes, "they become enemies, and . . . endeavor to destroy or subdue one another."[8] Moreover, human desire is insatiable: every man is driven by "a perpetual and restless desire of

[7] *Human Nature,* in *ibid.,* IV, p. 53.
[8] *Leviathan, op. cit.,* p. 111.

power after power, that ceaseth only in death."[9] Thus impelled, everyone will naturally prey upon his fellows, and be preyed upon in turn. The consequence is "such a war as is of every man against every man"—a state of anarchy described in a very famous passage:

In such condition there is no place for industry, because the fruit thereof is uncertain: and consequently no culture of the earth; no navigation, nor use of the commodities that may be imported by sea; no commodious building; no instruments of moving, and removing, such things as require much force; no knowledge of the face of the earth; no account of time; no arts; no letters; no society; and which is worst of all, continual fear, and danger of violent death; and the life of man, solitary, poor, nasty, brutish, and short.[10]

This is the intolerable condition of men before they have created a civil state; and to end this condition men band together to establish a sovereign who shall have absolute power to enforce peace. The "social contract," which establishes the unlimited power of the sovereign, is an agreement among asocial, self-seeking individuals in the interests of self-preservation. Only the naked force of the sovereign power, set up expressly for the purpose, can compel egocentric human beings to live peacefully together, for "covenants, without the sword, are but words, and of no strength to secure a man at all."[11] Without the force of the state to compel men to civil obedience, they would relapse into the state of anarchy. Believing that the only possible choice is between extremes, men have preferred the whips of tyranny to the scorpions of anarchy. They have surrendered anarchic liberty for the sake of iron-clad security.

It is obvious that Hobbes is here stating an extreme form of individualism: man's basic nature is antisocial; social relations are merely artificial; the state is simply a contrivance

9 *Ibid.*, pp. 85-86.
10 *Ibid.*, p. 113.
11 *Ibid.*, p. 154.

invoked by fear and maintained by force. The absolute power vested in the sovereign is the price that individuals must pay to achieve security. All action, both private and public, is for the sake of the individual. Society is never more than a means.[12]

An ethical individualist need not agree with all the opinions of Hobbes—indeed, some of these opinions are obsolete and many are extreme. Yet the extreme doctrines of Hobbes serve to throw into bold relief the thesis of ethical individualism that intrinsic value is to be found solely in the individual. Let us now turn to the opposite point of view.

3. The Group as the Locus of Value

THE ETHICAL THEORY of extreme collectivism has evolved over a long period of time and has been expressed by innumerable writers. To a certain extent, Plato and Aristotle contributed to it; it was widely current in the Middle Ages; Rousseau, Hegel, Durkheim, Bosanquet, Gentile, and many other modern thinkers have promulgated it. It has been immensely influential in the formulation of fascist ideology and has tinged communist doctrine.

Its outstanding representative is Georg Wilhem Friedrich Hegel (1770-1831), the greatest German philosopher since Kant. Not only is he the most devoted and articulate spokesman of social organicism, but he is also the most influential. Before Hegel, philosophers had concerned themselves with practical affairs, and a few of them had made some little stir. Plato had a finger in the political intrigues of Syracuse; Hobbes' *Leviathan* was dangerous enough to arouse the ire of both Cromwell and Charles the Second; Locke did much to inspire the American Revolution, and

12 *Cf.*, George H. Sabine, *A History of Political Theory*, 2d ed., Holt, New York, 1950, pp. 467, 474-475.

Rousseau to inspire the French Revolution. But the influence of all these thinkers has been exceeded by that of Hegel. As Ernst Cassirer has remarked:

> No other philosophical system has exerted such a strong and enduring influence upon political life as the metaphysics of Hegel. . . . There has hardly been a single great political system that has resisted its influence. All our modern political ideologies show us the strength, the durability and permanence of the principles that were first introduced and defended in Hegel's philosophy of right and in his philosophy of history. . . . A historian recently raised the question whether the struggle of the Russians and the invading Germans in 1943 was not, at bottom, a conflict between the Left and Right wings of Hegel's school. That may seem to be an exaggerated statement of the problem but it contains a nucleus of truth.[13]

Hegel's fundamental philosophical standpoint is that of absolute idealism—the view that the whole of reality is a unified system of spirit or mind. The processes of nature are within the world mind—they are the very reasonings of that mind. The laws of science are the tracing of world thought—the stages of history are the unfoldment of that thought. Every spirit, and everything, is part of this vast whole—no part is really separate, like a hard impenetrable atom or an enclosed self-subsistent mind; every part possesses its meaning and character in its relations to the other parts and to the whole. In expressing these views Hegel was giving voice to the dominant philosophical movement of the Germany of his day.

He was also influenced by the expanding knowledge of organisms. Biological science was beginning to develop rapidly, and Buffon, Erasmus Darwin, Lamarck, and Goethe had supplied much new insight into the structures and functions of organic life. In his *Critique of Judgment,* Kant had pointed out the distinctive characteristics of an organism as involving a systematic interdependence of its parts, which

13 *The Myth of the State,* Yale University Press, New Haven, 1946, pp. 248-249.

are thus the causes and effects of each other and of the whole
—the leaves of a tree, for example, depending upon the
trunk; the trunk, in turn, depending upon the leaves; and
both the leaves and trunk contributing to and being governed by the dynamic equilibrium of the whole.

This doctrine of organic part-whole relationships is fundamental in Hegel's philosophy. The universe, he believes, is
an immense organic unity made up of component organic
unities. In any organic unity, each part is through and
through relational; it cannot be isolated without altering its
character or destroying it; its value and character are like
those of a single musical phrase in a sonata, dependent upon
and derivative from its relations to the whole. The pattern
of the whole is prior to and immanent in the parts, just as
the plan of the whole human body dwells within and governs
all its parts.

Since things are essentially related to one another, they
cannot be understood truly apart from such relationships.
The truth is a whole, each integral part of which is mutilated
when considered in isolation. To see things together, therefore, is to enrich vision, to see things apart is to impoverish it.
No proposition taken in isolation is wholly true because no
thing taken in isolation is wholly real.

This point of view is basic in Hegel's social philosophy.
He believes that individualism is false because separate individuals are unreal. Apart from their social relations, human
beings are as artificial and insubstantial as the personifica-
tions in an allegory. They are shaped and constituted by the
social forces penetrating into them—by the customs, traditions, institutions, and cultural life of the society.

A social group is more than a mere aggregate, an arithmetical sum total of its parts. The mark of an aggregate is
that its parts can be joined or separated without essential
change in their internal characteristics. No genuine social
group is such an aggregate—its members are too interdependent; they are sustained in their activity by one another

and by the whole. The group has a total character impressed on every member—a concrete and ineluctable unity of its own, with an organized social structure and distinctive social functions. The common interests of a group regarded as a single individual, therefore, cannot be identified with the several interests of its members. A mob, acting as no individual would act, is simply the more pathological embodiment of a basic and universal fact: that every group has an *esprit de corps,* a common interest, a collective will, a kind of group mind. All of us have experienced such group feeling and group thought, the experience of being merged in something greater than ourselves, the experience of being dominated by the group spirit.

From these premises, Hegel derives a doctrine of freedom. He rejects the view that freedom could be anything merely negative, such as an absence of restraint. We cannot find freedom in detachment from all connections that make demands upon us. Such freedom is illusory, because the detached individual is lonely, empty, unreal. Nor can we find freedom in self-assertion. A man is as big as his interests; if he asserts only his own worth, he shrinks to the vanishing point. Nor can we find freedom in capricious interests, because then we garner no coherent happiness. Freedom requires organization and discipline, a coherence of personality that expresses itself in coherent action and striving. The only real freedom is to be found in social participation. The way for a man to become free is to achieve a deep and comprehensive self through many sympathetic relations to other things, other people, and the institutions which embody their collective life.

But what if a person's will is opposed to society? What if he is essentially an individualist and does not want to identify himself with social institutions? Does not his freedom then require an assertion of his private and individual will? In answering this question, Hegel distinguishes between a man's "real will" and his "apparent will." Each individual exhibits two wills, one irrational and immediate, and the other real, rational, long-sighted. The former is individualistic, the latter is social. My real will and your real will are the same, and the combined wills of all the citizens go to make up the "general will" of society, which is, as Rousseau said, more than the sum of its parts, a creative synthesis, a real organism in its own right. This real will, willing what is best for you and me, is the guardian of the moral values in society and is embodied in its traditions, its institutions, and above all, in the state. When we merge ourselves with these traditions and institutions and identify ourselves with the state, we are obeying our own real will, achieving that universality and social-mindedness in which true freedom consists.

Hegel distinguishes three stages in the realization of freedom. The first stage is the participation of the individual in the family. By living in the family circle, individuals lose their stultifying independence and participate in a wider and deeper whole. Every family has its distinctive character and atmosphere: no two homes are exactly alike. The union of its members creates a little social organism, a kind of collective personality, an *esprit de corps*. By sharing in this common life, each member learns the meaning of love as a loosening of the bands of selfhood. Declares Hegel:

> Love means in general the consciousness of my unity with another, such that I am not isolated from myself, but win my self-consciousness only by giving up my explicit being or independence, and thereby know myself as the unity of myself with the other and the other with me.[14]

The freedom of each member of the family lies in just this differentiation and union within the common life.

The second stage is the participation of the individual in civil society. This is the realm of institutions wider than the family but narrower than the state. It includes school and church and economic group and cultural association. Within

14 *The Philosophy of Right*, section 158 note. Quoted by Hugh A. Reyburn, *The Ethical Theory of Hegel*, Clarendon Press, Oxford, 1921, p. 208.

its wide ambit, the individual finds less intimacy but a larger scope than in the circle of the family. Hegel's analysis of civil society, in which he is especially concerned with economic activities and property rights, is characterized by his unsparing recognition of anarchic tendencies—the conflict of private interests, the clash of economic groups, and the welter of competing institutions. Yet all is not anarchy; each individual or group, in pursuing its private or particular interest, helps to create a system of social interdependence, as embodied, for example, in the division of labor. In so doing, it enlarges the area of freedom and rational association. Because of the anarchic tendency within society, however, it is necessary to achieve a binding force or synthesis which will integrate all divergent individuals and institutions into a supreme social organism. This unification is achieved in and through the state.

The third stage of freedom, therefore, is the participation of the individual in the state. It is here that the culmination of freedom is reached, because the state, in providing the widest and deepest integration of interests, supplies the individual with the richest form of social participation. Hence its claim upon the individual is higher than that of civil society. Hegel explains:

Were the state to be considered as exchangeable with the civil society, and were its decisive features to be regarded as the security and protection of property and personal freedom, the interest of the individual as such would be the ultimate purpose of the social union. It would then be at one's option to be a member of the state. But the state has a totally different relation to the individual. It is the objective spirit, and he has his truth, real existence, and ethical status only in being a member of it. Union, as such, is itself the true content and end, since the individual is intended to pass a universal life. His particular satisfactions, activities, and way of life have in this authenticated substantive principle their origin and result.[15]

15 *The Philosophy of Right,* translated by S. W. Dyde, Bell, London, 1896, p. 240.

In the ideal state, Hegel goes on to explain, "the private interest of its citizens is one with the common interest of the state," and "the one finds its gratification and realization in the other."[16] Although the ideal has not been fully attained, the actual state provides its individual citizens with their essential values.

> The state, its laws, its arrangements, constitute the rights of its members; its natural features, its mountains, air, and waters, are *their* country, their fatherland, their outward material property; the history of this state, *their* deeds; what their ancestors have produced, belongs to them and lives in their memory. All is their possession, just as they are possessed by it; for it constitutes their existence, their being.[17]

The worth of the state, according to Hegel, is not merely that it affords a better life for its citizens, but that it has a supreme intrinsic value. In rhapsodic language, he extols the state as "the march of God in the world" and as the "absolute, stable, end-for-itself."[18] He describes it as an organism, attributes to it will and thought, and reveres it as a thing divine.

> No predicates, principles, and the like suffice to express the nature of the state; it must be comprehended as an organism. . . . To the complete state belongs, essentially, consciousness and thought. The state knows thus what it wills, and it knows it under the form of thought. . . . We must therefore worship the state as the manifestation of the divine on earth.[19]

"This final end" of the state, Hegel explains, "has the supreme right against individuals, whose supreme duty it is to be members of the state."[20]

Although he thus apotheosizes the state, he does not seek to abolish individual distinctions. Unlike a modern fascist,

---

16 *The Philosophy of History,* translated by J. Sibree, Collier, New York, 1900, p. 70.

17 *Ibid.,* pp. 102-103.

18 J. Macbride Sterrett, *The Ethics of Hegel: Translated Selections from his "Rechtphilosophie,"* Ginn, Boston, 1893, pp. 189, 245.

19 *The Philosophy of Right,* translated by J. Loewenberg, in *Hegel Selections,* Scribner's, New York, 1929, pp. 446-447.

20 Sterrett, *op. cit.,* p. 189.

he believes that freedom requires the differentiation of the
parts.

The one essential canon to make liberty deep and real is to
give every business belonging to the general interests of the state
a separate organization wherever they are essentially distinct.
Such real division must be: for liberty is only deep when it is
differentiated in all its fullness and these differences manifested
in existence.[21]

He even reserves to the individual a sphere of private conscience "which as such does not come within the sphere of
the state."[22] Despite these qualifications, he remains the supreme representative in modern philosophy of the theory
that values are essentially social and that the group, rather
than the detached individual, is the locus of value.

4. *The Theory of Integrative Levels*

IN THE LIGHT of what we now know about human nature,
we should avoid an exaggerated individualism such as that
of Hobbes and an overpowering collectivism such as that of
Hegel. Society should be conceived neither as a monstrous
superorganism of which individuals are but cells, nor as a
mere arithmetical sum of self-enclosed egoists. We should
reject the concept of a "state organism," "race soul," or
"group mind" but should also reject the concept of independent selfish individuals, connected by no real ties to one
another. We should try to do justice to both sides of human
nature, the individual and the social.

A third view, that will avoid the pitfalls of both social
atomism and social organicism, is therefore required. Such
a view will carefully distinguish between the various types
and grades of integration and will point out the kinds of

21 *Encyclopaedia of the Philosophical Sciences,* section 541. Quoted in
Cassirer, *op. cit.,* p. 276.
22 Dyde, *op. cit.,* p. 264.

unity that characterize human groups and the kinds that do not. In the light of this analysis, it will be possible to indicate the fundamental errors of extreme individualists such as Hobbes and extreme collectivists such as Hegel. This alternative view I shall call the theory of integrative levels.

In the first place, this theory points out that unity permits of infinite degrees. If by unity we mean, as I shall mean, the integration of parts within a whole, the unity may be very slight or very intense. Any quality can thus vary from little to great. For example, there may be a very faint degree of light, so faint as to be scarcely distinguishable from total darkness; or there may be a brilliant intensity of light, blinding in its terrific luminosity. In between these two extremes are infinite gradations of intensity from least to greatest. Similarly, there may be a very slight degree of unity, so slight that one may hesitate to say that the parts are joined together at all; and at the opposite extreme, there may be a very intense and tight coherence. In between these extremes, there are again infinite gradations, and any given group may be low or intermediate or high on the scale. The mere fact that a group is a group indicates very little concerning the degree of its integration.

In the second place, it is important to remember that there are different kinds of integration. The integration that an organism or a mind exhibits is not the only kind, and it may not be the kind that a group or society exhibits. Let us now consider different kinds of unity, ranged in a scale of intensity. As we consider these kinds, we should remember that they are not mutually exclusive, and that the intenser kinds of unity may include the less intense. Moreover, within each kind there are infinite gradations in degree of integration, so that the lowest degree of one kind may be no more intense than the highest degree of the kind immediately preceding.

(1) Mere Adjacency. Things may form a group in the sense that they are juxtaposed in time and space. A pile of

miscellaneous rubbish forms a group in this sense: there is no real connection between the objects except that they are heaped together. A merely accidental and heterogeneous collection of individuals, indifferent to one another, is a human group of this type. A number of people, for example, may happen to be passing each other on some busy streetcorner. In such a casual group, each person is going his own separate way and is very slightly affected by the other people in the immediate vicinity. Such a group has a very low level of integration, so low that we hesitate to call it a group at all: it is a mere aggregate or collection.

(2) External Association. Things may be grouped together, not because they are related to each other, but because they are all related to something outside the group. The pieces of driftwood that litter a beach, for example, are grouped together, not because they are interrelated, but because they have all been cast there by the ocean tide. Similarly human beings may be held together, not because they have any concern for each other, but because they are all related to some common external factor. For example, the crowd that sits in a moving picture theater forms a group of this sort. With the exception of friends or lovers in the audience, who go less to see the show than to enjoy each other's company, the bulk of the onlookers ordinarily do not know or care about one another; but they are held together because they are all interested in a common object, the story on the screen.

(3) Mechanical Interdependence. At this level of integration, there is no mere relation to an external factor but a functional interaction of parts. In an engine, for example, cylinder, piston, connecting rod, flywheel, and shaft act upon one another and "cooperate." Part acts and reacts upon part, directly or through some transmission mechanism. Now such a part is, in one sense, *more,* and in another sense, *less* of an "individual" than is the part of an organism. It is more of

an individual in the sense that it is more independent: it has a certain determinate shape and composition that remains relatively unaltered when it is added to or subtracted from the machine. A gear, for example, can be taken out of a machine, and it still remains substantially the same gear; but a foot cannot be cut off a human body without ceasing to be a foot. On the other hand, the gear is less of an "individual" in the sense that it is standardized and replaceable, whereas the foot is unique and irreplaceable. It is characteristic of a machine part that it is made in accordance with exact specifications; it can usually be ordered by number from a catalogue; and it can be replaced by another part made according to the same precise specifications.

Human beings are never exactly like the parts of a machine, but they sometimes function mechanically. For example, a Roman galley slave pulling his oar in monotonous rhythm, was picked and trained essentially for this machine-like function and quickly replaced by another galley slave if he failed to perform according to specifications. Likewise acting mechanically are the modern workers on an assembly line, each performing some minute, monotonous task over and over again, day in and day out. From the standpoint of the "scientific manager," the inner life of the worker does not matter: all that matters is his external function and his externalistic relations to the other workers on the assembly line. If he breaks down, he is quickly replaced by another human robot who carries out the same monotonous motion in the same precise manner.

(4) Essential or "Organic" Interdependence. At this level, there is not only an interaction of parts, but the essential characteristics of the parts are modified by the interaction. The relations between the parts, therefore, are not external but internal. A relation is internal if it substantially influences the nature of the things which it relates. Such internal or essential relations, as opposed to merely external and

inessential, are often called "organic"; but it should be remembered that individuals can be thus related without constituting an "organism" in the literal sense of that term.

Everything is probably related to everything else—every time you nod your head, for example, you affect every star in the universe, but the relation, in this case, is so slight that it is negligible. Human relations, however, are very often not of this superficial character. A person is a son, a brother, a husband, a friend, an enemy, a citizen, a trade unionist, a church member, etc.; and stripped of all such relations, he would not be a human being. Some of these relations are so essential to his personality that they can properly be called internal. You do not greatly change a bolt when you destroy the machine from which you have removed it, but you do profoundly change a person when you destroy his family.

(5) Existential Interdependence. At this level, the parts depend upon one another not only for their functions but for their very existence. The parts of an organism are usually related in this manner. (Alexis Carrel managed to keep a chicken's heart beating for several years after he removed it from the chicken's body, but this feat is the exception.) Existential interdependence, however, is not limited to the parts of an organism. A very young animal, for example, may depend for its life upon its relations to its family, but this does not mean that it is not a separate organism. Or again, a soldier may lose his life if he becomes separated from his regiment, but this does not indicate that the regiment is a single organism. Generally, if the members of a group are existentially dependent upon one another, there is an intense degree of integration.

(6) Configurational Unity. The term *configuration* is now commonly used to designate a unity in which the parts are not merely interdependent but are determined by the character of the whole. We owe particularly to the Gestalt psy-

chologists the insistence that oftentimes the whole determines the existence and nature of the parts: the parts do
not simply combine to make a whole, but the whole expresses
itself in and through the parts. In this sense, the whole is
prior to, imminent in, and more than the sum of the parts.

Any well-composed work of art is such a unity. Some of the
details may seem to precede the whole, but the total effect
determines whether they will have to be altered or omitted.
Every inconsistent detail, as for example an inappropriate
chord in a musical composition, cries out for change or elimination; if it is finally included, the structure of the composition must be readjusted so as to achieve a consistent effect.
The chord, when fitted into this new context, sounds different
than it did before: it is not heard as a detached set of tones
but as an integral part of the total composition. Once the
total form is perfected, moreover, it has a certain relative
independence of its constituents. A melody, for example,
can be transposed into a different key, as from C to C sharp,
even though not a single tone of the original arrangement
recurs. Therefore the form, or configuration, is not simply
the arithmetical sum of the constituents.

Likewise in the case of human groups, there exist more or
less well-defined wholes and characteristics of wholes, and
these are impressed upon the parts. The parts are therefore
to be conceived as parts within the configuration of the
whole. Moreover, as in the case of a melody, the parts can
change and the form remain fairly constant. A national
culture, for example, is such a configuration: it is the common possession of all the individuals within the nation but is
relatively independent of any of them. It is a unique pattern
of religion, art, language, morality, ideology, history, etc., embodied in customs, traditions, institutions, and such artifacts
as books, laws, and works of art. Impressed upon individuals,
it pervasively molds their mentality and behavior; but it
endures and develops, even though individuals come and go.

"Americanism," for example, is something relatively independent of any one individual or any single generation. Moreover, no person is merely an American: he participates in other cultural configurations, perhaps in what we call Christianity. Every individual is at the focal point of various social patterns or systems of culture, each contributing to his personality.

(7) Biological Unity. A relatively intense degree of integration is achieved at the level of the biological organism. By an organism I mean a unity composed of a number of cooperative and mutually dependent parts constituted for subserving vital processes. Thus there is a single unity, the life of the whole, which is the end of its parts. It involves the organic and existential interdependence of the parts and the configurational unity of the whole. But it involves something more: the intense degree of integration that is realized in the unity of a life, though perhaps only the life of a vegetable or a very simple animal.

For reasons that I shall indicate, I do not believe that a group of human beings attains this level of integration.

(8) Psychological Unity. A higher animal is not only organic after the manner of a vegetable or a very simple animal, but is *consciously* organized, with a core of self-identity. It has a mind that expresses itself through what it experiences and what it does. In human beings, mind reaches the level of self-consciousness. Animals probably have experiences without being aware that they have them; but a man is aware of himself as the subject of experiences; he can consider himself as himself, the same thinking being, in different times and places. He thereby attains a capacity for self-direction and self-criticism.

As I shall later contend, a group does not attain the level of integration represented by a mind. In a group, there are the minds of the individual members, but no other mind.

In the light of this theory of integrative levels, we can now expose the fundamental fallacies of both extreme individualism and extreme collectivism.

5. *The Refutation of Extreme Individualism*

THE BASIC FALLACY of individualists such as Hobbes is that they deny that groups can be characterized in terms of any of the higher and intenser levels of integration. They represent a reductive or *leveling down* type of theory: they interpret groups in terms of mere adjacency or external association or mechanical interdependence, to the neglect or exclusion of higher types of unity.

This failure to recognize the intenser forms of integration is a necessary consequence of extreme individualism. In its very nature, this type of theory exaggerates the independence of individuals. It supposes that individuality largely excludes sociality, that each human being is self-centered, self-seeking, and mainly self-sufficient. Anyone who, in contrast, emphasizes the intenser types of social integration is by reason of that very emphasis not an extreme individualist.

At times the individualist may speak as if human groups are mere fortuitous collections, the members of which are connected by nothing more than temporal and spatial adjacency. Although this interpretation may more or less apply to very casual groups, it is obviously inadequate when applied to organized groups. Consequently the individualist must rely upon some other kind of explanation.

This he can find in the second type of integration, which I have called external association. In this type of group, as the reader will recall, the members are no more than superficially related to one another, but they are nevertheless bound together by their common relation to some external factor. For example, according to the philosophy of Leibniz, all finite beings have no direct relations to one another but nevertheless fit together into a harmonious whole, because they are all related to a common external factor, God, who predetermines each of them to be in harmony with every other. Somewhat similarly, Hobbes maintains that human beings within a state are all self-centered egoists, without any deep intrinsic relations to one another, but they manage to live together with a fair degree of peace and security, because they are all related to a common external factor, the absolute sovereign set up by the "Social Contract." Other individualists fall back upon similar mechanisms to hold together their separate human atoms. Turgot and Quesnay, for example, speak of the "laws of nature" that promote and maintain a harmony of egoisms; Adam Smith writes about the "invisible hand" of economic competition that reconciles the gain of each self-seeking individual with the gain of every other; Jeremy Bentham discusses the system of "sanctions," of rewards and punishments, that induces unmitigated egoists to work together harmoniously; and Friedrich Hayek maintains that the separate efforts of individuals are harmoniously coordinated by the self-equilibrating mechanism of the market system. In each instance, there is some common external force or agency that brings about an artificial harmony among self-centered individuals.

Extreme individualists also tend to interpret human relations in terms of mechanical interdependence. They admit that human beings functionally interact, but they think that the interaction is like that of the parts of a machine, which are not essentially altered by their interconnections. This view has traditionally been expressed by the myth of the "state of nature": individuals are said to have inherited their fundamental characteristics from a primeval, precivilized state, and these characteristics are thought to be constants throughout the social process. Each human being, like a hard impenetrable atom or a cog in a machine, remains fundamentally the same whether he is fitted into or is removed from a particular social mechanism. This theory of the immutable natural man—as promulgated in the works of Hobbes, Locke, Paine, Godwin, and the earlier books of Rousseau—had a profound influence upon the development of individualistic liberalism.

In economic theory of this type, the mechanistic nature of the doctrine becomes more obvious. Again there is a myth— the myth of the "economic man," an abstract, artificial, dehumanized individual, concerned solely with economic gain and controlled by impersonal economic forces. From this point of view, human beings are judged all alike; their individual emotions and aspirations do not matter; the difference between them is reduced to a merely quantitative difference, expressed in terms of their cash value. As Hobbes unsentimentally noted:

The *Value,* or Worth of a man, is as of all other things, his Price; that is to say, so much as would be given for the use of his Power; and therefore is not absolute; but a thing dependent on the need and judgment of another.[23]

From this standpoint, workers are commodities, and value is determined by the impersonal mechanism of the market.

Like the economic theories to which it has been linked, modern industry has been individualistic, externalistic, and mechanical in its mode of organization. Technology, with its tendency toward mechanical "rationalization," and finance capitalism, with its development of credits and abstract expense accounting, have depersonalized human relationships. The tendency of capitalism has been to exalt acquisitive above creative and sympathetic impulses, and to develop a narrow self-seeking, a hard, grasping egoism. The impersonal cash nexus has tended to replace the intimate human community. Here we discover the same tendency as in mechanistic philosophy, to dissolve wholes into self-enclosed monads, into "atoms" related externally without any deep internal connections. Extreme individualism has reflected these tend-

23 *Leviathan, op. cit.,* Chapter X.

encies and has thus expressed some of the fundamental aspects of modern life. If it recognizes any higher types of integration, such as intimate communities, it does so only inadequately and grudgingly.

Now it must be said emphatically that this is an inadequate interpretation of human nature. Men and women are not mechanisms nor parts of mechanisms. As William Ellery Channing, one of the great New England preachers of the early nineteenth century, declared:

I do not look on a human being as a machine, made to be kept in action by a foreign force, to accomplish an unvarying succession of motions, to do a fixed amount of work, and then to fall to pieces at death.[24]

Workers must not be conceived *abstractly* as *machines* or commodities but concretely as persons, who bleed when they are pricked, who dream and love and suffer. Human beings must not be regarded as social atoms, as isolated, egocentric individuals, each going his solitary way, but as members one of another. Individuals they are, and as individuals they are ends in themselves; but they are effective and happy only in relation to one another and to the social wholes of which they are members. The notion that an individual is complete in himself, and that the relationship between individuals is necessarily external—the notion of Hobbes and Bentham and Spencer—is inadequate and erroneous.

So long as such individualistic notions prevail, it is impossible to explain why human beings continually gather in societies. The extreme individualist tries to explain the formation of groups by the self-interest of each member. The group, he says, is only an artificial contrivance created by a "social contract" or similar agreement among self-seeking individuals. Now some groups, of course, are formed in this way; but other groups, and indeed most groups, arise out of

24 "Self Culture," lecture delivered at Boston, September 1838. Quoted in S. Giedion, *Mechanization Takes Command*, Oxford University Press, New York, 1948, p. 127.

the fundamental and essential nature of man as a social being. Men often are born into a group—into a family, tribe, clan, nation, etc.—and even when they join a group voluntarily, they may be impelled by their social nature and not simply by individual selfish calculations. Sociality is an essential human trait, and if it were not for man's social propensities, it would be impossible to account for that degree of trust and cooperation necessary for the formation and functioning of most human groups.

We are here touching upon the very essence of the human. Aristotle defined the essential nature of man as rationality; but more profoundly human, because more integral to man's whole nature, is the capacity for self-transcendence, of which reason is but a part. In his challenging book, *Man the Measure,* Erich Kahler gives the name of "spirit" to this faculty of going beyond oneself. It is the faculty, he says, of "detaching and discerning a definite non-self from a definite self," and of identifying oneself, in sympathy and understanding, with the non-self.

Thus spirit is not only the faculty of discerning and detaching but, at the same time, of establishing a relation between a self and a non-self, the faculty of overstepping the limits of the self. It is discerning and uniting in one. It is the very essence of a being concerned with more than itself. A person leads a spiritual life in so far as he rises above his personal "practical" interests, as he is able to detach himself from his own and conceived self and to grow more and more objective, to integrate himself in a higher, comprehending objective.[25]

Absorbed in himself and in the present moment, a man is just a transient flash of consciousness; but in so far as he transcends himself, he escapes from the petty compass of his own momentary identity and lives in the ample world that is brought into view by love, imagination, knowledge, and foresight. The *human* world, above all, emancipates the spirit. As David Hume wrote:

[25] *Man the Measure,* Pantheon Press, New York, 1943, pp. 11-12.

Let all the powers and elements of nature conspire to serve and obey one man: Let the sun rise and set at his command: The sea and rivers roll as he pleases, and the earth furnish spontaneously whatever may be useful or agreeable to him: He will still be miserable, till you give him some one person at least, with whom he may share his happiness, and whose esteem and friendship he may enjoy.[26]

Jailers have learned how important man is to his fellow man —they know that one of the most exquisite forms of torture is prolonged solitary confinement.

The effect of the inability to make sympathetic contact with other people is illustrated by an interesting type of neurosis which psychologists call "depersonalization." A neurotic of this type finds it very difficult to experience other human beings as real personalities; they seem to be mere automatons, toward whom he can feel no personal warmth. Moreover, he has the odd impression that his own personality has become purely mechanical. He seems to himself a puppet, a soulless automaton; he cannot find or acknowledge his own personality; there is no "real me." All things, including his own nature, seem to belong to the kind of depersonalized world so profoundly depicted in the novels of Franz Kafka. This type of mental illness illustrates the fact that no one can be fully a person unless he acknowledges others as persons. Full personality requires self-transcendence, appreciative awareness of other things and especially other people.

Morality too requires that the individual should overstep the boundaries of self. If all of us were sealed within ourselves we could not comprehend or respond to the moral injunction: "Be unselfish." If we did not feel the ties that bind us to others, we would not feel a sense of social obligation. The essential reason that a person feels obligated to others is that he is part of a larger whole. He is committed by his social nature to moral obligation, and he cannot deny the claims of

26 *A Treatise of Human Nature,* Clarendon Press, Oxford, 1896, p. 363.

social morality without denying an essential part of himself and without violating the society of which he is a constituent. Deep down in his mind he realizes the truth of Donne's oft-quoted words:

> No man is an Iland, intire to it selfe; every man is a peece of the Continent, a part of the maine. . . . any mans death diminishes me, because I am involved in Mankinde; and therefore never send to know for whom the bell tolls; It tolls for thee.[27]

As I shall endeavor to make clear in Chapter Eight, the sense of duty is the internalized "voice" of society exercising a "pull" or inner compulsion upon the individual. This explains why it is felt as a kind of external influence, yet as also internal. Freud's theory of the "super-ego" recognizes that moral obligation should be thus interpreted. The super-ego is the inner censor, the conscience, the embodiment of moral standards, checking a man's egoistic and instinctive impulses; yet it also represents the influence of society, so deeply imbedded within the individual's mind that it is largely subconscious. Freud tends somewhat to depreciate its value, but certain other psychologists, such as Henry A. Murray, regard it as a necessary constructive force that should be strengthened and reformed by critical intelligence.

Some such theory must be accepted if we are to explain moral obligation. It cannot be explained upon the basis of extreme individualism. Jeremy Bentham, who denied that society was more than a fiction and conceived of individuals as entirely egoistic, drew the correct implication from his own doctrine when he declared that *ought,* if it has any meaning at all, ought to be expunged from the dictionary.

Our criticism of extreme individualism amounts to this: it tries to explain social life in terms of only the relatively low forms of integration—mere adjacency or external association or mechanical interdependence—and in so doing it fails

---

[27] John Donne, *Complete Poetry and Selected Prose,* Random House, New York, 1936, p. 538. I have omitted italics found in the original.

adequately to explain why men congregate in societies, why men are so necessary to one another, and why men are moral.

6. *The Refutation of Extreme Collectivism*

WHEREAS extreme individualism is a *leveling down* theory, extreme collectivism is a *leveling up* theory. Just as the individualist insists upon interpreting groups in terms of the low levels of integration, so the extreme collectivist insists upon interpreting groups in terms of the high levels of integration. Some of these levels—organic interdependence, existential interdependence, and configurational unity—really do apply to human groups. In emphasizing this fact, collectivists have corrected the errors of extreme individualism. But other more intense forms of integration—the forms that characterize a living body and a mind—do not apply to groups; and extreme collectivism commits a fundamental mistake in supposing that they do apply.

To discover the nature of this error, let us consider the family, which is a relatively simple group and therefore less difficult to analyze than the state, nation, or race. Each member of the family is an organism, mind, or personality, but this does not mean that the family is an organism, mind, or personality. A group, in many respects, does not have the same characteristics as its members; a pile of bricks, for example, may be six feet high but no individual brick is that high. Likewise a human group is made up of organisms, but this does not make *it* an organism.

I admit that there are organic relations among its members. An "organic relation," as we have said, means an internal or essential relation. Now a husband, a wife, a son, or a daughter is affected through and through by family relations and would be a very different being apart from them. Moreover, these relations may involve not merely functional but existential dependence or interdependence. The children, at least, would not have come into existence apart from the family relations, and while they are still infants, they might not continue to exist if separated from the family. But there may be organic or existential relations between the members of a group, without the group being an organism. The father is an organism, the mother is an organism, and each of the children is an organism, and there are organic interrelations between them; but there is no group organism over and above the individual, or as the result of any fusion of individuals. To speak of a "family organism" is to use a metaphor.

It is also true that the family has a kind of configurational unity: it is not a mere sum of individuals but a synthesis, a *Gestalt*, a unique form or pattern. Every family is bound together by common goods, common memories, common hopes, common ideals, and common deeds. These coalesce into an *esprit de corps*, a kind of spirit that impresses itself upon each of its members and that gives a spiritual significance to the home. In these respects, the family has some sort of corporate character. The social organicists, such as Hegel, have performed a real service in emphasizing this fact, but they have not correctly analyzed what it means.

It does not imply that there is literally a family mind or a family personality. Even a work of art, as we have pointed out, has a *Gestalt* or configuration; but this does not imply that it has a life, a mind, or a personality. Of course, in the case of the family the constituents are minds or personalities, but this does not mean that the *configuration* of the family is a personality or a mind. The extreme collectivists have muddled their heads into supposing that the organization of individuals is itself an individual, that the organization of minds is itself a mind, that the organization of personalities is itself a personality. Admitting that the organization has configurational characteristics, we must still reject the mystical theory that there are group minds and collective souls, equipped with interests of their own.

Nothing can literally have an interest except an individual.

Within the family, each member has interests, and these interests are affected by the family *esprit de corps* and by the relations between the members of the family. But the interests of the family are nevertheless the interests of the father, the mother, and each of the children—these and nothing more. There are no family interests over and above these individual interests. And what is true of a group of a few members is also true of a group of many members, even a vast nation. It too has no interests that are not the interests of its members, because it has no mind apart from the minds of its members.

Certain philosophers, such as Emile Durkheim, have argued that it is impossible to explain the moral and religious life without supposing that society is an actual organism or group mind. They argue that religious and moral experience represents the pull of society upon the individual, and that society must be a real agency with objectives of its own to exert such a pull. Now I have contended that neither morality nor religion can be adequately explained in terms of extreme individualism, but I think that we need not fly to the opposite extreme and assume that society is an organism or a mind. The moral and religious pull of society upon the individual can be explained if we recognize that individuals are internally related to one another, that they can feel and enjoy and celebrate these intimate relations, and that society has a pattern of organization, a real configuration, that deeply impresses itself upon its members. All this can be recognized without assuming that society is literally a superorganism or group mind; and to make the assumption is to "multiply entities beyond necessity."

If groups cannot literally have a mind, they cannot be said to have intrinsic value. As we have said, there can be no intrinsic value where there is no interest, and there can be no interest where there is no mind. In the next chapter, I shall maintain that intrinsic value resides in interest, primarily in the fulfillment of interest. It follows that the locus of intrinsic value is the individual because the individual, after all, is the seat of interest. The group exists for the sake of the individual, and not the individual for the sake of the group. The welfare of human beings, therefore, is what counts, and not the "good" of the state, the nation, the race, or the "working class."

I do not deny that a group may be an *object* of interest, and in that sense the cause or occasion of intrinsic goodness. It is a familiar fact that a group, whether large or small, may be an object of human affection. We may love individuals not only for themselves but as members and representatives of a group; and, what is more to the point, we can love the group as having characteristics not to be found in the individuals taken severally. Affection toward the group, such as patriotism, can extend to its traditions, institutions, and symbols. As objects of intrinsic satisfaction some groups rank among the very highest of human values. I am, therefore, not denying for an instant that they are *objects* of value, but I am denying that they are *subjects* of value. No group, as distinguished from its members, can have an interest; and since I maintain that the seat of intrinsic value is interest, I deny that groups have intrinsic value. My position is different from that of Perry, because he speaks of intrinsic value as the object of interest. A group is often an object of interest, and hence on Perry's definition, it would possess intrinsic value, not independently of individuals, of course, but relative to the interest of individuals. My own view is different: as I shall make clear in the next chapter, intrinsic value is the interest in an object rather than the object of an interest; and hence, as I see it, no group can have intrinsic value.

It is of course true that a group has intrinsic value, if we mean that its *members* have; but it is false to say that a group as such has intrinsic value. It is also true that the interests of the group should take precedence over the interests of the individual, if we mean that the interests of the *many* individuals in a group should take precedence over the interests of *one* individual; but this is because they are many *individuals* as opposed to one. The group as such is not intrinsically higher than the individual; it has no intrinsic value at all. Hence the tendency to worship the state or the race or any other group, large or small, is a form of idolatry. As the philosopher McTaggart has declared:

A religion which fastens itself on a means has not risen above fetish-worship. Compared with worship of the state, zoolatry is rational and dignified. A bull or a crocodile may not have great intrinsic value, but it has some, for it is a conscious being. The state has none. It would be as reasonable to worship a sewage pipe, which also has considerable value as a means.[28]

The state may have a vast amount of instrumental value, but its value is that of a means and not that of an end.

This conclusion is worth emphasizing, because the contrary view has had great influence. The notion that a race or a state or a society can have intrinsic value is one of the great social myths—a myth that has had a terrific impact upon mankind. We need only remember that it is the myth of Mussolini and Hitler to realize what a stupendous role it has played. In rejecting this myth, we must not embrace its opposite—the myth of extreme individualism—the myth of the isolated, egocentric, self-sufficient man. The real individual is a profoundly social being: it is he alone, and not his mythical counterpart, that is the locus of value. It is only a false individualism and a false collectivism that are pitted against one another. Individuality and sociality, instead of being incompatible, are necessary to one another. The more men are truly united the more they respect each other's differences. People who are in love treasure each other's individualities. Human beings should be both more differentiated and more united than they are now; and the unity that is the legitimate goal of human aspiration is the unity of difference.

28 J. M. E. McTaggart, *Philosophical Studies*, Arnold, London, 1934, p. 109.

Chapter Seven

THE MEANING OF WELFARE

1. *Interest and Its Objects*

IN OUR PURSUIT of the meaning of a good society, we have begun to close in upon our quarry. We have abandoned the false paths of relativism and absolutism, recognizing that the good is universal but immanent in men's lives. We have discovered that both extreme individualism and extreme collectivism lead in the wrong direction, and that the right path is one that combines the individual and the social. The locus of intrinsic value, we have discovered, is the individual personality; but since individuality and sociality are inextricably mingled, the ideal is the fulfillment of personality in society. We have also suggested that what is intrinsically good in personality is interest or some object of interest. It is down this path, therefore, that we must hunt our quarry.

What, then, is interest, and how is it connected with value? It is, we have said, an attitude of favoring or disfavoring—a state of nonindifference. To consider an example, let us suppose that we have a white rock and a black rock, and let us ask which one should be to the right of the other. Does it really matter? It does not matter to the *rocks.* They have no consciousness, no feelings, no desires, and therefore nothing that could be called an interest; and where there is no interest, there is no distinction between better and worse, or good and bad. A universe made up of nothing but rocks would be without value.

Suppose we ask some person whether the white rock should be to the right of the black, or vice versa? He might reply,

"I do not care the least bit one way or the other." He would be conscious of the rocks but totally indifferent. Now suppose *all* conscious states were of this type. In a universe devoid of all but indifferent conscious states, there would be no more value than in a universe made up of unconscious objects, because in both there would not be the slightest interest.

But let us suppose that the person replies, "I like the black rock to the right of the white one. It looks better that way." He is conscious of the alternatives and is not indifferent. He likes or favors one rather than the other. Positive interest is just such a state of liking or favoring; negative interest is the opposite state of disliking or disfavoring; and both are distinguished from unconscious states and from conscious indifferent states. An interest is a conscious state distinguishable from indifference, and wherever there are interests there are values.

The relation between interests and values, however, requires a rather subtle analysis. We cannot simply say that value, or intrinsic goodness, *is* interest. To say this would be to commit what Professor G. E. Moore, in his *Principia Ethica,* calls "the naturalistic fallacy."[1] Moore's main contention in pointing out this fallacy is that intrinsic goodness cannot be identified with any mere matter of fact. It is not a datum of any natural science, such as psychology or biology. I cannot "find" it merely by inspecting my sense data or introspecting my mental states. It has an ethical significance other than merely factual. Value is *imputed* to an object or quality and is not factually discovered, hence an assessment is different from a mere description or factual inventory. It would be a fallacy, consequently, to *identify* goodness with interest. To do so would imply that the proposition, "Goodness is interest," is equivalent to the tautology, "Interest is interest," which obviously is not the case. To overlook the ethical character of goodness, and to identify it with a merely

[1] *Cf., Principia Ethica,* Cambridge University Press, Cambridge, 1922, pp. 13-14, 38-39, and *passim.*

factual property such as interest, is to commit "the naturalistic fallacy."

The reason for the irreducibly ethical character of goodness, so it seems to me, is to be found in its normative character. It involves not simply *what is* but what *ought to be*. The ought, as Kant insisted, is not identical with what is. Hence if goodness involves an "ought," it cannot be detected by a mere inspection of what is. Intrinsic goodness, I believe, is meaningless apart from the "ought to be," just as right is meaningless apart from the "ought to do." The nondescriptive, specifically ethical factor in good and right comes in with the "ought" and only with it.

Intrinsic goodness is that which ought to be unless its existence would involve the sacrifice of something better. Other things being equal, it ought to be. To say that it is nonindifferent, however, might seem to imply that it is a state of interest; but we need to distinguish between two kinds of nonindifference. The first is psychological, the second ethical. Psychological nonindifference is simply the state of being interested: of liking or disliking, of favoring or disfavoring. It can be described factually. *Ethical* nonindifference occurs whenever there is an "ought." To say that something is intrinsically good is to say that it ought to be in comparison with an ethically indifferent state. To say that something is intrinsically bad is to say that it ought *not* to be in comparison with an ethically indifferent state.

Now we would commit the naturalistic fallacy if we simply defined goodness as a *psychological* state of nonindifference, such as positive interest, the attitude of liking or favoring. But we would not commit the naturalistic fallacy if we defined it as a kind of *ethical* nonindifference: a state or quality or property that in some sense *ought to be*. Goodness is a *positive* state of ethical nonindifference: a state that, other things being equal, ought to be. Badness is a *negative* state of ethical nonindifference: a state that, other things being equal, ought not to be.

Having thus defined good and bad in ethical terms, I am entirely consistent in maintaining that *only* psychological states of nonindifference are good or bad, or ethically nonindifferent. It does seem to me that a world with no interests whatsoever would be ethically neutral. It is psychological nonindifference that *makes* a thing ethically nonindifferent. Whenever in this book I seem to identify value, or goodness, with interest, I should be understood as speaking elliptically: I mean that interest *ought to be,* and in that sense, is good.

The question that I want to answer in the present chapter is this, What *does* make something good? Is it the *interest itself,* or the *object* of interest? For example, is it my liking for an apple, or is it the apple as the object of my liking? In a sense, value involves both of these factors. The interest might be called the subjective value, and the object might be called the objective value; and the entire situation—interest related to object—might be called the complete value. Since a person is often interested in introspective data, the object may be internal to the interested organism, for example, a feeling, an image, an idea, a kinesthetic sensation, or even the ego as the object of its own awareness. Although the fact is difficult to analyze, one may love or hate "oneself." It is still true that the total value situation has a twofold character: an *interest* in an object and an *object* of an interest.

An apparent exception is a subjective attitude that has not yet found its object, as when we awake in the morning with an objectless grouch: we do not as yet know *what* we are angry at but we are angry. In many cases, however, psychoanalysts have discovered that there is a real subconscious object; and in these cases, if we eventually pick an object of which we *are* fully conscious, an inoffensive thing or person upon which we vent our spleen, we are making a substitution and are thus sublimating the anger that otherwise would be pent up. The process of sublimation, however, proves that an interest, without being completely altered, can be detached from an object and attached to another. It may thus be relatively independent of any specific object.

In analyzing the meaning of value, Professor DeWitt H. Parker points out that there may be desires or emotions without any corresponding objects:

> It is notable . . . that there exist rare cases of value without corresponding valuable objects. One of the most interesting examples is music. When we listen to music desires are now aroused, now satisfied, but the desires are not desires *for* anything or the satisfactions, satisfactions *in* anything. The sounds heard are not the objects of these desires any more than words that express longing are the objects longed for; they are expressions, embodiments of desire, not objects of desire. In music desires are objectless; we desire, but desire nothing, and are satisfied, but satisfied over nothing. In the musical experience, there are also no explicit objectives or goals; desire has not formulated whither it is tending or what would satisfy it.[2]

I am not sure that this is an adequate analysis. When we hear the initial phases of a musical composition, the mind is set vibrating with expectation and desire; certain tones demand and naturally lead into other tones. For example, dissonances must be "resolved"; there are "upleader" or "downleader" notes which naturally lead into the tonic; and the finale may be an answer to much premonition and desire. Hence we can be said to desire what satisfactorily completes and fulfills the cravings earlier aroused; and if so, the later phases of the music may be said, in some measure, to be the *objects* of the desires evoked by the earlier phases. Yet we cannot be said to desire the *exact* tones which we hear—since these particular tones are unexpected, and indeed their delightfulness depends partly upon their novelty. Music is partly an object of desire but partly an expression.

Let us suppose that it is merely the expression of desire and emotion. Even so, by stretching our terms a little, we can still speak of an "interest" and an "object." The emotion

2 *Human Values*, Harper, New York, 1931, p. 23.

or desire felt in the presence of the music *is* a state of psychological nonindifference, a value that *moves* the mind, and in this sense an *interest*, even when it is not an interest in anything specific. Moreover, the word "object" can be retained if we mean by it either that which we are interested in, *or* that which is an expression of an interest. The music, as a free creation of the imagination, illustrates this latter type of object. We often use the term "esthetic object" in this way, so we are not violating English idiom when we extend the term "object" to cover instances of this type—to denote, in other words, *expressive* objects—objects that are the expressions and embodiments of emotions, desires, or feelings.

It would seem possible, moreover, to use the term "potential interest" to designate a subjective emotion such as an "objectless grouch." An emotion of this sort is not an actualized interest in the sense of being directed toward a definite object, but it is a potential interest in the sense that it tends to become attached to an object. We could thus use "interest" as a convenient blanket term to include all feelings, emotions, volitions, and judgments, whether they are actually or only potentially attached to objects. Such broad usage is necessary if we are to have an "interest theory" that will be inclusive enough to cover all the phases of ethical life.

Does the value, in the sense of that which ought to be, lie in the interest or in the object? In trying to answer this question, philosophers do not always agree. Some declare that the value is the *interest* in the object; some say it is the *object* of the interest; others say it is the *relation* between the interest and the object; and still others say it is a character of the *entire interest-object situation*. The full discussion of these alternatives requires an intricate analysis that would be out of place in this book.

I shall try merely to clarify the issue with a few remarks. By "intrinsic value" I mean that which is an end in itself or good for its own sake. An object of interest may, in an inexact sense, possess intrinsic value. It may be said that, for example,

I am treating a piece of candy as an "end in itself" when I eat it, not for the sake of some future consequences, but simply because it is delicious. When I say that a personality has intrinsic value, however, I am using the terms in a different way. I do not mean that he acquires such value, for example, when a cannibal decides to eat him! He has intrinsic value in a more inward and essential sense. Intrinsic value, in this stricter meaning, seems to me to attach to the inner quality of experience, and the outward object seems to me valuable *not* intrinsically but instrumentally, as a means of arousing or expressing this experience.

I desire a book, for example, but the book is not good in itself. Suppose the book is painfully desired and not secured. Then it is instrumentally bad in the sense that it causes me suffering. Or suppose I obtain the book and read its contents. It would still be instrumentally bad because it displeases me. Suppose I enjoy its contents. It would then be instrumentally good—good as a means to the end of instructing or delighting me. But it is never, so far as I can see, good in itself, good intrinsically. So it is with other objects. Of course, when the object itself is an interest, it possesses intrinsic value, but *qua* interest and not *qua* object.

Intrinsic value, therefore, is interest, positive or negative. Whenever there is interest, there is value. If the interest is positive, a state of liking, the value is positive, good rather than evil. If the interest is negative, a state of disliking, the value is negative, evil rather than good. These remarks need to be qualified. Positive interest may involve moments of uneasiness and painful tension—the pangs of desire. To this extent, it involves evil and is therefore not an unqualified good. Unalloyed goodness consists primarily in the *fulfillment* of interests, whereby desire, in the process of being satisfied, becomes enjoyment. More inclusively stated, the human ideal is not only the fulfillment but the *cultivation* of interests. It is important not merely to fulfill interests but to get more interests to fulfill: to pass from a narrower to a wider range of interests and to fulfill this wider range. As John Stuart Mill remarked, "the cultivated mind . . . finds sources of inexhaustible interest in all that surrounds it; in the objects of nature, the achievements of art, the imaginations of poetry, the incidents of history, the ways of mankind, past, present and their prospects in the future."[3] The truly happy life is experienced by the man who responds with positive interests to a great range of objects and who fulfills these interests in activity that brings the full flavor of enjoyment. If we were to sum up the good in a few words, we would say that it is *the cultivation and fulfillment of positive interests.* Conversely, the sign of an unhappy or intrinsically evil life is the predominance of negative interests, and the noncultivation and frustration of such interests as are positive. The remainder of this chapter is largely an elucidation of the meaning of good and evil as thus conceived.

Although intrinsic value seems to me to reside in interests rather than in their objects, these interests are not blind and directionless and isolated, with an esoteric ghostly abstraction from the real world; they find expression *in* objects or are directed *toward* objects and are publicly describable in terms of their objective references and behavioral manifestations. I enjoy *this* painting. I love *this* person. I admire *this* act. The objects can still be spoken of as values in the light of their capacity to evoke and express interests, and even if they do not possess intrinsic value in the strict essential meaning of the term, they may still possess *terminal* value in the sense that interest is consummated in and through them. They are of course ethically very important, especially as the ends and goals of aspiration.

A man's personality, as the locus and center of interests, has three fundamental sides or capacities: knowing, feeling, and striving—or in more academic language, cognition, affection, and volition. What is the relation of interest and value to each of these capacities? Can we say that human welfare

3 *Utilitarianism,* Dutton, New York, 1910, p. 13.

consists in the fulfillment of all these capacities, or is it to be found in the fulfillment of some one capacity?

Again, the answers given by philosophers differ. An intellectualist, such as Aristotle, finds goodness essentially in the life of reason and maintains that the interest in knowledge takes precedence over every other. A hedonist, such as Epicurus, contends that intrinsic goodness is to be found exclusively in the feeling of pleasure, and that nothing else matters except as a means. A voluntarist, such as Nietzsche, maintains that intrinsic goodness is to be found in volition, and that feeling and intellect are entirely subordinate to it. Other philosophers, such as Plato, contend that human welfare involves the fulfillment of all sides of a man's nature. Let us now consider each of these alternatives.

2. *Welfare as the Life of Reason*

THE CLASSIC EXPRESSION of intellectualism is to be found in the ethics of Aristotle (384-322 B.C.). I shall begin with an exposition of his ethical philosophy and then make some comments and criticisms.

His conception of ethics is essentially humanistic. The knowledge of man, he believes, is the basis of establishing norms and values. Ethics is based upon psychology and not upon theology or transcendental metaphysics.

It is a branch of practical science and a part of politics. The business of the ethical philosopher is to determine the qualities in human life that the educator and the statesman should cultivate in the people. Its principal object is to find out what is man's highest good.

What, then, is the best kind of life? Aristotle answers that, so far as the name is concerned, there is general agreement to call it "happiness." The real question, however, is one of fact. What kind of life deserves to be called happy?

He lays down three criteria for determining happiness.

First, it must be desirable for its own sake—an end, and not just a means. Hence it cannot consist of merely external goods, such as wealth. Second, it must be self-sufficient; it must be adequate in itself to satisfy us. Hence it cannot be pleasure or honor, because these, he believes, are not sufficient. Third, it must be found in the life and work peculiar to man. Every creature has a characteristic function, and the good for that creature is to exercise this function. A bear, for example, should be a bear: it should express a bear's function. A man should likewise be a man: he should so far as possible express his specifically human function.

Beginning with the last criterion, what is it that *only* man can do? The capacity for growth and reproduction we share even with plants; the capacity for feeling, sensation, and impulse we share with animals; these cannot be the differentiating function and characteristic work of man. In human beings there is superimposed upon these faculties a higher faculty, the capacity to reason. This is man's distinctive gift, his essential attribute, his differentiating characteristic. Reason is the power to calculate, reflect, and know, to understand relations and universal qualities, to live by rule instead of being swayed by appetite.

Happiness is the life of reason—not the mere potentiality of reasoning, which a man may possess when he is fast asleep, but the active exercise of intelligence. It must also, Aristotle adds, be in accordance with virtue, or, if there is more than one virtue, with the best and most perfect of them. It must be manifested not merely for short periods but in a complete life; for one swallow does not make a summer, nor does a snatch of happiness make a happy life. To sum up, happiness is an active, virtuous, and sustained mode of living which calls into play the specifically human capacities of man, above all, his rational nature.

When thus defined, happiness satisfies not only the third criterion but the other two. It is desirable for its own sake—

an end or ultimate good and not merely a means. Also it is self-sufficient, and it is preferable to any other kind of life that might be proposed. It is the only life that can permanently satisfy man.

This conception has the merit of including other common conceptions of happiness. Some say that happiness is virtue; others say it is pleasure; still others say it is external prosperity. Now virtue is the spring from which happiness flows, pleasure is its natural accompaniment, and prosperity is its normal precondition.

It should be noted that Aristotle is not a hedonist but believes that pleasure is intrinsically good. It is good but not the supreme good. Animals also experience pleasure; and Aristotle is confident that the good for man must be higher than the good for lower animals. Pleasure is the *accompaniment* of the happy life, not the main substance of it. It is the "bloom" upon life; it perfects and completes the activity it accompanies; it attains its maximum with the freest and healthiest functioning of the soul. Hence the life of reason is not only the best and noblest but the most pleasant of all lives.

It should also be noted that external goods, although not good for their own sakes, are the necessary conditions of the good life. A certain amount of wealth, security, and comfort are essential for the noble employment of leisure, without which man's highest nature cannot attain expression.

There are two forms of goodness corresponding to the two main divisions of man's personality, the rational and the subrational. The first form is intellectual goodness, corresponding to the rational part. It consists in the exercise of reason for its own sake. The second is moral goodness, corresponding to the subrational part. This part Aristotle subdivides into the "vegetative," which consists of the elementary vital functions of nourishment, growth, and reproduction, and the "appetitive," which consists of perception, emotion, pleasure and pain, desire and aversion. The vegetative part is beyond the pale of reason, but the appetitive part is rational to the degree that it obeys the dictates of reason. Moral goodness consists in the guidance of the appetitive part by reason.

Let us first consider moral goodness, which is a kind of excellence or virtue. We inherit little more than a capacity for virtue, and the actualization of this capacity requires much practice. As a result of habit and education, however, the mere capacity becomes a developed disposition; and such a disposition is what we mean by virtue. Moral goodness is the disposition to choose moderation rather than some extreme. It is destroyed equally by excess or deficiency.

We may see this illustrated in the analogous case of bodily strength and health: strength is as much destroyed by an excess as by a deficiency of bodily exercise, health by too much as by too little food; but both are produced, developed, and preserved by a moderate amount. So with temperance, courage, and other virtues: the man who flees and fears everything and never stands his ground is a coward, while he who fears nothing at all and is ready to face everything is rash. Similarly, the man who partakes of every pleasure and abstains from none is profligate, while he who boorishly shuns all pleasure may be called insensible. Thus temperance and courage are destroyed by excess and deficiency but are preserved by moderation.[4]

This principle of moderation is not limited to actions, but applies also to emotions.

We can feel fear, confidence, desire, anger, pity, and in general pleasure and pain, either too much or too little, and in either case not well; but to feel them at the right times, with reference to the right objects, towards the right people, with the right motive, and in the right manner, is to strike the mean, and therein to follow the best course—a mark of virtue.[5]

This latter quotation clearly implies that the right mean is not a fixed point between extremes but a sliding, adjust-

---

[4] Aristotle, *The Nicomachean Ethics*, translated by Philip Wheelwright, in *Aristotle*, Doubleday, Doran, Garden City, 1935, p. 136. Quoted by permission of the Odyssey Press, Inc., New York, present holder of the copyright.
[5] *Ibid.*, p. 143.

able mean relative to the time, the place, the circumstances, the person who acts, and the persons affected. Such a conception pushes aside rigid moral laws, like those of Kant, and makes morality a subtle intellectual art governed by a feeling for proportion and harmony and by a calculation of consequences.

One part of the life of reason is the practical wisdom involved in moral virtue, which we have just discussed. This involves instrumental goods and not simply intrinsic. Another part is the exercise of reason for its own sake; this Aristotle calls intellectual virtue. Since man's chief intrinsic good is the perfect development of his rational nature, it must be found primarily in intellectual virtue, or the free exercise of reason.

We may apply here, too, the principle already laid down, that whatever is proper to the nature of each thing is best and pleasantest for that thing. Since it is reason that is most truly man, a life according to reason must be at once best and pleasantest for that thing. Such a life, therefore, will be the most truly happy.[6] The highest law of ethics is the love of intellectual virtue. Satisfaction of this love means the life of intellectual contemplation—the life that finds godlike expression in science and philosophy.

I shall now turn from exposition to comment and criticism. Let us inquire what is the relation of reason to value and interest, and in the light of this inquiry, let us determine whether the life of reason deserves Aristotle's unstinted praise.

His contention that reason is man's exclusive attribute, and that it must therefore constitute man's chief good, is fallacious. As the psychologist Wolfgang Köhler has proved in a number of experiments, chimpanzees also have the capacity of reason. For example, in front of a cage containing a chimpanzee, a banana is lying beyond its reach. Inside the cage is a stick by means of which the banana can be reached.

6 *Ibid.*, p. 226.

The animal, obviously using intelligence, will pick up the stick and rake in the banana. Thus it can be proved that intelligence or reason is not exclusively human. What fundamentally distinguishes man is the whole remarkable development of human culture, expressing his capacity for creativity and self-transcendence. For example, Bach, the man of art, is as profoundly human as Kant, the man of reason. Jesus, the man of religion, towers as high above the brutes as Aristotle, the man of science and philosophy. Moreover, what truly matters is the *worth* of a faculty at the human level; and it does not detract from that worth for the faculty to have its first beginnings in the prehuman life. Is love, for example, any the less valuable because dogs display affection? I think no one would say so.

The valuable is not necessarily the distinctively human: it is what is *worthy* of being human. Only man among animals knows the difference between right and wrong, and hence only man can act immorally—fiendish immorality is a distinctively human trait—yet it is not the good for which Aristotle searches. He asks, "What is man's proper function?" But if "proper" means simply distinctively human, it is not necessarily relevant to the moral ideal of happiness. On the other hand, if "proper" means *morally* proper, the attempt to get at its nature by reference to human function constitutes a begging of the question: the assumption, which begs the question, is that the human *is* the morally proper. This assumption, moreover, is unwarranted. Goodness does not reside in whatever is distinctively human: it resides in the *part* of human nature that is the locus of value, whether this part be distinctively human or not. That part, I have maintained, is interest; and we must therefore examine interest if we are to determine whether Aristotle's emphasis upon reason is justified.

Let us consider what connection reason may have with interest. It is at least a factor in interest. We can distinguish between thoughtless and thoughtful interest, between esteeming and estimating, between prizing and appraising. When we estimate or appraise, reason modifies and controls the interest. Judgment is simply reason when it so operates. But if we are asked if judgment is the most basic factor in interest, we must reply in the negative. Since there are nonrational or irrational likings, interest often does not include judgment. Judgment supervenes upon and qualifies interest rather than constitutes its innermost essence. In this sense judgment is less fundamental as a factor in interest than are feelings and desires.

It is nevertheless indispensable to the good life. Before an object of interest can be considered a trustworthy value, we must determine whether it is merely "liked" or is genuinely "likable," merely "desired" or is really "desirable," merely "admired" or is truly "admirable." There may be a vast difference between what is prized and what is prizeworthy and between thoughtless prizing and thoughtful appraising. Unless we recognize these distinctions, our lives will be thoroughly anarchic. As John Dewey has said:

There is nothing in which a person so completely reveals himself as in the things which he judges enjoyable and desirable. Such judgments are the sole alternative to the dominion of belief by impulse, chance, blind habit and self-interest. The formation of a cultivated and effectively operative good judgment or taste with respect to what is esthetically admirable, intellectually acceptable and morally approvable is the supreme task set to human beings by the incidents of experience.[7]

One of the great merits of Aristotle as an ethical philosopher is that he, in effect, recognizes the truth of these remarks. He realizes that without judgment, or practical wisdom, life would not be distinguished from madness. The main practical function of reason, he believes, is to govern our feelings and appetites. If it does not do so, the human personality cannot function in a normal, satisfactory, healthful, and harmonious way.

[7] *The Quest for Certainty*, Minton, Balch, New York, 1929, p. 262.

Not only is reason a factor in interest, it is one of the main objects of interest. Aristotle again and again points out that the life of reason is what men are really interested in—what they fundamentally want and crave—what fully and deeply satisfies them. There is much truth in this point of view. Most men are deeply averse to going insane, especially if the insanity should be permanent. Admittedly, insanity is only one form of irrationality—and a person, such as a mad genius, may be remarkably rational in certain respects even though he is insane—yet there is a radical impairment of reason in his nature, an impairment that no man would choose. The explanation of this aversion surely is that rationality is one of the things we most value and the loss of rationality one of the things we most dread. Moreover, wonder or curiosity— the desire to know—is a very basic human trait. It may be observed in young children, who ask innumerable questions and have an unquenchable curiosity about animals, machines, people, and such natural objects as stars and thunderstorms. Lucky is the man who retains this curiosity and whose sense of wonder develops into wide and vivid intellectual interests!

Aristotle's conception of science, it will be noted, is primarily intellectual contemplation rather than active experiment. Moreover, he exalts pure rather than applied science. His point of view contrasts sharply with Francis Bacon's aphorism that "knowledge is power" and with Robert Boyle's contention that true science is such knowledge "as hath a tendency to use." It is closely connected with his contempt for physical labor and his aristocratic predilection for "the noble employment of leisure." His bias in favor of pure science is condemned by a democrat and socialist such as Lancelot Hogben, who points out that it is typical of aristocrats in a slave-owning society, and who argues as follows:

Science thrives by its applications. To justify it as an end in itself is a policy of defeat. The fullest use of science cannot be made by society in which the pursuit of discovery is the toy of a privileged class, or by a society which restricts the benefits of its application to a relatively small group of individuals. Science advances most rapidly when its benefits are keenly recognized because widely shared, especially when it brings new prosperity to a previously unprivileged class. It will attain its highest dignity in a classless society which demands the means of an advancing standard of leisure and well-being for *all its members*.[8]

In defense of Aristotle, it can be urged that the love of knowledge for its own sake is one of the great sources of happiness, and that the applications of knowledge to life have very frequently been unsatisfactory or positively mischievous. In modern times, applied science has multiplied trivial amusements, rendered much labor monotonous, made war diabolical and infinitely dangerous, and produced, among other things, a vast quantity of ill-distributed and shoddy commodities. If it is to be a vast boon to mankind, men must change their ideals and direct it to human uses.

Despite Aristotle's fine appreciation of pure science and philosophy, his outlook in certain other respects is narrow. One may scan the pages of his *Ethics* in the vain attempt to find any mention of esthetic values. In his *Poetics,* it is true, he displays keen insight into the qualities of great poetry, and in his *Politics* he shows some understanding of the educational function of music and other forms of art. But he ranks art far below science and philosophy, and he exhibits little awareness of the immense contribution that beauty and art can make to happiness. In his discussion of moral virtue, moreover, he is almost exclusively concerned with pointing out the value of "the golden mean." This value, however, is instrumental and relative; there is a golden mean of the villain as well as the virtuous. "Be cautious; avoid extremes; follow the mean" is a counsel of prudence and not necessarily of morality—the wicked and crafty can find it useful. The main value for a good man in observing the mean is that it promotes the harmony and hence the maximum realization

[8] *Science for the Citizen,* Knopf, New York, 1938, p. 726.

of the various interests of the personality; but this value is negligible unless the interests thus harmonized are themselves rich in quality. Taken by itself, moderation makes for tameness and insipidity; and it contributes greatly to happiness only when it is counterbalanced by a relish for adventure and the careless rapture of intense moments of experience. Although Aristotle discusses friendship at length, his remarks never rise above the level of common sense nor indicate any realization of the value of passion. Also he shows very little appreciation of the importance of sympathy; and like other aristocratic Greeks, he condones slavery and regards manual workers with considerable disdain.

As we reflect upon his ethics, we find that most of it is sensible, but that it is marred by a too-exclusive intellectualism. "The life of reason," as Santayana remarks, "will mark a real progress whenever it gives fuller expression to the interests that prompt its gropings."[9] Apart from this vital background of interests, it is too dry and abstract a thing to speak for the human heart. No man would choose a life of mere intellectual activity devoid of feeling and satisfied desire.

3. Welfare as the Maximum of Pleasure

AT THE OPPOSITE EXTREME from intellectualism is the ethical theory called hedonism, a word derived from the Greek term *hedone,* which means pleasure. Hedonism maintains that pleasure alone is ultimately good and unpleasure alone is ultimately evil; and since pleasure and unpleasure are feelings, it maintains that feelings are the sole locus of ultimate value.

In the Occident, hedonism has flourished from the time of Democritus (*circa* 460-362 B.C.) until the present day. In the early part of the fourth century B.C., Aristippus of Cyrene, a pupil of Socrates, founded a school of hedonism which main-

9 *The Life of Reason,* Vol. I, Scribner's, New York, 1927, p. x.

tained that the pleasure of the moment is alone worthy of consideration. Epicurus, who went to Athens in 306 B.C., established a much more famous school of hedonism, which flourished for nearly nine centuries. Unlike Aristippus, whose motto was, "Eat, drink, and be merry, for tomorrow we die," Epicurus believed that pleasure and the avoidance of pain could best be attained by a simple, austere life, in which more emphasis is put upon the avoidance of evil than the attainment of good. Typical of his viewpoint are these words from one of his letters:

> By pleasure we mean the absence of pain in the body and of trouble in the soul. It is not an unbroken succession of drinking-bouts and of revelry, not sexual love, not the enjoyment of the fish and other delicacies of a luxurious table, which produce a pleasant life; it is sober reasoning, searching out the grounds of every choice and avoidance, and banishing those beliefs through which the greatest tumults take possession of the soul.[10]

In the Middle Ages, hedonism suffered an eclipse, but it reappeared with the revival of classical learning in the Renaissance. In England, where it enjoyed its greatest vogue, it was represented in various degrees and in divers manners by a great succession of philosophers, including Thomas Hobbes, John Locke, David Hume, Jeremy Bentham, James Mill, John Stuart Mill, and Henry Sidgwick. It is less widely held today than it was in the nineteenth century, but it has been represented in this century by many thinkers, including such American philosophers as Durant Drake, F. C. Sharp, William Savery, and Curt John Ducasse. It is still being vigorously advocated by men of great ability, and it still requires a hearing.

Among the modern proponents of hedonism, one of the most important and typical was Jeremy Bentham (1748-1832), founder of the important philosophical movement called Utilitarianism and the equally important political movement

---

[10] *Letter to Menoeceus,* Hicks' translation, in Gordon H. Clark and T. V. Smith, *Readings in Ethics,* Crofts, New York, 1935, p. 91.

called Radicalism. The keynote to his philosophy is struck in the opening sentences of his *Introduction to the Principles of Morals and Legislation:*

Nature has placed mankind under the governance of two sovereign masters, *pain* and *pleasure*. It is for them alone to point out what we ought to do, as well as to determine what we shall do. On the one hand the standard of right and wrong, on the other hand the chain of causes and effects, are fastened to their throne.[11]

Bentham is here stating two quite distinct doctrines, one psychological and the other ethical. The psychological doctrine states that every man is so constituted that he always seeks his own pleasure, or the avoidance of his own pain, in every action. The ethical doctrine states that happiness, consisting in the maximum surplus of pleasure over pain, is the sole standard of welfare and the goal of right action. The first doctrine is called psychological hedonism. It is formulated with great precision by Bentham as follows:

On the occasion of every act he exercises, every human being is led to pursue that line of conduct which, according to his view of the case, taken by him at the moment, will be in the highest degree contributory to his own greatest happiness.[12]

The second doctrine is called ethical hedonism. It maintains that pleasure always is good for its own sake, and that nothing else is ever good for its own sake. Pleasure, moreover, is judged purely in terms of quantity. All that matters is that we should get the greatest possible amount of pleasure: not that we should get any certain *kind* of pleasure, nor that we should get it in any particular way. Quantity is determined by two factors: duration, or the length of time the pleasure lasts, and intensity, or the relative strength of the pleasure at any one moment. Similarly pain alone is bad for its own sake,

[11] *An Introduction to the Principles of Morals and Legislation*, Hafner, New York, 1948, p. 1.
[12] *The Works of Jeremy Bentham*, Vol. IX, W. Tait, Edinburgh, 1843, p. 5.

and it too is to be judged solely in terms of the quantitative standards of intensity and duration.

The two doctrines, psychological hedonism and ethical hedonism, are logically quite separate. Bentham believed that ethical hedonism rests upon psychological hedonism: that pleasure must be good because it is always desired; but it is possible that something may be good even though it is not desired, and desired even though it is not good. Indeed, in recent years psychological hedonism has been almost universally rejected by psychologists and philosophers, whereas ethical hedonism is still widely maintained. Moreover, if we agree with the psychological hedonist that we *must*, by the compulsion of our own nature, pursue pleasure, we cannot logically agree with the ethical hedonist that we *ought* to pursue pleasure. "Ought" implies choice, not necessity. Hence there is a logical incompatibility between psychological and ethical hedonism.

Bentham has formulated ethical hedonism inaccurately. The real opposite of pleasure is not pain, as he maintains, but unpleasure. Pain is usually unpleasant, but it may be pleasant. A youngster with a loose tooth, for example, may put his tongue to his tooth and wiggle it, finding pleasure in the interesting painful sensation that he thus derives. The masochist's enjoyment of pain is a well-known psychological fact. As the psychologist Edward Titchener remarks: "Pain ... is a sensation, and it is a sensation that at different intensities and under different circumstances, may be pleasant, indifferent, or unpleasant."[13] Bentham should have defined "happiness" as the maximum surplus of pleasure over unpleasure.

Let us now inquire as to the relation of pleasure to interest. Is it the sole or main factor in interest? Is it the sole object of interest? If not, is it the sole object of *reflective* interest?

Pleasure and unpleasure certainly are forms of interest,

13 *Text-book of Psychology*, Macmillan, New York, 1910, p. 227.

but they are not the only forms. Judgment, as we have re-marked, is a factor in reflective liking or disliking. Emotion is also involved in interest and is more indispensable. An emotion is a complex state of consciousness, which contains pleasure or unpleasure as a constituent but which contains other constituents besides. Reverence, for example, is a blend of pleasure, awe, and affection. Wonder is a fusion of pleas-ure, curiosity, insight, and a sense of mystery. Love involves pleasure, tenderness, and appreciative awareness of the char-acteristics of the beloved. Loathing is a compound that in-cludes unpleasure, fear, and disgust. Every emotion, even the simplest, has some distinctive quality by which it can be recognized apart from its pleasantness or unpleasantness.

Interest also involves volition—that is, impulse, desire, wish, or will. Most psychologists at the present time, more-over, maintain that volition is causally the most basic factor in interest, since feeling and emotion arise from, and depend upon, the success or failure of the organism's volitional striv-ing. Since interest includes judgment, emotion, and volition, it cannot be reduced to pleasure and unpleasure. Let us now consider hedonic feelings as *objects* of interest.

Pleasure is an object of positive interest (liking), and un-pleasure is an object of negative interest (disliking). For ex-ample, a person may yearn for the pleasure of sexual love; in fact, he likes many kinds of pleasure. But it would be a mis-take to maintain, as the psychological hedonist does, that pleasure, or the avoidance of unpleasure, is the *sole* object of liking or desire. Actually, there is a great deal else that people desire, such as knowledge, security, honor, or power.

To suppose that pleasure alone is *always* the object of desire is the result of a confusion of thought—the failure to distinguish between the desire for pleasure and the pleasure of fulfilled desire. I always get some pleasure from realization of my desire, but this does not mean that the pleasure is neces-sarily the object of my desire. Because pleasure arises when we get what we want, we suppose that it is pleasure alone that we want. For example, when I am lonely, I desire companion-ship, and when I satisfy this desire, I get pleasure. But the craving for companionship comes first, and the pleasure is a *consequence* of the satisfaction of this craving, rather than the object of the craving. Actually, we often forget all pleas-ure, and strive after other things; and we are very apt to obtain more pleasure if we do forget it. There is a profound truth in the old saying (known as the "hedonistic paradox") that "the way to get pleasure is to forget it." The secret of happiness is the power of impersonal interests to make men happy, such as self-less devotion to a cause or absorption in creative work.

Most ethical hedonists would now admit that men desire other things besides pleasure; but they may still insist that pleasure is the only object of a *reflective* desire. For example, Professor F. C. Sharp, a defender of hedonism, asserts:

The good . . . is not the desired as such. It is that which is desired when we "sit down in a cool hour," reflect upon the rela-tions that obtain between the various ends that appeal to us, and squarely face the fact that attainment of some is incompatible with that of others. We thereupon find ourselves cleaving to some while the attraction of others may vanish. That which maintains its place in our affection under these conditions is what we call good. If a definition must be packed into a single phrase, we may say that an experience is intrinsically good when it is capable of becoming the object of a reflective desire, as the term reflective has been used in the preceding description.[14]

In moments of such reflection, he declares, he finds that pleasure, and nothing else, is intrinsically good.

Now it does seem to me that we have no other way of deter-mining what is good than to "sit down in a cool hour," reflect very carefully upon all the possible ends of life, and discover by means of critical introspection what we really and truly want. The definition of goodness proposed by Professor Sharp seems to me therefore a good working definition. But I be-lieve that pleasure is *not* the sole object of reflective desire.

14 *Ethics*, Century, New York, 1928, pp. 410-411.

It seems to me true that sanity is one thing that men want even when they carefully reflect. There are some forms of insanity, involving delusions of grandeur, that are pleasant; yet most thoughtful persons would not want to go insane, even if they could be positively assured that they would thereby achieve more pleasure and less unpleasure than they would otherwise experience.

Even pleasure and sanity taken together are not sufficient. An oyster is sane, and it may be that oysters feel pleasure; but most men, when they reflect, want a mental life above the level of an oyster. If oysters can feel, it is perfectly possible that a world made up of oysters would have a greater surplus of pleasure over pain than a world made up of human beings. But human beings, as Plato pointed out in the *Philebus,* want something more than this: they demand intellectual activity as well as feeling to satisfy them. A life with nothing but feeling—without memory, expectation, awareness of oneself, or understanding of one's environment—is not the ample life that a human being craves.

I believe that there are other things that men desire even when they reflect. To determine whether this is the case, let us try a mental experiment. Imagine two worlds *equal in amount of pleasure* but otherwise different. In the first world, the only creatures that exist are just sufficiently conscious to feel pleasure; but they are not conscious of one another or of what kind of world they live in. They have no insight into truth, love, imagination, awareness of beauty, or excellence of character. In the second world, there are human beings who not only experience pleasure but achieve knowledge, love, beauty, virtue, and the full expression of human capacities. Is not the second world, though equal in amount of pleasure, more desirable than the first? I think most reflective persons would say yes.

Or let us consider a single life. If someone could prove that a certain drug would put a man's faculties permanently to sleep except for the capacity to feel pleasure, this loss of varied human capacities would not be a matter of sheer indifference, even if the total amount of his pleasure would remain the same. In saying this, I am thinking of the *intrinsic* values of the person's life and not the instrumental values which would, of course, be reduced or eliminated.

The reply of the hedonist is that love, knowledge, beauty, and so forth, are indeed good, but good merely as sources of pleasure. This answer seems to me inadequate, because it is not simply desirable that one should feel pleasure, but that one should feel pleasure in certain ways and with certain accompaniments. In all of the foregoing examples, we have supposed that the less attractive alternative is equal or greater in amount of pleasure, but it lacks certain other things that men really want.

John Stuart Mill (1806-1873), in his *Utilitarianism,* admits that almost anyone would prefer to be a wise man than a fool, even if the fool experiences a bit more pleasure, and that almost no one would choose to be changed into a lower animal even for the fullest allowance of a beast's pleasures. Nevertheless, he tries to rescue hedonism by a distinction between quantity and quality of pleasure, and by an emphasis upon quality:

It would be absurd that while, is estimating all other things, quality is to be considered as well as quantity, the estimation of pleasures should be supposed to depend on quantity alone. If I am asked, what I mean by difference of quality in pleasures, or what makes one pleasure more valuable than another merely as a pleasure, except its being greater in amount, there is but one possible answer. Of two pleasures, if there be one to which all or almost all who have experience of both give a decided preference, irrespective of any feeling of moral obligation to prefer it, that is the more desirable pleasure. If one of the two is, by those who are competently acquainted with both, placed so far above the other that they prefer it, even though knowing it to be attended with a greater amount of discontent, and would not resign it for any amount of the other pleasure which their nature is capable of, we are justified in ascribing to the preferred enjoyment a superiority in quality, so far outweighing quantity as to render it, in comparison, of small account.[15]

Mill's position is more adequate but less consistent than Bentham's pure quantitative hedonism. In the first place, it is questionable if pleasures, taken by themselves, differ in kind or quality. Titchener, in his *Textbook on Psychology*, for example, denies that there are any such differences; and he suggests that the apparent difference in kind is really a difference, not in the pleasures but in the very different *contents* of consciousness that have the common property of pleasing.[16] According to this interpretation, the pleasure of a fast game of tennis is no different qualitatively than the pleasure of reading a book by the fire; but otherwise the two experiences differ greatly.

On the other hand, it is questionable if we can thus sharply separate the pleasure from the content to which it is attached. "Pure pleasure," it would seem, is an unreal abstraction. No doubt we can mentally abstract the pleasantness of an experience; but what we can thus *consider* separately is in fact not separated. What occurs in real life is pleasant experience and not bare pleasure. We never find pleasures "flocking all alone"; we find them as constituents of emotions, or intertwined with desires, or fused with ideas, images, or sensations. Such pleasant experiences do have qualitative differences. There is a difference in quality, for example, between the pleasant experience of listening to a symphony and the pleasant experience of scratching one's own back. The feelings involved in each experience are subtly interfused with the total content. As Felix Krueger, an eminent German psychologist, has written:

Never are the differentiable parts or sides of real experience as isolated from one another as the parts of physical substance, *i.e.,*

15 Mill, *op. cit.*, pp. 7-8.
16 *Cf.*, Titchener, *op. cit.*, pp. 256-257.

its molecules or its atoms. All things that we can differentiate there, by comparison, always grip into one another and around one another in the greatest elaboration. And every time it is, without exception, imbedded within a total whole, by which it is penetrated and more or less completely enclosed. Feelings are the qualities of experiences of this total-whole.[17]

Mill was right in maintaining that pleasures differ in kind if by a pleasure is meant not a pleasure abstracted from all content, but a pleasant state of experience. This is because the experience contains more than pleasure and the pleasure is fused with the other constituents. Mill's language inadvertently bears witness to these facts. He speaks, for example, of the greater "dignity" or "intellectuality" of the pleasures that he prefers. This implies that not only is pleasure good, but also the dignity or intellectuality that serves to differentiate one pleasant experience from another. In admitting these differences, Mill is tacitly abandoning strict hedonism.

To summarize, pleasure is not the only form of interest or the only object of interest or even the only object of *reflective* interest. I therefore conclude that it is not sufficient to constitute welfare.

Happiness—the ultimate good of life—is more readily recognized than defined. We generally know when we are happy, but we are baffled when we are asked to define happiness. But it can be described volitionally as what we like and want in the way of immediate experience; just as unhappiness is what we dislike and do not want. What we want is activity that is free from irreconcilable conflicts and frustrations, enjoyable and emotionally gratifying, satisfying without loss of interest or satiety. "Pleasure" as the sole word to apply to such experience will always seem inadequate to many people. So at least it seems to me for the reasons I have given.

If some philosophers persist in employing the word *pleasure* so as to cover all such intrinsically valuable experiences,

17 "The Essence of Feeling," in *Feelings and Emotions,* edited by Martin L. Reymert, Clark University Press, Worcester, Mass., 1928, p. 67.

it may be that the difference in point of view is merely verbal. Some prefer to use the term in a very wide sense, others in a narrower sense. But the extremely broad usage is ordinarily misleading, if not positively false; and therefore I think another term should often be used.

In asserting that welfare includes more than pleasure, I am not maintaining that pleasure is neutral in value. Although it is not exhaustive of intrinsic goodness, it *is* intrinsically good. When I try critically to introspect, it does not seem to me that any experience *wholly* lacking in pleasure is ever intrinsically good, even though other factors add to and heighten the value. Moreover, I am inclined to believe that pleasant experience is *always* intrinsically good. Kant's attempt to prove the contrary seems to me fallacious. He argued that pleasure must be combined with good will to be intrinsically good; that the pleasure taken in an act of torture, for example, is bad for its own sake. It is certainly true that pleasure of this sort is bad; but it is bad, not because it is pleasure, but because it is symptomatic of an immoral disposition and entails more evil than good. Its bad effects and accompaniments vastly outweigh its intrinsic goodness, but it is, *as pleasant,* intrinsically good. But I am not *certain* that I am right in this contention. It is possible that the pleasure is so infected through and through by its morally evil accompaniments that it is intrinsically evil.

In general, however, the liberal unpuritanical moralist will have a bias in favor of pleasure rather than against it. No one has more truly indicated the value of pleasure than the great liberal philosopher, Benedict Spinoza, although he was no hedonist.

Nothing but a gloomy and sad superstition forbids enjoyment. For why is it more seemly to extinguish hunger and thirst than to drive away melancholy? My reasons and my conclusions are these:—No God and no human being, except an envious one, is delighted by my impotence or my trouble, or esteems as any virtue in us tears, sighs, fears and other things of this kind, which are signs of mental impotence; on the contrary, the greater the joy with which we are affected, the greater the perfection to which we pass thereby, that is to say, the more do we necessarily partake of the divine nature. To make use of things, therefore, and to delight in them as much as possible (provided we do not disgust ourselves with them, which is not delighting in them), is the part of a wise man. It is the part of a wise man, I say, to refresh and invigorate himself with moderate and pleasant eating and drinking, with sweet scents and the beauty of green plants, with ornament, with music, with sports, with the theatre, and with all things of this kind which one man can enjoy without hurting another.[18]

Yet Spinoza believed that the good is the exhilaration of the whole organism and that the greatest delight is not mere passive localized pleasure but the joy of total organic fulfillment. It is this integral joy, rather than bare pleasure, that constitutes the surest mark of welfare.

4. *Welfare as the Satisfaction of Desire*

EXTREME VOLUNTARISM represents an exclusive emphasis upon volition, just as hedonism represents an exclusive emphasis upon feeling. A broader type of voluntarism is to be found in the view that volition includes moments of thought and feeling, and that the satisfaction of desire brings pleasure and agreeable emotions. To illustrate a few types of voluntarism, let me turn to some historical examples.

One of the most famous of all voluntarists was Arthur Schopenhauer (1788-1860), the outstanding pessimist in the history of Western philosophy. He believed that life, fundamentally and pervasively, is "will"; and he included under "will" any kind of appetite, impulse, urge, desire, or craving that impels any creature to strive and to act. As an idealist, he believed that all nature is pervaded by will. "Before this peo-

---

[18] *Ethic,* translated by W. Hale White and Amelia H. Sterling, Oxford University Press, London, 1930, pp. 217-218.

ple have subsumed the concept of will under the concept of force," he explained. "I do just the contrary, and would have every force in nature thought of as will."[19] The action of gravity, the expansive force within a crystal, and the tropic response of a plant, for example, are all manifestations of will. At the lower stages of existence, the will is blind craving; but in man it becomes conscious. All other mental functions are subordinate to it. Will is the captain, reason is the obedient steersman—will determines the ends sought, reason merely discovers or invents the means. Similarly, feeling and emotion are functions of volition.

With such a view, he was bound to make will central in the theory of values. "Everything conformable to the striving of an individual will," he contended, "is called good in relation to the will in question—good food, good roads, good portents—and the opposite bad or, in the case of animate creatures, evil."[20] As a pessimist, he believed that will involves far more evil than good. It is an irrational, insatiable rage for life, and it springs from unrest, demand, suffering. "Willing is need, lack, therefore pain," he declared. "Life vibrates between pain and ennui."[21] The only refuge from the restless avidity and long torture of desire is to be found in rapt moments of esthetic contemplation or rare states of passionless peace—the perfect equanimity of nirvana—attained by the ascetic saint.

Friedrich Nietzsche (1844-1900) agreed with Schopenhauer's doctrine of the transcendent importance of will, but he substituted a defiant optimism in place of a submissive pessimism. He maintained that will—above all, the will to power—is the fundamental driving force of life; and that it not only is, but ought to be, the ruling faculty within the personality. He exalted, above all other human types, the strong, proud, self-assertive, domineering aristocrat, whose

19 *Werke,* Vol. II, Leipzig, 1873-1874, p. 362.
20 *Ibid.,* IV, p. 265.
21 *Ibid.,* section 57.

ideal is to master and exploit; not the happy man, not the man of reason, nor the man of love.

In both Schopenhauer and Nietzsche—although they differ greatly in other respects—we find an extreme expression of the primacy of the will. The fascists and nazis made this principle one of their fundamental doctrines. Highly typical is the remark of Benito Mussolini, that fascism "denies the validity of the equation, well-being equals happiness," and discovers its "value" in "a will to exist and a will to power."[22] The subsequent history of fascism, with its destructive activism and anti-intellectualism, may be sufficient indication of the social dangers of such an exaggerated voluntarism. No ethics is adequate that neglects the intrinsic values of feeling and thought. As Bertrand Russell has said, "The good life is one motivated by love and guided by knowledge"[23]—any ethics is bound to be cruel and irrational if it fails to recognize this fact.

We can again refer to the philosophy of Benedict Spinoza for a comprehensive interpretation of welfare. His ethics was fundamentally voluntaristic: he believed that the essence of every being is a "conatus" or volitional drive, a propensity for self-conservation and self-enhancement, an urge to increase the plenitude of one's being. This "effort" or "endeavor," he wrote "when it is related to the mind alone, is called will . . . when it is related at the same time to both the mind and the body, is called appetite"; and when we are conscious of the appetite, it is called "desire." Volition is the basis of all our evaluations: "we neither strive for, wish, seek, nor desire anything because we think it to be good, but, on the contrary, we adjudge a thing to be good because we strive for, wish, seek, or desire it."[24] Thus good springs from desire and not desire from good.

Since man's basic urge is life enhancement, to be good

22 "The Political and Social Doctrine of Fascism," *International Conciliation*, January 1935, pp. 9, 13.
23 *What I Believe*, Dutton, New York, 1925, p. 20.
24 Spinoza, *op. cit.*, pp. 115-116.

means primarily to enhance life, to facilitate human powers. "A thing is called by us good or evil," Spinoza declared, "as it increases or diminishes, helps or restrains, our power of action."[25] Thus he built his ethics upon the distinction between descendent and ascendent life. The ethical problem is to make the transition from lowered to heightened vitality—to become more and more energized, organized, projective, alive as a whole, because such triumphant vitality is what we fundamentally desire.

The fulfillment of appetite, desire, and will involved in the transition to enhanced life, has its accompaniments of thought and feeling. Intellectually, it means replacing muddle and confusion with order and rational arrangement, and identifying ourselves in thought with the whole, the abiding. The development of thought is an ascent through three levels of knowledge. The first level is "imagination," which includes both sensation and imagery: it gives us separate, fragmentary, superficial glimpses of reality. Reason, or the second level, is more adequate: it gives us science; and its effect is to unify but incompletely. Intellectual mastery is not attained until we reach the third kind of knowledge, intuition, an "intellectual vision" which starts with the whole of things in order to understand the part, since the part is implicated in the whole. At this level, the certainty and necessity of scientific demonstration unite with a concrete, immediate, spiritual sense of the whole. At the summit of his mental development, man grasps the unity of the "Whole of Being": he achieves his health and freedom by living consciously as a whole man within a cosmic all-embracing whole.

Keeping pace with this fulfillment of desire and this widening of thought is the transformation of our emotional life, a transition from passive to active emotions. A passive emotion is localized, disengaged, unfused with the personality as a whole—a mere response to external forces dominating us—not an assertion of individuality and integrity, not the result

25 *Ibid.*, p. 186.

of organic fulfillment. Such passive emotions include panic fears, overmastering loves and hates and jealousies, and every immoderate passion. They correspond to the confused and inadequate ideas of the first kind of knowledge: detached sensory impressions, popular opinions, conventions, and superstitions. In contrast, the active emotions arise from the free, integral expression of the whole man. They spring from the maximum fulfillment of desire and will and are correlated with reason and intuition. They involve the love of great objects—nature and the universal human community—and they yield the maximum of happiness, for our happiness depends upon the quality of the objects upon which our love is fixed, and love toward the greatest of objects feeds the mind with a profound joy.

Such was Spinoza's view of the transition from human bondage to human freedom—a transition motivated and propelled by volition, but including both intellectual and emotional fulfillment within its wide arc.

We can best judge the validity of such doctrines, if we consider the relation of volition to interest and value. This requires an analysis of the component factors in the expression and fulfillment of desire. The following factors can be discriminated:

(1) Impulse or Drive. Volition is the dynamic element in personality: it is impulse, drive, movement, or tendency. A living organism, whether because of instinctive or acquired characteristics, has appetitions and governing propensities— physiological drives, such as hunger, thirst, sex appetite, and the urge to rest or sleep; and psychical dispositions, such as curiosity, desire to play, interest in security, and artistic impulse. The values of our bodies and minds are primarily the fulfillments of these needs, urges, and tendencies.

(2) Thought. If there is not to be mere blind impulse but conscious desire, thought must become aware of the impulse, or drive, and must envisage, truly or falsely, the supposed goal of the activity—either an immediate or more remote goal. In

the case of hunger, for example, the eating of food is the conscious goal of the impulse. The goal may be critically scrutinized by intelligence, and judged worthy or unworthy. Such an act of judgment frequently involves choice, and sometimes thoughtful reorientation of desire.

(3) Striving. Between the inception of an impulse and its appeasement, there is usually an interval of tension, unrest, and seeking. It is often, but not invariably, accompanied by unpleasure, which is a sign of lack and restlessness. As the seeking passes over into consummation, the unpleasure and accompanying negative emotions change to pleasure and positive emotions. But sometimes, as in the case of an agreeable appetite for food, there is no painful sense of deficiency, and the phase of seeking is pleasant throughout.

(4) Anticipation and Memory. The consummation of desire is not instantaneous: there is a foretaste of satisfaction in anticipation and an aftertaste of satisfaction in memory. Moreover, each new satisfaction may revive the memory of similar past satisfactions and may evoke the yearning for possible future renewals. As Professor Parker points out:

> Every value contains . . . echoes out of the past, and itself provides new overtones of new values in the future. A value is a harmonic system, like a tone sounding with all its partials. Through the imaginative anticipation of satisfaction, we enjoy before we have enjoyed; through memory we enjoy after we have enjoyed; and every joy contains a before and after joy. It follows from the role played by imagination in value—by anticipation and memory—that value does not pertain to the terminus of the experience, to consummation alone, but to the entire process of desire-seeking-fulfillment.[26]

(5) Consummation or Frustration. If the desire is consummated, the result is satisfaction; conversely, if it is frustrated, the result is dissatisfaction. Satisfaction brings relief from tension, pleasure, and positive emotions such as love and joy; dissatisfaction brings aversion, unpleasure, and negative emotions such as hate and disgust.

[26] Parker, *op. cit.,* p. 25.

Value consists primarily in the whole complex process of satisfying desire. As we have pointed out, it involves impulse, thought, imagination, emotion, and pleasure or unpleasure. The good is mainly the total satisfaction, with its emotional and hedonic ingredients; the evil is mainly the dissatisfaction, with its corresponding ingredients. When desire is analyzed in this inclusive way, it contains within it the intellectual, hedonic, and emotional factors in interest which we have discussed. It is only when desire is thus broadly conceived that it may properly be called the basis and content of value. Abstract desire, apart from all thought, emotion, and feeling, is no more real than pure pleasure and is therefore not the content of value experience. Consequently, Spinoza was a realist in emphasizing the interrelatedness of mental functions.

Since *desire* is very often conceived abstractly and narrowly, it is perhaps better, in indicating the psychological basis of value, to employ the word *interest*. And it is perhaps better to understand that positive interest is an inclusive attitude of liking involving intellectual, volitional, emotional, and hedonic elements, and that negative interest is a similar attitude of disliking and is likewise inclusive.

5. *Welfare as the Fulfillment of Personality*

THE HUMAN PERSONALITY, in its fundamental dynamic character, is an organization of interests, and the enrichment and fulfillment of these interests constitutes its welfare. As an organization of interests, it differs from a mere collection; it is more like a miniature community. The thought is an ancient one: Plato, in *The Republic,* taught that the state is the individual writ large and that the individual is the state writ small. Just as he wanted his ideal state to be a real community, with genuine interdependence and mutuality among its components, so he wanted the individual soul to be a kind of "community" of its parts, with a harmonious interplay of all its faculties. One may restate Plato's point of view in modern psychological terminology. The good personality, one can maintain, is the well-organized personality, in which all the sides of a man's nature—the volitional, intellectual, hedonic, and passional—form a community, an organic unity in which part is harmoniously related to part and part to whole, and in which all these interrelated parts, expressing themselves in manifold interests, are cultivated and fulfilled.

If we are morally wise, so it would seem to me, this is what we value as a proper goal. We are interested in interests; we have a commanding interest in the cultivation and fulfillment of interests; we have a supreme interest in personality, as the sole locus and dynamic center of interests. To the living being, therefore, all values must be contributory. The whole of human culture—science, art, religion, morality—must serve and facilitate life. The basic human aspiration, to quote the eloquent words of D. H. Lawrence, is to awaken "the unborn body of life hidden within the body of this half death which we call life."[27]

I do not mean to deny that we should be interested in more than man. Nothing contributes more to happiness than impersonal interests, self-transcending and even life-transcending, such as the astronomer's interest in probing the mysterious universe or the ordinary man's sense of the beauty and fascination of nature. Yet these interests are valuable to us because they enrich life. When we are thus engrossed, we open wide the windows of our minds and let fresh winds play upon our spirits from the far corners of the universe. We fulfill life by transcending life; the effect is life enhancement.

If the enrichment of life is indeed our goal, it is found in the realization of the whole man: not in reason alone, nor the will, nor the emotions, but in the full expression and realization of human nature as a dynamic organization of interests.

The meaning of welfare can perhaps best be understood in

27 "Glad Ghosts," *Dial,* Vol. 81, July 1926, p. 2.

contrast with evil. Let us take an example from literature: the terrible moment when Macbeth realizes the utter futility and meaninglessness and misery of his own existence. Disaster after disaster has come upon him; Lady Macbeth is dead; all his hopes and dreams lie in ruins; he knows at last that the witches have betrayed him, that defeat and death, are fast approaching. With the merciless candor of despair, he then sums up the evil of life:

> Tomorrow, and tomorrow, and tomorrow,
> Creeps in this petty pace from day to day
> To the last syllable of recorded time,
> And all our yesterdays have lighted fools
> The way to dusty death. Out, out, brief candle!
> Life's but a walking shadow, a poor player
> That struts and frets his hour upon the stage
> And then is heard no more: it is a tale
> Told by an idiot, full of sound and fury,
> Signifying nothing.[28]

What is this appalling realization of evil? It is not, as the hedonist would say, that life is simply unpleasant. The un-pleasure might be more intense if Macbeth had hit his thumbnail a sharp blow with a hammer; but there would have been lacking that deeper and wider realization of evil—the sense that all meaning, all dignity, all worth has dropped out of existence; the sense that life is nothing but a noisy, idiotic tale. It is in this mood, when one's life seems to be an affair of absolute inconsequence, with no pattern for the intelligence, no attraction for the will, and no delight for the feelings and emotions, that a man commits suicide.

It might be objected by a hedonist that Macbeth, in mental retrospect, is realizing the evil of a great span of life, whereas a man with a crushed fingernail is experiencing only a tran-sient unpleasure, and that the relative insignificance of the unpleasure is due entirely to its evanescence. But my point is that, *at any one moment,* Macbeth is experiencing a more

[28] *Macbeth,* Act V, Scene V.

comprehensive and massive evil, a more pervasive soul sickness, enveloping his whole personality and gnawing into the
innermost vitals of his being. Given an equal duration, the
unpleasure taken alone is less damaging, because of its single-
ness, its peripheral and localized character, its failure to en-
velop all dimensions of one's being, and to strike at the soul
of life's plot. A personality that is defeated in every essential
respect and in its innermost nature *loathes* itself more profoundly than a personality that is injured in only one respect,
as for example, hedonically.

The same thought may be put in other words: as we have
said before, not only do "interests" include more than feelings, but its "objects" include more than feelings. If we substitute the word *judgments* or *emotions* or *volitions* in place
of the word *feelings,* in the preceding sentence, the statement will still be true. Therefore an *exclusive* hedonism, or
voluntarism, or emotionalism, or intellectualism, is ethically
inadequate, and the only valid ethical theory is one which
admits that the whole personality is sometimes brought into
play in the act of being interested *and* as the object of
interest.

What I have just said holds true if we turn from the evil of
life, as illustrated by Macbeth's black mood, to the good of
life. When a person looks at his life and finds it truly glorious,
he is expressing and valuing all sides of his nature—the volitional, intellectual, hedonic, and passional. But these "sides,"
although they must be separated for purposes of analysis, are
not realized separately: in actuality they interpenetrate and
enrich one another within the organic unity of the personality. The highest good, I believe, is the exhilaration of the
whole organism, the joy of total organic fulfillment. The
intellectual, the volitional, the hedonic, and the passional
merge in a core of unity or self-identity—the man becomes
one and relatively complete. He is not just a bundle of changing states but a continuing and evolving *I*. This *I* becomes
the master of change; it expresses itself through what it does,

through its acts and thoughts. Such a personality is well integrated, and the elements thus unified are rich and various. They form, as I have said, a kind of "community," characterized by the interdependence and mutual enhancement of its members.

So far I have described the fulfillment of the personality in terms of its conscious faculties—feeling and emotion, volition, and intellect—and of their interpenetration in the organic unity of the purposive self. This account is incomplete unless we include physical and subconscious and low conscious levels. Not being a psychologist, I shall make no attempt to explore the obscure labyrinthine realm of the "Id," with its congerie of biologically determined wants, or to harmonize the rival claims of the "id-needs," the "ego-needs," the "super-ego-needs," and the "enlarged-ego-needs," as Tolman has done in an admirable analysis of "Psychological Man."[29] Also I do not wish to commit myself to the paradoxical doctrine that there are literally unconscious experiences—the meaning of "subconscious" is puzzling. It will be enough to emphasize the basic fact that every person is a psychophysical organism with body and so-called "subconscious mind" and conscious mind so intimately connected as to constitute a single system. As a result of the work of innumerable physiologists, such as Jacques Loeb and Walter Cannon, and of the work of many psychologists, such as Pierre Janet and Sigmund Freud, we can now assert the close linkage of body and mind and consciousness and "subconsciousness" in almost every aspect of life. Just as the physical hormones, for example, have a decisive influence upon man's temperament, so psychic conflict may profoundly disturb physical functions. The unity of the psychophysical organism is now fully recognized in psychiatry and psychosomatic medicine. Even though intrinsic value is to be found only in conscious states of interest, we must bear in mind the interdependence of mind and body if we are adequately to interpret physical and mental health.

29 Cf., *Journal of Social Psychology*, Vol. XIII, February 1941, pp. 205-218.

I am pleading for an ethics of the whole human organism rather than an ethics of a mere fragment of it. From the standpoint of such an integral humanism, the fundamental biological values, such as good nutritious food, rest, decent shelter, warm clothing, exercise and physical play, sex-expression, pain avoidance, and health care, must be considered basic to the personality and therefore to the good life. But the more "ideal values" of man, such as beauty, knowledge, love and cooperation, security, adventure, and creative work, are, if less basal, no less indispensable to the human organism. The two sets of values—the biological and the psychological—must be regarded as interactive, interdependent, and often coalescent. They are elements in the total organic fulfillment—the complete physiological and psychological health of the personality—which is the norm of human welfare.

The detailed definition of that norm requires the co-operative insight of many "experts"—the physician, the hygienist, the dietitian, the psychologist, the esthetician, the philosopher, the educator, the social welfare worker, and the community planner. The humane arts and sciences must pool their wisdom in defining the human goal—the total health and welfare of the personality. This is not a task for quacks or vague "idealists." It is possible to employ the methods of empirical science in finding out what human drives are so basic that their satisfaction leads to happiness and fulfillment and their denial to physical disease, insanity, suicide, or, in society, to war, economic collapse, and mass sadism. It is not true that the table of values is eternally fixed —it is necessary for man to extend and deepen his acquaintance with values, and by informed insight and critical judgment to test and improve the table. For the present, however, I wish to insist only upon the central concept: that the norm of aspiration is the health and happiness of the *total* personality, emerging in the harmonious cooperation of interrelated physical and mental activities.

No supernatural oracle reveals that such total fulfillment

is the highest good. The only witness to value is man himself. The *"summum bonum"* is defined by man's most careful
judgment *after all the available evidence is in.* The *highest*
good—not the *"bonum"* but the *"summum bonum"*—is what
morally wise men crave when they sit down in a cool hour,
reflect upon a full gamut of experience, consider the alternatives as defined by science and vivified by art, and decide what
it is that they basically and truly want. Value judgment should
rest upon all the insight that a man can summon, upon
science, imaginative sensitivity, practical experience, and
critical introspection. I believe that morally sensitive people,
if they thus reflect, want a life that is well integrated and rich
and various in experienced quality. They want the comprehensive and harmonious realization of their potentialities,
not pleasure or passion if it means insanity, not intellectuality
if it means emotional frigidity, not cultivation of the mind to
the neglect of the body or the body to the neglect of the mind.

6. *Social Value—The Meaning of Justice*

So FAR we have been discussing the welfare of the individual
personality, which, as we have seen, is the sole locus of intrinsic value. We have insisted in the preceding chapter, however, that human beings are profoundly social, and that their
fulfillment is possible only within a society or community.

The two great concepts in moral reconstruction are *personality* and *community*—our ideal should be the development of *total* persons united in a rich community of experience. There are out-of-date "liberals" who deny community
for the sake of "personality," and up-to-date "totalitarians"
who deny personality for the sake of "community"; but the
valid ethical solution is to assert their interdependence. In
terms of personality, life enhancement—interpreted as the
qualitative enrichment and satisfaction of interest—is *the*
supreme end or goal of aspiration. But to achieve such pleni-

tude of being, men must be united by sympathy and sharing for nothing, as Spinoza said, is so important to man as his fellow man. If it is true that personality shrivels into nothingness when separated from the community, it is likewise true that community evaporates into monotony when its component personalities are stultified. "The *great* community," as Whitehead has said, "is the community of vivid individualities connected in the unity of a background."[30]

Long ago Plato used the term *justice* to denote the harmony among individuals and groups within a wider community. He employed the same term to denote the harmonious development of all the basic parts of a single mind. It would be more in accord with common linguistic usage if we should use another term, such as self-realization, to denote the harmonious fulfillment of individual personality. Moreover, the word *justice,* unless it is to be understood in an exceedingly wide sense, represents one of the values of community life but not the only value. Nevertheless, it will be useful for the moment to consider justice in its wide Platonic meaning, namely, the working harmony, the organic unity, of the community. With this meaning in mind, I maintain that justice and self-realization are more or less interdependent, that they reciprocally determine and enhance one another. I do not mean that justice and self-interest *always* coincide. The demands of justice, or duty to others, may require the sacrifice of self-interest, even to the point of death. But I would deny that justice and self-realization are necessarily or even usually opposed. The moral ideal is to bring about the maximum harmony between individual and social welfare—between self-realization and justice.

The utter incompatibility of justice and self-realization, however, has frequently been asserted. For example, Glaucon, a character in Plato's *Republic,* recalls the story of Gyges' magic ring that could make its wearer invisible, and he asks

[30] Alfred North Whitehead, *Adventures of Ideas,* Macmillan, New York, 1933, p. 362.

what the ordinary man would do if he had such a sure and handy way of escaping the consequences of his social misdeeds. If, being invisible at will, we could steal or kill or take unfair advantage without the slightest risk of being apprehended, how many of us would tread the straight and narrow path of a moral life?

Friedrich Nietzsche believed that no *superior* person would do so. He maintained that self-realization normally requires the violation of justice. Fulfillment for the born aristocrat is achieved through power and domination, through the exploitation and subjugation of one's inferiors. A vast number of people in the modern world, without being so candid as Nietzsche, agree with him that justice and self-realization are incompatible. Innumerable human beings seek their own fulfillment, or the fulfillment of the restricted group to which they adhere, by unjust and antisocial methods.

This denial of justice assumes two forms. The first is personal egoism. Individuals seek private advantage at public expense. They seek it by political graft, by false advertising, by manufacturing shoddy products, by exploiting their employees, by soldiering on the job, by filing false income tax reports, by monopolistic price-fixing, by innumerable types of chiseling and racketeering. In extreme instances, they turn to violent crime, or to war, as a means of self-aggrandizement.

The second form is group egoism. Just as an individual may adopt the ideal of "myself alone," so a group functioning within a wider society can fanatically assert the ideal of "ourselves alone." This has been the cardinal sin of the fascists, but it has been by no means confined to fascism. In every land, there is a tendency to deny the wider justice, or the rights of the more inclusive community, in the interests of some restricted and divisive loyalty.

The effect of personal and group egoism is to destroy justice. Complete destruction means anarchy—the war of each against all. That is why, as Plato pointed out, there must be some degree of justice in any coherent group. There must be justice even among thieves if they are to hold together as a band. Injustice is the very essence and principle of anarchy in the sense in which Hobbes spoke of the anarchy of "the state of nature."[31] His account of this anarchical state—"solitary, poor, nasty, brutish, and short"—made clear that it is incompatible with self-realization. The individual life is intolerable when the only rule of life is that man is a wolf to man.

If self-realization usually requires justice, it is no less true that justice usually requires self-realization. The great social harmony is the harmony of cooperative individuals, each realizing his potentialities to the maximum and each acknowledging the right of others to do so. Justice cannot be described externally and negatively as the mere absence of friction. There is no friction among the dead, but there is also no justice. Justice means that human beings acknowledge and respect each other as persons.

Self-realization—the good of the individual personality—and justice—the basic value of the community—therefore tend to be interdependent. They constitute the two great objectives of moral reconstruction. They are to be conceived in terms of the cultivation, fulfillment, and reconciliation of interests, first within the personality and then within the society. The nature of such reconciliation will be pondered in the next chapter.

7. The Capacity for Improvement

IF WE CONSIDER not simply the present but the future, we must reckon with another important factor: the capacity to develop into something better. Some societies remain fairly static, showing little tendency to advance or decline. Others may have a fairly high level of well-being but are headed for

---

31 *Cf., Leviathan* in *The English Works of Thomas Hobbes*, Bohn, London, 1839, III, p. 113.

disaster. Still others are lower on the scale of immediate welfare but are progressive. Sacrifice, hard discipline, grim struggle, utmost devotion to duty, are sometimes required if a society is to avoid eventual collapse.

One of the great dangers of any tight, orderly, rationalized system is its tendency to remain static and eventually to decline. As Arnold J. Toynbee, perhaps the greatest living historian, has pointed out, this is the fatal defect of most Utopias, such as Plato's Republic:

> To arrest a downward movement is the utmost to which most Utopias aspire, since Utopias seldom begin to be written in any society until after its members have lost the expectation of further progress. Hence in almost all Utopias—with the noteworthy exception of that work of English genius which has given this whole genre of literature its name—an invincibly stable equilibrium is the aim to which all other social ends are subordinate and, if need be, sacrificed.[32]

Plato's tendency to ban poets, to censor artists, to forbid "dangerous thoughts," to disapprove innovations, to tell "noble lies" for the sake of preserving a class hierarchy, makes his Republic, despite the greatness of its conception, a static and even decadent ideal.

In accepting Plato's plea for justice, it is important that we should not make his mistake of sacrificing the dynamic to the orderly. Our ideal should not be a neat, tidy, tight system but a changing, dynamic equilibrium, combining integration and progress.

A healthy society, therefore, will nourish and protect freedom, spontaneity, and creative impulses. It will encourage artists and thinkers. It will stimulate inquiry, experiment, and invention, not only in physical science and technology but also in the humanities and social sciences. It will study and avoid the mistakes of the past and project its purposes clearly and boldly into the future. It will inspire men with a

[32] *A Study of History,* one-vol. ed., Oxford University Press, New York, 1947, p. 183.

vigorous faith in a better life and thus engage their energies
in the great tasks of social improvement.

We are now prepared to gather together the threads of
our discussion and to define, in the light of our argument,
the meaning of a good society. The intrinsic goodness of a
society consists in the well-being of those who compose it: it
has no intrinsic goodness of its own apart from its members.
These members, as bearers of values, can best be characterized in terms of a complex, dynamic fusion of interests; and
their welfare consists in the harmonious cultivation and fulfillment of these interests, involving pleasure, joyous emotion, and maximum satisfaction of desire. The good, as thus
conceived, involves both the *qualitative* enrichment and the
quantitative fulfillment of interests. Such an ideal, I have
contended, implies the realization of all the fundamental
sides of human nature—sensuous, intellectual, volitional, and
passional. Human nature, moreover, is fundamentally social,
and therefore the maximum fulfillment and qualitative cultivation of interests require a just society, in which human
beings acknowledge one another as precious, autonomous
personalities. In terms of immediate values, a good social
order is achieved when well-being, so described, is the possession not of one race, one class, one privileged group, but
of the maximum number of people within the society. But
since the future should also be taken into account, we must
consider whether the society is progressive or retrogressive.
The good society is that which is most efficacious in promoting welfare, all people considered and in the long run.

Chapter Eight

RIGHT SOCIAL ACTION

1. *The Basis of Social Obligation*

WE HAVE SAID that this book is primarily concerned with two great questions: "What is the nature of a good society?" and "What is right social action?" In the last several chapters, we have dealt with the first of these questions at considerable length, and it is now time to return to our second question. I say "return," because in Part One we considered and finally rejected law as the ultimate standard of right action. We shall now try another approach and attempt to find a teleological rather than a formalistic sanction for conduct.

Any adequate interpretation of right action must explain the meaning of the statement: "You ought to do so and so," when the *ought* is moral. The concept of "right" is inseparable from the concept of the moral "ought." It is never right to do what one ought not to do, and what one ought to do is always right. Apart from the sense of duty or obligation, right would lack all meaning and cogency.

We owe to Kant, more than to any other thinker, the recognition that "ought" is a crucial ethical concept. But as we have seen in Chapter Four, his attempt to derive the binding force of the ought from the logical principle of noncontradiction is a failure, and his abstract formalistic interpretation of obligation does far less than justice to the importance of consequences and the facts of human individuality.

In Chapter Six, we suggested an alternative interpretation: that obligation, in great part, represents the pull of society upon the individual. This interpretation means that a human being, in his innermost nature, is social, and feels the tug of society as the internalized "voice" of conscience. All men are involved in a complex network of social forces; these gradually build up within each one of us a social ego, the accumulation and internal deposit of innumerable social attitudes and emotions. When we have an impulse to act in harmony with these social forces, we feel the strong inner support of the social ego; when we have an impulse to act in a contrary manner, we feel its curb and restraint. "To cultivate this social ego," declares Bergson, "is the essence of our obligation to society. Were there not some part of society in us, it would have no hold on us."[1]

I believe this is a partial but not a complete explanation of obligation. It seems to me that the "ought" is to be explained primarily by a combination of two factors: first, the influence of society; and second, the attempt to escape bias and to attain moral objectivity. Both of these factors are included in the interpretation of right that we find in Adam Smith's *Theory of the Moral Sentiments* and in David Hume's *Treatise of Human Nature* and *Enquiry Concerning the Principles of Morals.* Although they seldom use the word *ought,* they provide the basis for a clear and cogent doctrine of obligation.

These two fast friends, who agreed in many of the essentials of their ethical doctrines, believed that the spring of the moral life is sympathy. All of us, to some degree, have a "fellow feeling" for the weal and woe of others—through such means as pity and kindness and imagination, we come to understand and to be affected by what others feel. Emotions and feelings are infectious and tend to flow, in a sense, from person to person. When some one is in agony, for example, we suffer at the very sight and thought of his suffering.

By the imagination [writes Smith] we place ourselves in his

[1] Henri Bergson, *The Two Sources of Morality and Religion,* Holt, New York, 1935, p. 7.

situation, we conceive ourselves enduring all the same torments, we enter as it were into his body, and become in some measure the same person with him, and thence form some idea of his sensations, and even feel something which, though weaker in degree, is not altogether unlike them. His agonies, when they are thus brought home to ourselves, when we have thus adopted them and made them our own, begin at last to affect us, and we then tremble and shudder at the thought of what he feels. For as to be in pain or distress of any kind excites the most excessive sorrow, so to conceive or to imagine that we are in it, excites some degree of the same emotion, in proportion to the vivacity or dullness of the conception.[2]

Sympathy is the main basis of our moral concern for others; and it is because of innumerable sympathetic experiences that altruistic dispositions are built up within the mind. These dispositions, along with other social attitudes, coalesce to form the social ego whose voice is conscience.[*]

Sympathy, however, needs to be controlled by critical intelligence. It is most intense toward our intimates and our own kind, and it fades or vanishes when distance, prejudice, or unfamiliarity blunts our feelings. Hence reason is morally necessary to correct our biases and to extend the range of our moral concern. To quote Hume:

Sympathy, we shall allow, is much fainter than our concern for ourselves, and sympathy with persons remote from us much fainter than that with persons near and contiguous; but for this very reason it is necessary for us, in our calm judgments and discourse concerning the characters of men, to neglect all these differences, and render our sentiments more public and social.[3]

Since everyone is strongly influenced by the accidents and perspectives of his own experience, he should try to attain a more objective point of view.

[*] Hume and Smith do not bring in the concept of the "social ego," and the present use of the term therefore represents an extension of their theory.

[2] Adam Smith, *The Theory of the Moral Sentiments,* Cadell and Davies, London, 1804, p. 3.

[3] David Hume, *An Enquiry Concerning the Principles of Morals,* Open Court, La Salle, Ill., 1938, p. 64.

Every particular man [declares Hume] has a peculiar position with regard to others; and 'tis impossible we could ever converse together on any reasonable terms, were each of us to consider characters and persons, only as they appear from his peculiar point of view. In order, therefore, to prevent these continual *contradictions,* and arrive at a more stable judgment of things, we fix on some steady and general points of view; and always, in our thoughts, place ourselves in them, whatever may be our present situation.[4]

Similarly Adam Smith recognizes that sympathy is very often distorted by favoritism or callousness, and that we must therefore achieve a more fair and unbiased basis for moral choice. He suggests that this higher standard is to be found in the point of view of the "supposed well-informed and impartial spectator," who considers the total effect of each alternative and decides upon the best course of action with a just regard for all the parties concerned. Such a completely wise and unprejudiced judge does not exist; but as an imaginary being, he represents an ideal or standard that we should try to attain. In so far as our action conforms to what he would recommend, we may be said to act rightly.

Now I believe that these theories of Smith and Hume provide the necessary clues for an accurate interpretation of moral obligation. The "ought," as a moral imperative, is both a rational and a social demand—the internalized pull of society regulated by reason. I shall now define a little more precisely the two aspects of obligation: the social and the rational.

The social pull of obligation arises when a person feels that he should relinquish his own lesser good for the sake of the greater good of others, or that he should sacrifice the lesser good of some restricted group for the sake of the greater good of some wider group. The interests of society are pulling a man away from something good toward something better.

Suppose a person is taking a stroll in the woods upon some

[4] Hume, *A Treatise of Human Nature,* Oxford University Press, London, 1896, p. 581.

fine summer day. He happens to be walking past a pond when he suddenly sees a child floundering in the water and in danger of drowning. He at once sympathizes with the plight of the child, and at the cost of sacrificing a carefree stroll and wetting his clothes, he plunges into the water to save the youngster. Can we say that the sympathy of the moment impels him to act, and that obligation means no more than this? The matter is by no means so simple! The man's feeling that he ought to rescue the child is called into play by the momentary sympathy; but the present and particular sympathy is merely the nucleus around which gravitate feelings and attitudes implanted in the mind by many past experiences of a kindred sort. All these experiences have left memories and traces that have long since united to form the social ego, a fusion and organization of countless sympathetic attitudes. It is this whole complex that is called into play by the sight of the child in distress; and therefore the pressure of the immediate sympathy is reinforced by the cumulative pressure of innumerable past sympathies. This pressure is felt as duty or obligation; and it arises whenever a person is being internally influenced toward an objective that seems not to be his own but to which he responds because something arouses the social ego within him.

The emotions and attitudes that coalesce to form the social ego and thus to constitute the sense of obligation are no doubt of composite origin. Following the lead of Hume and Smith, I have put special emphasis upon sympathy, but there are many diverse reactions that result from social command and prohibition, praise and blame, taboo and charm, punishment and reward. Such attitudes as disapproval, abhorrence, dread, a sense of constraint, or their opposites, are aroused within the mind. By accretion and fusion, these attitudes are finally synthesized into the dynamic psychological complex that Freud calls the super ego and that I have called the social ego. It is the internal pressure from this ego that primarily constitutes the sense of obligation.

Yet even this is not the whole story. As Hume and Smith point out, sympathy may be wrongly directed: it may be excessive, inadequate, or misplaced; it may be confined within too narrow limits; it may be distorted by bias or based upon a misconception. The reinforcement provided by the social ego, moreover, is no guarantee against misdirection, since it increases the pressure rather than guarantees its right application. Hence sympathy and the social ego need to be regulated and supplemented by reason in the sense of thoughtful and unbiased moral judgment.

Let us return to our illustration. Suppose the child who is in danger of drowning is a Negro, and the stroller who sees him is a white man with a strong racial prejudice against Negroes. In these circumstances so little sympathy may be aroused that the man may callously walk past. Or if he does stop to rescue the child, it may be because reason checks his spontaneous emotional reaction.

Let us again alter the illustration. Suppose that the man cannot swim and that the attempt at rescue will endanger his life. Suppose also that he is an important public official, whose life is not only precious to himself but valuable to others. Then the decision whether to risk his own life in the hope of saving the child might require intense reasoning.

In these instances, there is a need to control emotion by judgment. So it is in the many situations in life requiring moral choice. If sensibly employed, rules assist us in attaining a more steady and impartial point of view, and reason intervenes to broaden and regulate our sympathies and correct our biases. It is thus that action ceases to be merely sentimental and becomes principled.

If the only problem were to exercise sympathy or *feel* conscientious, any action so motivated would be right. But it is common knowledge that the motive may be *inwardly* or *subjectively* right, in the sense of being well intentioned, and yet the act not *outwardly* or *objectively* right, in the sense of bringing about the best possible consequences. An *act* cannot be *wholly* right unless it combines good intentions and good results. Therefore it is not enough to be motivated by sympathy or a sense of obligation: it is important to act without bias, with a keen appreciation of ends, with adequate knowledge of means, so that the act will be objectively right. "Ought" expresses the demand for moral objectivity and not simply the subjective feeling of obligation. When we say that a certain act ought to be performed, we mean that it is, so far as foreseeable consequences are involved, objectively the best choice.

To sum up, the sense of obligation involves two elements. First, the emotions and volitional attitudes that become crystallized in the social ego and that give one, on occasion, such a strong *feeling* of obligation. Second, the rational aversion from an act which would produce harmful consequences, and the rational approval of an act that would produce beneficial consequences. This rational factor in obligation is expressed in the demand to escape from bias and to achieve moral objectivity. As morality becomes more reflective, this rational side of morality becomes ever more prominent. It is important, of course, not to uproot the powerful motivation provided by love and a strong sense of obligation, but to make this motivation harmonize with intelligence.

What I have been saying applies whether the choice is to be made by an individual or a society. The issues confronting a society may be much more complicated than the issues facing an individual; but there is the same need to combine reason and good will. The policy makers for the society—whether they be many or few—should not only be conscientious and sympathetic but should understand what welfare means and how to attain it. They should avoid any bias, such as an undue preference for a certain race, nation, or class that would warp and distort their judgment. Thus only can they heed the call of obligation.

But it might be asked, why should either an individual or a society heed this call? Why not prefer our own lesser good to the greater good of society? Why not choose the lesser good of our own little group to the greater good of some larger group?

A partial answer is to be found in the fact that morality is a fundamental part of our nature. Society is too much with us, the social ego is too much an essential part of ourselves, flagrantly to deny its claims; or if we *can* override the claims of sociality, we can do so only by suppressing an essential part of ourselves. As Walt Whitman has said: "Whoever walks a furlong without sympathy walks to his own funeral dressed in his shroud."[5]

But to some extent, as Kant maintained, morality consists in going against the grain of human nature. It consists in curbing our inclinations, resisting our biases. To this extent morality is somewhat foreign to our nature, but it is still the case that we ought to be moral. The ultimate reason why we should be moral is simply that good, being good, ought to be maximized, and evil, being evil, ought to be minimized. It seems to me self-evident that we ought to perform any act the total content and consequences of which stand higher in the scale of intrinsic value than those of any other act which might have been chosen. Instead of yielding to some bias in favor of a less valuable alternative, we should bring about the most good and the least evil in our power. There is no more fundamental principle of ethics than this. If we do not accept this principle, we can have no basis for an objective teleological ethics, whether for an individual or a society.

We can now define the meaning of right action. An act is objectively right if, so far as one can reasonably foresee, it brings about the maximum surplus of good over evil. The intrinsic value or disvalue of the act itself must, of course, enter into the calculation. For example, if we are to judge whether the waging of war is right, we would have to include in our calculation not only all the eventual consequences of

[5] "Song of Myself," in *Leaves of Grass,* Heritage Press, New York, no date, p. 79.

such waging but the immediate values and disvalues of the waging itself. But when we have calculated what an act or a course of action involves both immediately and eventually, intrinsically and instrumentally, we can determine its objective rightness or wrongness by the good and evil which it thus inclusively involves.

In the last chapter, I defined good as the fulfillment of interests and evil as the frustration of interests. I explained that fulfillment means not only the satisfaction of desire but pleasure and agreeable emotion, and that frustration means not only the frustration of desire but displeasure and disagreeable emotion. For the sake of simplicity of expression I am going to use *happiness* to denote the good as thus defined and *unhappiness* to denote the evil. Now since happiness is the good, the more the better; and since unhappiness is the evil, the less the better. Therefore that act is objectively right that involves and brings about the maximum surplus of happiness over unhappiness, all people considered and in the long run. The *aim* to produce such a state is subjectively right. It would also be subjectively right conscientiously to choose a wrong ultimate ideal. The sign of objectively wrong action is the *increase* of unhappiness and the *decrease* of happiness. The *aim* to produce such an overbalance of unhappiness is subjectively wrong.

2. Invalid Standards of Right

MISTAKEN CONCEPTIONS of right are of four sorts: hypothetical, formalistic, dysdemonic, and biased eudemonic. I shall deal with each in turn.

(1) Hypothetical Theories. These deny the objectivity of duty and insist that morality always takes the form, "*If* I want X, *then* I ought to do Y"; or "*If* my group wants X, *then* the group ought to do Y." According to this view, nothing is right or wrong unless thinking makes it so, and the

thinking is simply inclination or subjective approval. Such a purely hypothetical or subjective conception of right, for example, is implied by the contention of Hobbes that moral goodness or badness is determined by each man's appetite or desire, or by the arbitrary command of the sovereign. In general, relativistic theories can be reduced to this type: they maintain that right is determined either by *individual* approval or inclination, or by *group* approval or inclination. They refuse to admit that there is any ultimate standard whereby right and wrong can be universally and objectively determined.

This subjective or relativistic view, in my opinion, is mistaken. Since "ought" denotes not merely subjective but objective rightness, there is a categorical and not merely a hypothetical element in morality. Morality depends not simply upon inclination but upon what is objectively right. It imposes claims or demands upon the individual, and these are not simply to be shirked or turned aside by saying that "I am not so inclined," or "My group is not so inclined." If I should commit a murder, I could not validly excuse myself on the plea that I or my group was so inclined, and that my action was consistent with this inclination. Kant was perfectly right in distinguishing between duty and inclination and in maintaining that a moral injunction is a categorical and not a hypothetical imperative. His mistake was simply in accepting a *formalistic* criterion for determining the categorical imperative. In a teleological ethics, such as we are outlining in this book, only that which contributes to welfare is categorically imposed. Our duty, I maintain, is to bring about the maximum surplus of happiness over unhappiness; but it really *is* our duty and not just a subjective fancy or inclination. A society that should deliberately set out to do the opposite, to maximize unhappiness and minimize happiness, would not be equally right; it would be morally deranged. Similarly a sadist is pathological, and his sadistic inclination does not make the deliberate inflic-

tion of suffering morally right. Unless we take an objective
view of morality, we are left with nothing but moral anarchy
and nihilism. We have no rational basis for objecting to
torture chambers.

(2) Formalistic Theories. Since we have discussed these
theories in Part One, we need only reaffirm our criticism. To
all such theories, we can make two objections. First, they
tend to lack driving force because they are not based upon
the consciousness of ultimate value. He who truly appreciates
goodness and strives to increase it finds that his action is
motivated by love and sympathy; whereas he who seeks
merely observance of the "moral law" may be inwardly cold,
a "Pharisee" at heart. Second, they fail to provide a reasonable objective basis for ethics. "Law for law's sake" is not
rational; and the attempt of Kant to base moral law upon the
abstract principle of noncontradiction likewise fails. I can
find no valid test of right and wrong except welfare. To the
extent that obedience to law promotes welfare, law should
be obeyed, but not otherwise. To maintain that it is absolutely always our duty to obey rule or law, even when the
results are bad, seems to me a false and mischievous doctrine.
I agree with G. E. Moore when he says:

> It seems to me to be self-evident that knowingly to do an action
> which would make the world, on the whole, really and truly
> *worse* than if he had acted differently, must always be wrong.
> And if this be admitted, then it absolutely disposes of the view
> that there are any kinds of action whatever, which it *would*
> always be our duty to do or to avoid, *whatever* the consequences
> might be.[6]

I think the acceptance of formalistic doctrines is usually
due to a deep irrational tendency in human nature to turn
means into ends. Some "practical" people, for example, are
so preoccupied with means as to mistake them for ends; they
become so enamored with "efficiency" or the "bitch god-
dess success" that they forget to be happy or to make others

6 *Ethics,* Oxford University Press, New York, 1912, p. 181.

happy. Similarly a miser covets money, which is merely a means, and treats it as an end, gloating over it for its own sake. So likewise the ethical formalist takes rules, which are merely a means, and treats them as an end, revering them for their own sake. In this, there is nothing wise, but only a form of idolatry.

(3) Dysdemonic Theories. I borrow the terms *eudemonic* and *dysdemonic* from Professor F. C. Sharp's *Ethics.* He defines a "eudemonic" standard as that which "approves conduct for its good effects and disapproves it for its harmful effects." In contrast, the "dysdemonic" standard "reverses the relationship of good and harm found in the first, in that it approves of doing harm and disapproves of doing good to one who has wronged another, not as a means to some further end, such as the protection of society, . . . but as an end in itself."[7] Such a standard is accepted by all those who maintain that enemies or criminals or "bad men" should be made to suffer, not because it will help them or society, but because they "have it coming to them."

The dysdemonic standard is very widely accepted, especially during a war or fierce struggle when the impulse to retaliate is strong. It has had a profound influence upon our whole system of criminal justice: it helps to explain the barbarous conditions that prevail in most of the prisons of the world. It inspires the plots of innumerable plays, novels, and moving pictures in which the "villains" are killed or severely chastised, to the evident satisfaction of the readers or the audience. It is explicitly defended by such sophisticated philosophers as Kant and Hegel, who maintain that criminals should be punished regardless of whether it helps them or society. On the other hand, it is rejected by the character Socrates in the first book of Plato's *Republic,* in which he maintains that it is wrong to harm anyone, friend or foe; and it is contrary to Christ's injunction to return good for evil.

[7] *Ethics,* Century, New York, 1928, p. 33.

Unquestionably it is plausible to maintain that good men are more deserving of happiness than bad men, and that bad men are more deserving of unhappiness than good men, and that we should therefore aim at a "just" distribution of happiness and unhappiness, rewarding the virtuous and punishing the wicked. Even God has supposedly been motivated in this way, elevating good men into a never-ending heaven and casting bad men into a never-ceasing hell.

Now the standard of right that we have adopted condemns such gratuitous increase of misery in any circumstances. It maintains that *everybody* should be made as happy as possible in so far as this is consistent with the happiness of others. This standard, however, does not *wholly* condemn rewards and punishments. If moral goodness is rewarded with happiness, goodness will be encouraged, and men will tend more often to serve their fellows; and if moral badness is punished by unhappiness, badness will be discouraged, and men will tend less often to injure their fellows. Hence if there is no better alternative, punishment will be justified.

But the word *punishment,* as most people understand it, does not mean preventive and remedial penalty for the purpose of maximizing welfare. It means suffering deliberately imposed upon "bad men" because they "deserve" it. In *this* sense of the word, *punishment* should be completely expunged from our moral code. It is a relic of primitive moral systems, such as "an eye for an eye, a tooth for a tooth." It is often the expression of malevolent impulses such as revenge and sadism. Its effect is to decrease human welfare.

What we really need is not "punishment" but "treatment." Just as a physician must sometimes inflict suffering for the sake of health, so a judge must sometimes inflict suffering for the sake of welfare. In Samuel Butler's satirical utopia, *Erewhon,* physicians of the mind, called "straighteners," deal with crime in this way, trying impartially to understand and eliminate its causes rather than to make people suffer. This attitude is sometimes adopted in our society toward juvenile delinquents, and in consequence, considerable progress has been made. In some cases, the treatment has resulted from a careful scientific study. The child's difficulties have been expertly diagnosed as a result of searching investigation and analysis of his intelligence, physical disabilities, character traits, psychological conflicts and abnormalities, and the manifold aspects of his environment. Upon the basis of the knowledge thus gleaned, a prescription—as scientific as a physician's prescription—is written out for his care, and this prescription by no means always advocates "punishment." Painstaking study is made of the effectiveness of the treatment thus prescribed, and a different treatment is undertaken if the first fails. This procedure employs the manifold resources of social, psychological, and medical science and brings great benefit to both the individual and society. It seems to me that such humane and scientific methods should be extended not only to all youthful offenders but also to adults. We should endeavor scientifically to discover the causes of crime, both in the individual case and in society at large, and we should carry out a well-considered plan for the elimination of crime and the reformation of the criminal. The effect of this rational approach, I am confident, would be greatly to increase the sum of human happiness; and in the long run it would be far less expensive even financially than our present crude methods of dealing with crime.

(4) Biased Eudemonic Theories. Doctrines of this type recognize, within limits, that the proper standard of right action is the increase of welfare, but they all exhibit a preference for a narrow spread of good (as, for example, egoism, racialism, nationalism, etc.). Such doctrines are extremely common and are often followed when they are not openly advocated. It is only the rare man who lives according to a universalist standard; and even he, being human, does not always do so.

I have already touched in Chapters Five and Seven upon the need for a universalist rather than a constricted standard of welfare. In view of the social importance of the topic, however, it is well to dwell upon it at greater length, particularly in connection with the meaning of right and wrong social action.

A narrow standard of welfare is to be condemned because, being narrow, it makes us sacrifice the greater good. In practice, moreover, favor toward a limited group is very often combined with *disfavor* toward those "outside the pale." A narrow eudemonic standard is combined with a dysdemonic standard. For example, racism ordinarily means that one not only favors the members of one's own "race," but that one tramples upon the members of the "inferior races." Similarly bias in favor of one's own nation is often combined with bias *against* other nations; or bias in favor of one's class or caste is combined with bias *against* other classes or castes. Hence group wars with group, cause with cause, loyalty with loyalty.

So common is this pattern of conflict that Carl Schmitt, a German political scientist, has argued that all political relationships are organized upon this basis.

The essential political distinction is that between *friend* and *foe*. It gives to human actions and motives their political significance. All political actions and motives can be traced back ultimately to this distinction.[8]

Upon this basis, he regards conflict and even war as the normal and inevitable expression of political and social relationships. There is no universal norm or impartial standard, Schmitt insists, whereby such conflicts, if extreme, can be resolved, and hence, "a World State, comprising the totality of human beings, is an impossibility," and "the political domain is a pluriverse, not a universe."[9]

Now this sort of view has not only been very prevalent but has led to some very nasty social behavior, which reached its climax in World War II. Especially among the fascists

8 *Der Begriff des Politischen,* Hanseatische Verlags-Anstalt, Hamburg, 1933, p. 7.

9 *Ibid.,* pp. 35-36.

and nazis but also among many like-minded people in our own ranks, there was a fanatical assertion of the ideal of "ourselves alone." The Occidental and the Oriental, the Gentile and the Jew, the white man and the black, the *Herrenvolk* and the vassal races, were sharply distinguished, the one eulogized and exalted, the other despised, tortured, and even murdered.

Applied to the various spheres of culture, such tribalism has involved the most intolerant doctrines. The German people, for example, were told that there is an exclusively "Aryan" physics, mathematics, history, anthropology, a peculiarly "Aryan" art, music, literature, a distinctively "Aryan" law, morals, religion—and that no non-Aryan culture is truly valuable or important. In Italy and Japan, likewise, the idea of a universal humanity was renounced in favor of racial and nationalistic bias.

This strategy of hatred, with its intolerant culture and its fantastic myths, served the purposes of the fascist demagogues: to divert the masses from the real causes of their woe, to foster a sense of national solidarity by cultivating herd-mindedness and hatred of all "alien" groups, to prepare the minds of the people for a campaign of war and violence, and to inspire the hope among innumerable victims of the Great Depression that the "destruction of the enemy" would prove a social panacea. Insecurity, unemployment, poverty, and international strife provide the soil in which these pathological attitudes flourish.

When we turn to the democratic nations, there are many whose position is, in spirit, not so very different from the fascist. Our cities swarm with anti-Semites; the defenders of "white supremacy" are to be numbered in the millions; during the war and even the postwar period, we have frequently heard the Japanese denounced as "yellow." The average American, if told that the Puerto Ricans are starving, shrugs his shoulders and turns to matters of "real" concern.

Nationalistic and racial bias has clearly not been confined

to the fascist countries. It can be shown historically that nationalism has grown more and more intense in almost every country, and that imperialism, with its cruel exploitation of subject races, is a well-nigh universal phase in the development of modern capitalism. The slogans that have led to bloody conflict are all too familiar: "Britannia rules the waves!" "Deutschland über alles!" "France d'abord!" "America first!" "My country, right or wrong!" The fascists carried these tendencies to mad extremes of sadism and xenophobia, yet we need to pluck the motes from our own eyes and to see how deeply the cancer of racialism and nationalism has eaten into the healthy tissue of the democratic organism.

Among the great thinkers of the nineteenth century, Karl Marx devoted especial attention to the problem of conflicting group loyalties. He believed that history is largely the record of bitter antagonisms: the conflicts between rich and poor, freeman and slave, ruler and ruled, exploiter and exploited, "master race" and subject peoples, manual and intellectual labor, town and country, man and woman. He maintained that the root conflict is the struggle between the economic oppressors and the oppressed, and that this conflict is, in our age, based upon the ownership of the means of production by private individuals. Until this conflict is resolved by the establishment of a classless society, with social ownership of the means of production, the derivative antagonisms are bound to remain. So long as the basic economic conflict is unresolved, there cannot be a united mankind, because there can be no real cooperation between master and subject, exploiter and exploited. I shall not undertake at this stage to evaluate Marx's argument; but we can at least grant that economic conflict is *very* fundamental, and that class bias is not less important than racial and nationalistic bias.

To such forms of group bias must be added the individual bias of egoism: the preference for "myself alone." I call this an "individual bias," but it is fostered by a competitive social order, and it is comparatively rare in such highly cooperative societies as the Pueblos and Arapesh among primitive peoples or in such friendly groups as the Quakers among more civilized people. The findings of sociology and anthropology conclusively prove that selfishness is not an unalterable human trait, and that its intensity varies with social conditions. It is far less acute and frequent in an essentially cooperative, as contrasted with a ruthlessly competitive, society.

Egoism, therefore, is difficult but not impossible to avoid. Every man is, in a sense, the center of his own little world—he lives within his own skin, sees with his own eyes, feels with his own feelings. Unless we suppose that he has the power of mind reading, he never *directly* experiences anyone's values but his own. He sees the *symptoms* of someone's happiness, and this may make him happy, but he never directly enjoys another person's happiness. This fact has led some writers to defend egoism. Since each of us is in the "egocentric predicament," why should any person bother with anyone's good but his own?

As we have seen, however, people are not only selfish but social. Sympathy is a basic fact of human life; love, according to many psychologists, is the root impulse of life. These emotions break down the walls between human beings and thus are the great solvents of conflict and selfishness. "Love consists in this," Rainer Maria Rilke has written, "that two solitudes protect and touch and greet each other."[10] To this extent people *do* transcend the egocentric predicament.

As an ethical theory, moreover, egoism is essentially contradictory. It maintains that *each* man's good is the *sole* good; but since there are many men, this is to assert that there are *many* sole goods—which is an absolute contradiction.[11] If I expect other men to recognize *my* good, moreover,

[10] Quoted by Walter De La Mare in *Love,* Morrow, New York, 1946, p. 11.
[11] *Cf.* G. E. Moore, *Principia Ethica,* Cambridge University Press, Cambridge, 1922, p. 99.

it is equally incumbent upon me to recognize *their* good. If my good ought to be promoted, by the same token their good ought to be promoted. Good, being good, ought to be promoted, wherever possible. This appears unreasonable only when we *are* overmastered by selfishness. As we expand our sympathies, as we attain a livelier appreciation of the weal and woe of others, it seems more and more unreasonable to harden our hearts and to confine our ethical aspirations within the narrow limits of selfhood.

The reasonable way to avoid selfishness is not to crush or harass the self, but to expand it until the good of oneself and others coincide. A man should not despise himself but should have wide and vivid interests in what is not himself. As Spinoza maintained, a man is as great as his interests, and mere self-seeking, because it narrows the range of interests, impoverishes the self. The problem of social control, in great measure, is to eliminate the conflict between self-interest and social interest. This is to be done by changing both the self and society: by making society more cooperative, and the individual more altruistic and far-ranging in his interests.

Just as there is nothing wrong with self-interest if it is not a barrier to social interest, so there is nothing wrong with group interest if it is not an obstacle to still wider interests. Indeed, the rich and multifarious growth of human associations, with all the various forms of love and loyalty that they evoke, is a prime requirement of any vital civilization. It is only when group loyalty turns into group egoism, or worse still, into group aggressiveness, that it is immoral. What we need, as Josiah Royce maintained, is loyalty that is deeply tolerant, loyalty that respects the loyalties of others, loyalty that is thus "loyal to loyalty."[12]

The basic moral issue of our times is whether we believe in the widest possible community of human beings, recognizing their common destiny and cultivating their common

12 *Cf., The Philosophy of Loyalty,* Macmillan, New York, 1909, especially Chapter III.

humanity; or whether we believe only in rootless, isolated, private individuals, struggling in a disorganic system of devil-take-the-hindmost; or again whether we believe only in a multiplicity of races and nations and classes, warring against one another in meaningless strife.

3. *The Moral Task—The Choice and the Integration of Values*

I AM PLEADING for more order and less anarchy. The essence of the moral task is the achievement of a more inclusive and harmonious integration of interests, so that impulse will no longer war with impulse, or individual with individual, or group with group. As Ralph Barton Perry has said:

The moral drama opens only when interest meets interest; when the path of one unit of life is crossed by that of another. Every interest is compelled to recognize other interests, on the one hand as parts of its environment, and on the other hand as partners in the general enterprise of life. Thus there is evolved the *moral idea,* or principle of action, according to which *interest allies itself with interest in order to be free-handed and powerful* against the common hereditary enemy, the heavy inertia and incessant wear of the cosmos. Through morality a plurality of interests becomes an *economy,* or *community of interest.* . . . The fulfillment of a simple isolated interest is good, but only *the fulfillment of an organization of interests is morally good.* . . . Moral principles define the adjustment of interest to interest, for the saving of each and the strengthening of both against failure and death. Morality is only the method of carrying on the affair of life beyond a certain point of complexity. It is the method of concerted, cumulative living, through which interests are brought from a doubtful condition of being tolerated by the cosmos, to a condition of security and confidence. The spring and motive of morality are therefore absolutely one with those of life.[13]

Morality does not exist for a being that does not experience the hazard and adventure of living. A static being such

[13] *The Moral Economy,* Scribner's, New York, 1909, pp. 13, 15, 19.

as Aristotle's God—an eternal being eternally thinking his eternal thoughts—cannot be moral, because he is not confronted by choice. It is the temporal and on-going character of life that poses problems: our existence is charged with moral concern because we must look before and after. We ponder the lessons of the past, we choose with an eye to the future, we consider the interests of our neighbors, so that conflicts and incompatibilities can be resolved by a working harmony.

Choice is made much simpler for us by the fact that we live in an organized society, with customs, rules, laws, and institutions based upon long and varied experience. That kindness is better than unkindness; that lying is a poor practice; that one ought not to steal; that one ought in general to keep one's promises—these and kindred conceptions we imbibe in childhood. As we grow older, we become aware that certain sources of happiness have been accepted by the common sense of mankind; that such goods as health, security, knowledge, freedom, love, beauty, and fine workmanship are, by common consent, the principal sources of human happiness; and that their opposites, ill health, insecurity, ignorance, tyranny, hate, ugliness, and drudgery, are, by common consent, the principal sources of unhappiness. In addition, we can deepen and extend this table of values by reflecting upon the opinions of ancient thinkers and recent experts.

Nevertheless, we ourselves must choose among various and conflicting values. Every value is subject to criticism in the light of its intrinsic merit and its consistency or inconsistency with other values. How shall we determine which values are choiceworthy? What are the principles whereby we may construct our moral economy?

One of the classical attempts to answer such questions is to be found in the "hedonic calculus" of Jeremy Bentham. The intrinsic value of a pleasure or pain, he maintained, is determined by its intensity and duration. If a *future* pleasure or pain is to be considered, we must add its certainty or uncertainty and its propinquity or remoteness. If, in addition, we wish to consider the *consequences* of a pleasure or pain, we must calculate two other factors: first, its "fecundity" (that is, the likelihood that the pleasure will be followed by more pleasure, or the pain by more pain), and, second, its "purity" (that is, the freedom of a pleasure from subsequent pain, and of a pain from subsequent pleasure). Finally, if we are considering an action affecting a group of individuals, we must consider the number of persons who will experience pleasure or pain. Bentham summed up his advice in a little ditty:

> Intense, long, certain, speedy, fruitful, pure—
> Such marks in pleasures and in pains endure.
> Such pleasures seek if private be thy end:
> If it be public, let them wide extend.
> Such pains avoid whatever be thy view;
> If pains must come, let them extend to few.[14]

He proposed to calculate the worth of action in terms of all the plus values in way of pleasure and all the minus values in way of pain, subtracting the latter from the former.

Bentham's "calculus" has frequently been attacked as impractical; and no doubt it is impossible to calculate with arithmetical precision the surplus of pleasure over pain or of pain over pleasure resulting from any act. But we can often judge that one pleasure (or pain) is greater in duration or intensity than another, and we can roughly estimate the consequences that will ensue. Some such weighing of values and consequences is required for any teleological ethics, and Bentham at least deserves credit for recognizing the nature of the problem and trying to solve it.

If we should attempt to formulate standards not for a hedonistic ethics such as Bentham's but for an ethics based upon the broader concept of the cultivation and fulfillment

---

[14] *Principles of Morals and Legislation,* Hafner, New York, 1948, p. 28. I have omitted italics that appear in the original.

of interests, our problem is even more complex. Nevertheless, the following standards are suggested:

(1) The Standard of Duration. President Charles W. Eliot of Harvard University was fond of the phrase, "the durable satisfactions of life." He was pointing to an important standard—the temporal span of value.

Other things remaining equal, satisfactions or enjoyments that are durable—that do not, for example, quickly turn to the dust and ashes of boredom—are to be preferred; and the interests that yield such satisfactions are to be cultivated. Such interests are those that are deeply based, that express major rather than minor cravings, and that are supplied with the instrumentalities necessary for their realization and maintenance. An interest that is superficial or unrealistic soon lapses or turns to aversion.

(2) The Standard of Intensity. Other things remaining equal, the more intense enjoyments and satisfactions are to be preferred to the less intense. Intensities cannot be exactly measured, but we can sometimes confidently say that one enjoyment is more intense than another, and still more intense than a third. They can thus be ranked in an order of intensive magnitudes, each separated from the next in the hierarchy by some noticeable difference.

Just as profound interests generally yield more durable enjoyments, so they likewise yield more intense enjoyments. When such fundamental interests are frustrated, the resulting misery is correspondingly intense and prolonged. We already have enough psychological data, gathered by such psychologists as Freud, Adler, Hamilton, Murray, Hollingworth, and Tolman, to conclude that certain interests are extremely fundamental, and that these include the interest in love and friendship, in security, in productive occupation, in constructive expression of one's talents, in status and good repute, in freedom of expression, and in a considerable variety of stimulation. To realize intense happiness, and to avoid intense unhappiness, it is particularly important to satisfy major cravings.

(3) The Standard of Quality. John Stuart Mill invoked this standard when he maintained that some kinds of pleasure are preferable to others quite apart from the question of intensity or duration. We have already pointed out certain inconsistencies in Mill's argument, but what now concerns us is simply the contention that qualitatively higher enjoyments are to be preferred to qualitatively lower.

In judging quality, we must distinguish between the preferred and the preferable. There are passionate and irrational cravings, such as masochistic and sadistic desires, that are not objective measures or determinants of value-quality. "To crave that which is harmful," as Erich Fromm has said, "is the very essence of mental sickness."[15] The preferences of a diseased, superficial, or ignorant mind are not necessarily indicative of higher quality. Any preference, since it is a form of interest, involves *some* value, but not necessarily a value that is choiceworthy or morally permissible; nor is the *object* of that preference, if it be itself an intrinsic value, necessarily of a qualitatively superior or choiceworthy type.

How then can we judge what is qualitatively superior? This is a difficult question. It may be that the standard of quality will turn out, upon adequate analysis, to be ultimately reducible to quantitative standards, such as intensity. Nevertheless, it is a widely held belief that certain types of satisfactions and enjoyments, such as the values of art, of science, of philosophy, of religion, of love and friendship, are qualitatively higher than purely bodily or sensual enjoyments. Perhaps the main justification for this belief is that the "higher" values represent the mind as a whole, and thus more nearly express the essence and totality of a man's personality, whereas the "lower" values are less rich, complex, full-bodied, integral to the whole self, resonant of every corner of the personality. For example love, at its best, is

15 *Man for Himself,* Rinehart, New York, p. 179.

not only an intense sensuous experience but an emotional, imaginative, and intellectual experience as well, and hence it concentrates within it the flavor of the whole personality, whereas mere physical lust, though perhaps yielding enjoyment as intense, expresses only one isolated side of a man's nature, his bodily appetite. It is this kind of standard that DeWitt Parker has in mind when he declares:

That interest is higher which is a better representative of the value of the self as a whole, giving to the whole what the whole wants. The claim of any one of the major interests to be superior to the others can be established, therefore, only by showing that it is more adequate to the value of the self as a whole.[16]

If this be correct, the higher interest is the more inclusive, expressing a larger segment of the self or even the self as a whole. Inclusiveness might appear to be purely quantitative, and therefore reducible to the quantitative standards of duration, intensity, and number. But when we examine the higher values, such as love or beauty, there seems to be a qualitative difference, too. This matter of quality is very difficult to analyze, and the interpretation I have suggested is purely tentative.

(4) The Standard of Number. Other things remaining equal, an aggregate of many values is better than an aggregate of few values. In general, a life in which there are many joys is better than a life in which there are few joys, and a society in which there are many happy people is better than a society in which there are few happy people.

One of the implications of this standard is that one should prefer concordant rather than discordant interests. The effect of discord is to decrease the number of enjoyments and increase the number of miseries. As Bertrand Russell has wittily remarked, love is better than murder because love suits both parties whereas murder suits only one. Selfish, greedy, predatory, sadistic, or intemperate interests breed conflict, whereas unselfish, generous, noncompetitive, and temperate

16 *Human Values,* Harper, New York, 1931, p. 97.

interests produce harmony. Moreover, costly social conflicts should be avoided; from the standpoint of internal harmony, the best of all groups is the community in which the good of each is the good of all.

Another implication of the standard of number is that the good things of life should be extended to as many people as possible. This means that wide democratic sharing is better than narrow exclusiveness. To try to increase happiness by lavishing attention upon one or a few members of a community when all the members might be cultivated is very much like trying to grow a bumper crop of wheat by cultivating one acre when a hundred acres might be cultivated.

(5) *The Standard of Fruitfulness.* Values must be judged not only in terms of their immediate worth but in terms of their instrumental value, or fruitfulness in producing future values or disvalues. Upon this basis, certain external goods, which are of little or no value intrinsically, may be judged choiceworthy. This consideration, for example, justifies us in putting a great deal of emphasis upon the basic essentials of life, such as food, clothing, and shelter. As Helen Lynd has remarked: "Decent food and decent housing do not give men spiritual life, but they are a better basis for it than starvation."[17] For similar reasons, health and good education deserve great emphasis, because without them men are fettered in all their pursuits. The first charge upon any society should be to supply these five essentials to its citizens—food, housing, clothing, health services, education. Similarly fundamental is the achievement of an economic and social system that will avoid the terrible waste of economic depression and war and that will yield every man, woman, and child security against poverty and reasonable opportunity for the pursuit of happiness.

In considering instrumental values, we must take account of the factor of risk. In general, the more probable satisfac-

---

[17] *England in the Eighteen-Eighties,* Oxford University Press, New York, 1945, p. 424.

tions and enjoyments are to be preferred to the less probable. Therefore, we must ask, to what extent is it probable that the future values that we aim to achieve will actually be realized. This consideration justifies a certain preference for values near us in time and space, because temporal and spatial distance renders more obscure and uncertain the effects of our actions. But there is a marked tendency in human nature to overrate this factor—the bias in favor of the near is one of the most mischievous forms of bias. For example, like spendthrift children, Americans have denuded forests, exhausted soil, and wasted mineral supplies to the tune of colossal loss. One of the main values of social planning, especially if based upon the careful estimates provided by social scientists, is that it can greatly reduce such waste.

As we have seen, values may differ as more or less durable, more or less intense, more or less high in quality, more or less numerous, and more or less fruitful. It is difficult to assess the worth of alternatives in terms of any or all of these standards, and more difficult to balance these standards against one another. Indeed, the latter problem, how to compare standards, is very difficult indeed. For example, let us suppose that we are considering which of three alternatives to choose when the first is preferable in terms of the standard of intensity; the second, in terms of the standard of duration; and the third, in terms of the standard of quality. How can we compare these standards and decide which should be given priority in the given situation? Much would depend, of course, upon the extent to which each alternative is superior or inferior to the others in respect to each standard. If one alternative, for example, is *greatly* superior in intensity and *very slightly* inferior in duration and quality, it would seem to be, so far as these three criteria are concerned, the best alternative. But if there is no such decisive superiority in favor of any one alternative, and each is superior in some different respect, it may be impossible to choose upon the basis of any clear or rational grounds. In these circumstances we might as well flip a coin. I would like to say much more about the problem, but it is so difficult and involved that I have chosen not to discuss it except in this brief paragraph.

If the worth of alternatives is hard to assess for a single life, it is even harder to assess for the many lives that comprise a society. Social morality is a subtle and difficult art that cannot be reduced to rote; yet if men take time and care, they can at least make their choices much more intelligent and, on the average, much more fruitful of good consequences.

REVIEW OF PART TWO

In part one, I maintained that the ethics of formal laws is inadequate and that the appeal to ideals and consequences is ethically necessary. In Part Two, I have examined the ethics of ideals.

This kind of ethics, which I have called "teleological," maintains that actions are right in proportion as they tend to promote intrinsic goodness, wrong in proportion as they tend to promote intrinsic evil. It seeks to define intrinsic goodness and intrinsic evil and to determine the best means to promote the good and curtail the evil.

There are various theories of what is intrinsically good. The relativist denies any universal good; the absolutist asserts that the good is not only universal but eternally fixed. The extreme individualist seeks the good in the self-sufficient individual; the extreme collectivist regards the group or society as intrinsically good. The intellectualist finds the good in reason; the hedonist, in pleasure; the voluntarist, in desire or will. Or, seeking a broader psychological conception of goodness, some philosophers find the good in interest or its objects. I have explored these various interpretations.

In Chapter Five, I have examined the contention of relativism, that goodness has no universal import—that it varies from time to time and from place to place. Such a theory is at the opposite pole from absolutism, which maintains that ethical standards are unconditional and invariable.

Relativism has been most prevalent in periods of conflict, such as the age of the Sophists or the present age of crisis. Ancient relativism is represented by Protagoras, who taught that each man or group is "the measure of all things," or by the more radical Thrasymachus, who maintained that justice is merely "the interest of the stronger." Among modern relativists, Pareto and Westermarck have maintained that ethical concepts rest upon variable "sentiments" or "emotions" without rational justification. But, like many relativists, Westermarck is inconsistent and admits an element of impartiality in moral judgment.

In attacking the nonempirical premises and implications of absolutism, relativism joins forces with science and liberalism. Its weakness is that it denies all objective basis for human norms and thus cuts the heart out of ethics.

To avoid the extremes of both absolutism and relativism, we should combine the old and the new, the spirit of change and the spirit of conservation, the enduring ideal and its variable applications. Similarly, we should combine particularism and universalism, catholicity and local patriotism, world citizenship and regionalism, loyalty to the great state and loyalty to the small community.

There is a basis in human nature for this "union of opposites." Human beings are neither utterly changeable nor completely fixed and static; they are neither merely alike nor merely different. They share basic needs, but they express them in different ways. World unity is imperative in an age of scientific warfare; but there is no possibility of achieving unity without a recognition of common needs and legitimate differences.

In Chapter Six, I have discussed the question: Does intrinsic goodness occur in the individual or in the group? Individualists sometimes point out that there can be no intrinsic value apart from interest (feeling, emotion, desire, will, or some similar attitude of prizing or disprizing), and that the locus of interest, and hence of intrinsic value, is always the individual. In contrast, ethical collectivists, such as Rousseau, contend that a group may have a collective interest quite different from a mere sum of individual interests, and that the fulfillment of this interest constitutes a distinct good that is not the sum of individual goods.

Hobbes is a representative of extreme ethical individualism. He maintained that man's fundamental nature is egocentric, that societies are "artificial bodies" designed to aid or protect individuals, and that the state is essentially a contrivance to avoid the suicidal anarchy of man's natural condition. On his view, the locus of value is the self-seeking individual.

Hegel is an example of an extreme ethical collectivist. He believed that the supreme values of life are social, that the freedom of the individual is to be attained only through participation in society, and that the family, the church, the state, or any similar coherent group is a kind of social organism with intrinsic value.

I have argued that we should avoid both an exaggerated individualism such as that of Hobbes and an exaggerated collectivism such as that of Hegel. In formulating an alternative view, I define the various grades of integration and distinguish between the ones that characterize human groups and the ones that do not. The following grades are noteworthy: (1) Mere adjacency in time and space, as in the case of an accidental and heterogeneous collection. (2) External association, which occurs when things are grouped together not because they are related to one another but because they are all related to something outside of the group. (3) Mechanical interdependence, in which there is a functional interaction of parts, but in which the parts are not *essentially* altered as a consequence of this interaction. (4) Organic interdependence, in which there is not only an interaction of parts, but in which the essential characteristics of the parts are altered by the interaction. (5) Existential interdependence, in which the parts depend upon one another not only for their essential characteristics but for their very existence.

(6) Configurational unity, in which the parts are not merely interdependent but are determined by the character of the whole. (7) Biological unity, in which there is a single unity, the *life* of the whole, which is the end of its parts. (8) Psychological unity, in which this vital unity attains the level of consciousness.

By reference to these integrative levels, we can expose the main fallacies of both extreme individualism and extreme collectivism. Extreme individualism interprets groups in terms of mere adjacency or external association or mechanical interdependence, to the neglect or exclusion of higher types of unity, and it thus exaggerates the independence of individuals. Extreme collectivism, on the other hand, attributes to human groups the most intense forms of integration. Some of the higher levels—organic interdependence, existential interdependence, and configurational unity—really do apply to some human groups; but other more intense forms of integration—namely, biological and psychological unity—do not so apply, and extreme collectivism commits a fundamental mistake in supposing that a group is literally a living organism or a mind.

But if a group cannot literally have a mind, it cannot possess intrinsic value. There can be no intrinsic value where there is no interest and no interest where there is no mind. Hence the locus of intrinsic value is in the individual and not in the group. But the real individual is a profoundly social being, and it is he, and not his mythical counterpart, the pure egoist, that is the locus of value.

In Chapter Seven, I have examined some of the classical theories of welfare and have analyzed, in particular, the relation of welfare to interest. Wherever there are interests, there are values; but we would commit "the naturalistic fallacy" if we should simply *identify* value with interest. To avoid this mistake, we must distinguish between *psychological* nonindifference—namely, interest—and *ethical* nonindifference—namely, oughtness. However, it is psychological nonindifference that *makes* anything ethically nonindifferent. Positive interest *ought to be* and, in that sense, is good.

Intrinsic value, in the strict sense, attaches to the interest and not to the object of interest. For example, it is the enjoyment that I get from candy, and not the candy, that is intrinsically good. To generalize, we can say that human welfare can be found in the cultivation and fulfillment of positive interests (states of liking) and human misery in negative interests (states of disliking) and the frustration of positive interests.

A man's personality has three fundamental sides: cognitive, affective, and volitional. What is the relation of interest and value to each?

Aristotle is the classic exponent of cognitive values. He maintained that the supreme good is the life of reason, corresponding to man's essentially rational nature. He divided the good into two parts: first, moral goodness, which is the guidance of appetite by reason, and, second, intellectual goodness, which is the free exercise of reason for its own sake. The first is exhibited in the wise choice of the golden mean, the second, in the noble cultivation of science and philosophy.

Aristotle was mistaken in supposing that reason is exclusive to man, since chimpanzees, for example, also exhibit intelligence. It is true that reason in its higher forms is exclusively human, but so are the higher forms of love and religion and art. Moreover, goodness does not reside, as Aristotle supposed, in the exclusively human, but in the part of human nature that is the locus of value, whether distinctively human or not. That part is interest; and reason, although it qualifies interest, does not constitute its core. Without intellectual judgment, however, life would not be distinguished from madness; and knowledge is one of the supreme objects of interest. Although reason is indispensable, no man would choose a life of mere intellectual activity.

Hedonists, such as Epicurus and Bentham, maintain that pleasure alone is intrinsically good. To evaluate this contention, we need to consider the relation of pleasure to interest. It is a form of interest, but interest also includes judgment, emotion, and volition. Moreover, pleasure is not the only object of interest. Indeed, there is a great deal else that people desire. But ethical hedonists may still insist that pleasure is the only object of *reflective* desire. Men want sanity, however, and they want love, beauty, knowledge, and other substantial goods, *even when they carefully reflect.*

Since pleasure is not the only form of interest or the only object of interest or even the only object of reflective interest, I believe that hedonism is too narrow in its conception of the nature of goodness.

An extreme voluntarism, such as that of Nietzsche and Schopenhauer, is likewise too narrow. Much more adequate is Spinoza's conception of welfare as primarily based upon volition but as involving the fulfillment of man's whole being. It is only when desire is thus broadly conceived as including intellectual, hedonic, and emotional factors that it may properly be called the basis and content of value. But desire, so described, can best be termed interest.

The fulfillment of the personality, as a dynamic focus of interests, involves feeling and emotion, volition, and intellect; but it also requires the support and cooperation of physical and subconscious levels. The norm of human welfare thus becomes the complete physiological and psychological health of the personality.

Our social ideal should be the development of *total* persons united in a culturally rich community. Personality and community are essential to one another: personality shrivels into nothingness when separated from community, and community evaporates into monotony when its component personalities are stultified. Self-realization, the good of the individual personality, and justice, the basic value of the community, thus tend to be interdependent. But we should avoid the mistake of Plato, whose conception of social justice is too static. Our ideal should be a dynamic equilibrium, combining integration and progress. The best social order is most efficacious in cultivating and fulfilling human interests, not only immediately but in the long run.

Having thus answered the question, "What is the nature of a good society?", I return in Chapter Eight to our other basic question, "What is right social action?"

We cannot answer this question without an interpretation of the *ought*. Following the lead of Adam Smith and David Hume, I have interpreted obligation as both a social and a rational demand: the pressure of the social ego regulated by intelligence.

The social aspect of obligation primarily explains the *feeling* of moral compulsion. Innumerable social attitudes and emotions, such as sympathy, leave their traces upon the mind; and, by a gradual process of accretion and fusion, these traces unite to form the social ego. Under appropriate stimulus, this ego exerts internal pressure felt as obligation. The pull of society thus becomes internalized as a sense of duty.

But obligation as a psychological event is distinct from obligation as a moral fact. To say that a person *ought* to act in a certain way is not the same as to say that he *feels* like so acting. Duty as an objective moral fact may exist in the absence of such internal pressure, and we may act wrongly even when we act conscientiously. Reason must intervene, therefore, to broaden and regulate our sense of obligation and correct our moral biases.

The sense of being morally well-intentioned I call "subjective rightness," and the *fact* that the alternative chosen is morally best I call "objective rightness." *Ought* and *right* when thus interpreted express the rational demand for moral objectivity, and not simply the subjective feeling of obligation. This demand for objectivity is ultimately based upon the self-evident ethical principle that good, being good, ought to be maximized and that evil, being evil, ought to be minimized. Social action is objectively right if it brings about the maximum surplus of good over evil (defining these terms as we have in Chapter Seven).

Invalid standards of right are of four sorts: hypothetical, formalistic, dysdemonic, and biased eudemonic. (1) Hypothetical theories deny the objectivity of duty and insist that *ought* always depends upon inclination—a merely subjective choice of ends. (2) Formalistic theories, which were criticized in Part One, interpret right nonteleologically as mere obedience to "moral laws." (3) Dysdemonic theories assert that enemies or criminals or "bad men" should be made to suffer because they "deserve it." (4) Biased eudemonic theories, such as egoism, racialism, and nationalism, exhibit a preference for a narrow spread of good. Opposing all of these invalid standards, I have advanced an unbiased eudemonic standard —the universalist standard of maximum welfare.

The essence of the moral task is to achieve the most welfare through an inclusive and harmonious integration of interests. A teleological morality consists in the cultivation of such a moral economy, whether for a single life or for the many lives that comprise a society.

The elements in this moral economy are satisfactions of interest, and the more choiceworthy of these satisfactions are the more durable, intense, high in quality, numerous, and fruitful. I have discussed these grounds of choice and have pointed out how difficult it is to decide which should be given priority in the event of conflict. Yet we can make our personal decisions and social policies much more intelligent if we take time and care and do not act blindly.

We have now defined the meaning of a good society and right social action. It is time to turn to a more concrete delineation of social ideals.

Part Three

SOCIAL IDEALS

INTRODUCTION TO PART THREE

In part two, we have surveyed various interpretations of welfare, and we have concluded that it consists essentially in the cultivation and fulfillment of interests, evaluated both quantitatively and qualitatively. The ultimate test of any social order is its efficacy in promoting such happiness among its members. (When I use the word *happiness,* of course, I am employing it to denote the good as I have defined it in Part Two.)

The test of happiness is to be applied not only to the social order as a whole but to its main parts. An economy, or polity, or legal system that unnecessarily thwarts interests—that favors the interests of the few rather than the interests of the many, that realizes the lesser happiness when it might realize the greater—cannot, in these respects, be justified.

Let us consider, as an illustration, the question of the proper balance between work and leisure. Up to a certain point, the longer the working day, the greater will be the volume of goods and services; but the advantages that would accrue from this increased production must be balanced against the disadvantages that would result from diminished leisure. To maximize welfare, men should work as long as each added increment of work would increase the total surplus of happiness over unhappiness, but they should cease work when they have reached the point at which an added increment of work would diminish rather than increase this surplus. In practice, it might be impossible to determine with any degree of exactitude whether the men in a certain industry should work eight hours, or more, or less; but the principle for judging the issue is clear and would serve to guide social policy.

If we deal not with a single issue such as the proper length of the working day but with the evaluation of a comprehensive social ideal, the problem is much more complicated. But the *principle* for determining social policy remains the same: How can we maximize welfare? We must ask, in other words, what kind of social order *is* best fitted to cultivate and fulfill human interests. The answers currently given to this question differ fundamentally, and the differences depend in great measure upon competing sets of values. A communist and a liberal, for example, differ in their interpretations of freedom, in their estimates of equality, and in their conceptions of the state as an instrument of social policy. Most of these differences probably resolve themselves into questions of means, but some of the differences may involve questions of ends or ultimate goals.

Social intelligence depends upon our capacity to know both the proper goals of our social order and how we ought to seek them. It is unlikely that we can avoid catastrophe in this supremely critical period of history if we have no clear objectives or well-conceived plans.

In Part Three, I shall briefly examine a few of the principal ideals of a social order—aristocracy, democracy, liberalism, fascism, and socialism—so as to suggest some of the main problems that confront us in this difficult age of crisis and reconstruction. The questions discussed will be of the greatest practical importance—about as important as any questions can be. I believe, however, that we can best resolve these questions if we consider them calmly and impartially. The intense fervor of partisanship, although at times morally commendable, is not usually conducive to philosophical inquiry.

Chapter Nine

THE ARISTOCRATIC IDEAL

1. *Socrates and the Ideal of Aristocracy*

ALTHOUGH most Americans consider themselves democrats, there are some among us who are essentially aristocrats. Influential American writers, such as Irving Babbitt, Ralph Ames Cram, and George Santayana, have criticized democracy and inclined toward aristocracy. In a challenging book, *Patterns of Anti-Democratic Thought,* David Spitz has discussed some of these thinkers. I shall not deal with the details of such recent doctrines but discuss the ancient and broad ideal of aristocracy.

By an aristocrat I mean one who habitually prefers the choice goods as opposed to the common goods. The essence of the aristocratic ideal is the emphasis upon quality rather than upon quantity. The aristocrat agrees with Spinoza that "all excellent things are as difficult as they are rare."[1] He contends that democracy involves sharing without excellence. Its effect, he declares, is to popularize and thus vulgarize. In its lust for equality, it levels all distinctions and exults in the average. This indictment of democracy, although as ancient as Socrates, seems to be especially applicable to a complex industrial society. As the problems of this society become ever more technical and recondite, the opinions of the average man seem to be ever more inept and irrelevant. Consequently the political ideal of Socrates and Plato—the rule of the wise—still has a deep appeal. Moreover, the broad

[1] *Ethics,* Dutton, New York, 1910, p. 224.

245

ideal of aristocracy—the cultivation of excellence—retains its vitality throughout the centuries.

There is no better expression of the aristocratic ideal than the life and ideas of Socrates. Born in 469 B.C., about eleven years before the defeat of the Persians at the naval battle of Salamis, and died in 399 B.C., four years after Athens had surrendered to Sparta at the conclusion of the Peloponnesian War. He saw Athens at the height of her glory and at the depth of her humiliation. Scarcely a year passed without some notable victory or defeat; and the excitement was heightened by a grim struggle between the democratic and oligarchical parties within the walls of the city. In this age of conflict, any secure repose in established ways was most severely shaken. Men of unstable character, as represented for instance by Alcibiades, appeared on the scene in increasing numbers. Released from bondage to custom, some of the more daring philosophers, who acquired the name of Sophists, insisted upon a new, radical theory of value. Since truth in moral matters is impossible of attainment, good and evil, they thought, are simply matters of arbitrary convention, which no man should observe unless it serves his purpose to do so. Hence they advocated that men renounce human laws to follow the law of "nature":

> . . . the good old rule
> . . . the simple plan,
> That they should take who have the power,
> And they should keep who can.[2]

In politics, this meant that might is right, and that the power state is the only realistic and natural polity.

Within this society of tottering ideals Socrates spoke out with quiet but deep conviction. Odd in appearance, he was a barefoot man with snub nose, protruding eyes, and a shambling gait. His words were usually plain and simple, but

2 William Wordsworth, "Rob Roy."

he spoke the language of religious love. He combined a shrewd common sense and a flair for ironical humor with a mystical absorption in the unseen world of contemplation. He went unpretentiously about the streets of Athens, engaging people in conversation. His discourse was not an idle pastime, for he had a "mission" to which he was devoted with intense earnestness. His purpose was to awaken in his fellow citizens a sense of their profound ignorance of good and evil. He did not himself pretend to wisdom but observed that others did. Yet these pretenders when cross-examined turned out to be sunk in an abyss of ignorance. Some would abandon themselves to cynicism or moral nihilism, others to crude selfishness, still others would repeat the conventional formulas. Socrates rejected this unthinking acceptance of custom and the alternative plea that might makes right.

His deepest conviction was that reflection is the duty of man. "The unexamined life," he said, "is not worth living."[3] He passionately championed alertness and inquiry and faith in the venture of thought. He therein contrasted sharply with the contemporary dogmatist and agnostic. The dogmatist emphatically said, "It is so," or "It is not so." The agnostic—a disguised dogmatist—asserted no less emphatically, "We never can know." Socrates pleaded, "Let us take nothing important for granted, but let us be hopeful and try to find out." He defended this ideal of inquiry with all his might; his earnestness rings in the words that Plato has attributed to him:

Some things I have said of which I am not altogether confident. But that we shall be better and braver and less helpless if we think that we ought to inquire, than we should have been if we indulged in the idle fancy that there was no knowing and no use in seeking to know what we do not know;—that is a theme upon

[3] Plato, *Apology*, in *The Dialogues of Plato*, translated by Benjamin Jowett, Oxford University Press, London, 1924, II, p. 131.

which I am ready to fight, in word and deed, to the utmost of my power.[4]

The inquiry which he advocated was not a cloistered research but the igniting of mind against mind—inquiry in common, dominated by love, and directed to the establishment of the great ends of life. For this ideal he was willing to die. Thus he spoke to the Athenian citizens at his trial in reply to Anytus, his accuser:

If you say to me, Socrates, this time we will not mind Anytus, and you shall be let off, but upon one condition, that you are not to inquire and speculate in this way any more, and that if you are caught doing so again you shall die;—if this was the condition on which you let me go, I should reply: Men of Athens, I honor and love you; but I shall obey God rather than you, and while I have life and strength I shall never cease from the practice and teaching of philosophy.[5]

Angered by this intransigence, the citizens of Athens condemned him to death.

What was the ideal for which he drank the fatal hemlock? It was the ideal of philosophy in its ancient original meaning: "the love of wisdom." He agreed with the Sophists that the business of man is not to follow custom; but unlike them, he believed that wisdom rather than power should be the supreme aim of man. He taught men to look within their own minds, not to find what is individual and subjective and relative but what is universal and basically human. The fundamental element in man he believed to be reason, and he maintained that wisdom is the essence of virtue, both for the individual and the state. The only valid solution for political ills, he thought, is to work out a rational science of politics and to vest political control in the wise men of the state.

Plato's ideal of the Republic, in which philosophers are

4 *Meno*, in *ibid.*, p. 47.
5 *Apology*, in *ibid.*, pp. 122-123.

kings and in which the whole state is based upon a rigorous and comprehensive system of education, is in some respects the logical extension of the Socratic ideal of inquiry. Many aspects of Plato's ideal state have turned out to be open to grave objections. His tripartite division of the soul into appetite, spirit, and reason; his corresponding division of the social classes into workers, soldiers, and philosopher-kings; his recommendation that the ruling class should employ myths and "noble lies" to deceive and subdue the people; his views about censorship of religion and the arts, about eugenics, about the community of property, or the community of wives and children—all are open to severe criticism. The greatness of *The Republic,* however, depends less upon these details than upon the principal ideal introduced by Socrates and imaginatively expanded by Plato: the ideal of the educational state—the rule of wisdom. This ideal has lost none of its vitality.

Some recent writers, such as R. H. S. Crossman and K. R. Popper, believe that Plato's portrait of Socrates in *The Republic* greatly distorts the facts.[6] They think that the real historical Socrates was at heart a liberal and a democrat, whereas the Socrates depicted by Plato was not merely an aristocrat but even something of a fascist. I believe it is very difficult to know the kind of person that Socrates actually was, and I do not intend to discuss the question here. I suspect that Socrates was more democratic and open-minded than Plato, but that Plato, if we think of him within the context of his own age, was not so reactionary as he is sometimes depicted as being. In any event, the portrait of Socrates to be found in Plato's dialogues is profoundly impressive and, in most respects, credible. Whether fictional or not, this Socrates has deeply impressed mankind; and it is this sort of

6 *Cf.,* R. H. S. Crossman, *Plato Today,* Oxford University Press, New York, 1939, and K. R. Popper, *The Open Society and Its Enemies,* Routledge, London, 1945, I.

character, unhampered by some of the more totalitarian ideas attributed to him in *The Republic,* that I have in mind in my present discussion.

2. *An Imaginary Dialogue*

IF SOCRATES could return to earth, his criticism of American democracy would not be different in principle from his criticism of Athenian democracy. Let us imagine that he has somehow escaped from limbo and that, disguised in modern attire, has found his way to some city in the United States, where he has gradually mastered our language. His conversation with a modern democrat might run somewhat as follows:

Socrates: If you had a pair of sandals that needed repair, would you hand them to just anyone who would be willing to tinker with them, or would you take them to a sandal-maker who knows the art?

Democrat: No, indeed, if I had sandals—or more likely, shoes—that needed fixing, I would take them to a shoe repairman, who would know what to do.

Socrates: Now suppose you were seriously ill. Would you listen to an old wives' tale as to how you should doctor yourself, or would you go to a physician—a man who is wise in these matters?

Democrat: To the physician, of course.

Socrates: Or suppose you owned a boat with a precious cargo, and that you wanted to sail it through a perilous strait. Would you allow it to be manned by a crew of landlubbers and permit them to choose one of their own number to pilot the boat?

Democrat: Of course not. I would want a trained crew, and above all, I would want a pilot who would know how to run a ship.

Socrates: Very well. Now let's consider the most important

art of all—the art of arts—the art that controls and directs all
the other arts.

Democrat: What is that?

Socrates: It is the art of government—the most complex
and difficult of all the arts, and the most important, because
it determines the goals of the state.

Democrat: How strangely you talk! You who come from
Athens, the tiny city-state, how little you know of the com-
plexities of government. Think of our immense sprawling
state, with one hundred and fifty million inhabitants, and
with scores of cities much larger than ancient Athens.

Socrates: Quite right! And it is not just a matter of size.
You have invented and multiplied cunning machines beyond
our wildest dreams, and you have bound the whole world
together by your methods of communication and transit.
You have also invented methods of waging war of the most
ghastly effectiveness. All of these changes fill me with profound wonder and fear. I speculate how even your wisest
statesmen can understand a system so vast, so complex, so
technical, and so dangerous. How baffled your average man
must be!

Democrat: It is not easy, I know, to understand matters so
difficult. But the people can determine the broad general
policy, and the experts can work out the details.

Socrates: Our Athenian democracy never worked that way.
All of our citizens had the right to sit in the legislative assembly, and even our executive officials were selected by lot. But
I realize that your state is so vast that such methods are impossible, and if they were possible, they would not be wise.

Democrat: Very true. We have learned to temper our
democracy and to avoid, for the most part, the direct rule
of the people. The masses decide the general policy by voting
for a body of representatives. If they are mainly impressed
by economic evils and social injustices, they vote for the Left.
If they wish to conserve traditional ways, they vote for the
Right. Then the body of elected representatives decide upon

the details of governmental policy. These representatives may not be experts, but they are better qualified than the ordinary voters.

Socrates: I can see that you have mitigated some of the evils of democracy; but the main policy, which your voters indirectly decide, is the most difficult of all, because it is the most inclusive and should take account of the widest variety of factors. It is often hard for a man to manage his own household. How very much harder it is to decide upon a comprehensive policy for a whole state! Even in Athens, small though it was, it was difficult enough; yet to decide upon a general program for your mammoth state is vastly more difficult.

Democrat: Yet it seems as though common men have a kind of instinct or knack for knowing what is good for them. As we say, it is the man who wears the shoe who knows how it pinches.

Socrates: I don't believe in your so-called "instinct" or "knack." Religion may be a matter of intuition, but statesmanship is a rational art. The common man, I grant, may know that his shoe pinches, but he won't know how to fix it. Please recall what you have already granted. You have admitted that in the ordinary business of life you need the services of those who really know. But what happens when it comes to the most important and difficult of all the arts—the art of government. What do you do then? You merely count heads, which is almost as silly a procedure as breaking heads.

Democrat: What you say sounds rather sensible, but we distrust a government of the few, however "expert," because it always turns out to be a government *for* the few. Despite all the hazards, we let the people decide.

Socrates: How can even a popular government be "for" the people, if they do not *know* what is good for them. Let me ask you again, do they—the general run of people—know how to make sandals?

Democrat: No.

Socrates: Do they know how to cure the sick?

Democrat: No.

Socrates: Do they know how to pilot a boat?

Democrat: No.

Socrates: Do they know how to do what is far more difficult than any of these—to run and direct the ship of state?

Democrat: I suppose not. But then, as I have said, they choose leaders who determine the details of policy.

Socrates: Yes, but in choosing leaders, they are deciding policy. Moreover, if they themselves are ignorant, how can they choose wise leaders?

Democrat: Well, we educate our voters so that they can choose wisely.

Socrates: But do you? I have already wandered about the streets of your city, and I have talked with many of your citizens, and they seem as ignorant and conceited as were the citizens of Athens. Yet the matters that they are asked to decide, as I have said, are far more complex. Moreover, I have seen what happens when you have an election. Last week the people in your city went to the polls. For several weeks before this happened, I heard the speeches of your politicians, and I read your newspapers, and I saw everywhere on town walls the same names blazoned in an endless round of repetition. I listened to those strange uncanny machines of yours, which you call radios, and again there was the same stupefying device of repetition and the same lack of cogent reasoning. It seemed to me that your politicians, advertisers, publicists, and broadcasters had merely mastered the art of the Sophists—to make the worse appear the better cause. They knew how to appeal to prejudice and misinformation, how to stupefy and hypnotize the popular mind by endless repetitions or by fomenting extravagant desires or by creating an atmosphere of delusion. A philosopher who wished to illustrate the nature of logical fallacies could find no end of examples in the outpourings of these demagogues. I have heard it rumored that rich men buy the services of these clever deceivers, and that they also buy those mighty machines, the press, the moving pictures, and the broadcasting stations, which are used to instruct your people how to think fallaciously, whom to love and hate, when to laugh or cry. Philosophers and statesmen are powerless against these mechanical monsters. Your boasted "democracy" is therefore really a plutocracy rendered more vicious by inciting the passions of the multitude.

Democrat: You paint a dark picture. I think it is exaggerated, but there is some truth in what you say. Yet have you anything better to offer?

Socrates: There will be no cure for these evils until men learn that statesmanship is a rational science, requiring careful training and special aptitudes. Until this happens, your democracy will drag all standards down to the cheap mediocre level of the average. A real aristocracy would strenuously guard a high standard of culture, and it would insist that only the best representatives of this standard be intrusted with the very important and difficult task of government.

Democrat: What you say sounds fine, but I am skeptical. I doubt if any such ideal rulers could ever be produced; and even if they were produced, how could they be brought to power?

Socrates: The first requirement is that education be made the basis of the whole art of government. Your voters, if you still insist upon them, should be well educated, and your rulers especially should be cultivated. As Plato, my most talented pupil, was fond of saying, in a good state the Minister of Education is far more important and influential than the Minister of War.

Democrat: But Plato made the mistake of reserving a thorough education to the few, whereas I would extend it to everybody.

Socrates: As if everybody were capable of receiving it! And what would you teach your wonderful mob?

Democrat: We live in a scientific age, and I think, therefore, that all the citizens should know the fundamentals of science.

Socrates: Ah, yes, so that all the people, and not just the few, can help to blast you and your cities to smithereens. I have heard about the hellish devices your scientists have concocted, and I know that your science threatens to annihilate everything you hold dear. You have gained vastly in factual knowledge and technical proficiency, but you are no *wiser* than the men of Athens. In knowledge and power, you are like giants, but in wisdom, you are like pygmies. Your science is not to be despised, of course, but it can be used for either good or ill.

Democrat: I am afraid that what you say is only too true.

Socrates: It *is* true. And when I say, therefore, that only education can save you, I mean that you should have not only a scientific but a philosophical education. You need to ponder the most fundamental questions: What is man? Whence does he come, and whither does he go? What is his proper business? How shall he find happiness? What kind of state is good, and what kind is evil? The man who has never grappled with these questions is but a kind of earthworm, unfit to govern human beings. Only the rule of wise men—men who have inquired deeply into the meaning and value of life— will save your cities from becoming heaps of blackened rubbish strewn with millions of shattered skeletons. So at least it seems to me, a visitor from afar, who knows very little, but knows the importance of being wise.

Chapter Ten

THE DEMOCRATIC IDEAL

1. *Sharing and Excellence*

IT WOULD BE a great mistake to suppose that the democrat must reject the aristocratic ideal of excellence. He is bound to maintain that the aristocratic ideal is not adequate; and he is necessarily opposed to overprivilege and underprivilege. He believes in the equal satisfaction of equal needs, the equal recognition of equal abilities, and an equality of opportunity. However, he need not despise excellence in any of its manifestations. He is not compelled by his democratic faith to prefer mediocrity—it would be foolish and vulgar for him to do so—but as a consistent democrat, he cannot be satisfied with excellence alone. He wishes excellence to be widely and equitably shared.

Sharing and excellence—these are the two great values that must be combined and cultivated. The civilized world has experienced much of each individually but not much sharing of excellence. This kind of sharing represents the valid reconciliation of democracy and aristocracy. First, we must share the good things of life, and second, we must make the things shared just as good as possible. If democracy is to be adequate, it must, in this sense, embrace and include the aristocratic ideal.

The timeworn charge against democracy is that it involves sharing without excellence. This was the criticism of Socrates and Plato, and in our own day it is the criticism of men such as Dean Inge. The impossibility of reconciling excellence

and sharing has been asserted, for example, by George Santayana in these words:

> Culture is on the horns of this dilemma: if profound and noble
> it must remain rare, if common it must become mean. These
> alternatives can never be eluded until some purified and high-
> bred race succeeds the promiscuous bipeds that now blacken the
> planet.[1]

There is, of course, a certain amount of truth in this statement. Many forms of excellence involve such difficulty that
they will always be more or less rare. Yet it is doubtful if
there is any soil more congenial to high attainment, and certainly to the sharing of its benefits, than a political and social
democracy. Wide differentials in opportunity, such as occur
in an undemocratic society, prevent the maximum attainment of both sharing and excellence. The underprivileged
are seriously handicapped, the overprivileged are preferred
to their betters. Only in a democratic society, where opportunity is the heritage of all, can there be the most effective
development, and the best use, of talent. As Ralph Barton
Perry has well said:

> In democracy it is not a question of giving room and authority
> to the genius which has already declared itself, and of sacrificing
> thereto the residual mass of mediocrity, but one of tapping new
> sources, and discovering genius in obscure and unsuspected quar-
> ters. By giving light and air to the hitherto buried masses of
> mankind, democracy hopes to enrich human culture in the quali-
> tative, and not merely in the quantitative sense.[2]

*To enrich culture in both a qualitative and quantitative
sense*—this is indeed the proper goal of a democracy. But such
enrichment is possible only if the democracy is of a high type,
only if the democratic society itself adopts the aristocratic
goal of excellence. It must not sacrifice the choice goods out
of love for the common goods; it must not value mere size,
speed, and power. If Western democracy is not to go the way

1 *Reason in Society*, Scribner's, New York, 1927, p. 111.
2 *Puritanism and Democracy*, Vanguard Press, New York, 1944, p. 453.

of Babylon and Rome, it must cultivate intellectual discrimination, esthetic sensitiveness, and moral refinement.

The nature of the problem—how to combine excellence
and sharing—is revealed in the life and correspondence of
that brilliant, almost legendary figure, T. E. Lawrence (1888-
1935). After his astonishing feats as a leader of the Arabs in
World War I, he became profoundly disgusted with the
failure of the Allies to fulfill their promises to the Arab people, and in 1922 he sought escape from mental turmoil by
enlisting under an assumed name as a mechanic in the Royal
Air Force. The following year in a continued attempt to
elude publicity, he transferred to the Tank Corps. The ensu-
ing experience as an ordinary enlisted man brought deep
anguish, almost to the point of madness and suicide. Being
an Oxford graduate, an archeologist, man of letters, and lover
of music, he was wounded to the quick by the indifference
of his new companions to beauty and culture. In a letter to
Lionel Curtis, the editor of the quarterly *Review of Politics,*
he poured forth his bitter questions and doubts.

Can there be profit, or truth, in all these modes and sciences
and arts of ours? The leisured world for hundreds, or perhaps
thousands of years has been jealousy working and recording
the advance of each generation for the starting-point of the
next—and here these masses are as animal, as carnal as were their
ancestors before Plato and Christ and Shelley and Dostoevsky
taught and thought. In this crowd it's made startlingly clear
how short is the range of knowledge, and what poor conductors
of it ordinary humans are. You and I know: you have tried to
tell all whom you can reach: and the end is here, a cimmerian
darkness with bog-lights flitting wrongly through its gas.[3]

Lawrence's realization of the pervasive animality of his
companions was no more shocking to his personality than the
doubts that assailed him as to the role of such artists and intellectuals as himself. Without any deep foundation in the
masses, the cultivated *élite* seemed to him rootless, and there-

[3] *The Letters of T. E. Lawrence,* Doubleday, Doran, New York, 1939, p. 413.

fore lacking the pristine health and virility of his carnal companions. In the same letter from which I have quoted, Lawrence declared:

These fellows are the reality, and you and I, the selves who used to meet in London and talk of fleshless things, are only the outward wrappings of a core like these fellows. They let light and air play always upon their selves, and consequently have grown very lustily, but have at the same time achieved health and strength in their growing. Whereas our wrappings and bandages have stunted and deformed ourselves, and hardened them to an apparent insensitiveness . . . but it's a callousness, a crippling, only to be yea-said by aesthetes who prefer clothes to bodies, surfaces to intentions.[4]

This letter is a vivid presentation of perhaps the supreme problem of human culture: How can the uprooted intelligentsia strike roots in the soil of humanity? How can mankind, split into the *élite* and the masses, be harmonized and made whole? How can the leaven of culture enter into the lump of common life? How can we attain a culture that is high in its vertical thrust and broad in its horizontal spread?

In Lawrence's letter, we can see him groping toward the combination of excellence and sharing, which is the only valid solution of the problem of aristocracy *versus* democracy. The first stage of Lawrence's mental history was the experience of the choice goods—the cultivation of excellence in poetry, art, music, and philosophy. This was followed by a shocking reversal: the apparent negation of all that he most valued—the discovery that the common goods, which lack refinement but have intense vitality, are sharply opposed to his aristocratic values. The resulting conflict forced him to think back over the whole of his previous experience. His letters written at this stage implied that mankind must not sacrifice the common goods out of love for the choice goods, or vice versa; and consequently the goal is neither excellence alone nor sharing alone but the sharing *of* excellence. His

[4] *Ibid.*, p. 414.

whole view of life was being broadened and transformed; he
was reaching out toward the ideal of a high yet classless
culture.

Such a culture would be a deep organic part of common
life and "as wide and varied as humanity itself." It would
not be a toy of the rich and the sophisticated—"a thing added
like a sauce to otherwise unpalatable stale fish." Culture as
a "separate commodity"—"something to be acquired by superior people with sufficient time and money," and described
in the "society section" of our Sunday newspapers—would
not even exist in a thoroughly democratic society. To continue in the words of Herbert Read:

> A democratic culture—*that is not the same thing as a democ-
> racy plus culture.* The first important point that I must make
> and keep on stressing, is that culture in a natural society will not
> be a separate and distinguishable thing—a body of learning that
> can be put into books and museums and mugged up in your
> spare time. Just because it will not exist as a separate entity, we
> had better stop using the word "culture". . . . To hell with
> culture![5]

A democratic culture, which is the only kind that we should
not consign to hell, is no mere by-product of democracy. It
is democracy itself as a creative and articulate way of life.

It was toward such a conception of culture that Lawrence
was groping. He was too individualistic and unpolitical in
his interests, however, to push the implications of his thinking very far into the field of fundamental social reconstruction. It was characteristic of him to think in terms of personal
action, such as the attempt, by sharing his phonograph record
collection, to stimulate the appreciation of fine music among
the enlisted men. But at least *we* can appreciate the broad
implications of his more mature insight; we can understand
that the valid ideal for human culture, in its many diverse
aspects, is the interpenetration of excellence and sharing.

[5] *The Politics of the Unpolitical,* Routledge, London, 1946, pp. 47, 50-51.

This means a culture high in its vertical thrust into excellence and yet broad in its horizontal spread among the masses.

An undemocratic state, such as Czarist Russia, may be content with a vertical culture. The old Russian empire achieved a narrow kind of eminence. Names such as Dostoevsky and Tolstoy in literature, Moussorgsky and Tschaikowsky in music, Pavlova and Nijinsky in dancing, and the Moscow Art Theater in drama, testify to the heights of the Russian achievement. Even in science there were such illustrious figures as Lobatchewsky, the mathematician, Mendeleef, the chemist, and Pavlov, the physiologist. But only the few could participate in art and science. The overwhelming mass of the population was filthy, illiterate, and half starved. The vertical culture was enviably high, but the horizontal culture was insufferably narrow. Similarly wealth and political power were the monopoly of the few.

I do not believe that Soviet Russia represents such a high vertical culture as did Czarist Russia, but, with all its grievous faults, the Soviet Union represents an immense gain in the horizontal spread of culture. The rapid reduction of illiteracy among one hundred and eighty millions of the Russian people is one of the heroic achievements of history. The circulation of individual books has increased from a few hundred or thousand copies to millions; the universities and scientific institutes have had an amazing growth; the popular circles for drama, singing, music, dancing, and the graphic arts attract innumerable participants. As a consequence, a writer such as Sholokhov, a musician such as Prokofiev, a scientist such as Kapitza, is known to millions of his countrymen; and a great many more people directly participate in creative activity. A similar achievement occurred in the United States in the founding and rapid extension of the free public school system. In our case, however, this democratization of culture occurred under a government that is not controlled by a single, highly disciplined party exercising a severe censorship, and in this sense, our achievement is much more healthy and democratic than is the Russian.

We cannot afford to be too complacent, however, as to the state of our own nation. We still exclude vast numbers of our people from any effective share in our cultural achievements. Not only, in any normal times, do we keep one third of our people ill housed, ill fed, and ill clothed, but we keep them without even the rudiments of high and generous culture. If any one doubts this I suggest that he ride on the "Elevated" through the south side of Chicago. Let him see mile after mile of blighted area, much of it incredibly ugly and shabby and poor, with human morale so low that garbage, tin cans, and blackened rubbish are strewn indiscriminately in innumerable backyards and empty lots. Ruskin maintained that ugliness in the works of man is a symptom of disease in the state. If this is true, there is a great deal of disease in Chicago and in other comparable American cities.

The United States, moreover, has yet to achieve a culture as high in some respects as that of Czarist Russia. We likewise have not attained, except in science, to the heights of other historical periods—Athens in the time of Pericles, Florence in the time of the Medicis, London in the time of Queen Elizabeth. The achievement was high but restricted to narrow limits. We democrats want no such restriction. Ours is a dual demand: give us *both* excellence and sharing.

We should, therefore, encourage the people of unusual ability—the artists and the thinkers—and we should increasingly use our public institutions—schools, forums, libraries, museums, theaters, and concerthalls—to diffuse the benefits of this stimulated talent and to evoke the latent talents of the people. We should multiply our public technical exploits, such as the Grand Coulee Dam, and we should so stimulate and control invention that it will be available, not to restrictive private monopolies, but to an expanding public economy.

Whatever be the form of sharing, there is a corresponding form of excellence—political intelligence, economic efficiency, or cultural eminence. We must strive to achieve and share all of these forms of excellence. These values will thereby be embodied not merely in institutions but in the hearts and minds of the people. Democracy, as a way of life, is the self-realization of cooperative human beings—the interpenetration of excellence and sharing.

2. Social Intelligence

THE ARISTOCRAT might concede that our goal should be the sharing of excellence, a civilization rich both quantitatively and qualitatively, but deny that political democracy is the proper means to achieve this end. He might say that we should have a government *for* the people but not *of* and *by* the people. He might contend that "experts" rather than a "bungling" democratic electorate and their "incompetent" representatives are the fit instruments to achieve social welfare.

Max Lerner has answered those who reason in this manner.

The reasoning has started with the rather sensible proposition, as its major premise, that government must rest on intelligence; and then has quietly asserted, as a minor premise, that intelligence is necessarily limited to the few; from which it has marched to the conclusion that government must rest on the select few. The undistributed middle, of course, from a strictly logical standpoint, is the term "intelligence." If it means wealth, success, and formal education, the minor premise is justified. If, however, it means something closer to social intelligence and therefore more widely distributed among the sons of Adam, the whole syllogism crashes to the ground.[6]

What is "social intelligence"? Is it something reserved to an élite or something possessed by common men? Can democracy summon the intelligence to set its society in order? Among political philosophers, no one has answered these

[6] *It Is Later Than You Think,* Viking Press, New York, 1943, p. 246.

questions more illuminatingly than Jean Jacques Rousseau
(1712-1778). I am thinking less of the earlier Rousseau, who
glorified the unspoiled innocence of the primitive natural
man, than of the later Rousseau, who envisaged the "freedom
under law" enjoyed by the civilized citizen as a responsible
member of the body politic. To find the more mature thought
of Rousseau we must turn to his *Social Contract*.

Far from maintaining that there are "natural rights" that
exist in a presocial "state of nature," Rousseau in the *Social
Contract* contends that all rights are essentially social.

> The social order is a sacred right which is the basis of all other
> rights. Nevertheless, this right does not come from nature, and
> must therefore be founded on conventions.[7]

As a result of social conventions, a human being ceases to be
"a stupid and unimaginative animal" and becomes "an intelligent being and a man."[8]

The fundamental convention, which Rousseau calls "the
social contract," is that which creates the state. He tells us that
the-question of its historical origin is unanswerable and irrelevant, and proposes to discuss its legitimacy.

> The problem is to find a form of association which will defend
> and protect with the whole common force the person and goods
> of each associate, and in which each, while uniting himself with
> all, may still obey himself alone, and remain as free as before.[9]

To this problem, the social contract provides the solution.

> Each of us puts his person and all his power in common under
> the supreme direction of the general will, and, in our corporate
> capacity, we receive each member as an indivisible part of the
> whole.[10]

The body politic thus created is a society of free assent and
not of force, and a union of each with all on equal terms for

---

7 *The Social Contract,* Dutton, New York, 1913, p. 6.
8 *Ibid.,* p. 19.
9 *Ibid.,* p. 14.
10 *Ibid.,* p. 15.

the common welfare. Although individualistic "freedom," the mere isolation and independency of the "natural man," is surrendered to such a union, a far more substantial freedom, the power and prerogative of the citizen, is thereby attained.

Each man, in giving himself to all, gives himself to nobody; and as there is no associate over whom he does not acquire the same right as he yields others over himself, he gains an equivalent for everything he loses, and an increase of force for the preservation of what he has.[11]

Professor Ernest Hunter Wright, in his excellent book, *The Meaning of Rousseau,* supplies a "homely illustration" of the terms of this exchange.

When there was no society, of course I paid no taxes, and now I have to do so. That is my loss. But all the other members also pay taxes, and the amount of their tribute that is used for my benefit should equal the amount I pay to benefit them all. So my gain is equal to my loss. But together we can do things with our taxes that would be impossible in any other way; so by joining forces we have each inherited a power hitherto unknown. Extend the illustration, and the principle would seem to hold. Every duty that I owe the other members of society is balanced by a duty they perform in part for my benefit; and meanwhile we have all gained the strength that comes from union.[12]

Such union creates the democratic state. In the active exercise of its functions, the state is called a sovereign; and the sovereign is the general will, exercised by the single collective body of all the citizens. Law is the voice of the general will, and it alone provides security in human rights. Liberty under law is the only kind that is not illusory.

The general will, which thus expresses itself in law, is "general" in two senses. It is general in its object: its aim, in the language of the United States Constitution, is "to promote the general welfare." It is also general in expressing the will of all. The Constitution begins: "We, the people of the

11 *Ibid.*
12 *The Meaning of Rousseau,* Oxford University Press, London, 1929, p. 73.

United States . . . do ordain and establish. . . ." The will of a whole people is being expressed.

The general will is not the sum of particular wills. In so far as a person is expressing only his separate identity, his selfish interest, he is not functioning as a citizen, and no summation of the votes of private self-seeking individuals can speak for the general will. Rousseau insists that a political community is a union that binds men organically together, their wills merged and transformed in a corporate will.

At once in place of the individual personality of each contracting party, this act of association creates a moral and collective body, composed of as many members as the assembly contains votes, and receiving from this act its unity, its common identity, its life and its will. This public person, so formed by the union of all other persons, formerly took the name of City, and now takes that of Republic, or Body Politic.[13]

Just as this corporate personality transcends all purely individual interests, so it transcends all limited group interests. Rousseau rejects the "pressure group" theory of the state no less emphatically than he rejects the purely individualistic theory. A state is not an arena of conflicting groups, each expressing its bias, but an organic body of disinterested citizens intent upon the general welfare.

If the clashing of particular interests made the establishment of societies necessary, the agreement of these very interests made it possible. The common element in these different interests is what forms the social tie; and, were there no point of agreement between them all, no society could exist. It is solely on the basis of this common interest that every society should be governed.[14]

The clear implication of this passage is that there must be no "house divided against itself," no fundamental cleavage into classes or other divisive groups. "If the general will is to be able to express itself," declares Rousseau, "there should be no partial society within the state."[15] The prime requirement

13 Rousseau, *op. cit.*, pp. 15-16.
14 *Ibid.*, p. 22.
15 *Ibid.*, p. 26.

for such unity is the abolition of special privilege, and hence
the establishment of social equality.

From whatever side we approach our principle, we reach the
same conclusion, that the social compact sets up among the citizens an equality of such a kind, that they all bind themselves to
observe the same conditions and should therefore all enjoy the
same rights.[16]

Long before Marx, Rousseau had sketched the ideal of a
classless society. That it is an ideal, and not an actuality,
Rousseau would be the first to admit. He would agree with
the words of Walt Whitman in his *Democratic Vistas* that

We have frequently printed the word Democracy. Yet I cannot
too often repeat that it is a word the real gist of which still sleeps,
quite unawakened, notwithstanding the resonance and the many
angry tempests out of which its syllables have come, from pen or
tongue. It is a great word, whose history, I suppose, remains
unwritten, because that history has yet to be enacted.[17]

If the history of democracy remains largely unenacted, can
we still say that societies, in so far as they approach the democratic ideal, exhibit social intelligence? The theory of Rousseau will help us to answer this question.

The first point to make is that no other kind of intelligence
is truly *social* in the sense of representing a real community
of interests. The private interests of individuals, competing
in a system of devil-take-the-hindmost, are not in this sense
social. Among interests of this sort there can be conflict or
domination or compromise but not a real integration and
mutual enhancement. Again, the interests of the most powerful class, or of a dominant elite, are not truly social, in the
sense of representing the society as a whole. They involve a
separation of the part from the whole, and to this extent, they
are outside the society, imposing patterns upon it. All such
interests, whether of private individuals or of partial groups,

16 *Ibid.*, p. 28.
17 *Democratic Vistas*, in Floyd Stovall, *Walt Whitman: Representative Selections*, American Book Co., New York, 1939, p. 409.

are *special* interests seeking *special* privileges. Quite different are the interests involved in and evolved by a community of interacting and interdependent individuals, consciously acknowledging the mutuality of their interests.

I mean by community something so ordinary, indeed, so common, so elemental, that nobody can fail to experience it. It is a simple fact that human beings are interdependent. In a family, a neighborhood, a circle of friends, in a cooperative activity of any sort, men experience the fact of mutual aid and personal interdependence. A community exists when this experience is made the voluntary basis of group coherence. Such a group is held together and unified by the attitude and practice of cooperation, collaboration, and sharing.

The word *community* comes from the Latin *communitas,* which in turn is composed of two roots, *com,* meaning *with,* and *munis,* meaning *ready to be of service.* With these meanings in mind, we can say that a person belongs to a community when he is "with" others, when he is "ready to be of service" to them, and when they reciprocate the attitude.

Thus a community differs from a mere collection of individuals, each member of which is pursuing his own separate interests. In a community, the members are functionally dependent upon one another, either because they possess something in common or because they complement and enrich one another by their differences. The oneness of a community does not exclude differentiation: the greater closeness of the unity may even involve the greater individuality of its members. As I remarked at the conclusion of Chapter Six, we may love people all the more because of their uniquenesses. But some real unity, some touch of organicity, every community must possess.

A community differs from an association in which some are using others as mere tools. A man may look at another and say to himself, "You are for my use." His attitude is different when he says, "We can help one another." The first attitude excludes mutuality, the second is based upon it. The first leads to exploitation, the second to fellowship. In an acquisitive society, the first is predominant; hence men are divided into classes, and to this extent democracy is lacking. In a real community, which is always democratic in essence, the second is fundamental; men regard each other as ends and not as mere means; hence class divisions and other barriers tend to disappear.

A community differs from an involuntary association. The complex division of labor in modern industry, for example, may force men to cooperate, each person performing some minute operation in the total productive process. Yet the men may remain essentially strangers to one another, each motivated by a purely private interest, each cooperating because he is forced by necessity to do so. A community, on the other hand, is a voluntary fellowship bound together by mutual aid. So understood, it does not exclude the more fruitful kind of competition, such as the friendly rivalry of scientists in the discovery of truth. Such competition contributes to the common cause and is not an alternative to cooperation but an aspect of it.

Men need not be intimate to combine in a community. In large communities intimacy among all the members is impossible, but they must at least voluntarily enter into mutually serviceable relations, and they must have some sense of "belonging" or group identity. To some extent, they must be bound together by common goods, common memories, common hopes, common ideals, and common deeds.

Democracy is essentially that political form which molds and expresses the life of a community. Rousseau's greatest achievement as a political philosopher is that he elaborates the meaning of the political community, indicating its democratic roots. For this reason, he deserves to be called the philosopher of democracy. It is true that he exaggerates: he insists that the community is a social organism with a supreme intrinsic value—a view that I have criticized in Chapter Six. Also he is more deeply attached to fraternity and equality than he is to liberty; and hence his ideal may be called one-sided. Yet whatever may be his incidental exaggerations or mistakes, his theory of community makes clear the profound difference between the interest of a private individual or special group and the interest of the whole community. When reason is brought into conformity with community interest, there is, as Rousseau realized, social intelligence. Such intelligence is indigenous to democracy, because only a democracy can be a true political community. It is therefore idle to argue that an aristocracy is more intelligent than a democracy and is therefore better. The proper reply is that the type of intelligence involved is quite different and serves different ends.

A democracy, moreover, need not be stupid. In the first place, it can make full use of experts so long as they remain public servants and do not become masters. While retaining its essence, democracy can delegate its powers. The delegates can be of high competence; and adequate staffs of experts and technicians can advise congressional committees and governmental administrative agencies so that the representatives of the people may base their decisions upon accurate knowledge and expert technical planning rather than upon hearsay and the mere special pleading of lobbyists. Indeed, there should be far more of such expert advice than there is at present.

Moreover, democracy should fully embrace, and adapt to its own purposes, Plato's ideal of an educational state. Education is at the very heart and core of democracy, and without it civilization cannot survive in a world as complex and dangerous as ours. As Whitehead has said, civilization is "the victory of persuasion over force";[18] and such victory requires, above all, the arts of the teacher. In this Atomic Age, when the capacity both to destroy and to construct has increased by leaps and bounds, we need a gigantic effort at synthesis and liberal education, so that human knowledge can be directed

18 Alfred North Whitehead, *Adventures of Ideas,* Macmillan, New York, 1933, p. 105.

to life enhancement rather than to life destruction, and so that the vast and ever-accumulating mass of scientific information can be integrated into a unified interpretation of nature and man. This great task in itself depends upon a broad community of effort, transcending the specialisms of research, scholarship, and teaching. It calls not only for the expert and the technician but for an open forum of discussion and socially elaborated judgments, to which every man can contribute his little stock of talent and wisdom for the common good. It calls for a juster and wider employment of human resources than any aristocracy can ever boast. Democracy does not mean that all men will be treated alike: it means that all will be given a chance to prove themselves, and that preference will be given only to those who can contribute most to human well-being. Democracy believes not in the absurd doctrine of an equality of native capacities but in the sensible ideal of an equality of rights and opportunities. The very fact of psychological inequality is all the more reason for equal opportunity, since without it, able men will often be handicapped and the less gifted will often be preferred to their natural betters. A wise democracy will be eager to develop its geniuses, but it will recognize that genius crops up in lowly places.

Jesus was the son of a carpenter and Leonardo da Vinci the illegitimate son of a domestic servant; . . . Shakespeare's father was a butcher and glover; Beethoven's, a "confirmed drunkard"; Schubert's, a peasant; Faraday's, "a poor blacksmith"; Carlyle's, a stone-mason; Lincoln's, a "roving carpenter"—"poor white trash"; Pasteur's, a tanner; Browning's, a clerk; . . . Socrates' mother was a mid-wife, Beethoven's, the "daughter of a cook"; and Schubert's, "an ignorant drudge."[19]

The democrat's reply to the aristocrat is that he does not want art or science or education for the few any more than government for the few. He recognizes the importance of

[19] F. W. Coker, *Recent Political Thought,* Appleton-Century, New York, 1934, p. 361.

cultivating intelligence, but he wants it to be social, expressing the interests of the community rather than the interests
of privilege. Democracy, as Rousseau divined, is essentially
the ideal of community, in which all men, without invidi-
ous distinction of class, are bound together by relations of
mutuality.

Chapter Eleven

THE LIBERAL IDEAL

1. *The Tradition of Individualistic Liberalism*

ALTHOUGH "democracy" and "liberalism" are closely related, it is possible to distinguish them. Whereas the essence of the democratic ideal, it seems to me, is equality and fraternity, the essence of the liberal ideal is freedom. The term *freedom* is often used to mean government by popular consent; in this sense, it is inseparable from political democracy. But there is another kind of freedom—civil liberty—that does not necessarily characterize democratic theory and practice. Alexis de Tocqueville, in his famous study of *Democracy in America,* had in mind the difference between liberalism and democracy when he declared:

> I think that democratic communities have a natural taste for freedom; left to themselves, they will seek it, cherish it, and view any privation of it with regret. But for equality, their passion is ardent, insatiable, incessant, invincible: they call for equality in freedom; and if they cannot obtain that, they still call for equality in slavery.[1]

As a historical movement, liberalism has often insisted that democratic equality must be restricted in the interests of personal freedom and civil rights. It is therefore possible to distinguish, historically as well as theoretically, the liberal from the democratic ideal and to discuss each separately. Indeed, there may be an undemocratic liberalism or an illiberal democracy.

Until the present century, the main tradition of liberalism

[1] *Democracy in America,* Oxford University Press, New York, 1947, p. 310.

273

has conceived of freedom in individualistic terms—the liberty of the enterprising individual free from the trammels of social organization. Summing up the liberal thought of his day, Tom Paine declared that even the best government is a necessary evil. Thomas Jefferson similarly distrusted strong government. Thoreau went so far as to declare that not merely is the government best which governs least, but that the government is best which governs not at all. Southern aristocrats like John C. Calhoun and Jefferson Davis thought of freedom in terms of local autonomy free from governmental restraint. Abolitionists such as William Lloyd Garrison and Wendell Phillips conceived liberty as the right of every man, black or white, to own and control his own person. Frontiersmen such as Davy Crockett and Daniel Boone identified freedom with the hard-hitting individualism of the West. In England, thought took a parallel course. For example, William Godwin, in his famous book *Political Justice,* declared that "government is, in all cases, an evil," and that "it ought to be introduced as sparingly as possible."[2] Likewise, the famous Victorian Herbert Spencer was so averse to governmental activity that he refused to transmit his manuscripts through the government post office and carried them to the printer himself.

When I call such viewpoints "liberal," I am not thinking of the broadest meaning of the term. In its more inclusive meaning, liberalism involves open-minded and critical inquiry; tolerance toward unorthodox opinions; desire to employ persuasion rather than force; opposition to arbitrary or unwarranted use of power; preference for variety rather than a regimented uniformity; liberation from oppressive social conditions; desire to achieve a genuine equality of rights and opportunities; opposition to any form of discrimination, whether on grounds of race, religion, political belief, or economic status. These values are not confined to any particular

[2] *Enquiry Concerning Political Justice,* University of Toronto Press, 1946, II, p. 215.

time or place. They are the values of reason and sympathy as opposed to hate and violence. Although they are construed differently in successive ages and are never realized completely, they are the enduring marks of civilized existence. Nothing that I shall say in this chapter, or indeed in this book, should be construed as calling these essential liberal values into question.

In the narrower sense, however, liberalism is the ultra-individualistic philosophy of the middle class in its rise to power. The product of many factors—religious reformation, scientific discovery, technical invention, geographic expansion, etc.—it has been mainly the result of economic revolution, the transition from feudalism to laissez-faire capitalism. Its period of maximum ascendancy was about 1600 to 1900 in England and the United States, a shorter time in France, and a much more limited interval in Germany and Italy.

In rationalizing a "free-enterprise" system, the liberal philosophers and social theorists such as John Locke and Adam Smith conceived of the economic order as an impersonal, self-regulating, and natural equilibrium. The model in nature for this concept of the economic system was the Newtonian world order, which had been expounded not only in Newton's *Principia* but in various popularizations, which ran through many editions. The great discovery of Newton was that terrestrial and celestial motions all obey the same uniform law, that every particle of matter attracts every other particle of matter with a force varying directly with the mass and inversely with the square of the distance. This one grand generalization embraced all phenomena from the motion of the most distant star to the falling of a pin. Social theorists, looking at the contrast between the concrete muddle of human affairs and the abstract economy of Newton's physical universe, tried to formulate kindred laws for man.

For example, in France, Turgot, Quesnay, and other "physiocrats" endeavored to extend "the rule of nature" from the physical order to society—they were the first to represent the economic system as a unity, having a rational consistency and governed by an immutable system of "natural laws." In opposition to the "mercantilists," who upheld the traditional practice of state regulation of economic affairs, the French physiocrats maintained that the economic system, *if left to itself*, would produce the best possible results by the free and unfettered operation of impersonal economic forces. To one of the group, Vincent de Gournay, is attributed the classical slogan *laissez faire, laissez aller* (let do as you please, let go as you please). In defense of their ideal of *laissez faire*, the physiocrats maintained that every man has a "natural right" to pursue his own self-interest, which by reason of a natural harmony in the economic sphere, necessarily promotes the common good. Reflecting the rural life of eighteenth-century France, they also contended that the land and its produce are the only ultimate sources of wealth and that agriculture should be the basis of the nation's productive system.

The classical English economists, Adam Smith and David Ricardo, adapted the physiocratic ideal of free competition to the relatively commercial and industrial economy of England. They worked out the detailed theory of a self-regulating, self-equilibrating economic order, governed by no over-all plans or purposes but by the "impersonal" factors of free competition. According to this theory, selfish interest is the best guide to social interest. Smith, for example, declared:

> Every individual is continually exerting himself to find out the most advantageous employment for whatever capital he can command. It is his own advantage, indeed, and not that of the society, which he has in view. But the study of his own advantage naturally, or rather necessarily, leads him to prefer that employment which is most advantageous to society. . . . By pursuing his own interest he frequently promotes that of the society more effectually than when he really intends to promote it. I have never known much good done by those who affected to trade from the public good. It is an affectation, indeed, not very common among

merchants, and very few words need be employed in dissuading them from it.[3]

Bernard Mandeville, in his *Fable of the Bees,* expressed the same thought more pungently and half satirically:

> Thus every part was full of Vice;
> Yet the whole Mass a Paradise; . . . .
> This, as in Musick Harmony,
> Made Jarrings in the main agree;
> Parties directly opposite,
> Assist each other, as 'twere for Spight.[4]

Believing that a competitive economic order would thus take care of itself, the liberals defined freedom negatively as the absence of restraint and opposed the interference of government in economic affairs. Thereby they hoped to achieve what Adam Smith called "the obvious and simple system of natural liberty." The fundamental principle of this system he described as follows:

> Every man, as long as he does not violate the laws of justice, is left perfectly free to pursue his own interest his own way, and to bring both his industry and capital into competition with those of any other man, or order of men.[5]

There were others, less concerned with justice or more confident that self-interest could not conflict with social interest, who did not thus qualify their individualism. Frederic Bastiat, the French economist, summed up the optimistic tenets of such liberalism in the slogans, "Competition is Liberty" and "Liberty is Harmony."[6] In the spirit of this theory and the later theory of Social Darwinism, Herbert Spencer contended that political control must limit itself to the elimination of evil and must leave the achievement of good entirely

[3] *The Wealth of Nations,* Modern Library, New York, 1937, pp. 421, 423.
[4] *The Fable of the Bees,* 6th ed., J. Tonson, London, 1732, pp. 8-9.
[5] Smith, *op. cit.,* p. 651.
[6] Quoted in Sebastian de Grazia, *The Political Community,* University of Chicago Press, Chicago, 1948, p. 53.

to individuals. In the United States, these ideas were widely propagated by such influential social theorists as William Graham Sumner, who declared: "At bottom there are two chief things with which government has to deal. They are the property of men and the honor of women. These it has to defend against crime."[7]

No one today would phrase his political negativism and economic "liberalism" so naïvely, but many influential economists, such as Ludwig von Mises and Friedrich A. Hayek, are still dominated by the conception of the competitive economic order as a self-equilibrating harmony. The "free competitive system," they believe, should be repaired and protected, but not impeded, by governmental action. For example, Hayek in his widely acclaimed *The Road to Serfdom,* maintains that the separate efforts of individuals are harmoniously coordinated by the self-equilibrating mechanism of the market system, and that the only alternative to the "impersonal and seemingly irrational forces of the market" is the arbitrary, tyrannical rule of "bureaucrats" and "dictators."[8]

The liberal theory of economics was paralleled by a liberal theory of politics, which was supposedly based upon immutable "natural law" as distinguished from transient man-made law. The concept of natural law as the basis of human rights is traceable to such ancient philosophers as Heraclitus, the Sophists, the Cynics, and the Stoics. In Chapter Three, I have discussed the Stoic doctrine that "the whole universe is one commonwealth" governed by natural laws, and that every human being, as a citizen of this commonwealth, is born with inalienable natural rights discoverable by reason. In the Middle Ages, this doctrine of nature was combined with Christian theology. God, it was said, created nature, and nature is an immutable providential order. The "Eternal Law of God," declared St. Thomas Aquinas, has been revealed

---

[7] *What Social Classes Owe to Each Other,* Harper, New York, 1883, p. 101.
[8] *Cf., The Road to Serfdom,* University of Chicago Press, Chicago, 1944.

directly in the Bible and indirectly in nature. It has also been written in the hearts of men, where its general precepts can be deciphered by reason. During the Renaissance and the Enlightenment, men's confidence in the "natural light" of human reason increased, and the reliance upon divine "revelation" in the form of sacred scriptures correspondingly declined. The physics of Newton, in particular, seemed a marvellous disclosure of a rational order established by God.

Influenced by this tradition, John Locke (1632-1704) maintained that there is a "natural order" designed by God, that men by natural law possess certain rights, that these rights are discoverable by reason, and that they furnish an immutable standard for testing political institutions. Human beings, Locke contended, existed before civil society, and their natural state was not, as Hobbes had described it, a brutal war of each against all but a peaceful and friendly existence. All men in this pre-civil state possessed certain rights in virtue of being rational creatures and children of God. Declared Locke:

> The state of nature has a law of nature to govern it, which obliges everyone; and reason, which is that law, teaches all mankind, who will but consult it, that being all equal and independent, no one ought to harm another in his life, health, liberty, or possessions.[9]

The main defect of the state of nature was insecurity, which resulted from the lack of any civil authority to enforce the natural law. Hence government, resting upon the consent of the governed, was set up to protect these natural rights. "The end of law," Locke declared, "is not to abolish and restrain but to preserve and enlarge freedom."[10] If the sovereign should signally fail to respect the natural rights of the citizens, he is guilty of a breach of contract, and the people have the right to revolt. For no one ought to be "subject to the

9 *An Essay Concerning the True Original, Extent, and End of Civil Government,* Appleton-Century, New York, 1937, section 6.
10 *Ibid.,* section 57.

inconstant, uncertain, unknown, arbitrary will of another man."[11] The dissolution of government, which may occur in the event of revolt, is not the dissolution of moral responsibility, which is antecedent to, and independent of, the political institutions of mankind.

These ideas had a very profound influence and were echoed in such great historic documents as the American Declaration of Independence and the French Declaration of the Rights of Man. In course of time, however, they were severely attacked. Among the attackers were the utilitarians, such as Jeremy Bentham and John Stuart Mill, who rejected Locke's reasoning while retaining many of his conclusions. Bentham stated:

> *Natural rights* is simply nonsense: natural and imprescriptable rights, rhetorical nonsense—nonsense upon stilts. . . . What is the language of reason and plain sense upon this same subject? That in proportion as it is *right* and *proper*, i.e., advantageous to the society in question, that this or that right . . . should be established and maintained, in that same proportion it is *wrong* that it should be abrogated: but as there is no *right*, which ought not to be maintained so long as it is on the whole advantageous to society that it should be maintained, so there is no right which, when the abolition of it is advantageous to society, should not be abolished.[12]

According to Bentham, the only rule of action which is true unconditionally is that which bids us maximize the surplus of pleasure over pain—only in so far as, and as long as, "rights" and "liberties" have this effect, are they justified. Thus Bentham resolutely substituted a utilitarian, in place of a natural rights, theory.

Yet Bentham, in his own way, was as individualistic as Locke. He conceived of individuals as utterly egoistic and of society as a mere association of atomic individuals. Moreover, he partially adopted the doctrine of the natural harmony of

11 *Ibid.,* section 22.
12 *Anarchical Fallacies,* in *The Works of Jeremy Bentham,* W. Tait, Edinburgh, 1843, p. 501.

interests—with some reservations, he justified *laissez faire* in economics on the assumption that human selfishness harmonizes with social interests. However, he modified this doctrine to a considerable extent: he wished, through legislation, to establish a system of rewards and punishments which would more perfectly induce individuals, while remaining wholly egoistic, to further "the greatest happiness of the greatest number." But he never doubted that a multitude of egoists could form an ideal society.

The classic utilitarian defense of freedom is to be found in the essay *On Liberty* by John Stuart Mill. There is no one whose name more instantly occurs to the mind as the symbol and embodiment of the liberal ideal. Like his liberal predecessors, he sought to define the *negative* conditions of freedom, to determine the extent to which the individual is entitled to claim freedom from interference by the state or public opinion. "The subject of this Essay," he declared, "is . . . Civil or Social Liberty; the nature and limits of the power which can be legitimately exercised by society over the individual."[13] His approach shows the influence of the traditional doctrine that the individual, as such, is free, and that his freedom will be beneficially exerted if society will not interfere. Mill primarily defended the individual, as against government and public opinion, in his right to be let alone.

He avowedly based his argument not upon natural rights but upon "utility, in the largest sense, grounded on the permanent interests of man as a social being."[14] Without freedom the individual cannot be happy or society progressive. "Mankind," he declared, "are greater gainers by suffering each other to live as seems good to themselves, than by compelling each to live as seems good to the rest."[15]

With respect to his own affairs, the individual and not society should be sovereign.

13 *On Liberty*, edited by Philip Wheelwright, Doubleday, Doran, Garden City, 1935, p. 301. Quoted by permission of the Odyssey Press, Inc., New York, present holder of the copyright.
14 *Ibid.*, p. 312.   15 *Ibid.*, p. 314.

The only part of the conduct of anyone, for which he is amenable to society, is that which concerns others. In the part which merely concerns himself, his independence is, of right, absolute. Over himself, over his own body and mind, the individual is sovereign.[16]

In thus contending that the individual's "own good, either physical or moral, is not a sufficient warrant"[17] for social control, Mill seems to be departing from his strict utilitarianism. Likewise, he seems to be asserting liberty as an absolute principle when he declares that mankind has no right to silence a lone dissenter.

If all mankind minus one were of one opinion, and only one person were of the contrary opinion, mankind would be no more justified in silencing that one person, than he, if he had the power, would be justified in silencing mankind.[18]

On the whole, however, he argues that individuality and diversity are justified by their utility. In his *Autobiography,* he states that the central truth of his essay *On Liberty* is "the importance to man and society, of a large variety in types of character, and of giving full freedom to human nature to expand itself in innumerable and conflicting directions."[19] In the essay itself, he superbly contends that "a State which dwarfs its men in order that they may be more docile instruments in its hands even for beneficial purposes, will find that with small men no great thing can really be accomplished."[20] He is especially anxious to defend the exceptional individual against "the collective mediocrity" of public opinion. In this respect, there is an aristocratic, as well as an individualistic, cast to his thought.

The initiation of all wise or noble things comes and must come from individuals: generally at first from some one individual. The honour and glory of the average man is that he is capable

16 *Ibid.,* p. 311.
17 *Ibid.,* p. 310.
18 *Ibid.,* p. 318.
19 *Autobiography,* Columbia University Press, New York, 1924, p. 177.
20 *On Liberty, op. cit.,* p. 396.

of following that initiative; that he can respond internally to wise and noble things, and be led to them with his eyes open. . . . It does seem . . . that when the opinions of masses of merely average men are everywhere become or becoming the dominant power, the counterpoise and corrective to that tendency would be the more and more pronounced individuality of those who stand on the higher eminences of thought. It is in these circumstances, most especially, that exceptional individuals, instead of being deterred, should be encouraged in acting differently from the mass.[21]

Mill's essay, as Professor George H. Sabine has well said, "is in a sense a defense of liberty against democracy."[22]

Applying his liberal principles, Mill eloquently defends "the liberty of thought and discussion." Progress is desirable, he maintains, and the suppression of ideas is almost certain to impede progress. In the first place, the suppressed idea may be true. To assume that this cannot be the case is to assume our own infallibility; and history is replete with examples of ideas which, seemingly absurd or noxious, have turned out to be highly salutary. Even the best and wisest of men, such as Marcus Aurelius, who unfortunately tried to suppress Christianity, have been mistaken in what they have regarded as certain. In the second place, the suppressed idea may contain a part of the truth. Only by the collision between opinions can the whole truth be brought out. Half-truths asserted as dogmas, without the opposition being permitted to speak, are often as deadly as errors. In the third place, the suppressed idea may be wholly false. Yet its advocacy is still valuable, because without opposition and controversy, even a true doctrine degenerates into a lifeless dogma. Indeed, the very meaning of the truth may be lost, since its meaning is best brought out by contrast and controversy. Mill declares:

The peculiar evil of silencing the expression of an opinion is, that it is robbing the human race: posterity as well as the existing generation; those who dissent from the opinion, still more than

21 *Ibid.*, pp. 362-363.
22 *A History of Political Theory*, Holt, New York, 1937, p. 667.

those who hold it. If the opinion is right, they are deprived of
the opportunity of exchanging error for truth; if wrong, they lose,
what is almost as great a benefit, the clearer perception and livelier impression of truth, produced by its collision with error. . . .
We can never be sure that the opinion we are endeavoring to
stifle is a false opinion; and if we were sure, stifling it would be
an evil still.[23]

Mill likewise vigorously defends "the liberty of action,"
although he recognizes that actions can sometimes be rightly
prohibited even when their advocacy cannot. He believes that
experimentation in many modes of living is socially advantageous; and he has a deep and generous respect for the independent, or even eccentric, personality.

It is not by wearing down into uniformity all that is individual
in themselves, but by cultivating it, and calling it forth, within
the limits imposed by the rights and interests of others, that
human beings become a noble and beautiful object of contemplation; and as the works partake the character of those who do
them, by the same process human life also becomes rich, diversi-
fied, and animating, furnishing more abundant aliment to high
thoughts and elevating feelings, and strengthening the tie which
binds every individual to the race, by making the race infinitely
better worth belonging to.[24]

Yet even in this passage, he recognizes that personal freedom must be limited by "the rights and interests of others,"
and in another passage, he admits that the freedom of each
must be limited so as to avoid "harm to others."[25] Within a
complex and highly interdependent society, this limitation
may call for a very considerable amount of social control.
After writing *On Liberty,* Mill became increasingly aware of
the social context within which human liberties function
and the brutalizing effects of gross inequalities in wealth and
economic power. In his *Autobiography,* the last edition of his
Principles of Political Economy, and his posthumous work,

23 *On Liberty, op. cit.,* pp. 318-319.
24 *Ibid.,* p. 358.
25 *Ibid.,* p. 314.

Socialism, he considerably modified his earlier individualism and even accepted a half-socialistic outlook. He had no sympathy for extreme socialism, with its concentration of almost all powers in the state, but he approved of voluntary cooperation and a very considerable amount of common ownership. The great problem of the future, he declared, is "how to unite the greatest liberty of action, with a common ownership in the raw materials of the globe, and an equal participation of all in the benefits of combined labor."[26]

Mill's social philosophy has stimulated the two main currents of recent liberal thought. His earlier individualistic liberalism has contributed to the staunch defense of "individualism" and "free enterprise" by statesmen such as Herbert Hoover, publicists such as Walter Lippmann, and economists such as Lionel Robbins. Mill's later social idealism has likewise found many sympathizers, ranging from moderate, social-minded liberals such as L. T. Hobhouse to more outright socialists such as John Dewey and Harold Laski. A great ideological battle is in progress between the "old" and the "new" liberalism, between those who insist that freedom is inconsistent with planning and collectivism and those who contend that freedom will be greatly increased in a planned social democracy. So elastic has the term *liberalism* become in view of these conflicting opinions, that it has been used to designate almost every shade of social theory from archconservativism to archradicalism. Yet there is considerable continuity in the liberal tradition as I have sketched it.

2. *Evaluation of the Liberal Tradition*

THE TRADITION of individualistic liberalism contains very precious truths, but also very serious errors. Interpreted non-teleologically, the natural rights theory contains more error

26 *Autobiography, op. cit.*, p. 162.

than truth. The laws of nature, as merely descriptive of what exists, do not provide reliable norms for human conduct. As I have maintained in Chapter Three, we must distinguish between *what is* and *what ought to be,* between fact and norm. Not to do so constitutes "the fallacy of factualism." The liberals, in effect, committed this fallacy when they described the competitive economic order as an "obvious and simple system of natural liberty." They supposed that man's nature is selfish, and that there is an identity between his selfish proclivities and social welfare. Yet in so far as the self is centered in itself, it does not necessarily serve the public weal. The perfect accord of self with self and self with society is an ideal and not a fact; and to base economic and political theory upon the identity of fact and ideal, when that identity does not exist, is to make a very costly mistake. It makes virtue out of selfishness, and glorifies greed as obedience to nature's law.

Moreover, there are no inalienable or inviolable "natural rights." To quote Professor A. C. Ewing:

> Is the right to property inviolable? If so there could be no social reform that would involve any sacrifice of wealth on the part of the rich unless all who had to make the sacrifice consented. Is the right to free speech inviolable? Then I ought not to be prosecuted for saying without a shred of evidence that my neighbor is a murderer or by false stories inciting people to kill him. Or the right to free assembly? Then the state ought not to prevent the holding of a public meeting under circumstances where it is practically certain that it will lead to a sanguinary riot.[27]

In practice, the United States Supreme Court has discovered that all such rights must be hedged by qualifications and exceptions. To deny that such reservations are ever necessary is to maintain that the laws of social morality admit of no

---

[27] *The Individual, the State, and World Government,* p. 12. Copyright 1947 by The Macmillan Company and used with their permission.

conceivable exceptions. In effect, this is to adopt the theory of Immanuel Kant that rights and duties are absolute. In Chapter Four, we have criticized this sort of absolutistic ethics—a type of ethics that has been almost universally repudiated by philosophers.

Most of the proponents of the natural rights theory have committed other fallacies. They have assumed that natural rights are "self-evident," that there is, consequently, some easy method of insight or immediate intuition whereby rights can be determined; but, in truth, long investigation and deep reflection are required to ascertain the nature, limits, and conditions of human rights. The proponents of natural rights tend to conceive these rights abstractly, each independently of the others and independently of concrete historical circumstances, whereas rights are profoundly conditioned by their interrelations and historical circumstances. They tend to connect these rights with mythical history—a primitive "state of nature"—whereas rights, far from being complete in some mythical golden age, are achieved only by the long, hard, difficult ascent of man out of barbarism. They tend to conceive these rights too negatively and individualistically, as inherent in the individual apart from positive social action; whereas freedom is positive and not merely negative—the presence of opportunity rather than the mere absence of constraint. There is no liberty of the "natural man," inherent in the isolated individual, to be uncovered merely by stripping away the "yoke" of social relations. The individual, apart from society, is never free; he is profoundly and ineluctably social in his nature, and he can never achieve real and substantial freedom except by mastering social forces.

Having made these criticisms of the theory of natural rights, we must turn to the basic truth which it expresses. As defenders of natural rights, Locke and Jefferson were maintaining, in effect, that there is a higher and more ultimate court of appeals than ordinary human conventions and laws;

that there are rights that are deeply embedded in the very nature of things; that whenever government violates these rights, it stands condemned before men's reason and conscience; that the individual is consequently more than a creature of government and can never wholly surrender his independence; that the state does not create morality but must be judged by it; and that the citizens owe obedience to the state only if it is, on the whole, a guarantor of basic human rights. When properly interpreted, these contentions are true and extremely salutary.

In a sense, therefore, there *are* natural rights. We can scarcely doubt that there are relatively constant characteristics of human nature, of the physical environment, of the conditions of social existence, which have been and will continue to be fundamental factors in the pursuit of happiness. Natural laws, so far as they define natural rights, are these permanent and general conditions of human happiness; and natural rights are the claims that human beings can legitimately make in view of these natural laws. It is not fantastic to say, for example, that the nazis, with their callous disregard of human sympathy, reason, and the fundamental conditions of happiness, violated the natural rights of man and therefore forfeited all moral claim to remain in power. So interpreted, natural rights are teleological rights; and to insist upon them is to deny that all values are merely relative, merely the creations of the government in power or the existing society. These natural rights, far from being unfounded or obsolete, are antitotalitarian and have never been more timely than in the present century when political totalitarianism has encroached so greatly upon freedom. They are the necessary defenses against tyranny.

If natural rights are thus to be interpreted as teleological rights, they are not essentially different in kind from the rights that Mill so ardently defended. His method, as I have said, was to show that the permanent welfare of mankind is bound up with the rights of the individual, and that the individual can be happy and progressive only if he is free. Mill is right: freedom is as necessary to man as bread and air. Without civil rights—such as free speech and assembly— human beings are dehumanized, and a society made up of such ciphers lacks all the essentials of greatness. Without freedom, the methods of persuasion are abrogated, the channels of peaceful adjustment are blocked. No country, in these conditions is safe; social lags and injustices will pile up, resentments will mount, until violent explosion is inevitable. In an Atomic Age, when the need of adaptation to unprecedented and rapidly changing situations is acute, free speech may be a matter of life or death. Without freedom, we cannot achieve the peaceful, orderly, and flexible adjustment to rapid technological change—and without such adjustments, there is little chance to avoid an eventual world war or violent revolution.

Free speech, like other basic human rights, should not be denied to those who do not believe in it. Professor Ewing has well said:

The right should be allowed even to those people who would not themselves allow it if in power. For the reasons for allowing it are not dependent on the opinions of those to whom it is allowed being right, and it would be inconsistent for the advocate of free speech to exempt his own principles from the free discussion which he advocates as the best means of finding and confirming the truth. To repress the free expression of opinion is either to treat force, not reason, as the supreme arbiter, or to claim infallibility.[28]

Yet I think there are profound crises in human life, such as occur if powerful antidemocratic cliques are threatening to destroy democratic processes, when we are justified in suppressing the freedom of some in order to save or regain the freedom of most. A democracy, for example, may need to

[28] *Ibid.*, pp. 55-56.

curtail liberty to survive at all; but the policymakers should be reasonably sure that the crisis is deep enough to justify suppression of the antidemocratic forces, and that these forces really *are* antidemocratic and not merely allegedly so.

If they do not exercise extreme caution, however, they will, by suppression, create greater evils than they are seeking to avoid. As Mr. Justice Oliver Wendell Holmes wrote:

> I think we should be eternally vigilant against attempts to check the expression of opinions that we loathe and think to be fraught with death, unless they so imminently threaten interference with the lawful and pressing purposes of the law that an immediate check is required to save the country.[29]

It would seem safest to rely upon repression only when free discussion no longer remains as a practical alternative. To use the slogans of "Americanism" to justify a greater repression is specious indeed. As Mr. Justice Louis Brandeis has eloquently written:

> Those who won our independence by revolution were not cowards. They did not fear political change. They did not exalt order at the cost of liberty. To courageous, self-reliant men, with confidence in the power of free and fearless reasoning applied through the processes of popular government, no danger flowing from speech can be deemed clear and present, unless the incidence of the evil apprehended is so imminent that it may befall before there is opportunity for free discussion. If there be time to expose through discussion the falsehood and fallacies, to avert the evil by the processes of education, the remedy to be applied is more speech, not enforced silence. Only an emergency can justify suppression. Such must be the rule if authority is to be reconciled with freedom. Such, in my opinion, is the command of the Constitution. It is, therefore, always open to Americans to challenge a law abridging free speech and assembly by showing that there was no emergency justifying it.[30]

[29] Myer Cohen, editor, *Selected Supreme Court Decisions,* Harper, New York, 1937, p. 9.
[30] *Ibid.,* p. 19.

Such tenacious attachment to the methods of free discussion is the indubitable mark of a liberal mind.

Living in an age of comparative peace and security, Mill did not see fit to discuss the problem of preserving liberty during a crisis so profound that it shakes the social order to its very foundations. He did not witness the deep international crisis that led to the downfall of the Spanish republic, the German Weimar republic, and the Czechoslovakian republic. He was not constantly reminded, as we have been, that tolerance is a function of security, that intolerance thrives upon crisis, and that, consequently, "freedom from fear" is a condition of all other kinds of freedom. He was unaware of the strong measures that must sometimes be taken to prevent men like Hitler from storming the citadels of power. One of the limitations of Mill's essay is that he could not sufficiently take account of such facts.

The limitation, however, is not his alone: one of the chief shortcomings of the liberal tradition has been its tendency to overestimate the power of reason as a solvent of social conflicts, especially when the conflicts involve the most fundamental issues, such as the main prerogatives of a dominant class. The tendency of many liberals to shrink from a realistic analysis of the role of force in society does not help to eliminate violence. On the contrary, the beginning of social wisdom is realism. And if we do not overestimate the compelling power of reason, we have a better chance to avoid violent disasters that have crushed the democratic and liberal forces in a number of countries.

Another limitation of traditional liberalism has been its middle-class bias. In this respect, it has not been liberal enough. It has tended to restrict freedom to particular races, nations, or classes; it has too often withheld its bounty from the poorer workers, the colonial peoples, the Negroes and other racial and religious minorities. For example, Locke, in his *Thoughts on Education,* advocated an essentially servile

training for working-class children and referred contemptu-
ously to "the abhorred rascality" of the common people.[31]
Burke, a more conservative liberal, spoke of the people as "a
swinish multitude . . . born to consume frugally";[32] and
Alexander Hamilton declared, "The People, Sir, is a great
beast."[33] Even such radical revolutionary leaders as Tom
Paine and Robespierre thought in terms of a middle-class
revolution, which would safeguard the rights of property;
and the best representative of liberalism, John Stuart Mill,
was fearful that democracy would subjugate exceptional
men to the "collective mediocrity" of the masses. Some of the
more recent apologists for "liberalism" have defended the
"right" of the great monopolists to create an artificial scarcity
of goods and the "right" of the wealthy to exploit native
labor in the colonies.

I see no reason why the "right" thus to injure human
beings should be glorified by the name of liberty. Those who
would extend freedom to all, moreover, are far more liberal
in spirit than those who would restrict freedom to the holders
of power and riches. The issue is whether we are willing to
democratize freedom. The liberal ideal of freedom and the
democratic ideal of equality should be combined. Liberalism,
when sundered from democracy, is an upper-class privilege—
far too limited to satisfy the demands of justice. Democracy,
when sundered from liberalism, might be called "totalitarian
democracy"—democracy based upon majority rule without
civil rights—and this, tyrannical in itself, will almost inevitably degenerate into the deeper tyranny of totalitarian
autocracy. We must, therefore, create a social structure that

31 *Cf.*, Alexander Meiklejohn, *Education between Two Worlds*, Harper,
New York, 1942, pp. 31-33.

32 *Cf.*, Harold Laski, *The Rise of Liberalism*, Harper, New York, 1936, pp.
225, 231. The phrase *"fruges consumere nati,"* which occurs in Burke's
Thoughts on Scarcity, I have translated as "born to consume frugally."

33 Quoted by Merle Curti, *The Growth of American Thought*, Harper, New
York, 1943, p. 192.

will ensure the creative interplay of freedom and equality, a society of free men united in a democratic community.

3. *Freedom and Organization*

IN A TOTALITARIAN DICTATORSHIP or a totalitarian democracy, the man of independent opinions and talents is a pariah. Mill, above all, dreaded this type of regime, and it seems to me that he had good reasons for dreading it. But it is important to see that there are two sides to the individual: the side that separates and isolates, and the side that unites. The full development of individuality includes the expression of self-transcending, and not merely self-asserting, interests. Historically, individualistic liberalism has been so intent upon emphasizing the latter type of interest that it has grossly underestimated the importance of the former. It has tended to think of the individual as self-complete, self-enclosed, and self-centered; consequently it has conceived of freedom as inherent in the individual apart from his social relations and has regarded freedom and social organization as antithetical terms. This aspect of liberalism requires careful and extended consideration.

Although such individualistic liberalism contains a precious element of truth, it is inadequate, and, in its traditional insistence that freedom is inconsistent with organization, it survives mainly as an anachronism. It provides the main slogans for those who are endeavoring to divert the people from fundamental social reconstruction. Everywhere they are telling the voting public that "freedom," especially "the freedom of enterprise," is opposed to "the tyranny of planning." They often declare that planning is "un-American" and contrast it with the liberty to which the Founding Fathers of our republic were devoted.

Actually, planning, whether it be by civic groups, business

organizations, or governmental bodies, is quite as much a part of the American tradition as "rugged individualism." Americans have not acquired their world-wide reputation for efficiency by mere caprice or a tendency to drift. From the time of the Mayflower Compact to the recent reports of our planning boards, our citizens have known how to sit down together, to talk over their mutual problems, to reach intelligent understanding upon the basis of exact information, and to achieve coherent social action which integrates divergent interests and activities in the light of a common knowledge and a common design. Planning, so far from being a new kind of disease imported from Soviet Russia, is American to the core. The sensible attitude is not to flee it as a foreign plague, but to use and control and democratize it.

The truly democratic choice is neither the "liberal" nor the fascist position. Freedom without organization is a delusion; organization without freedom is a strait jacket. These two values, instead of being pitted against each other, must be interfused, so that freedom is no longer merely freedom and organization merely organization. There must be a new quality in both and a new ideal as a result of their fusion: *organized* freedom and *free* organization.

Anything so precious as freedom exacts a price—it can be achieved only when we plan and organize to achieve it. Being *legally* "free" to do what we choose and being *actually* free and *able* to do so are not equivalent. We tend to think of freedom abstractly, as mere absence of legal restraint, as "the freedom of both rich and poor to sleep under bridges"; we too seldom think of it concretely and operationally as the opportunity to do what we like, which depends upon planning and organization. In considering a problem of this kind, it is very important that we should get down, as William James would put it, to the pressing concrete particulars of the matter. When we think in these terms—of remunerative work, good food, decent clothing, and adequate shelter, of sufficient rest and carefree holidays, of education sufficient to evoke one's talents, of the right to speak one's mind on the job without fear of economic reprisal, of the right to a happy and secure old age with more than a beggarly pension—we realize that a welter of competing selfishness or mere absence of legal restraint does not constitute a free society. The failure to think in this manner betrays itself in confused and sentimental ideas. For example, a prominent official once said, in the depth of the Depression, that it is a blessing we have our national parks, because the unemployed are now *free* to amuse themselves in these public playgrounds. This official apparently conceived of freedom negatively as the mere absence of external restraint.

A far more adequate and less naïve conception of freedom is contained in the definition of Ralph Barton Perry: "the absence of external obstacles which prevent, and the presence of resources and capacities which promote, the power of any individual to realize his desires or execute his will."[34] This definition combines two concepts: negative freedom, the absence of external restraints, and positive freedom, the presence of resources and capacities to effectuate one's choices.

With this definition in mind, we can understand two basic mistakes that many so-called liberals commit. First, they interpret negative freedom too narrowly as involving merely governmental restraint, whereas there are other important forms of restraint, such as physical force, social ostracism, or economic coercion. Whoever wields power can restrain those who lack power. When there are wide class differentials in society, some will possess a greatly disproportionate share of power and will be able to restrain those who lack such power. A government actively devoting itself to the protection of the weak and the removal of these wide differentials may greatly increase the amount of negative freedom even when it sternly restrains unduly powerful members of the society.

Second, "liberals" often stress negative freedom to the relative neglect of positive freedom. They conceive of freedom

[34] *Puritanism and Democracy*, Vanguard Press, New York, 1944, p. 512.

as consisting almost exclusively of "civil rights," such as we
find stipulated in the first ten amendments to the American
Constitution. These rights are very necessary to a free society
—there should be no misunderstanding on this point—but
they are not *sufficient* to constitute real freedom. A man is
only nominally free if he is "allowed" to make a choice but
lacks the instruments to effectuate the choice, or if his personality is so undeveloped that he can make few wise or
ample choices. As Helen Lynd has said, in so far as liberalism
emphasizes only negative freedom it leaves "men free to live
without the material basis of life, free to speak, but with
nothing of their own to say, free to believe but with nothing
positive to believe in, free to worship but with nothing in
which to place their faith."[35] To possess any large measure of
positive freedom, men must satisfy fundamental needs, such
as for food, shelter, clothing, health, education, security, play
and recreation, the creative expression of one's talents, the
enjoyment of beauty and art.

Thinking in these positive terms, Franklin D. Roosevelt
urged an "Economic Bill of Rights," which included the
following provisions:

> The right to a useful and remunerative job in the industries
> or shops or farms or mines of the nation; the right to earn
> enough to provide adequate food and clothing and recreation;
> . . . the right of every family to a decent home; the right to
> adequate medical care and the opportunity to achieve and enjoy
> good health; the right to adequate protection from the economic
> fears of old age, sickness, accident and unemployment; the right
> to a good education.[36]

Such rights, which have been embodied by the United Nations Assembly in its International Bill of Rights, are necessary if freedom is to constitute the essential texture of men's
lives.

Even the traditional civil rights require positive conditions

[35] *England in the Eighteen-Eighties,* Oxford University Press, New York,
1945, p. 348.
[36] Message to Congress, January 1944.

to realize them. Free speech, for example, demands much besides the legal right to speak. As the Office of War Information declared during World War II:

> The first condition is that the individual have something to say. Literacy is a prerequisite of free speech, and gives it point. Denied education, denied information, suppressed or enslaved, people grow sluggish; their opinions are hardly worth the high privilege of release. Similarly, those who live in terror or in destitution, even though no specific control is placed upon their speech, are as good as gagged. Another condition necessary for free speech is that the people have access to the means of uttering it—to newspapers, to the radio, the public forum. When power or capital are concentrated, when the press is too closely the property of narrow interests, then freedom suffers. There is no freedom, either, unless facts are within reach, unless information is made available. And a final condition of free speech is that there be no penalties attached to the spread of information and to the expression of opinion, whether those penalties be applied by the Government or by any private interests whatsoever.[37]

Thus supplied with the instrumentalities for their full and effective expression, human rights are very real and precious; but if they are not thus buttressed by the necessary social organization, they may be good as resolutions but barren of results.

Many books on politics and economics are vitiated by the failure clearly to recognize these facts. For example, Professor Hayek's argument in *The Road to Serfdom*, that a planned economic order is incompatible with freedom, is plausible only because the concepts of "freedom" and "organization" are left unanalyzed. In the absence of such analysis, it is reasonable to equate "economic liberalism" with "freedom" and a "planned society" with "totalitarianism," and to argue that "ne'er the twain shall meet." The effect is to obscure the fundamental differences between fascism and socialism, or between socialism and a mixed program such as Franklin D.

---

[37] Quoted by Abraham Edel, *The Theory and Practice of Philosophy*, Harcourt, Brace, New York, 1946, p. 261.

Roosevelt's New Deal. The argument, in this form, is very confused and consequently very dangerous. Any adequate analysis, in contrast, would have revealed that governmental organization, which Professor Hayek so constantly equates with regimentation, *can* be free, and that "freedom" in the absence of such organization, is often merely negative and nominal. Moreover, in his eagerness to defend "business enterprise," he overlooks the prime conditions for the realization of his own ideal of individualistic freedom. He does not understand that, in the words of Perry:

The greatest force for regimentation is a maldistribution of wealth which binds men to the routines of livelihood, reduces life to those animal functions in which men most closely resemble one another, exposes men to the pressures of group opinion and sentiment, and excludes that free play of imagination, thought, and choice which is the most fruitful source of individual differences.[38]

The truth is that we cannot achieve a decent measure of individuality, we cannot achieve real, effective, operational freedom, without deep-ranging and far-reaching plans. If we should mobilize our national resources for public welfare as effectively in peacetime as we do in wartime, but on a stable and lasting basis, we could work a wondrous transformation in a single generation and thereby enormously increase the amount of positive freedom. We know from our wartime experience what a vast deal we can produce, and we begin to see that it is sheer folly and cruelty to perpetuate poverty when we have the necessary resources to eliminate it. Our planning, of course, must counterbalance directives from the leaders above with initiatives from the masses below. It must unite free men within an organized community.

The fact that real freedom is not inconsistent with organization is indicated by many ordinary activities. Consider, for example, two people dancing together. They move together according to a pattern which is their cooperative deed. They dance in time and in step—the motion of one dancer is con-

[38] Perry, *op. cit.*, p. 464.

tinually responsive to the motion of the other. They dance in this manner, not because they are compelled to do so but because they want to move in just this way. Their desires are fulfilled in and through this very pattern. The result is a fusion of law and impulse, a reconciliation of the two fundamental aspects of man's nature, the spontaneous and the orderly, the impulsive and the rational.

True individuality, moreover, is enhanced, not repressed, by the right kind of organization. As Felix Cohen has remarked, there is more true individuality, more scope for diverse talents, in the superb coordination of a baseball team, than in a field of nine runners each pursuing his separate course. "Social harmony," therefore, "no more requires that each individual play a simple tune, much less the same tune, than does orchestral harmony."[39]

It may be objected that in these examples of free organization no restraints are imposed upon the individual, whereas social planning usually requires such restraints. This sort of objection is frequently based upon the assumption that any type of coercion decreases the amount of freedom. If this were the case, there would be little justification for laws with police to enforce them. Traffic regulations, for example, impose curbs and require enforcement, but without them the lives of many people would be less free and more hazardous. Similarly, when a public meeting is governed by Roberts' Rules of Order, it may be necessary to supply the chairman with a gavel and to provide a sergeant at arms, but the effect of such enforcement is usually to expedite the freedom of those who wish to deliberate and vote in a fair, democratic manner. Coercion is often necessary to "keep the peace," without which real freedom is impossible.

It may also be objected that freedom and organization can be reconciled only if the group is small. We must admit that if a large group, instead of a small, move and act together, the problem of reconciling freedom and organization be-

[39] In *American Philosophy Today and Tomorrow,* edited by H. M. Kallen and Sidney Hook, Furman, New York, 1935, p. 92.

comes more subtle and complex; but the harmony, when achieved, may be correspondingly richer, the resulting freedom more profound and exhilarating.

An excellent example of such free social organization has been provided by the Tennessee Valley Authority. As I read David Lilienthal's *T.V.A.: Democracy on the March*[40]—a book that retains its interest despite the passage of years—I am deeply impressed by the success of this great social experiment in achieving the ends of freedom *by the methods of freedom*. The basic objective—the elevation of living standards throughout the great valley by the unified development and conservation of resources—means the increase of positive freedom—opportunity for greater happiness and richer experience. The methods have been to stimulate grass-roots democracy, to bring the people and the experts together, to enlarge the people's alternatives by revealing to them what technology makes feasible, to achieve a community of persuasion by the methods of free discussion, to avoid undemocratic centralization by maintaining regional autonomy and employing local resources and agencies. Here is a vivid example of the interpenetration of freedom and organization. Here is a demonstration that planning can make use of the immense power of science and technology for the enhancement of freedom. I realize, of course, that T.V.A. has its detractors, and I recognize that the experiment, like every human enterprise, is not perfect; but I believe that it is a valid example of free social organization.

In this chapter, I have given an exposition and criticism of liberalism. I have tried to make clear that freedom is very precious, but that it has often been misconceived and fallaciously defended. Opposing an exaggerated individualism, I have contended that freedom without organization is a delusion. In the next two chapters, we shall look at the other side of the coin; organization without freedom, I shall maintain, is a strait jacket.

[40] Harper, New York, 1944.

Chapter Twelve

THE FASCIST IDEAL

1. *The Main Characteristics of Fascism*

THE DEFEAT of the fascist powers in World War II does not remove the need for a critical evaluation of fascism. As a phase in the life of the human spirit, as a force which dangerously lingers on after the war, and as a tendency at work even within the democracies, fascism must still be discussed. As an example, moreover, of organization without freedom, it is decidedly instructive.

By fascism I shall mean the kind of right-wing totalitarianism that dominated Germany, Italy, and Japan and that has found expression, in less pure form, in Spain, Portugal, Greece, Argentina, and a number of other countries. There are some profound differences among these various forms of fascism, but there is enough similarity to justify the common name. My brief discussion will be mainly concerned with nazi Germany and fascist Italy, as typical examples of fascism.

In practice, fascism is a "command economy" based upon the interpenetration of three groups: the militarists, the industrial monopolists, and the political bosses and bureaucrats. As Franz Neumann, in his superb book, *Behemoth,* has pointed out, each member in this alliance needed the others. The army needed the party and the bureaucracy, because modern war, being total, requires the mobilization of the entire population. The army could not mobilize the nation into a single disciplined whole; that was left to the party and the bureaucrats. The party, on the other hand, needed the army to stabilize the rule of force, to prepare for war, and eventually to fight. Both needed the big monopolists to form the economic basis of a totalitarian economy; and economic privilege, in turn, relied upon the army and the party to put down opposition and to further its imperialistic aspirations. All three groups were united by their antidemocratic bias and by the need to pool their forces in a period of intensifying social crisis. The frequent attempt to interpret fascism in terms of a single one of these factors, whether it be economic, political, or military, represents an oversimplification. Fascism was, in short, a complex alliance of antidemocratic rightist forces intent upon consolidating their power and impelled to act mainly by the profound economic and cultural crisis.

Admittedly, this was always an uneasy alliance. To a great extent, the army and "big business" became subordinate to the party machine and political directives; but there were always internal rifts. As the strain of war and deepening crisis went on, the members of the alliance began to fly apart. How deep the schism eventually became is illustrated by Liddell Hart's revealing book, *The German Generals Talk,* and by numerous other accounts of disaffection among the fascist ruling cliques.

Fascist theory was largely a cloak and rationalization for the totalitarian alliance. The basic concept of totalitarianism is expressed in Mussolini's famous slogan, "Nothing outside or above the State, nothing against the State, everything in the State, everything for the State." The nazis nominally rejected such political totalitarianism, maintaining that the state is merely an instrument of the Nazi party and the German race; but actually they adopted it under the disguise of the "racial community" and the "people's state" and transformed it into an even more drastic totalitarian creed.

The Italian theory, as articulated by such fascist philosophers as Alfredo Rocco and Giovanni Gentile, was mainly a perverted Hegelianism. The individual, it was said, is saved from incompleteness only by entering into social relations. By engaging in the life of the community, he achieves ethical salvation. All the manifold interests of the community, however, are integrated within the state. When the citizen obeys the state, therefore, he is obeying his own deeper will, achieving that social-mindedness, that identification with a larger whole, in which true freedom and welfare consist. The state, however, does not exist simply for the sake of the citizens, since, as a kind of group mind or social organism, it has a supreme intrinsic value not to be found in the individual minds of its members. Hence the government, within which the state's power resides, has the right and duty to coerce recalcitrant citizens into obedience, and to coordinate all aspects of the national life within its comprehensive, monistic integration.

The German theory of totalitarianism, as expressed by Hitler and Alfred Rosenberg, was based upon the concept of the racial community. The theory can be traced to various antecedents, such as Fichte's Germanic nationalism, Wagner's folk mysticism, and Gobineau's Aryan myth; to some extent its pattern of thought is to be found even in the Old Testament. Although they tortured and murdered the children of Israel, the nazis revived something of the ideology of ancient Judaism—the myth of the chosen people and its Messiah, who is destined to lead them from bondage. As the new Messiah, Hitler emphasized the tribal values implied by his Teutonic adaptation of this myth—the supreme worth of the German folk-community, the spiritual unity of the chosen people. In their intense, intolerant tribalism, however, the nazis departed from the sublime element in the ancient Jewish creed: the doctrine that the chosen people will prepare the way for a realm of true brotherhood among all human beings, a united humanity under a universal God. In practice, therefore, the nazi creed was quite different; it

meant anti-individualism and vague racial mysticism, employed to justify the forceful coordination of all activities
within the ambit of an exclusive, savage, militarized state.

The Nipponese people were similarly taught that "Japan
is the only divine land," inspired by a god-emperor, and
providentially destined to dominate the world. To achieve
such hegemony, the people must be molded by the state into
herdlike unity.

In its concrete aspects, fascism represented, as we have said,
a managed economy in which authoritarian economic, political, and military interests coalesced and interpenetrated—a
kind of collectivism, if you please, but very far from a democratic socialism. The fascists abolished "free enterprise"—and
to this extent they abolished "capitalism"—but they retained
a kind of monopoly capitalism subject to the state's commands. This fact is made crystal clear in such books as Franz
Neumann's *Behemoth,* Carl Schmidt's *The Plough and the
Sword,* and Robert Brady's *Business as a System of Power.* In
consonance with its basic hierarchical structure, fascism represented a will to power—the power of the few over the many,
the power of the victorious class or race or nation over its
subjugated victims.

In some measure, however, fascism disguised its antidemocratic character. A total war cannot be fought by a few
"select" champions: it must engage, so far as possible, the
total will and energy of the people; but the people cannot be
won by an authoritarian creed which asserts the right of the
few to domineer over the masses. Consequently, the fascist
propagandists were somewhat chary of advertising the concepts of authoritarianism and advanced a popular ideology.

According to the tenets of this popular creed, Germany,
Italy, and Japan were represented as proletarian nations,
fighting for their rights against "plutodemocratic" enemies,
who had monopolized a vast inequitable share of the world's
territory and wealth. "Economic justice," so the argument
ran, "cannot be achieved so long as the 'have' nations selfishly

withhold the riches of the world from the 'have nots.' The Axis peoples are not only poor but racially superior, and hence have a biological as well as economic right to a greater share of the world's goods. If the world is divided up properly, with Europe for the Europeans, Asia for the Asiatics, and America for the Americans, the superior races within each area will find the *Lebensraum* for a new life of happiness and prosperity." Later, when it was discovered that Americans could not be placated by this argument, it was less often said that America should be reserved for Americans.

The argument has a triple character. In its economic phase, it appeals to the ideal of sharing, the right of the masses to economic goods and all that can therewith be purchased. In its biological aspect, it appeals to the pride of birth, the assumed racial superiority of certain peoples and their "right" to dominate others. Finally, in its geopolitical aspect, it maintains that there are vast regional areas that must be organized as a whole if the economic resources thereof are to be utilized effectively. This ideology, which combines gross errors and deceits with the rightful demand for sharing and broad regional integration, was abominably successful in winning support from the Axis masses, who tried to escape from the terrible suffering and frustration occasioned by the Great Depression and deepening cultural crisis. Without this appeal to the common man, fascism could never have put civilization in such awful jeopardy.

Despite its popular mask, the tyrannical character of the fascist regimes is now very evident. The spirit of such rule is best summed up in Machiavelli's famous advice to the Prince that he should combine the fierceness of the lion with the hypocrisy of the fox. As a lion, he will be ever ready to employ violence; as a fox, he will break his word whenever it is to his advantage to do so.

Beneath the mask of good will and honest dealing, there is fraud and cruelty and unscrupulousness; beneath the glove of diplomacy there is the red claw of the beast. In every age, there have been imperialists and despots who have behaved in accordance with Machiavelli's precepts, but the clearest recent example of this pattern of behavior has been supplied by the fascist dictators. There is one basic difference, however, between Machiavelli and the fascists. The Florentine was aware of a nobler code of ethics that he expounded in his other writings, and he conceived these base precepts as suitable only for an age of crisis and decadence, whereas the fascist dictators lost the sense of a higher standard. Their cynicism was carried to the point of nihilism.

Franz Neumann, in *Behemoth,* and Harold Laski, in *Where Do We Go From Here?,* have contended that this unprincipled opportunism and lawlessness, in the service of a limitless will to power, represents the most fundamental character of fascism. They discounted, therefore, the trappings of fascist "philosophy"—the tag ends of doctrine borrowed from Hegel, Nietzsche, Sorel, Gobineau, and innumerable other sources—and insisted that, in essence, fascism represents the outlaw and the nihilist. Neumann, for example, described German National Socialism as "a non-state, a chaos, a rule of lawlessness and anarchy, which has 'swallowed' the rights and dignity of man, and is out to transform the world into a chaos. . . ."[1] It seems to me that this interpretation is, on the whole, correct. In so far as fascist theory was used to bolster such lawlessness, it assumed the form of an extreme relativism, which eschews fixed principles and regards ideals as fictive constructions to be shattered, at any critical or opportune moment, by the decisive deed.

Although Mussolini played a pitiful and subordinate role in the last few years of his life, he can be regarded as an authoritative spokesman of this aspect of the fascist creed. He repeatedly stressed the extent to which principles are relative to changing moods and situations. For example, he declared:

Fascism has never attempted to clothe its complicated and powerful mental attitude with a definite program but has suc-

[1] *Behemoth,* Oxford University Press, New York, 1942, p. vii.

ceeded by following its ever changing intuition. . . . If relativism signifies contempt for fixed categories and men who claim to be the bearers of an immortal objective truth . . . then there is nothing more relativistic than fascist attitudes and activity. From the fact that all ideologies are of equal value, that all ideologies are mere fictions, the modern relativist infers that everybody has the right to create for himself his own ideology and to attempt to enforce it with all the energy of which he is capable.[2]

The fascists, in these terms, sought to excuse their unprincipled opportunism.

An elaborate metaphysical rationalization for opportunistic behavior is to be found in the "actualism" of Giovanni Gentile, the most reputable of Italian fascist philosophers. All reality, as he conceives it, is nothing but mind in flux. Man's whole life, including all standards, is reduced to evanescence and subjectivity—"the mind as pure act." Proclaiming ever-changing practice to be the only truth, Gentile announced that the true decisions of Il Duce were those simultaneously formulated and executed.[3]

Such apotheosis of the irrational deed, when applied to law and politics, means that a social policy is nothing more than the command of the leader—each man, each group, each situation, must be dealt with by an individual decision. It means that the Gestapo, or some other gang, is told: do not worry about legal precedents or principles; deal with each case as you see fit. "Science" is no longer objective, morals no longer impartial, art and religion no longer universal. "Culture" becomes nothing but propaganda—the subjection of all thought and expression to transient expediency.

A typical representative of this outlook was Hitler. For the most part, *Mein Kampf* is derivative and mediocre, but in one respect it is brilliant: discussing propaganda, the tactics of deceit, manipulation of symbols and shibboleths, the appeal to

[2] *Diuturna*, Milan, 1924, pp. 374-377.
[3] *Cf.*, "The Philosophical Basis of Fascism," *Foreign Affairs*, Vol. VI, January 1928, p. 300.

the fickle and irrational in man, it reveals something of the devilish cleverness of a modern Machiavelli, but of a Machiavelli who has cast aside all fixed ideals and has become, in the profoundest sense, an outlaw. Beyond a few fanatical tenets, such as racism, Hitler's whole "ideology" was pure hoax, the ruse of the gangster, the substitution of tactics for principles, the use of any expedient in the drive toward power. Here is opportunism pushed to the point of nihilism, the anarchy of the jungle as the rule of life.

I have spoken of the resemblances among the fascist powers, but I do not mean to deny the very substantial differences. In Germany, as contrasted with Italy, the social convulsion was more profound, the dictatorship was more ruthless, the masses were more fervent, the ideology was more mystical and barbaric, the racism was more intense and intolerant. The cynical opportunism of Mussolini was that of a reckless adventurer; the savage opportunism of Hitler was that of a fanatic. Although I know far less about Japanese fascism, I have no doubt that it also exhibited marked individual characteristics. The fascist regimes, however, were alike in other respects, such as their rightist totalitarianism, their hierarchical structure, their intense racialism or nationalism, their opportunism verging on nihilism, their reliance upon myth, propaganda, and the great art of bamboozling.

2. *An Appraisal of Fascism*

OUR HEALTHY DETESTATION of the fascist type of society should not blind us to the limited validity of its theory and practice. The fascists are, in a measure, right in denouncing the vast unregulated interplay of competitive interests and institutions which produce an anarchy as capricious, and therefore as destructive of true freedom, as the untamed natural forces which bedevil primitive man. Moreover, the order and design imposed by fascism, at least during the initial afflatus of the movement, gave to millions of people a sense of meaning and purpose generally felt to be lacking in modern life. Young men and women, who could not find employment and who felt frustrated and baffled by a world which apparently had no use for them, suddenly felt that they were wanted, that they had a role and a function transcending anything that they had known before. They participated in the emotional excitement of a great collective movement; they found escape from petty and selfish preoccupations in the wider ethos of tribal solidarity; and they were willing and happy to sacrifice many things for what *seemed* to them the glory of the nation or the race. In the early stages, moreover, the state seemed to prosper: under the impetus of national planning, unemployment first diminished and then disappeared, and productivity leaped upward.

Admitting the transient successes of fascism, we must insist that its ideals were demonic and tyrannical. We scarcely need to emphasize the lack of freedom that characterized fascist regimentation—the deliberate extermination of spontaneous thought and autonomous action, the treatment of human beings as products to be turned out en masse upon a social assembly line, cut and trimmed and patterned according to the latest blueprints of the ministry of propaganda. Waiting for orders and blindly obeying them, the citizens of the fascist state became atomized, dehumanized, self-alienated, and isolated from one another—mere mechanical replicas of an abstract mass-man. As if it were a grim satire, this *"Gleichschaltung"* was the terrible exaggeration of common tendencies in modern civilization: the mass hypnosis of propaganda and commercial advertising, the cunning manipulation of men's minds and wills by the "political machine," the mental treadmill of the overgrown bureaucracy, whether it be within a governmental office or an industrial corporation.

Such regimentation is a gross violation of the principles enunciated in Part Two of this book. Opposing every regi-

men not directed to human welfare, every glorification of a
collectivity for its own sake, we have contended that the individual is the sole locus of value, that he alone is an end in
himself, that he therefore has an indefeasible right to be
treated as an end and not as a means merely, and that no
state or race or ruling class has intrinsic value apart from the
welfare of its members.

Moreover, the nationalism or racialism of the fascist
regimes is a shocking example of a biased ideal. As I indicated in Chapter Eight, such loyalty must be rejected because
it wars upon the loyalties of others, and thus is not "loyal to
loyalty." It combines a narrow spread of good, an intense
group egoism, with a malevolent attitude toward those outside the pale. Indeed, in warring upon other groups, the
fascists reveled in fiendish cruelty. In Germany alone twelve
to fifteen million persons were executed in gas chambers, on
gallows, before firing squads, or through similar devices. Old
and young, male and female, were tortured and exterminated,
often without provocation. What happened, also, in the
ghetto of Warsaw, and in other extermination centers outside of Germany, beggars all description. Sadism could
scarcely have been carried to greater extremes. Such carnage
measures the terrible depths that human nature can reach in
periods of profound crisis and disorientation.

In Chapter Five, I have called such racialism and nationalism a kind of group relativism. A perfect example is the doctrine, advanced by fascist apologists such as Alfred Rosenberg, that all values are relative to the national or racial
"community." I also pointed out, in the same chapter, that
there is a relativism of the moment, a denial of enduring
norms. Just as fascist parochialism is a rejection of any
world-wide values, so fascist opportunism is a denial of any
lasting values. Fascism, in effect, maintains that all standards
vary from place to place and from time to time; and fascism
pushes this temporal and group relativism, as I have said, to
the very point of nihilism. My attack upon both types of

relativism in Chapters Five and Eight constitutes, by implication, an indictment of fascism. I shall not attempt to repeat that indictment.

I would point out, however, how tragically this twofold relativism constricts the fascist ideal of organization. Because of its unprincipled opportunism, fascism did not really succeed in imposing law and order upon the internal affairs of the fascist societies. There was savage repression but no stable moral or legal order, and beneath the surface, there was disorder, doubt, and uncertainty. In Italy, especially, cynicism gradually replaced any binding faith; the state, outwardly one, seethed with inner conflicts. But in Germany, also, belief systems eventually collapsed like houses of cards. There was a temporary hysterical faith in *Il Duce* or *Der Fuehrer*, but finally there was little but brutal force and desperate fanaticism to integrate the society.

In the field of international relations, moreover, fascism stood for anarchy. Rejecting international law and government, it refused to extend organization to the very sphere where it is most needed. Mussolini declared, "Internationalism is an absurd fable," and emphasized the "insuppressible datum of race and nation."[4] This is typical of fascism; and it means war or the constant threat of war. Unfortunately, such mentality is far from being dead, and its existence, in this age of incredibly potent weapons, constitutes a peril to all men everywhere.

The fascist mentality is a threat even within our democracy. If a great national calamity should occur, such as a war with the Soviet Union or a vast economic depression, this threat could become very serious indeed. A certain number of people, in a period of deep crisis, would favor a fascist type of "solution"—coercive right-wing organization to the exclusion of freedom. We would like to think that this number is very small, but we must not be too complacent about the

4 *Popolo d'Italia,* February 1, 1921; reproduced in Herbert W. Schneider, *Making the Fascist State,* Oxford University Press, New York, 1928, p. 275.

difficult years ahead. The outbreak of war, in an age of
fiendish scientific warfare, could very quickly produce a national hysteria with its concomitant of extreme repressive
measures. Moreover, if we should eventually have another
very profound depression—which many thoughtful economists regard as a distinct possibility—a "revolt of the masses"
might rapidly assume immense proportions, men of property
might fly into a panic, and demagogues might offer "crack-
pot" solutions. In these circumstances, can we be sure that the
dupes, the demagogues, and the monopolists will not combine
to create something like an American fascism?

Even without a dire crisis, the tendencies toward fascism
are ominous. This book was written while a wave of intolerance was sweeping through the land. Liberals, among others,
have been accused of being "subversive" and have been
pilloried by "loyalty boards" and "un-American activities
committees." In the hearings of such legislative committees,
the accused have been denied the right of full representation
by counsel, the right to cross-examine witnesses testifying
against them, the right to call witnesses in their own behalf,
and the right to testify freely in their own defense. At the
same time, the Federal Bureau of Investigation, although entirely proper in most of its functions, has been growing into
a kind of national secret police, collecting secret dossiers upon
many people suspected of being left of center. Such dossiers,
and other clandestine evidence, have sometimes been used as
the basis for dismissing men from public employment; the victims, in many cases, have not even been told what evidence is
being used against them. Many newspapers and periodicals
have joined in the hue and cry, and a new false standard of
Americanism—the uncritical and unquestioning acceptance of
things as they are—has been dinned into people's minds.

The men who conceive "loyalty" in these terms are
obviously not liberal, but neither are they conservative. True
conservatism would cling to the traditional principles of
Americanism, including the procedures prescribed by our

Bill of Rights and by Anglo-Saxon traditions of fair play. Any actions less conservative, such as intolerance and repression, give aid and comfort to extremists who seek to subvert American institutions. Naturally, we must guard against espionage and *real* treason, but we must also guard against the trend toward a Police State.

As Mr. Justice William O. Douglas of the Supreme Court has declared:

A people indifferent to their civil liberties do not deserve to keep them, and in this revolutionary age may not be expected to keep them long. A people who proclaim their civil liberties but extend them only to preferred groups start down the path of totalitarianism. They emulate either the dictatorship of the right or the dictatorship of the left. In doing this they erase a basic distinction between our system of government and totalitarianism. To allow this to happen is to lose by default. Far better to lose pleading the cause of decency and of justice. Then we win greatness even in defeat, and leave behind a rich heritage for those who later rebuild on the ashes of our lost hopes. But there will be no failure if we adhere steadfastly to our faith. For the goal of all races is toward a system which respects their dignity, frees their minds, and allows them to worship their God in their own way. None has yet designed an article of political faith more suited to those ends than our own Bill of Rights.[5]

The best defense against antidemocratic forces, whether of the extreme right or the extreme left, is a dynamic democratic program. Democracy can be defended only by *democracy:* it cannot be defended by tyranny, or preserved by fear of change. To the threat of revolution there is ultimately only one answer: the reforms that bring hope and exhilaration and happiness "in widest commonalty spread." If the people are happy and free, incitements to revolt will fall on deaf ears—and the revolutionists will rapidly diminish in number. The best of all recipes against subversive influences is given by the ancient sage who wrote the *Tao Te Ching,* the sacred book of Chinese Taoism:

[5] "Our Bill of Rights," *Vital Speeches,* Vol. XIV, February 1, 1948, p. 242.

Make the people's food sweet, their clothes beautiful, their houses comfortable, their daily life a source of pleasure. Then the people will look at the country over the border, will hear the cocks crowing and the dogs barking there, but right down to old age and the day of their death, they will not trouble to go there and see what it is like.[6]

[6] Translated by E. R. Hughes, in *Chinese Philosophy in Classical Times*, Dutton, New York, 1942, p. 164.

Chapter Thirteen

THE SOCIALIST IDEAL

1. *Historical Roots and Main Contributors*

THE CONCEPTION of a socialist society is not merely recent. Some elements of socialist or communist theory are to be found in such venerable classics as Plato's *Republic* or More's *Utopia*. A vague notion of socialism was, for example, in the mind of John Ball, the leader of a late medieval revolt of British peasantry, and the Diggers, a radical democratic faction, entertained socialist ideals during the Puritan Revolution. But it was not until the nineteenth century that socialist theory assumed definitive form in the works of such men as Charles Fourier, Louis Blanc, Robert Owen, Ferdinand Lasalle, and above all, Karl Marx and Friedrich Engels. In 1884, George Bernard Shaw and Sidney Webb organized the Fabian Society, and in the next year, the poet, William Morris became the head of the British Socialist League. Socialist ideas were also popularized in America by intellectuals, such as Edward Bellamy and William Dean Howells, and by radical labor leaders such as Daniel De Leon and Eugene V. Debs.

With the development of large-scale industrial capitalism and the appearance of a very powerful labor movement, socialist theory became immensely influential. The revolutionary establishment of the Paris Commune, first proletarian state, in 1871, dramatized the formidable character of the new ideals. By 1898, the cause of socialism had gained a large number of adherents: the Social Democratic party of Germany in that year polled two million votes and elected fifty-six parliamentary representatives; six years later Debs received four hundred thousand votes as socialist candidate for the Presidency of the United States. The first important attempt at revolution, accompanied by a general strike of three million workers, swept Russia in 1905. On the eve of World War I, the socialists polled a fifth of all Italian votes and a third of all German. The war, however, precipitated a split between the socialist parties and led to a temporary waning of socialist influence, but in 1917, the first great Communist revolution occurred in Russia. Subsequent events, such as the vast expansion of Communist power in Eastern Europe and Asia after World War II, and the upsurge of social democracy in Western Europe, are too familiar to require mention.

To evaluate these great historical events, we must understand the doctrines which have largely inspired them. Since my space is limited, I shall confine myself to the social philosophy of Marx and Engels. I shall not discuss their general philosophical doctrine known as "dialectical materialism," which is not strictly relevant to the theme of social ideals.

The lives and personal traits of Marx and Engels may throw some light upon their doctrines. Born in Trier, Prussia, in 1818, Karl Marx came from an upper middle-class Jewish family, but his father, a lawyer, abandoned the Jewish faith and joined the state church of Prussia. Karl Marx was sent to the universities of Bonn and Berlin, where he came into contact with the Young Hegelians, a group of left-wing philosophers and critics who deeply influenced him. After receiving the degree of Doctor of Philosophy, he found that his political ideals were too radical to permit an academic career. In 1842 he entered politics as editor of an opposition newspaper, the *Rheinische Zeitung*, which was soon suppressed by the Prussian government. Accompanied by his aristocratic young wife, Jenny von Westphalen, he chose to live as an exile in Paris and Brussels until a brief return to Cologne during the Revolution of 1848-1849. Exiled again for his revolutionary activities, he took his family to London, where they established a permanent home. It was there that Marx unremittingly toiled as a socialist writer and organizer for the remainder of his lifetime.

In the meantime, he had entered into a fecund and intimate friendship with Friedrich Engels, whom he had known in Paris during the fall of 1844. Engels, who became Marx's close collaborator, was born in 1820 in Barmen. His father was a well-to-do textile manufacturer of orthodox views, and the son eventually entered the family business of Ermen and Engels, cotton spinners in Manchester. While he was still living in Germany, he passed, as Marx had done, through left-wing Hegelianism into political heresy and became for a short time a radical journalist. In 1842, however, he took a position in the firm at Manchester but spared enough time to write a scathing indictment of British industrialism, *The Condition of the Working Class in England,* published in 1844. After meeting Marx in Paris, he spent the years from 1845 to 1850 in France, Germany, and Belgium, organizing socialist groups and collaborating with his new friend. It was in Brussels late in 1847 that they published the *Communist Manifesto.* Forced out of Germany in 1850 by a rightist reaction, he reluctantly went back to the family business in Manchester, but he kept in communication with Marx by mail and occasional visits until he himself moved to London in 1870. In 1865, the two friends helped to organize the International Workingmen's Association, known later as the First International; and they took an active part in its affairs until it was dissolved in 1872. After Marx's death in 1883, Engels completed, from Marx's notes, the second and third volumes of *Capital.* His own death occurred in 1895.

Despite their close friendship, the two men were in striking contrast. Engels was a blond German, tall and straight, carefully groomed. He was a convivial drinker, buoyant of temperament, yet an efficient businessman, a respected member of the Manchester Stock Exchange. When he grew tired of his "damned business," he would plunge into socialist activity or steal away to an Irish sweetheart, Elizabeth Burns, whom he eventually married. In time he rose to be a partner in the firm, but even when he was a simple employee with modest income, he assisted the poverty-stricken Marx family with a stream of five- and ten-pound notes. Despite his practical activities, he was a scholar of no mean range, being especially well versed in natural science, military tactics, and languages.

Marx was a swarthy Jew, whom his intimates nicknamed "the Moor," with a squat powerful body, thick black hair, and dark, flashing eyes. Careless of dress and bearing, he scarcely spared time from his tremendous labors to swallow his meals. With only a meager income as a correspondent for the New York *Tribune,* he could not keep himself and his family supplied with necessities, such as shoes or postage stamps. To the miseries of poverty were added the deaths of several of his children and, in his later years, the ravages of disease. In spite of these difficulties, he did a colossal amount of work and became well versed not only in philosophy, economics, and history, but even in literature, such as the Greek dramatists, Shakespeare, Goethe, and Balzac. His personal lot and fierce polemical spirit did not prevent him from being a tender father and a sympathetic friend to his chosen few. Many have complained of his vindictiveness, but as Edmund Wilson has pointed out:

> Only so sore and angry a spirit, so ill at ease in the world, could have recognized and seen into the causes of the wholesale mutilation of humanity, the grim collisions, the uncomprehended convulsions, to which that age of great profits was doomed.[1]

2. *Self-alienation and Fetishism*

THE EARLY WRITINGS of Marx, and to a lesser extent of Engels, exhibit an intense preoccupation with the problem of man's

[1] *To the Finland Station,* Harcourt, Brace, New York, 1940, p. 316.

self-alienation in a world of his own making. As Marx later declared:

In our days everything seems pregnant with its contrary; machinery gifted with the wonderful power of shortening and fructifying human labor, we behold starving and overworking it. The new-fangled sources of wealth, by some strange weird spell, are turned into sources of want. The victories of art seem bought by the loss of character. At the same pace that mankind masters nature, man seems to become enslaved to other men or to his own infamy. Even the pure light of science seems unable to shine but on the dark background of ignorance. All our inventions and progress seem to result in endowing material forces with intellectual life, and in stultifying human life into a material force.[2]

Marx contends that industry and technology, developing more swiftly than the forms of social control, turn against their human creators and subjugate them. In the words of Emerson:

> Things are in the saddle
> And ride mankind.[3]

Men become enslaved to machines and money, and things take on life and dominate human beings. Thus there is a twofold inversion of values: the dehumanization and depersonalization of mankind, and the attribution of social relationships and spiritual properties to material objects. The first Marx calls "self-alienation" and the second, "fetishism."

He very bitterly describes the "self-alienation" of the workers under capitalism. In the mechanized industries of capitalist civilization, ordinary workers sell their labor power and are handled as commodities; and the objects they create are not theirs to keep or to market. They work under a routinized system of a minute division of labor, which utilizes and develops only a fraction of their potentialities. Hence the worker does not realize himself, does not fulfill his *own* ends: he is used as a tool by his employer:

[2] "Speech at the Anniversary of the *People's Paper*," in *Selected Works*, Vol. II, International Publishers, New York, 1933, pp. 427-428.
[3] Ralph Waldo Emerson, "Ode to William Ellery Channing."

Instead of developing his free physical and mental energies, he mortifies his body and ruins his mind. . . . His working is, therefore, not done willingly but under compulsion. It is forced labor. It is, therefore, not the satisfaction of a need, but only a *means* for the satisfaction of wants outside of it.[4]

Still more dehumanizing is the unemployment and poverty, the waste and decay of man power, which results when machines compete against human beings, impoverish them, or cast them out of work. *"Not having,"* declared Marx, "is . . . an entire negation of the reality of the human being, a very positive *having,* a having of hunger, of cold, of sickness, of crime, of debasement, of imbecility, of all forms of inhumanity and pathology."[5] Marx and Engels substantiated this indictment by appalling descriptions of life among the poor.

Even the wealthy, we are told, are perverted and dehumanized by the profit system. Their absorption in moneymaking, business in itself, production of goods per se, their obsessive devotion to mammoth, inhuman, impersonal business organizations, stultifies their personalities and robs them of the fruits of any broad and generous culture. "Contempt for theory, for art, for history, for man . . . ," declared Marx, "is the real conscious standpoint and virtue of the monied man."[6]

If men are thus money-ridden and machine-dominated, it is because inanimate objects have taken on the qualities of persons: they have become, in Marxian language, "fetishes." Workers produce commodities, give them economic value as the result of their labor; but the commodities, once produced, rule the producers instead of being ruled by them. They appear as independent beings endowed with life, and enter into relations both with one another and the human race. Declared Marx:

[4] Marx, *"Ökonomische-philosophische Manuskripte,"* in Marx and Engels, *Gesamtausgabe,* Vol. III, Berlin, 1932, pp. 85-86; quoted by Herbert Marcuse, *Reason and Revolution,* Oxford University Press, New York, 1941, pp. 277-278.
[5] *Die Heilige Familie,* in *Gesamtausgabe, op. cit.,* Vol. I, Frankfurt, 1927, p. 212.
[6] *Selected Essays,* International Publishers, New York, 1926, p. 93.

The object which labor produces, its product, is encountered as an *alien entity*, a force which has become independent of its producer. . . . The more the worker toils, the more powerful becomes the alien world of objects he produces to oppose him, and the poorer he himself becomes.[7]

The tyranny of industrial processes, according to Marx and Engels, is intensified by the superstitious attitude which men assume toward economic commodities. The values of these commodities, which they possess only through their relations to persons, seem to be intrinsic properties exchanging on the market in terms of their fixed objective worth. A diamond, for example, seems *intrinsically* very valuable, whereas it would be as cheap as coal if it required as little labor to produce. Hence the human core and content of exchange values becomes depersonalized and, in consequence, heartless.

The inhumanity of capitalism is accentuated when the productive forces expand much more rapidly than the corresponding social controls. The economic system, thrown out of balance, then begins to run riot, driving men into and out of employment, dragging them through cycles of inflation and depression, casting them into the black hell of war. Nobody intends, plans, or organizes these developments. Consequences quite other than those intended result from "the innumerable intersecting forces."[8]

We can now understand the substance of Marxian ethics: the demand that human beings be treated as human beings, and things as things. In his own way, Marx is as insistent as Ruskin that "the only wealth is life." The advantage of socialism, as he sees it, is that it will end the "self-alienation" of human beings and the "fetishism" of commodities and industrial processes. It is "man's complete conscious . . . return to himself as a social, that is, human being."[9] He believed that such a return to man's essential humanity is

---

[7] *Gesamtausgabe*, Vol. III, p. 83; quoted by Marcuse, *op. cit.*, p. 277.

[8] *Cf.*, Marx and Engels, *Correspondence: 1846-1895*, International Publishers, New York, 1936, p. 476.

[9] *Gesamtausgabe*, Vol. III, p. 114; quoted in Marcuse, *op. cit.*, p. 286.

possible only if social relations are fundamentally reorganized to correspond to the more highly evolved productive forces. Self-alienation will not be terminated until human beings, under a planned economy for social benefit, regain mastery over the products of their labor. Real freedom means liberation from the bondage to material conditions, especially from poverty and excessive toil. Marx insisted:

The kingdom of freedom actually begins only where drudgery, enforced by hardship and external purposes, ends; it thus lies, quite naturally, beyond the sphere of proper material production.[10]

It lies in "the full and free development of every human individual"[11] which the shortening of the working day and the mastery of man's material environment will make possible. But "the true kingdom of freedom . . . can flourish only on the grounds occupied by the kingdom of necessity, which remains its basis."[12] It is not by turning away from material things, but by mastering them, that the spirit of man is to be freed. Man does not live by bread alone, but he must have bread to live for other things.

3. The Productive Forces and the Social Relations

THE FACT of man's self-alienation, Marx declared, should not leave us in a state of despair.

This antagonism between modern industry and science on the one hand, modern misery and dissolution on the other hand; this antagonism between the productive powers, and the social relations of our epoch is a fact, palpable, overwhelming, and not to be controverted. Some parties may wail over it; others may wish to get rid of modern arts in order to get rid of modern conflicts.

[10] Quoted from Marx, *Capital*, by K. R. Popper, *The Open Society and Its Enemies*, Routledge, London, 1945, p. 96.
[11] *Ibid.*, p. 107.
[12] *Ibid.*, p. 96.

Or they may imagine that so signal a progress in industry wants to be completed by as signal a regress in politics. On our part, we do not mistake the shape of the shrewd spirit that continues to mark all these contradictions. We know that to work well the new-fangled forces of society, they only want to be mastered by new-fangled men—and such are the working men. They are as much the invention of modern times as machinery itself.[13]

These sentences require elucidation. They presuppose the doctrine that economic conditions *primarily* determine historical events. Marx and Engels recognized, however, that a *purely* economic explanation is an illegitimate abstraction from the concrete fullness of history. Engels stated:

Political, juridical, philosophical, religious, literary, artistic, etc., development is based on economic development. But all these react upon one another and also upon the economic base. It is not that the economic position is the *cause and alone active,* while everything else has only a passive effect. There is, rather, interaction on the basis of the economic necessity, which *ultimately* always asserts itself.[14]

Thus Marx and Engels conceived of history as a very complex interaction of unequal forces, among which the economic causes are, in the long run, by far the most powerful. The historian should, therefore, look to the economic system for the primary causes of social change. When he does so, he discovers that there is not just *one* kind of economic system but a succession of types: primitive communism, slavery, feudalism, and capitalism, with historical forces moving inexorably toward socialism. Each stage is marked by a corresponding level of technological development. "The hand-mill," for example, "gives you society with the feudal lord; the steam-mill, society with the industrial capitalist."[15]

There is not only a development from stage to stage but a development *within* each stage. In the early expanding

13 "Speech at the Anniversary of the *People's Paper*," *op. cit.*, p. 428.
14 Marx and Engels, *Correspondence, op. cit.*, p. 517.
15 Marx, *The Poverty of Philosophy*, International Publishers, New York, no date, p. 92.

phases of an economy, the various interacting factors in a productive system—labor power, natural resources, instruments, and social relations—are in a state of relative equilibrium and therefore develop progressively and harmoniously. But sooner or later the social relations—the class structure and system of property—enter into conflict with labor and technology and the effective use of natural resources. Whereas initially these social relations were part of the forces of production, in time they become mainly *fetters* upon these productive forces. In the early phase of capitalism, for example, the rise of the capitalist class immensely facilitated the expansion of production; in the late phase of capitalism, the system of private ownership and the attendant class structure result in depression and war, and the enormous waste of labor power, natural resources, and technology. This catastrophic conflict between the forces of production and the social relations of production will persist until the social relations are reorganized so as to harmonize with the productive forces. Such a fundamental reorganization constitutes a revolution.

The nature of the conflict between the productive forces and the social relations, as envisaged by Marx, needs to be stated more precisely. The forces develop more rapidly than the relations. This means that the techniques, tools, and machines employed on the job change more quickly than the institutions of property and the distribution of wealth. New wine is poured into old bottles; the difficulties and dangers caused by the fermentation of the new wine cannot be avoided until new bottles are provided; new social relations, in other words, must be instituted to match the new productive forces. For example, the multiplication of inventions, the expansion of trade and manufacture, and the attendant development of urban life in the late period of feudalism could not be reconciled with the rigid, hierarchical structure of feudal society; a profound reorganization, which we call the rise of capitalism, was therefore necessary. Marx and Engels believed that the rapid development of technology in recent decades similarly necessitates the change from a capitalist to a socialist type of economy.

Henry Adams, who likewise believed that technology is the great dynamic factor in history, wrote:

> Bombs educate vigorously, and even wireless telegraph or airships might require the reconstruction of society. . . . The new American—the child of incalculable . . . electric power and radiating energy—must be a sort of God compared with any former creation of nature.[16]

Marx and Engels would reply that we need an embattled working class, rather than "a sort of God," to resolve our difficulties, but otherwise they would endorse this quotation from Adams.

Although they believed that technology is enormously important, their interpretation of history is not a mere technological determinism. Not only machines and techniques but class relations are fundamental. The great crises of history, they believed, are mainly the result of the conflict between rapidly changing techniques and slowly changing class stratifications. This conflict, moreover, is not subhuman, automatic: it always involves a contest of ideas and wills. Above all, it involves a struggle between opposing classes, such as masters and slaves, feudal lords and serfs, capitalist employers and workers. To understand the details of this theory as it applies to contemporary problems, we must turn to the Marxian economic theory.

4. A Brief Résumé of Marxian Economics

WE MUST REMEMBER that Marxian economics is extremely complex, and that an exposition in a few pages can mention only the barest essentials.

(1) The Labor Theory of Value. Marx distinguished be-

16 *The Education of Henry Adams*, Houghton Mifflin, Boston, 1918, p. 496.

tween "exchange value" (the economic value of goods or services) and "use value." Something may be very useful and still not worth buying. When it can be obtained without work, there is no sense in paying anyone for it, but it may be, nevertheless, very useful. Air, for example, has use value, since we cannot live without it, but it has no exchange value. In order that anything may have exchange value, it must be the product of labor power.

But, of course, it must also be of some use to the buyer. If it has no utility or only private utility, it will not bring a price. A prankster who, on a dark night, digs a big hole in a public park, would not be creating exchange value. No one would pay him for being a nuisance. Hence an article, if it is to possess economic value, must (a) be the product of labor power and (b) be socially useful.

Although market price is the monetary measure of exchange value, it is not identical with exchange value. Prices may represent fictitious values, since we often say that the rate of profit is too high. Because of fraud or the misrepresentations of advertising or monopolistic price fixing, prices are sometimes exorbitant. Hence we must distinguish between the real economic worth of a commodity, which Marx sometimes calls the "natural price," and the actual market price, which *may* depart greatly from the exchange value or "natural price."

What makes a commodity economically valuable is that it can only be obtained at a cost: the expenditure of a given quantity of unwasted labor power. This book, for example, has economic value, not only because it has use value, but because of the effort spent in writing and manufacturing it. All effort, whether of hand or brain, that goes to produce a socially useful article adds to its exchange value, which Marx defines as "congealed labor power." Such is the theory not only of Marx, but of the Physiocrats Adam Smith and David Ricardo and of almost all the economists who preceded him.

What he added was the limitation implied in his statement that exchange value is based upon "socially necessary labor time." This means that the value of a commodity is determined by "the quantity of labor necessary for its production in a given state of society, under certain social average conditions of production, with a given social average intensity, and average skill of the labor employed."[17]

This implies, in the first place, that the amount of labor power required to produce a given quota of exchange value is relative to the technological advancement of the society. As labor-saving devices are introduced, the exchange value of a commodity falls accordingly; but of course more such commodities can then be produced by a worker in a given time.

The theory means, in the second place, that economic value is determined by *average* conditions. The relatively unskilled worker will produce somewhat less, and the relatively skilled worker somewhat more, than the average; but the value is determined by the average amount of effort required at the given technological level. Again, since it is a theory of averages, it is not meant to apply to the concrete exceptional case, for instance, the pearl found by chance. The *average* labor time required to find a pearl is quite considerable, and this determines the exchange value.

Since exchange value is produced by labor power, it is not produced by absentee landlords or capitalists. If a capitalist produces economic value, he has actively used his hand or brain in "socially necessary" production; and if remuneration is to be based upon productivity, he is then entitled to the wages of management, but he is not entitled to the profit which he receives from dividend holding. In *Capital*, Marx admits the justice of "wages of direction or superintendence" which, while nominally a part of profit, are, in fact, remuneration for the necessary work of management. But in general,

17 *Value, Price, and Profit*, International Publishers, New York, 1935, p. 33.

according to Marx, the income of capitalists represents not a just remuneration for work done but an appropriation of the "surplus value" produced by their employees.

(2) The Theory of Surplus Value. The ordinary worker, lacking capital, is forced to sell his labor power as a commodity. Its exchange value, as in the case of every other commodity, is determined by the quantity of socially necessary labor power needed to produce it. This quantity is the amount of labor power required to maintain the worker, to train him for the given skill, and to bring up a certain quota of children who are to replace him on the labor market when he wears out. Under ordinary conditions, the wage that the capitalist pays is a rough measure of this exchange value.

The laborer, however, normally produces more value than is represented by the wages he receives. Labor power is thus a peculiar commodity, since it produces more value than it is worth on the market. If a man works eight hours, for example, he may in the course of six hours produce sufficient to pay the cost of his own wages; and in the next two hours, he will produce "surplus value" for which the employer does not pay him. The workers produce the wealth, Marx contends, but the capitalists appropriate a large part of it. This surplus is the source of rent, interest, and profit.

According to Marx, the conflict of interest between capitalists and workers is now evident. Since the capitalist wishes to obtain as great a surplus as possible, he is interested in paying wages as low as possible and selling the commodities as high as possible. The interest of the worker is diametrically opposite: to secure a wage as high as possible and to buy commodities as cheaply as possible. Conflict between the two classes, declares Marx, is therefore inevitable.

(3) The Concentration of Capital. As surplus value accumulates, wealth and economic value tend to be concentrated in fewer and fewer hands. Great corporations, trusts, associations, cartels develop. Large companies destroy or absorb small companies. Why is this concentration occurring?

Marx's answer is that the big companies are more efficient and powerful and can crush their smaller opponents. Large-scale production, at a higher technological level, is generally cheaper. But the smaller companies cannot afford mass production and expensive new machinery, hence they are eliminated in the fierce competition for profits.

When wealth and economic power become highly concentrated, the crisis of capitalism becomes acute. The wonderful new machines utilized in large-scale production represent an enormously augmented productive potential, but, under capitalism, they compete against the workers, displace and impoverish them. Receiving in wages a diminishing proportion of what they produce, the workers do not have the buying power to consume the products that highly mechanized industry can pour forth so plentifully. The result is a constant tendency toward overproduction in relation to effective demand and underproduction in relation to human need and the capacity to produce. As Engels declared:

> Too little is produced. . . . But *why* is too little produced? Not because the [technical] limits of production . . . are exhausted. No, but because the limits of production are determined not by the number of hungry bellies, but by the number of *purses* able to buy and to pay. The moneyless bellies, the labor which cannot be utilized *for profit* and therefore cannot buy, is left to the death-rate.[18]

Here is the source, Marx and Engels asserted, of the modern paradox of poverty in the midst of potential plenty.

It is not only the worker who is squeezed. As mechanized productive power increases and buying power decreases, the rate of profit falls. Less and less labor power is spent on each individual commodity, the creation of surplus value is correspondingly decreased, and the whole basis of profit shrinks. Although the *rate* of profit thus tends to fall, the *mass* of profit, under large-scale production, may rise. Nevertheless, the falling rate of profit, in the long run, is a mortal threat

18 Marx and Engels, *Correspondence, op. cit.,* p. 199.

to the capitalist structure. Moreover, the increasing disparity between the capacity of society to produce and its capacity to consume makes the system more and more erratic, and leads to a crazy succession of booms and depressions.

In the effort to counteract these tendencies, employers intensify the dog-eat-dog competition with other employers and the exploitation of their employees. They feverishly attempt to safeguard profits by finding cheaper labor and raw materials and capturing foreign markets. The nations dominated by capitalist interests are thus driven into commercial rivalry and imperialism, which, in turn, provoke military conflict. War may temporarily revive employment and profits, but at the cost of a deeper crisis in the postwar period. When conditions become sufficiently intolerable, and the counterorganization of the workers, arrayed in great trade unions, becomes sufficiently formidable, the age of revolution dawns.

(4) The Economy of Social Ownership. The rest is prophecy. After a protracted struggle, the workers will obtain control of the state and the instruments of production. The subsequent revolution will not be primarily a technological one but a social one. Even though there were no airplanes, dynamos, tractors, and atomic bombs during the lifetime of Marx and Engels, they believed that technology had made immense strides. Engels asserted:

We have subdued the forces of nature and have pressed them into the service of mankind; we have thereby infinitely multiplied production, so that a child now produces more than a hundred adults previously did.[19]

The main difficulty, according to this theory, is not that the forces of production are inadequate, but that the *relations* of production run counter to the maximum utilization of these forces for human welfare. Hence the revolution will be directed not against the techniques and instruments of pro-

[19] *Dialectics of Nature,* International Publishers, New York, 1940, p. 19.

duction but against the social relations that fetter and distort these productive forces. Since the root difficulty is the private ownership of the means of production, *social* ownership must replace private individual ownership. The economic system must be reorganized upon the basis not of individually directed production for profit but of socially planned production for use. With industry in the hands of the state or non-profit-making cooperatives, an individual will not be able to purchase a factory for the sake of making a profit, any more than he can now purchase a post office or a public school. Consumers' goods, of course, will be in private hands; and, in this sense, there will be, Marx believed, far more private property in the possession of the immense majority of people than under capitalism.

As a result of this revolution, comprehensive social planning will replace anarchic individual effort. Down to the present point in history, man has achieved control only of physical nature. In the control of industry and in the making of history, human action has achieved "its desired end only by way of exception and, much more frequently, the exact opposite."[20] "What each individual wills is obstructed by everyone else, and what emerges is something that no one willed."[21] But as a result of the social ownership of the means of production, and of planned production for social use, a new phase of history dawns—for the first time, man can plan his social existence for the sake of maximum welfare. The full productive capacity of society, no longer fettered by an obsolete system of property, will be employed to meet essential human needs. The exploitation of man by man will be abolished, and step by step the traces of the old class divisions will be erased.

Although differential wages, as incentives to greater effort, must for some period be retained, and although coercive power cannot quickly be eliminated, society will progress

20 *Ibid.*
21 Marx and Engels, *Correspondence, op. cit.,* p. 476.

toward genuine equality, freedom, and economic abundance.
In the first, or "socialist," phase of development, the principle of distribution will be based upon the slogan of St.
Simon: "From each according to his ability, to each according to what he produces." But when the era of abundance
has been securely established, and the old class antagonisms
have disappeared, a more generous system of distribution can
be inaugurated. According to Marx:

> In a higher phase of communist society, after the enslaving
> subordination of individuals under division of labor, and there-
> with also the antithesis between mental and physical labor, has
> vanished, after labor has become not merely a means to live but
> has become itself the primary necessity of life, after the produc-
> tive forces have also increased with the all round development
> of the individual, and all the springs of cooperative wealth flow
> more abundantly—only then can the narrow horizon of bourgeois
> right be fully left behind and society inscribe on its banners:
> from each according to his ability, to each according to his
> needs.[22]

5. *Political Theory and Tactics*

To COMPREHEND this theory of social revolution, we must
understand the Marxian doctrine of the state. Marx and
Engels reacted strongly against the idealistic political theory
of Hegel. According to this theory, all social organizations
except the state are partial and relatively biased. The state
alone provides a just balance between contending interests,
achieves an organic synthesis of the innumerable forces
within society, and gives to all citizens the fullest opportunity for self-realization. Marx and Engels believed that
this theory is unrealistic. Far from being above class bias,
the state "as a rule" is the instrument of "the most powerful
economic class that by force of its economic supremacy be-

22 *Critique of the Gotha Program,* in *Selected Works,* Vol. II, International
Publishers, New York, 1933, p. 566.

comes also the ruling political class, and thus acquires new means of subduing and exploiting the oppressed masses."[23] Since it is thus primarily an instrument of class domination, police and military power are at its very foundation.

Yet Marx and Engels qualified this theory. In the quotation that I have just cited, Engels declared that the state "as a rule" takes the form of class domination. He did not deny that in certain circumstances "the struggling classes balance each other so nearly that the public power gains a certain degree of independence by posing as a mediator between them."[24] Marx indicated, in *The Eighteenth Brumaire of Louis Bonaparte*, for example, that the government of Louis did for a time represent such a precarious equilibrium in French society.

He and Engels believed that the economic order, as the more powerful force, determines on the whole the political and legal structure, but that this structure may develop a certain relative independence or may react upon the economic system. Engels explained:

> The reaction of the state power upon economic development can be one of three kinds: it can run in the same direction, and then development is more rapid; it can oppose the line of development, in which case nowadays state power in every great nation will go to pieces in the long run; or it can cut off the economic development from certain paths, and impose on it certain others.[25]

In any of these three ways, political causes may have a momentous effect upon economics.

Since political power is by no means negligible, the workers must control the state to accomplish their social revolution. One of the crucial questions is whether such control can be achieved and maintained by peaceful means. The popular impression is that Marx and Engels are the apostles of violent revolution, and certain passages, especially in their

23 Engels, *The Origin of the Family, Private Property, and the State*, Kerr, Chicago, 1902, p. 208.
24 *Ibid.*, p. 209.
25 Marx and Engels, *Correspondence, op. cit.*, pp. 480-481.

earlier works, can be cited to support this interpretation. In the *Communist Manifesto,* for example, they wrote:

> The Communists disdain to conceal their views and aims. They openly declare that their ends can be attained only by the forcible overthrow of all existing social conditions.[26]

Likewise in *Capital* Marx stated that "force is the midwife of every old society pregnant with a new one."[27]

Yet there are other passages in which they speak of violent revolution as a necessary evil. In 1846, a little more than a year before the *Communist Manifesto,* Engels wrote a pamphlet entitled *The Basic Principles of Communism,* in which he asked the question, "Will the abolition of private property be possible in a peaceful way?" He gave the following answer:

> It is to be wished that this could occur, and the Communists would be the last to protest against it. . . . They also see, however, that the development of the proletariat in almost all civilized lands is violently suppressed, and that the enemies of the Communists are thus making with all their might for a revolution. Should the oppressed proletariat in this way finally be driven to a revolution, then we Communists will defend the cause of the proletarians quite as well with deeds as we now do with words.[28]

This was the attitude of Marx and Engels at a time when very little democracy existed in Europe.

In their later years, however, democracy had developed greatly, and they repeatedly expressed the hope that socialism might be achieved in the more democratic countries mainly by peaceful methods. For example, in his famous speech at Amsterdam on the morrow of The Hague Congress of the First International (1872), Marx declared:

> We know that we must take account of the institutions, customs and traditions of the various countries, and we do not deny that there are countries such as the United States and Great Britain—

---

[26] *Communist Manifesto,* in Emile Burns, *A Handbook of Marxism,* International Publishers, New York, 1935, p. 59.

[27] *Capital,* Kerr, Chicago, 1906, I, p. 824.

[28] Marx and Engels, *Gesamtausgabe, op. cit.,* Vol. VI, p. 513.

and if I knew your institutions better I should perhaps add Holland—where the workers will be able to achieve their ends by peaceful means.[29]

On several occasions Engels made similar pronouncements.

When the time arrives for decisive action, whether peaceful or violent, the proletarian masses must mainly be depended upon. Although Marx and Engels recognized other noncapitalist classes, they believed that only one class, the industrial workers, can be relied upon for revolutionary action. The peasants must at least be placated, the small tradesmen and poorer professional workers must be won over if possible, but the spearhead of the revolution must be the industrial workers. These workers alone, through their trade-union organizations, develop enough social consciousness and mastery of class struggle to be the trustworthy agents of revolutionary change.

After the revolution, there will be a difficult transitional period before a collectivist society can be securely established. In this period, we are told, the state assumes the form of "the dictatorship of the proletariat." Much has been written concerning the meaning of this phrase, yet Marx and Engels used it but rarely. Lucien Laurat, a French social democrat, has counted the number of times it is used, and he can find only three instances in the works of Marx and only two in the writings of Engels.[30] Moreover, there seems to have been no intention on the part of either Marx or Engels to contrast such "dictatorship" with the rule of the majority. For example, Engels stated:

If one thing is certain it is that our Party and the working class can only come to power under the form of the democratic republic. This is even the specific form for the dictatorship of the proletariat, as the great French revolution has already shown.[31]

Marx and Engels apparently meant by proletarian dictator-

29 Quoted by Lucien Laurat, *Marxism and Democracy*, Gollancz, London, 1940, p. 36.
30 *Cf., ibid.*, p. 40.
31 Marx and Engels, *Correspondence, op. cit.*, p. 486.

ship what I have called in Chapter Twelve "totalitarian democracy"—namely, democracy, in the limited sense of majority rule, without civil rights for dangerous opposing minorities.

They used the term *dictatorship* to emphasize their conviction that the socialist state, struggling into existence in a hostile world, must adopt stringent measures to safeguard itself against counterrevolution and war. In taking this view, they were greatly influenced by the bloody suppression of the Paris Commune: Following the Franco-Prussian War, "the first proletarian government," the Commune, was set up by revolutionists in Paris. The national government of France, under the leadership of Thiers, laid siege to the city, and in the week that followed the capture of Paris, it executed, imprisoned, and exiled more people than had the Terror of Robespierre in three years of the French Revolution. The losses to the Parisian proletariat have been estimated at one hundred thousand. These events, according to Marx and Engels, were a terrifying demonstration of the grave dangers of counterrevolution and the importance of strong protection against enemies from within and without.

They believed, however, that coercion would prove less and less necessary as security is achieved. Consequently, when socialism becomes very firmly established upon a world-wide basis, and the old class antagonisms vanish, political coercion will cease to be necessary. Men will no longer cringe to the powerful of the earth; genuine freedom—political, economic, and intellectual—will be the privilege of all men. Socialism will develop into a cooperative anarchism, and the state, as a coercive organization, will "wither away."

6. *The Schisms in the Collectivist Movement*

THE ANARCHISTS, such as Michael Bakunin (1814-1876) and Peter Kropotkin (1842-1921), contended that it is possible to achieve collectivist anarchism without a long transitional period. They opposed the socialist ideal of state ownership and operation of the means of production no less ardently than they rebelled against the capitalist economic order.

They contended that the evils of existing society are intolerable, but that these evils can be remedied only by a direct control of the economic system by the workers themselves, without the intervention of the political state. Hence "direct action," such as the general strike, rather than political campaigns and parliamentary procedures should be employed by the workers.

Industry should be controlled by voluntary associations of toilers, without political coercion or state centralization. There should be no compulsion, no law, no government exercising force. According to Kropotkin, moreover, the distribution of wealth should be based upon the principle: "To each according to his needs." There should be no compulsion to work; and not only necessaries but all commodities produced in sufficient quantities should be given freely to those who desire them.

Although Marx and Engels agreed that cooperative anarchism is the highest and eventual phase of communism, they opposed as suicidal the immediate abolition of the state. Engels, for example, declared:

The anarchists put the thing upside down. They declare that the proletarian revolution must begin by doing away with the political organization of the state. But after its victory the sole organization which the proletariat finds already in existence is precisely the state. This state may require very considerable alterations before it can fulfill its new functions. But to destroy it at such a moment would be to destroy the only organism by means of which the victorious proletariat can assert its newly acquired power, hold down its capitalist adversaries and carry out that economic revolution of society without which the whole victory must end in a new defeat and a mass slaughter of the workers similar to those after the Paris Commune.[32]

[32] *Ibid.*, p. 417.

Despite its extremism, anarchism has served to challenge the more authoritarian aspects of Marxism, and to vivify the ideal of a free, cooperative, and decentralized organization of society.

The ideal of combining freedom and collectivism found less intransigent expression in the social democratic movement. Moderate socialists, such as Edward Bernstein (1850-1932) and Jean Jaures (1859-1914), put their trust in a gradualist, democratic movement and rejected such Marxian doctrines as the increasing misery of the workers, the intensification of class struggle, and the dictatorship of the proletariat. In Great Britain, this gradualist type of socialism found congenial soil. The Social Democratic Federation, which was the only English working-class group with strong Marxist leanings, never attained popularity; and the trade unions formally renounced the doctrine of class war during the first great Trades Union Congress of 1869. When a distinctive British socialism eventually did arise, it took the form of the gradualist ideals of Fabianism and the British Labor party. The main theorists of socialism in England have been men like Sidney and Beatrice Webb, Graham Wallas, George Bernard Shaw, H. G. Wells, Harold Laski, and G. D. H. Cole—thinkers who have sought to combine the socialist and the liberal traditions.

This sort of socialism is intimately connected with the onward surge of democracy. One of the principal tenets of the democratic creed—that happiness should not be the monopoly or privilege of any one class—is written into basic democratic documents such as the American Declaration of Independence and the French Declaration of the Rights of Man. When the workers became more conscious and articulate, they demanded that this democratic ideal be translated into economic reality. They insisted that the distribution of wealth has a very real connection with the distribution of happiness, and that the poverty of the workers is therefore a fundamental negation of democracy. Much of the appeal of socialism depends upon its proposal more equitably to redistribute wealth and economic power, and thus indirectly to redistribute and augment happiness. The immense growth of democracy in the nineteenth century contributed to the strength of this appeal. In the more advanced democratic countries, such as France, Great Britain, Australia, New Zealand, and the Scandinavian nations, the attractiveness of socialism depended upon this democratic sentiment. In America, with its strong individualistic tradition, socialism has been less influential, but such movements as Wilson's "New Freedom" and Roosevelt's "New Deal" have been in part similarly inspired.

The conflict between the gradualists and the radical Marxians led to numerous splits in the socialist parties. The most fateful split took place in Russia when the Bolsheviks (the majority) under Lenin broke with the Mensheviks (the minority). As everyone knows, the Bolsheviks assisted in the overthrow of the Czar in 1917 and then waged a successful second revolution against the Mensheviks and reformists under Kerensky. This revolution "shook the world" as no other has ever done. I need not remind the reader of the subsequent remarkable expansion of communist influence in Eastern Europe, China, and, to some extent, in other areas.

The communists bitterly denounced the Social Democrats as "revisionists" and "renegades," unfaithful to Marxism. Yet Lenin, Stalin, and other communist spokesmen departed fundamentally from the teachings of Marx and Engels in a number of respects.

First, the very insistence on orthodoxy represents a rigidification of Marxian theory. Both Marx and Engels repeatedly declared that their theory is a guide to study, not a dogma to be repeated mechanically. "Every opinion based on scientific criticism I welcome," declared Marx.[33] Too many of his followers, including most communists, have lost his attitude of eager inquiry.

Second, the emphasis of Lenin and Stalin upon "the dictatorship of the proletariat" represents in effect a change in

33 *Capital, op. cit.,* Vol. I, p. 16.

Marxian doctrine. As I have pointed out, Marx and Engels used this phrase very rarely, and even then they identified "proletarian dictatorship" with a type of "democracy." In communist political theory, on the other hand, the phrase becomes a cliché. Moreover, in practice, it has meant the dictatorship not of a class but of a party. Lenin and Stalin created the highly disciplined Communist party backed up by a ruthless secret police, and thereby they departed from the more democratic aspects of Marxism. So far, there has been no hint in the Soviet Union of "the withering away of the state" which Marx and Engels believed would eventually occur.

Third, the emphasis upon Russian nationalism is quite different from the boast of Marx and Engels in the *Communist Manifesto* that the proletarian worker has been "stripped . . . of every trace of national character."[34] In the effort to win support, Lenin advocated the self-determination of national minorities. Stalin similarly proposed a new type of "multi-national state" which would encourage a diversity of language and folk cultures among the constituent nationalities of the Soviet Union. At the same time, he and his associates encouraged an upsurge of patriotism and Russian nationalism, which reached its climax during World War II.

In the most fundamental of all respects, however, the communists have been faithful to Marxism. Whereas the Social Democrats have temporized and compromised, the communists in Russia have executed a huge collectivist revolution. The importance of this revolution, achieved at the cost of a drastic uprooting of humanity, can scarcely be exaggerated.

7. *Criticisms and Conclusions*

No SOCIAL THINKERS have aroused more bitter and widespread controversy than Marx and Engels. Confining myself

34 *Communist Manifesto, op. cit.,* p. 35.

to a few important issues, I shall try fairly to state what seems to me to be the truth in the matter.

(1) Marxism and Ethics. Although many passages in the works of Marx and Engels burn with intense moral indignation, they were chary of stating explicit moral theory. They hated "preaching" and felt that moral exhortation was more sentimental than scientific. As environmentalists, moreover, they emphasized economic and political revolution rather than inward moral transformation. Nevertheless, their theory of "self-alienation" and "fetishism" constitutes a profound ethical critique of existing society and enunciates, implicitly, a humanistic ethical ideal.

Their ideal, however, is revealed only in scattered passages, never in an explicit and reasoned ethical theory. One consequence has been that Marxism, although its appeal has been partly moral, has masqueraded as an amoral doctrine. Marx's profound feeling of social responsibility, his love of freedom, his broad humanism, are submerged beneath a tough-minded "scientific" analysis of economic forces. This apparently nonmoral character of Marxian doctrine has avoided the taint of a sham righteousness but has encouraged moral callousness and cynical opportunism among some so-called followers of Marx. It helped to make possible Stalin's "nonaggression pact" with the nazis, the Soviet invasion of Finland, and other similar opportunistic maneuvers of the Soviet government and of Communist parties inside and outside of Russia.

We here touch upon the very important question of the relation between means and ends. John Dewey, Bertrand Russell, and various other liberals insist that the *means* of deceit, violence, and dictatorship are not only bad in themselves but are not compatible with the *end* of a free, peaceful, cooperative commonwealth. Evil tactics, these critics say, inevitably pervert and infect the goal. This criticism seems to me fully justified when directed at some radicals who are committed to the idea of doing evil that good may come. But if communists are much too prone to suppose that the end justifies the means, their critics sometimes fall into an opposite error. They are so intent upon the fact that ends are degraded by bad means, that they fail to realize that means are elevated by good ends. Consequently, they have not sufficiently realized that a good end *may* justify an intrinsically bad but *necessary* means to that end, as for example, the defeat of an evil enemy such as fascism may justify a determined waging of war, or the achievement of a social and economic democracy may justify an iron control in a chaotic period of transition. Also the ends have a relative independence and stability, and consequently we cannot say that the qualitative character of the means must always carry over to, and largely determine, the qualitative character of the end. For example, it obviously does not follow that, because a medical operation is painful, the consequent state of health is also painful, or that the American republic was doomed to be a regime of violence because it was created by violent revolution. The relation between means and ends is too complex and variable to be understood in terms of any simple or inflexible formula. The end *sometimes* justifies the means, but not always; and either the end or the means can be overemphasized at the expense of the other. The only safe generalization is that we should estimate very carefully the values and disvalues involved both in the end *and* the means, and that we should choose, to the best of our ability, the course of action which yields most value and least disvalue when both ends and means are thus carefully evaluated.

The absence of an explicit moral theory in Marxism not only leaves unclarified the relation between means and ends, but it leaves equally ambiguous the relation between the economic determination of morals and the moral determination of economics. On the whole, Marx maintains that inexorable economic forces determine the main pattern of culture and hence the essential content of morality. This would imply that we must submit to "inexorable laws" and that the most we can ever hope to accomplish is to modify, by reason and moral effort, the contours but not the course of history. It would imply that morality is always a reflection of, and relative to, the economic forces of the age.

There is, however, another vein in Marxian philosophy. Marx at times speaks not in terms of a purely relative morality but of a broadly human and universal morality. For example, he maintains that the proletariat, in emancipating itself, will emancipate all mankind.

This class must represent the dissolution of all classes. It must be a sphere of society of universal character as a result of its universal suffering, demanding no particular right, because no particular wrong has been done to it, but only wrong as such. It must no longer be able to appeal to a historical title, but to a human title only. . . . Finally it must be of such a nature that it cannot emancipate itself at all without emancipating itself from all other spheres of society, thus emancipating them at the same time. In a word, there must be a complete forfeiture of man as he is, compelling an equally complete rebirth of a new humanity.[35]

This ethical universalism, moreover, is sometimes combined with an insistence upon inward change and active moral effort. Marx, for example, criticized Feuerbach and other materialists who put all their emphasis upon the environment.

The materialist doctrine that men are products of circumstances and upbringing and that, therefore, changed men are products of other circumstances and changed upbringing, forgets that circumstances are changed precisely by men and that the educator must himself be educated.[36]

Although human beings, in other words, cannot change themselves without altering their environments, they cannot alter their environments without changing themselves. Marx adds: "The philosophers have only *interpreted* the world in various ways; the point however is to *change* it."[37] Such passages

---

35 "Introduction to a Hegelian Philosophy of Law," Paris, 1843; quoted in Franz Mehring, *Karl Marx*, Covici-Friede, New York, 1935, p. 95.
36 "Theses on Feuerbach," in Burns, *op. cit.*, p. 229.
37 *Ibid.*, p. 231.

imply that the economic determination of morals must be limited by the moral determination of economics. But Marx's activism is not entirely consistent with his historicism, as K. R. Popper, in *The Open Society and Its Enemies,* has shown.

I believe that socialist theory would have been strengthened if Marx and Engels had tried to formulate their ideas of a good society as explicitly as possible, and if they had made clear that a better social order is the result not of inexorable historical laws but of plan, effort, imagination, and deliberate moral choice, selecting among the alternatives that history makes possible.

(2) The Marxian Analysis of Social Crisis. The essence of the Marxian theory of crisis, as we have said, is that the forces of production—the techniques and instruments—change more rapidly than the relations of production—the class-structure and institutions of property—and that recurrent crises are primarily caused by this unequal development. The main emphasis in this theory is economic; in the multifarious drama of history, the economic process is the soul of the plot.

I sympathize with this emphasis upon the fundamental nature of the economic problem, especially in reference to the contemporary world, but I would insist that even this problem cannot be understood unless we look beyond the confines of economics. No part of society can be sharply isolated from the wider setting of history. The modern crisis must be analyzed, I believe, not *merely* in terms of the disproportionate development of the economic system, but of the disequilibrium which embraces the whole structure of civilization. Although I would agree with Marx that the conflict between dynamic economic technology and relatively static economic institutions is exceedingly crucial, I believe that other conflicts are perhaps no less crucial.

To illustrate, let us consider the supreme crisis of Greco-Roman civilization. This crisis was not merely economic but political. Economically and technologically the Greek cities became increasingly interdependent, but *political* evolution did not keep pace with these changes. As long as Greece was free and independent, it was not so much a single state as an anarchic bundle of independent city-states. For brief periods, the threat of Persian aggression forced parts of the Greek world into an uneasy alliance, but as soon as the danger subsided, the old economic and military conflicts among Athens, Sparta, Corinth, Syracuse, and other city-states broke out with renewed fierceness. Even when leagues of states were formed, these were pitted against each other, like the Allies and the Central Powers in World War I or the Axis and the United Nations in World War II. The conflict between the Athenian and the Spartan confederations, growing out of their failure to unite under a common sovereignty, was the principal catastrophe of Greek civilization. Similarly, the conflict between Rome and Carthage was protracted and very costly. Eventually, by grim force of arms, a wider unity was achieved, first and precariously in the Macedonian Empire and later and more permanently in the Roman. Nevertheless, political unification was never attained upon the basis of rational persuasion, and the anachronism of the sovereign city-state persisted until the creative energies of the culture were depleted by war and imperialistic conquest. The failure of political adjustment to keep pace with the development of communication and transport produced a very serious disequilibrium; states that had become interdependent in fact remained disunited in political structure. New wine was poured into old bottles, and the result was crisis and catastrophe. When political unification was at last superimposed by military might, the decay of the culture was already far advanced.

We are confronted by an analogous crisis. The little city-states of yore have now been replaced by great nation-states, *but even these are not large enough.* The world has become one in danger but not one in government. Transit, communication, and economic ties have developed much more rapidly than political unification. The resulting crisis is made immeasurably more serious by the swift and terrible development of modern technological warfare, such as the atomic bomb. As a consequence, the political anachronism of the absolute nation-state is as serious as any economic anachronism could possibly be. The danger of political nationalism is as great as any economic danger. The task of strengthening the United Nations and creating a real world government is as urgent as any economic task.

There are two essential mandates for human survival in this Atomic Age. One task is economic: to achieve a total use of resources for the satisfaction of fundamental human needs. Failure at this task means poverty, depressions, violent revolutions. A second task is political: to replace anarchy among nation-states by a real world community. Failure at this task means world war. These two tasks are closely interdependent, but neither is entirely reducible to the other.

If this analysis be correct, we cannot admit the Marxian contention that economic factors alone are fundamental. For the sake of a more complete interpretation, we should generalize the Marxian analysis and speak not only of economic but of moral, political, and sociological factors. We may say that modern technology tends to develop much more rapidly than social control, moral adjustment, the class structure of society, and the political relations among nations; and the result is disequilibrium and crisis. In stating this view, moreover, we should extend the concept of "technique" beyond economics to many fields. In recent years, there have been fundamental inventions outside the economic sphere—for example, in military and administrative techniques and in the psychological methods of propaganda—and all such inventions disturb the social equilibrium and act as dynamic forces in history. The rise of Hitler was the result of the cunning manipulation of propaganda as well as the result of older types of physical technology. The release of atomic power, although prepared by a great deal of previous research, resulted from the pressure of military exigencies rather than directly from economic motives.

It is well to remember, also, that the very rapid expansion of technology would have been impossible without the swift development of pure science. Is the disequilibrating effect of pure science confined to its influence upon technology? I believe not. The swift pace of scientific discovery, even apart from technology, has a profoundly unsettling effect upon modern thought. New scientific discoveries are made more rapidly than we can spiritually and culturally assimilate them. Confusion results when the new truth, itself too complex and abstruse for the laity to comprehend, supplants the old truth. If men at times seem to be plunged into extreme intellectual disorientation, one reason is the very rapid increase in factual knowledge without an equivalent advance in synthesis and a sense of values. We therefore lack an adequate spiritual assimilation of scientific ideas and techniques: and our wonderful new resources, for want of this right orientation, are linked to techniques of death rather than to arts of life. Marx and his more orthodox followers have not sufficiently recognized these intellectual and moral causes of social crisis.

(3) The Marxian Economic Theory. There have been innumerable criticisms of Marxian economics, some of which involve technical details of economic theory. Into the scholastic niceties of these controversies I cannot go, partly because I am not an economist and partly for want of space. But technicalities aside, there would seem to be considerable truth in the Marxian theses: that economic value is produced and measured by socially necessary labor power; that workers generally receive less in wages than they produce in economic value; that wealth and economic power tend to be concentrated in fewer and fewer hands; that the buying power of the public either shrinks, as in a period of depression, or expands less rapidly than the capacity of industry to produce; that

consequently there tends to be a critical overproduction relative to effective demand and a critical underproduction relative to human need; and that only basic changes in the economic order can remove the major paradox of poverty in the midst of potential plenty.

There is no doubt that Marx's ideas in these respects need qualifications and refinements and that he erred in some other respects, especially in his predictions. Except in war-devastated lands or during major depressions, there has not been the increasing misery of the workers that he predicted. Without glossing over the terrible poverty that exists in many places, we can safely assert that the lot of the average worker in industrialized nations has been greatly improved during the past hundred years, largely as a result of social welfare legislation, the growth of a strong labor movement, and the increasing productivity of industry. Although Marx and Engels rightly predicted the growth of monopolies and the decrease in the number of small entrepreneurs and independent tradesmen, they did not foresee the immense increase in the number of skilled and professional workers: lawyers, doctors, teachers, journalists, engineers, technicians, civil service employees, and administrators. Moreover, the increasing concentration of wealth has in some small measure been counteracted by the fairly wide sale of stocks and bonds and, in greater measure, by steeply graduated income taxes and inheritance taxes. To cite another example of wrong prediction, Marx and Engels supposed that, with possible rare exceptions, socialism would first emerge in advanced industrial countries as a result of the complete maturation of capitalism; but its first great conquest was semifeudal Russia and its more recent conquests have been in the retarded countries of Eastern Europe and the much more retarded areas of China. I think some very substantial changes need to be made in Marx's theory to account for these deviations from his predictions.

I am less interested, however, in debating the details of

Marxian economics than in considering the broad questions of economic policy. All but the blind would admit that we need to improve our economic system so as to avoid booms and depressions, to minimize the economic causes of war, and to meet more adequately basic human needs. The question is: What sort of economic changes do we require?

Marx and Engels would reply that we need a total economic revolution, but I believe that they underestimated the power of the democratic state to control and improve the economic order. I have in mind the type of comprehensive economic program advocated in England by John Maynard Keynes and in America by Alvin Hansen, who believe that government and private industry should work together to guarantee total production and full employment. This is the method of piecemeal social engineering, with a vigilant preservation of our essential democratic liberties rather than a swift and total revolution with its high probability of violence and dictatorship. Public projects, such as rural electrification and the building of great hydroelectric plants, slum clearance, highway and transportation development, flood control, conservation of natural resources, and extension of educational facilities, would be employed to take up the slack in employment and to prevent the piling up of stagnant savings —the idle money that means idle machines and idle men. Such devices as old-age pensions, social security, and "guaranteed annual wages" would be used to maintain public purchasing power and to establish a decent minimum standard of living for all citizens. Fiscal, monetary, and investment controls would be used to check an impending inflation or to mitigate, or prevent, a threatened deflation. Such methods have already led to very great improvements, especially in social democracies such as Sweden and New Zealand, and have achieved signal triumphs even in the United States.

Since I am not an economist, I do not know what are the best means of achieving a system of maximum use of our resources for human welfare. The methods of Keynes and

Hansen may prove inadequate, or some other gradualist methods may be much better, or possibly nothing short of a comprehensive program of socialization may ultimately prove sufficient. But in any event, we should be steadfastly devoted to the goal of human happiness and flexible and democratic in our employment of means. A society continually planning will more likely succeed than a society completely planned— an experimental approach is more apt to succeed than a dogmatic one.

(4) Marxism and Liberal Democracy. The greatest objection to the more extreme political tenets of Marxism is that they violate the ideals of liberal democracy. This objection applies particularly to the version of Marxism dominant in the Soviet Union and its satellites.

It is very difficult to obtain accurate information about the Soviet Union and other communist states: prejudice, propaganda, and misinformation obscure the truth. The wise reader will thread his way very carefully through the labyrinth of contradictory reports. On the one hand, he will note some very substantial gains, such as the immense increase in the number of schools, libraries, museums, theaters, concert-halls, and art circles; the widespread development of technical skills; the considerable increase in total productivity; the more equal treatment of women and of the formerly oppressed classes, races, and nationalities. On the other hand, he will note the suppression of civil liberties, the iron control by a single disciplined party, the ruthless activities of the secret police, maltreatment of political prisoners, and the bureaucratic control of science and the arts. He will conclude that the Soviet regime has been progressive in some respects and regressive in others, and that the dictatorship has not only persisted but in some respects has become accentuated. The illiberal character of the communist states is, in some measure, an inevitable result of the evil heritage of the past and the profound crises of revolution, civil war, and international war. The evidence clearly indicates, however, that socialism can be established in backward countries such as Russia and China only at a very considerable cost—namely, the carrying over into the new stage of the undemocratic features of the primitive presocialist society.

It is significant that the Communist party has achieved its most notable successes in the more backward nations and not in countries such as the United States, Britain, France, and Scandinavia—not in countries, in other words, that are relatively advanced educationally, economically, and democratically. Czechoslovakia might appear to be an exception, but the triumph of communism there was more in the nature of a *coup* than an indigenous popular revolution. There is strong reason to think that Soviet communism represents Marxism debased and distorted by contact with primitive social conditions.

Yet Marx and Engels are themselves partly to blame for the undemocratic features of such communist regimes. Although their ultimate ideal, as we have seen, is the fullest freedom achieved upon a cooperative basis, they were very insistent that any new socialist state must ruthlessly guard itself against counterrevolution. They did not sufficiently realize that there are other major dangers besides counterrevolution, and that the problem of tyranny may be even more acute after the means of production are socialized. They did not clearly understand that the unification of economic, political, and military power within the state can produce a repressive engine of terrible force, and that a new oligarchical class may use this engine for its own aggrandizement and increase of power.

The evils inherent in unlimited centralization and dictatorship were decried by Rosa Luxemburg, the intrepid revolutionary leader of the German Marxists, in the early days of the Soviet regime:

Freedom for supporters of the government only, for the members of one party only—no matter how big its membership may be—is no freedom at all. Freedom is always freedom for the man who thinks differently. This contention does not spring from a fanatical love of abstract "justice," but from the fact that everything which is enlightening, healthy and purifying in political freedom derives from its independent character, and from the fact that freedom loses all its virtue when it becomes a privilege. . . . The suppression of political life throughout the country must gradually cause the vitality of the Soviets themselves to decline. Without general elections, freedom of the press, freedom of assembly, and freedom of speech, life in every public institution slows down, becomes a caricature of itself, and bureaucracy rises as the only deciding factor. No one can escape the workings of this law.[38]

Rosa Luxemburg was a good Marxist who, in certain respects, saw more keenly than either Marx or Lenin the meaning of history. She recognized that the *only* guarantee against abuse of power is freedom and democracy, including institutions for keeping the public well informed.

The social democrats in France and England, such as Jean Jaures and G. D. H. Cole, have likewise recognized that the great objective for those who believe in a *democratic* socialism, is to conserve the basic liberal values—inquiry, persuasion, freedom, individuality—and to combine them with socialist institutions. Such a program requires the jealous preservation of civil rights, the provision for free discussion and political opposition, and the maintenance of varied decentralized centers of power. It would seem much more likely that these ends can be attained by the gradual methods of persuasion and experimentation rather than by sudden and violent means.

It is impossible to sketch in any detail the strategy for realizing a free, democratic, and cooperative social order. Great tact and adaptability are required, and unforeseeable circumstances must be met as they arise.

Freedom we must have, but not the kind of unlimited freedom which means that the strong are free to bully and

---

[38] Rosa Luxemburg, *Die Russische Revolution*, p. 113; quoted by Paul Frolich, *Rosa Luxemburg: Her Life and Work*, Gollancz, London, 1940, pp. 276-277.

exploit the weak. Planning we must also have, but not the unlimited planning that gives more and more power to a centralized state, thus undermining freedom. Tolerance we must cherish, but not the unlimited tolerance that leaves a democratic society wholly unprotected against the onslaughts of the intolerant. Democracy we must broaden and strengthen, but not the unlimited democracy that admits no checks upon the right of the majority to override the civil rights of individuals and minorities. No infallible recipe exists to strike the just right mean between too much and too little freedom, too much and too little planning, too much and too little tolerance, too much and too little democracy. It is clear, however, that no absolute principle can guide us. We should recognize that absolutist "solutions," such as unlimited *laissez faire,* or, at the opposite extreme, full state responsibility for all economic and social activity, are almost certain to prove disastrous.

Piecemeal democratic social engineering rather than quick and wholesale revolution would appear to offer most hope for mankind. A mixed economy, combining private enterprises, cooperatives, and state-owned or state-controlled establishments, would seem to provide the best basis for a happy and free society. We need a considerable extension of social ownership, control, and planning so as to eliminate unnecessary poverty and to avoid depressions; but planning for welfare must include planning for freedom, and the planners themselves must be held in leash by democratic safeguards. This means that the socialist ideals of Marx and Engels must be tempered by the great traditional ideals of liberalism and democracy.

REVIEW OF PART THREE

In PART TWO, I maintained that welfare consists in the cultivation and fulfillment of positive interests expressive of the whole nature of man, and that the worth of any social order is its efficacy in promoting such welfare. The question remains, What kind of social order is best fitted to cultivate and fulfill human interests? The answer depends upon differing interpretations of freedom, equality, planning, and other basic social values. The principal ideals of a social order—the ideals of aristocracy, democracy, liberalism, fascism, and socialism—represent contrasting interpretations of these fundamental values.

Chapter Nine is devoted to the aristocratic ideal. The aristocrat prefers the choice goods to the common goods and believes that excellence is incompatible with broad democratic sharing. In its original import, *aristocracy* means rule by the best, and, according to Socrates and Plato, the best are the wise.

There is no better expression of the aristocratic ideal than the life and thought of Socrates. His mission, to which he devoted the best part of his life, was to awaken in the minds of his fellow citizens a sense of the supreme importance of inquiry. Plato's sketch of a Utopia where philosophers are kings is partly an extension of Socratic ideals. Many features of Plato's Republic are open to grave criticism, but the basic

354

concept of the educational state—the rule of wisdom—has a deep and perennial appeal.

If one could imagine Socrates revisiting the earth and conversing with a modern democrat, his criticism of American democracy would not be different in principle from his criticism of Athenian democracy. He would point out that in all the ordinary arts, such as repairing shoes, healing the sick, or piloting a ship, we rightly insist upon expert knowledge; but in the art of government—the most important and difficult of all—we appeal to the suffrage of the unlearned crowd. He would remind us how terribly complicated and dangerous are the problems of modern statesmanship, yet how inept are the people's representatives. The remedy, he would insist, is a state based upon a thorough educational system. Such a state would elevate wise men to power and would apply expert knowledge to the many critical problems of modern government. Until the nations of the world adopt this remedy, there can be no sure protection against violent revolution or atomic warfare.

In Chapter Ten, I have considered the reply that an intelligent democrat might make. He would not despise the aristocratic ideal of high intellectual attainment or reject the choice goods out of love for the common goods. He would try to combine excellence and sharing. As T. E. Lawrence so poignantly realized, mankind is split into two parts, the élite and the masses; and our great problem is to end this schism— to achieve a culture high in attainment and broad in participation. An undemocratic culture, such as Czarist Russia, may reach an enviably high level, but it restricts its cultural values to the very few. Likewise one-sided is the kind of "democratic" culture that widely diffuses its benefits but remains mediocre. We in America want no such limitation. We want a high but truly democratic culture—rich both qualitatively and quantitatively.

The aristocrat might concede that this should be our goal and yet insist that the *means* to this end should be aristocratic.

He might say that we should have a government *for* the people but not *of* and *by* the people. But a government of the few is almost certain to be a government for the few. Democratic social intelligence, as the expression of the people's will and needs, is quite different from the intelligence of self-seeking individuals or pressure groups. As Jean Jacques Rousseau made clear, the general will is not the sum of particular wills, each bent on its separate goal; it is the corporate expression of a democratic community. A community exists when the common human experience of personal interdependence is the voluntary basis of group coherence. The bond of community involves a person-taken-as-person relation among free individuals, a relation of mutuality; it thus stands in contrast to the relation that exists when one person regards another as a mere tool. When reason expresses community interest, there is, as Rousseau maintained, *social* intelligence. The democrat's reply to the aristocrat is that such intelligence is indigenous to democracy, and that "aristocratic intelligence" is quite different and serves different ends. But to realize social intelligence, democracy should embrace, and adapt to its own ends, Plato's great ideal of an educational state.

In Chapter Eleven, I have examined the liberal ideal. Although democracy and liberalism are very closely related, the essence of the first is equality and fraternity and the essence of the second is freedom. As a body of theory that crystallized in the seventeenth and eighteenth centuries, liberalism is the ultra-individualistic philosophy of a competitive business civilization. The liberal theorists conceived of freedom primarily as the right of the enterprising individual to be let alone. In the field of economics, the French physiocrats Turgot and Quesnay and the English economists Smith and Ricardo worked out the theory of a self-regulating and "natural" economic order in which private profit is public benefit. In the field of politics, Locke maintained that natural rights exist before any political state and provide the immutable norms whereby the merits and demerits of government can be judged. Bentham and Mill, in contrast, rejected the theory of natural rights and defended freedom on utilitarian grounds. Mill's great plea for the liberty of thought, speech, and action is based upon the conviction that full and free discussion and experimentation are socially advantageous —that the independent, original, and even eccentric person enriches society far more than the tame conformist. His early individualistic liberalism, expressed in his essay *On Liberty,* has been a support to liberal individualism; his later socially minded liberalism, expressed in his subsequent works, has contributed to liberal socialism.

If we try to evaluate the theory of individualistic liberalism, we find that it contains both truths and errors. The historic theory of natural rights involves the false assumption, criticized in Chapter Three, that the laws of nature provide reliable norms for human conduct. It assumes a natural identity between self-interest and social interest and thus makes a virtue out of selfishness. It falsely supposes that natural rights are absolute, self-evident, independent of historical circumstances, and inherent in the isolated individual. If natural rights, however, are interpreted as social and teleological rights, based upon the relatively permanent and general conditions of human happiness, they are valid and necessary defenses against tyranny. So interpreted, they do not differ essentially from the rights that Mill advocated so eloquently. But Mill did not consider the problem of preserving liberty during a very profound social crisis. He did not sufficiently realize that, in a period of deep crisis, we may not be able to tolerate the enemies of tolerance, as for instance, men like Hitler. He did not remark that crisis brings insecurity and insecurity breeds intolerance, and that therefore freedom from fear is a very basic kind of freedom. Some liberals, moreover, have been loath to democratize freedom—to extend it to the poorer workers, the colonial peoples, or to certain racial, religious, and political minorities. Yet freedom, like education, should not be the exclusive privilege of any segment of mankind.

Individualistic liberalism has also erred in supposing that freedom and organization are antithetical. It has too often supposed that man was born free but has enslaved himself in a network of social relations, that freedom will be regained by striking off the coercions and ties of society. This is to conceive of freedom much too narrowly and negatively. *Real* freedom involves not merely the absence of legal constraints but the presence of resources and capacities. You cannot really be free when you are badly clad, underfed, wretchedly housed, without education, without money for medicine, living at a miserable wage, or haunted by the fear of war, unemployment, or a penniless old age. The material and cultural means to freedom cannot be realized without democratic planning and organization. Hence freedom without organization is a delusion, just as organization without freedom is a straitjacket.

In Chapter Twelve I have examined and criticized the fascist ideal. Fascism was a complex alliance of antidemocratic rightist forces—military, economic, and political—impelled to extreme action by a profound economic and cultural crisis. The theory of fascism was largely a mask to conceal the predatory nature of this alliance. The Italian theory was a perverted Hegelianism glorifying the totalitarian state. The German theory was the expression of an intense and intolerant tribalism. But fascism partly disguised its antidemocratic character by advancing a popular ideology, which represented Germany, Italy, and Japan as poor but superior nations fighting for their rightful place in the sun. Beneath all these theories was a lawless will to power.

While admitting the transient successes of fascism in ending unemployment and inspiring group loyalty, we must condemn its totalitarian regimentation and extreme racial and nationalistic bias, which run fundamentally counter to the ethical principles advocated in this volume. Its rejection of

world-wide and lasting values tragically constricted its ideal
of organization. Internally it achieved no stable moral and
legal order, and internationally it stood for anarchy.

The fascist mentality is by no means dead: it is a threat
even within our democracy. If a major war or a great depression should occur, this threat could become extremely serious.
Even now there are ominous fascistic tendencies in the widespread intolerance toward liberals and radicals and viola-
tions of civil rights. Such intolerance and repression are
themselves subversive because they erase a basic distinction
between our system and totalitarianism. The best defense of
democracy is to build a country where no one is cold or
hungry or sick for want of care. If the people are happy,
incitements to revolt will fall on deaf ears.

In Chapter Thirteen I have examined the socialist ideal.
This ideal is ancient and widespread; today it is a terrific
force in world affairs. Since Marx and Engels have been immensely influential, I have focused my attention primarily
upon their ideas. What follows is meant to be an exposition
and a criticism of their doctrines.

According to their theory of "self-alienation and fetishism,"
human beings are money ridden and machine dominated,
and machines seem to take on life and dominate human
beings. Under capitalism the worker becomes a kind of tool
and commodity; and technology, developing more rapidly
than social controls, runs riot and drags men through crises
and wars. The substance of Marxian ethics is that these conditions should cease—that human beings should be treated as
human beings, and things as things.

If this ideal is to be realized, men must understand and
master the forces of history. Marx and Engels conceived of
history as a very complex interaction of unequal forces, of
which the economic are by far the most powerful. History
exhibits a succession of economic systems: primitive communism, slavery, feudalism, capitalism, and, in the future,
socialism. The great crises of history, which result in a revo-

lutionary transition from one economic system to another, are mainly caused by the conflict between productive forces and social relations. The techniques and methods of production change more rapidly than the class structure, and this unequal development finally results in profound conflict. This conflict will grow more intense until finally the social relations are reorganized so as to harmonize with the productive forces.

The main factors in this revolutionary process are economic. They are analyzed in Marxian economic theory as follows: (1) *The labor theory of value.* A commodity is economically valuable because a certain quantity of unwasted labor power is expended in producing it. The *amount* of economic value is determined by average labor working with average instruments at a given technological level. (2) *The theory of surplus value.* The worker normally produces more economic value than is represented by the wages he receives. The difference between what he produces and what he receives is "surplus value." The capitalist strives to obtain a high surplus, because this is the source of profits; the worker strives to obtain high wages, thus reducing the surplus. The interests of worker and capitalist are opposed. (3) *The concentration of capital.* In the effort to increase surplus value, the larger, more efficient companies crush their weaker opponents and more intensively exploit their employees. Wealth and economic power thus become ever more concentrated, while the forces of production continue rapidly to expand. The result is a fundamental disparity between the capacity of the society to produce and its capacity to consume. This disparity, in combination with other factors, ultimately leads to a revolutionary crisis. (4) *The economy of social ownership.* After the workers seize control of the productive system, they substitute social ownership in place of private individual ownership and production for use in place of production for profit. Gradually the "socialist economy" evolves into a "communist economy" of cooperative anarchism.

As the economy alters, so does the political superstructure. The state is primarily an instrument of class domination. The workers must therefore control the state to complete their social revolution. In some of their writings, Marx and Engels speak of the necessity of violent revolution; but in later pronouncements, they express the hope that peaceful revolution can be achieved in democratic countries such as England and America. The initial form of the workers' state, they maintained, will be the "dictatorship of the proletariat"; but they used this phrase rarely and did not contrast it with majority rule. They employed it to emphasize the importance of strong protection against war and counterrevolution. But they believed that socialism would eventually develop into a peaceful and world-wide cooperative anarchism.

Nevertheless, the anarchists Bakunin and Kropotkin denounced the Marxian insistence upon a strong coercive state however temporary. Anarchism has thus challenged the more authoritarian aspects of Marxism and expressed the ideal of a cooperative economy. The social democrats, such as Bernstein, Jaures, and the English Fabians, have also been critics of orthodox Marxism. They have endeavored to combine socialism with liberal democracy and to use gradualist, parliamentary means. The conflict between the social democrats and the radical Marxists has led to numerous splits, including the momentous break between the Mensheviks and the Bolsheviks (the Communists) in Russia. But the Russian Communists have also fundamentally departed from Marxian teachings especially in the rigidity of their dogmas, their repressive totalitarianism, and their nationalism.

Turning from exposition to criticism, I believe that Marx and Engels erred in not stating an explicit ethical theory. Although their theory of self-alienation and fetishism constitutes a profound ethical critique of modern society, they have not explicitly set forth the ultimate norms for judging social actions and institutions. In particular, they have not sufficiently clarified the relations between means and ends and between relative and universal values. They have not clearly indicated whether the economic determination of morals precludes the moral determination of economics. This lack of a clear and explicit ethical theory has encouraged moral callousness and cynical opportunism among some so-called Marxists.

Moreover, the Marxian analysis of social crisis puts too exclusive emphasis upon economic factors. The economic problem *is* fundamental, but other problems are also basic. The supreme crisis of Greco-Roman civilization, for example, was *political* and not merely economic. Similarly, the crisis of this Atomic Age is not merely economic: the political anachronism of the absolute nation-state is as serious as any economic anachronism. We should realize that crisis is usually the result of a conflict between relatively dynamic inventions and relatively static traditions and institutions, but that neither the inventions nor the traditions and institutions are *necessarily* economic. Marx and Engels underestimated the historical role of these noneconomic factors.

The Marxian economic theory contains very important truths, but it is in need of qualifications and revisions. Since I am not an economist, I do not know whether the humanitarian aims of Marx and Engels can be achieved by an alternative economic program, such as the method of piecemeal social engineering advocated by John Maynard Keynes and Alvin Hansen. But an experimental approach is more likely to succeed than a dogmatic one.

As interpreted and applied in the Soviet Union, the political tenets of Marxism violate liberal and democratic ideals. Soviet communism, I believe, represents Marxism debased and distorted by contact with primitive social conditions; but Marx and Engels themselves were not sufficiently aware of the danger of producing a new kind of tyranny by the concentration of economic, political, and military power within a collectivist state.

The *only* guarantee against abuse of power is freedom and

democracy. The hope of the future lies in the achievement *within* nations of liberal social democracy and *among* nations of strong world government. The immediate imperative is to exercise great tact and determination in the pursuit of *peaceful* goals.

CONCLUSION

THE NEED TO MAKE THINGS
DIFFICULT

THE DANISH PHILOSOPHER, Sören Kierkegaard, remarked, "With everyone engaged everywhere in making things easier, someone was needed to make them difficult again."[1]

Most theories of social ethics try to make things too easy. Formalistic theories try to reduce right social action to obedience to law. Cut-and-dried maxims, rigid and inflexible rules, or even the more sophisticated rules of "intuition" and "practical reason," are too simple. They can never be adequate to deal with the subtle, variable, and complicated problems of modern society.

Most forms of teleological ethics are also too easy. Relativism emphasizes the differences among human beings and fails to note the resemblances; absolutism emphasizes the resemblances and fails to note the differences. An extreme individualism exalts the individual at the expense of the group; and an extreme collectivism exalts the group at the expense of the individual. Hedonism seeks the good in feeling; intellectualism, in reason; voluntarism, in desire. In stressing only one side of man's nature, each oversimplifies.

The real center of value is the personality-in-society, and this social personality, as a dynamic focus of interests, is the

---

[1] Quoted by William Barrett, "Dialogue on Anxiety," *Partisan Review*, XIV, March-April 1947, p. 152.

whole man. Only an ethics that does justice to every essential side of man's nature, as both individual and social, as mind and body, as thinking, feeling, and desiring, is complete and complex enough to be the basis of valid social ideals.

Likewise any theory of right is too narrow if it seeks the good of a particular race, class, sex, or nation exclusively. Only a universalist theory of right, intent upon maximizing welfare, is ample enough to span the wide realm of human obligation.

Likewise most social ideals make things too easy. This is frequently true even of radical ideals. A friend has said to me, "The trouble with the ordinary radical is that he is not radical enough." My friend meant that such a radical seeks to change society in only one fundamental respect, for example, in a transformation of the economic system, and that he fails adequately to recognize the need to change man and society in other fundamental respects. If we are to achieve a stable and lasting peace, we must act in many fields at once—economic, political, scientific, educational, and moral. There is no simple and easy solution, no single panacea.

We need to unite respect for individuality with a realization of social interdependence; to combine devotion to freedom and individual rights with loyalty to community plans and purposes; to link a democratic spirit of sharing with an aristocratic devotion to excellence; and to supplement economic and technological efficiency with a humane appreciation of moral, artistic, and cultural values. It is not easy to achieve a social synthesis so complex and inclusive.

Since it is not easy, free and democratic methods are imperative. A liberal democracy has this decisive advantage over any alternative: it can correct its own mistakes. In permitting debate and criticism, in allowing the free play of ideas, in stimulating the expression of popular grievances, in safeguarding the rights of minorities, it supplies the means to eliminate abuses and to respond flexibly to changing needs. Democracy is an open society; dictatorship is a closed society.

Democracy permits basic reform without violence. Dictatorship does not.

Even at best, the task of safeguarding peace and promoting welfare will not be easy. We live in a time of great fear. There is fear of depression, fear of war, fear of the loss of freedom. In an age of fear, it will not be easy to resist the hotheads and hysterics who will push us toward violence. As the great historian, Arnold J. Toynbee, has written:

> In some ways it is much more difficult to live with worries than to try to cut them short by some cutting of the knot, some short and easy solution. I believe if either we or the Russians try to solve the present situation by a shooting war, it merely will come back upon us ten times worse. . . .[2]

Who can doubt, now that both sides are terribly formidable, that Toynbee is right? The supreme imperative is that we keep the peace.

Some have sought an easy way out of modern perplexities by escaping into the subhuman, the bestial. The fascists are an obvious example of this tendency. In so far as they have revolted against the more dehumanizing processes of our machine civilization, they have combated the overly mechanical not by exalting the human but the subhuman, the bestial. The distinctive human traits in man—his rationality, humanitarianism, democracy—are conceived to be the source of evil, a weakening and debilitating of vital instincts. Nietzsche is the great prophet of this "transvaluation": he joyously forecast the "barbarians" of the twentieth century and declared that "the savage in every one of us" must be accepted, "even the wild animal."[3] Oswald Spengler, who considered Nietzsche his forerunner and master, likewise recognized the devitalizing effect of mechanization and sought escape in a new age of blood and iron: the only "creative" possibility, he tells us, that remains open in our "dying"

2 "Russian Catfish and Western Herring" (pamphlet), Oxford University Press, New York, 1949, p. 8.

3 Cf., The Will to Power, Macmillan, New York, 1910, Vol. II, p. 405.

Western civilization. He announced that man is a "beast of prey," despised "the toothless feeling of sympathy and reconciliation," and boasted that Germans have at last recovered "the ability to hate."[4]

Such an attempt to get back to the animal roots of life is bound to fail. Indeed, the very nature of animals is misconceived by Nietzsche and Spengler. Animals are violent, but they are also placid; they kill, but they also live by mutual aid. Those who have known and loved animals, such as St. Francis of Assisi and W. H. Hudson, have discovered much in them besides carnivorousness and ferocity. The defenders of the "beast of prey" as typical of "nature" are interpreting all life in terms of their own predatory impulses. When men seek the level of the bestial, they fall below the beast. When they strip off the human, they reach the subanimal level, the stage of nihilism, the inhumanity of the uncontrolled machine or the antihumanity of a diabolical sadism.

Likewise, the attempt of many individuals to escape into the transhuman, the supernatural, is bound to fail. Inevitably, a human being is the child of nature, and the earth, far from being alien to him, is the spring of all his life and hope. It is here that he finds his happiness or not at all. Moreover, to direct his aspiration toward some theological abstraction, "pinnacled dim in the intense inane," is to divert him from the terribly urgent tasks at hand.

We need something different, therefore, from an easy escapism, whether the attempted escape be into animalism or supernaturalism. We must find salvation, not by scorning human nature but by giving it a new expression, a higher level of realization. We must realize that all work and wealth find their end and justification in the many-sided cultivation of personality. We must achieve a larger scope for play and art and love and laughter, for creative thought and the pride

[4] *The Hour of Decision*, Knopf, New York, 1934, p. 21; *Man and Technics*, Knopf, New York, 1932, pp. 19 ff., 43; and *Politische Schriften*, Beck, Munich, 1934, p. 147.

of workmanship, for the cultivation of life in all its sparkle and diversity. Under a democratic economy, planned and operated for social welfare, men must achieve mastery over their machines. They must use mechanical techniques to enrich *human* values.

Out of the brains of scientists and engineers have sprung millions of machines with billions of horsepower. Because this prodigious energy has not been mastered, we have had war, revolution, economic chaos. Nevertheless, technology, if rightly employed, can eliminate poverty and the exploitation of man by man. It can bind all parts of the world together by transit and communication and thus create the indispensable basis of a universal community. Our machines, therefore, are too wonderful, too productive, too indispensable for us ever to destroy them. But we must have the will to conquer these mechanical monsters that have been running amuck, running wild. *This* is the great adventure of our age—to master the unlimited potentialities of science and technology—the boldest, the most exhilarating, the most promising and dangerous adventure that ever challenged the spirit and intelligence of man.

Mindful of the immense potentialities of science and technology, I have written not in a spirit of despair and hopelessness but of adventurousness and faith. What impresses me about the modern world is not merely the uncertainty and trouble but the immense hope that thrusts itself up through human suffering. Even the huge scale of modern calamities gives us grounds for hope: it is an indication of an immense tide of change which has been gathering force for more than one hundred years and has been rushing toward a climax. The terrific clash of interests which breeds strikes, riots, wars, and revolutions testifies to the radical nature and immense impetus of the transition. These changes are too pervasive and profound to be dismissed as temporary aberrations. They are clear announcements, so that those who run may read, of a profound alteration in human life.

We as individuals cannot prevent the coming of this new order, but we can understand its necessities, appreciate its potentialities, and contribute to its values. If we are guided by understanding and motivated by good will, we not only can mitigate the cruelty of the transition but can help to build a humane and rational society. It will not be easy, but it is not impossible.

The coming of a better world may be prevented by the hellish fury of scientific warfare, but mankind has exhibited an extraordinary capacity for survival. "It is not probable that war will ever absolutely cease," wrote W. Winwood Reade in 1872, "until science discovers some destroying force so simple in its administration, so horrible in its effects, that all art, all gallantry, will be at an end, and battles will be massacres which the feeling of mankind will be unable to endure."[5] As a result of scientific and technological developments, such a peak of destructiveness has now been reached; and it is quite possible that the human will to survival will forever revolt against so colossal a massacre as the next World War would bring.

In every country and in the interior of every mind, the struggle is continuing between the forces of chaos and the forces which may eventually produce a far better civilization. Despite tragedy and confusion, "the hope of the great community" gives a majestic significance and purposiveness to our age. There may be an incredibly devastating war or series of wars. There may be a new Dark Age such as followed the death of St. Augustine. But the hope of the good society will live on even as then. Those who love adventure and desire a better world are not sick before the prospect that looms ahead. If they keep bright the arrows of desire, they may eventually storm and occupy the citadels of power.

5 *The Martyrdom of Man*, Vol. III, 1872; quoted by James R. Newman and Byron S. Miller, *The Control of Atomic Energy*, McGraw-Hill, New York, 1948, p. 251.

SUGGESTIONS FOR FURTHER READING

FOR LIMITED SUPPLEMENTARY READING, some of the original classics are excellent. Such works as Plato's *Euthyphro** (on the problem of theological ethics), Epictetus' *Manual* (on naturalistic ethics), and Kant's *Fundamental Principles of the Metaphysics of Morals* (on rationalistic ethics) will introduce some of the fundamental types of ethics discussed in Part One. I would similarly recommend as supplementary reading for Part Two such classics as Aristotle's *Nichomachean Ethics,* especially Chapters I, II, and X; John Stuart Mill's *Utilitarianism,* especially Chapters I, II, and IV; and David Hume's *Inquiry Concerning the Principles of Morals.* To accompany Part Three, I would suggest Plato's *Republic,* for its delineation of the aristocratic ideal; Rousseau's *Social Contract,* especially Books One and Two, for its statement of the democratic ideal; Mill's *On Liberty,* for its defense of the liberal ideal; and Friedrich Engels' *Socialism: Utopian and Scientific,* and Engels' and Karl Marx's *Communist Manifesto,* for a sketch of the socialist-communist ideal.

Shorter selections from the great ethical and social philosophers are available in a number of anthologies. The best collection of the writings of the great ethical philosophers is A. I. Melden's *Ethical Theories* (New York, 1950). L. A. Selby-Bigge's *British Moralists* (London, 1897), Benjamin Rand's *Classical Moralists* (Boston, 1909), and Gordon H. Clark's and T. V. Smith's *Readings in Ethics* (New York, 1935) are also sourcebooks of ethical theories. Among the anthologies of political and social philos-

* In the case of well-known classics, which are available in a number of editions, I shall omit the date and place of publication.

ophy, Albert R. Chandler's *The Clash of Political Ideals*, rev. ed. (New York, 1949), D. O. Wagner's *Social Reformers* (New York, 1934), V. F. Calverton's *The Making of Society* (New York, 1937), and Michael Oakeshott's *The Social and Political Doctrines of Contemporary Europe* (Cambridge, England, 1939), provide readings from the classics, ancient and modern.

Surveys of Ethical and Social Theory

Henry Sidgwick's *Outlines of the History of Ethics* (London, 1886) and A. K. Rogers' *Morals in Review* (New York, 1927) are useful histories of ethical theory. George H. Sabine's *The History of Political Theory*, rev. ed. (New York, 1950) is the best book in its field. In their *History of Economic Doctrines* (London, 1915), Charles Gide and Charles Rist have written an authoritative survey, and Erich Roll's *History of Economic Thought* (New York, 1942) is liberal and informative. Among the many books that throw light on the history of social thought, one might cite Ernst Cassirer's *The Myth of the State* (New Haven, 1946), Erich Kahler's *Man the Measure* (New York, 1943), Karl Mannheim's *Ideology and Utopia* (London, 1936), Lewis Mumford's *The Condition of Man* (New York, 1944), F. S. C. Northrop's *The Meeting of East and West* (New York, 1946), John Hermann Randall's *The Making of the Modern Mind* (Boston, 1940), and W. Stark's *The Ideal Foundations of Economic Thought* (New York, 1944). The large volume edited by Feliks Gross, *European Ideologies* (New York, 1948), is a survey of twentieth-century political and social ideals by various authors, who emphasize the historical derivations of current "ideologies." C. E. M. Joad's *A Guide to the Philosophy of Morals and Politics* (New York, 1938) is a critical survey of ethical and political philosophy beginning with the ancient Greeks.

If we turn from such works of a general nature to the supplementary reading for each chapter, I would suggest the following:

Chapter One: The Laws of Society

In the opening chapters of their *Ethics* (New York, 1932), John Dewey and J. H. Tufts describe the transition from customary to reflective morality. L. T. Hobhouse's *Morals in Evolution* (New York, 1906) and Edward Westermarck's *The Origin and Development of the Moral Ideas* (London, 1906) trace much the same ground in scholarly detail. The older interpretations of primitive morality, found in such works as Walter Bagehot's *Physics and Politics* (London, 1915) and W. G. Sumner's *Folkways* (Boston, 1906), should be supplemented by more recent and accurate anthropological studies, such as Bronislaw Malinowski's *Crime and Custom in Primitive Society* (New York, 1926), which shows that blind custom has no exclusive sway over primitive peoples. The reader who would like to study Edmund Burke's defense of custom and tradition should turn directly to his great polemical works, *Reflections on the French Revolution, Appeal from the Old to the New Whigs,* and *Letter to a Noble Lord.* Illuminating passages from Burke are contained in Alburey Castell's *Introduction to Modern Philosophy* (New York, 1946). John Maccun's *The Political Philosophy of Burke* (London, 1913) is a good secondary source. Students of the philosophy of positive law will find a rich mine of interpretation in Huntington Cairns' *Legal Philosophy from Plato to Hegel* (Baltimore, 1949), Benjamin Cardozo's *The Nature of the Judicial Process* (New Haven, 1921), Felix S. Cohen's *Ethical Systems and Legal Ideals* (New York, 1933), Morris R. Cohen's *Law and the Social Order* (New York, 1933), Oliver Wendell Holmes' *Collected Legal Papers* (New York, 1920), Hans Kelsen's *General Theory of Law and State* (Cambridge, Mass., 1945), and Roscoe Pound's *Law and Morals* (Chapel Hill, 1924) and *Introduction to the Philosophy of Law* (New Haven, 1922). In *Civilization and the Growth of Law* (New York, 1935), William A. Robson has traced the gradual development of legal theories from very primitive notions to modern concepts.

Chapter Two: The Laws of God

As I have mentioned, Plato's *Euthyphro* is an interesting presentation of the conflict between a formalistic and a teleological conception of religious ethics. A. E. Taylor's *Plato: The Man and His Work* (New York, 1927) contains a helpful analysis of this dialogue. William Paley's theological ethics can be studied in his

Principles of Moral and Political Philosophy (Boston, 1811) or in Alburey Castell's more available volume, *An Introduction to Modern Philosophy* (New York, 1946), which quotes essential passages. Walter Lippmann's *A Preface to Morals* (New York, 1929) is a stimulating discussion of the perplexities of modern man in breaking away from a formalistic religious ethics. Students of the moral and social ideals of Catholicism cannot do better than to turn directly to the Papal Encyclicals, such as *Arcanum* (1880), *Diuturnum* (1881), *Immortale Dei* (1885), *Libertas* (1888), *Rerum Novarum* (1891), *Quadragesimo Anno* (1931), and *Divini Redemptoris* (1937), selections from which are reprinted in Michael Oakeshott's *Social and Political Doctrines of Contemporary Europe* (Cambridge, England, 1939). Liberal Protestant ethics and social ideals can be studied in such works as John Dewey's *A Common Faith* (New Haven, 1934), A. D. Lindsay's *The Moral Teachings of Jesus* (New York, 1937), John Macmurray's *Creative Society* (New York, 1936), Reinhold Niebuhr's *An Interpretation of Christian Ethics* (New York, 1935), George Santayana's *The Idea of Christ in the Gospels* (New York, 1946), and *Toward the Christian Revolution* (Toronto, 1936) edited by Gregory Vlastos and R. B. Y. Scott. W. R. Inge's *Christian Ethics and Modern Problems* (New York, 1930) and T. S. Eliot's *The Idea of a Christian Society* (New York, 1940) are representative of a more aristocratic and conservative religious outlook. Those who would like to study not only Christian ethics but the ideals of other religions will find that Robert O. Ballou's *Portable World Bible* (New York, 1944) is an excellent collection of the original scriptures and that John B. Noss' *Man's Religions* (New York, 1949) is a superb exposition and interpretation.

Chapter Three: The Laws of Nature

Whitney J. Oates' *The Stoic and Epicurean Philosophers* (New York, 1940) contains the complete extant writings of Epicurus and Marcus Aurelius, the two great Stoics. Michael B. Foster, in *Masters of Political Thought*, Volume I (Boston, 1941), has an excellent chapter on Cicero, including selections from *De Re Publica* and *De Legibus* (works which are available in their entirety in the Loeb Classical Library). Edwyn R. Bevan's *Stoics and Sceptics* (New York, 1913) is a good secondary source. The books of Friedrich Nietzsche, especially *Thus Spake Zarathustra, The Genealogy of Morals,* and *Beyond Good and Evil* (in his *Complete Works,* New York, 1910-1927), present an utterly different conception of naturalistic ethics. The best book on Nietzsche, I believe, is George A. Morgan's *What Nietzsche Means* (Cambridge, Mass., 1941), but Crane Brinton's *Nietzsche* (Cambridge, Mass., 1941) is also good. A laissez-faire interpretation of revolutionary ethics is contained in Herbert Spencer's *Social Statics* (New York, 1892) and *The Data of Ethics* (New York, 1879); and a contrasting interpretation can be found in Thomas Henry Huxley's and Julian Huxley's *Touchstone for Ethics* (New York, 1947). The conception of biological nature as mainly competitive is challenged in Peter Kropotkin's *Mutual Aid* (London, 1902), Patrick Geddes' and J. A. Thomson's *Life: Outlines of Biology* (New York, 1931), and W. C. Allee's *The Social Life of Animals* (New York, 1938). The attempt to base ethics upon nature is admirably criticized in John Stuart Mill's essay, "Nature," in his *Three Essays on Religion* (London, 1885). The volume edited by Y. H. Krikorian, *Naturalism and the Human Spirit* (New York, 1944), contains sophisticated recent interpretations of nature and naturalistic ethics.

Chapter Four: The Laws of Mind

The older English intuitionists are best represented by Joseph Butler, whose *Sermons* (London, 1726) are among the masterpieces of ethical theory. A revival of intuitionism is to be found in such comparatively recent works as H. A. Prichard's essay, "Does Moral Philosophy Rest on a Mistake?" in *Mind* (Volume 37, 1912), and W. D. Ross' *The Right and the Good* (Oxford, 1930) and *The Foundations of Ethics* (Oxford, 1939). An excellent summary and criticism of intuitionism is contained in Henry Sidgwick's *The Methods of Ethics* (London, 1922). Immanuel Kant's ethical and social philosophy is presented in his *Critique of Practical Reason* (New York, 1909), *The Fundamental Principles of the Metaphysics of Morals* (London, 1916), *Philosophy of Law* (Edinburgh, 1887), *Principles of Politics* (Edinburgh, 1891), and *Perpetual Peace* (New York, 1939). Since Kant's works are very difficult, the student may prefer to read the material on Kant in Castell's *Introduction to Modern Philosophy* (New York, 1946), which quotes copiously from the originals. H. J. Paton's *The Categorical Imperative* (London, 1947) is the best book on Kant's ethical theory written from a sympathetic standpoint. C. D. Broad, in *Five Types of Ethical Theory* (New York, 1930), ably interprets and criticizes both Butler and Kant. A. D. Lindsay's *Kant* (London, 1937) contains a good chapter on Kant's ethics, and A. C. Ewing's "The Paradoxes of Kant's Ethics" in *Philosophy* (Volume 13, 1938) corrects a number of common misinterpretations. Carl J. Friedrich interprets and edits Kant's moral and political writings in *The Philosophy of Kant* (New York, 1949), and discusses Kant's internationalism in his excellent book, *Inevitable Peace* (Cambridge, Mass., 1948).

Chapter Five: Relativism

Plato's *Gorgias, Protagoras,* and Book I of the *Republic* portray and criticize Sophistic ethics, which is an ancient form of relativism. Among modern books, Edward Westermarck's *Ethical Relativity* (New York, 1932) is perhaps the best-known defense of relativism based upon anthropological data. As an indication of the wide variations in human mores, such anthropological works as *Patterns of Culture* (New York, 1934) by Ruth Benedict or *Cooperation and Competition among Primitive Peoples* (New York, 1937) edited by Margaret Mead, should be consulted. An entirely different approach to relativism is to be found in A. J. Ayer's *Truth, Language, and Logic* (London, 1946), which uses the concepts and methods of "logical positivism" to attack the alleged objectivity of ethical values. Arguing from a similar standpoint, C. L. Stevenson has defended ethical subjectivism in his *Ethics and Language* (New Haven, 1944) and in a very clear essay, "The Nature of Ethical Disagreement," in *Readings in Philosophical Analysis* (New York, 1949) edited by Herbert Feigl and Wilfred Sellars. Another leading positivist, Moritz Schlick, in Chapter V of his *Problems of Ethics* (New York, 1939), cogently attacks ethical absolutism but adheres to hedonism rather than to a strict relativism. Charner Perry's article, "The Arbitrary as Basis for Rational Morality" in *Ethics* (Volume 43, January 1933), defends a carefully qualified relativism; and in the same issue, his argument is discussed and criticized by Shailer Mathews, G. Watts Cunningham, Frank H. Knight, Walton H. Hamilton, Max Ascoli, and David F. Swenson. One of the underlying premises of Vilfredo Pareto's massive work, *The Mind and Society* (New York, 1935), is ethical relativism. A criticism of Pareto's argument, and a defense of ethical objectivity, is to be found in Chapter III of Melvin Rader's *No Compromise* (New York, 1939). A clear and cogent argument that the majority of human beings can agree upon fundamental values is to be found in Theodore Brameld's *Ends and Means in Education*, Chapters V and XXI (New York, 1950). For additional arguments against relativism and subjectivism, the reader may consult A. C. Ewing's *The Definition of the Good* (New York, 1947), G. E. Moore's *Ethics* (New York, 1912), W. T. Stace's *The Concept of Morals* (New York, 1937), and James Bissett Pratt's *Reason in the Art of Living*, Chapters VI and VII (New York, 1949). At the opposite extreme from relativism is Nicolai Hartmann's argument for ethical absolutism in his *Ethics*, Volume I (London, 1932).

Chapter Six: The Group and the Individual

The ethical individualism of Thomas Hobbes, which is paradoxically accompanied by a defense of political absolutism, is stated not only in his *Leviathan*, but in his less-well-known work, *De Cive* or *The Citizen* (New York, 1949). An extreme laissez-faire type of individualism is expressed in Herbert Spencer's *The Man versus the State* (New York, 1891) and Max Stirner's anarchistic *The Ego and His Own* (New York, 1918). A contrasting point of view is found in Thomas Henry Huxley's essay, "Administrative Nihilism" in his *Critiques and Addresses* (New York, 1873). The argument for ethical collectivism is stated in such classic works as Rousseau's *Social Contract*, Hegel's *Philosophy of Right* (London, 1896), Bernard Bosanquet's *Philosophical Theory of the State* (London, 1899), and (with less emphasis upon the state) Josiah Royce's *Philosophy of Loyalty* (New York, 1908).

Impressive replies to Hegel and Bosanquet are to be found in L. T. Hobhouse's *The Metaphysical Theory of the State* (New York, 1918) and J. E. M. McTaggart's "The Individualism of Value" in *Philosophical Studies* (New York, 1934). Chapter XVI of Ralph Barton Perry's *Puritanism and Democracy* (New York, 1944) is an excellent defense of ethical individualism. W. E. Hocking mediates between individualism and collectivism in his *Man and the State* (New Haven, 1926) and *The Lasting Elements of Individualism* (New Haven, 1927).

Chapter Seven: The Meaning of Welfare

Plato's *Republic* and Aristotle's *Nichomachean Ethics* emphasize the ethical primacy of reason. A great intellectualist, in many ways comparable to Aristotle, is Confucius, whose writings are in part reproduced in *The Wisdom of Confucius* (New York, 1938) edited with an interesting introduction by Lin Yutang. A viewpoint similar to Aristotle's, although modified by Catholic supernaturalism, is to be found in such neoscholastic works as Jacques Maritain's *True Humanism* (New York, 1938). The place of reason in the good life is carefully appraised by L. T. Hobhouse in *The Rational Good* (New York, 1921), W. T. Stace in *The Destiny of Western Man* (New York, 1942), and Arthur E. Murphy in *The Uses of Reason* (New York, 1943). The doctrine that pleasure alone is ultimately good is represented by Epicurus' works (available in Whitney J. Oates' *The Stoic and Epicurean Philosophers,* New York, 1940), Jeremy Bentham's *Introduction to the Principles of Morals and Legislation* (Oxford, 1879), John Stuart Mill's *Utilitarianism* (many editions), and Henry Sidgwick's *The Methods of Ethics* (London, 1922). Among the more recent arguments for hedonism are F. C. Sharp's *Ethics,* Chapter XIX (New York, 1928), Ralph M. Blake's "Why Not Hedonism? A Protest," *International Journal of Ethics* (Volume 37, 1926), William Savery's "A Defense of Hedonism," *International Journal of Ethics* (Volume 45, 1934), and F. J. Schlick's *Problems of Ethics,* Chapter VI (New York, 1939). The contention of ethical voluntarism that impulse, desire, or will is the basic factor in value is expressed by Spinoza's *Ethics,* Schopenhauer's *The*

World as Will and Idea, and Nietzsche's *The Will to Power.*
More recent attempts to base ethics upon a "hormic" or voluntaristic psychology include E. B. Holt's *The Freudian Wish and
Its Place in Ethics* (New York, 1915) and W. Olaf Stapledon's
A Modern Theory of Ethics (New York, 1929). The ideal of "self-
realization" is represented by F. H. Bradley's *Ethical Studies*
(Oxford, 1927), T. H. Green's *Prolegomena to Ethics* (Oxford,
1884), George Herbert Palmer's *The Nature of Goodness* (Boston,
1903), and H. A. Reyburn's *The Ethical Theory of Hegel* (Oxford, 1921). Ethical pluralism, maintaining that a number of
things are ultimately good, is advanced by Hasting Rashdall's
Theory of Good and Evil (Oxford, 1906) and G. E. Moore's *Ethics*
(New York, 1912) and *Principia Ethica* (Cambridge, England,
1922). The conception of value as interest or its object is maintained in John Dewey's *The Quest for Certainty,* Chapter X (New
York, 1926), W. P. Montague's *The Ways of Things,* Chapters
VII and VIII (New York, 1940), DeWitt H. Parker's *Human
Values,* Part I (New York, 1931), Stephen C. Pepper's *A Digest
of Purposive Values* (Berkeley, 1947), Ralph Barton Perry's *The
General Theory of Value* (New York, 1926), D. W. Prall's *A
Study in the Theory of Value* (Berkeley, 1921), and W. M. Ur-
ban's *Valuation, Its Nature and Laws* (New York, 1909).

Chapter Eight: Right Social Action

As I have pointed out in the text of Chapter Eight, Adam
Smith's *The Theory of the Moral Sentiments* (London, 1892) and
David Hume's *Inquiry Concerning the Principles of Morals*
(Oxford, 1936) and Book III of his *Treatise of Human Nature*
(Oxford, 1928) provide the essential clues for a teleological inter-
pretation of right and obligation. F. C. Sharp's *Ethics,* Book I
(New York, 1928), elaborates a theory of right similar to Hume's
and Smith's. Henri Bergson's *The Two Sources of Morality and
Religion* (New York, 1935) emphasizes the concept of a social self
as the basis of obligation. James Bissett Pratt, in *Reason in the
Art of Living* (New York, 1949), especially in Parts II and III,
outlines a "principle of rationality and value" which is very
much like the conception of right that I have maintained in the

present volume. Ralph Barton Perry's *The Moral Economy* (New York, 1909) is an excellent comprehensive discussion of the meaning of right from the standpoint of an interest theory. Among recent psychological interpretations of moral obligation, Erich Fromm's *Man for Himself* (New York, 1947) is outstanding. L. A. Reid's *Creative Morality* (London, 1937), which surveys many of the problems of ethics, is especially noteworthy for its discussion of the relation between love and duty. Almost all the books mentioned above under Chapter Seven contain discussions of the concept of right.

Chapter Nine: The Aristocratic Ideal

The finest discussion of the ideal of aristocracy is Plato's *Republic*. The translation by F. M. Cornford (New York, 1945) is an excellent English rendering supplemented by very useful notes and introduction. Among the many commentaries, R. H. Nettleship's *Lectures on the Republic of Plato* (London, 1920) and Ernest Barker's *Greek Political Theory* (London, 1918) and *The Political Thought of Plato and Aristotle* (New York, 1906) are particularly good. R. H. Crossman's *Plato Today* (London, 1937) is a sparkling interpretation of the social ideals of Socrates and Plato, with reference not only to Greece but to our modern civilization. More difficult but challenging is K. R. Popper's *The Open Society and Its Enemies,* Volume I (London, 1945), which interprets Plato's thought as a forerunner of modern totalitarianism. Completely opposed to this interpretation is John Wild's *Plato's Theory of Man* (Cambridge, Mass., 1946), which finds in Plato many liberal and democratic tendencies. Somewhat akin to Plato's *Republic* in spirit is José Ortega y Gasset's *The Revolt of the Masses* (New York, 1932), the work of a modern intellectual aristocrat. B. F. Skinner's *Walden Two* (New York, 1948) presents in the guise of utopian fiction the Platonic contention that the wise man should rule, but contends that the modern social scientist, rather than the philosopher, fulfills the requirements. The best critical review of recent aristocratic and authoritarian theory is David Spitz's *Patterns of Anti-democratic Thought* (New York, 1949), which trenchantly criticizes the ideas of James

Burnham, Lawrence Dennis, Ralph Adams Cram, Madison Grant, E. M. Sait, and Irving Babbitt.

Chapter Ten: The Democratic Ideal

The Everyman's edition of Rousseau's *Social Contract* (New York, 1913) contains an excellent introduction by G. D. H. Cole. Ernest Hunter Wright's *The Meaning of Rousseau* (London, 1929) is a lucid and sympathetic interpretation of Rousseau's social philosophy. A fine essay on Rousseau is to be found in Harold Laski's *The Dangers of Obedience* (Harper, 1930), which also contains a number of other essays in defense of democracy. R. H. Tawney's *Equality* (New York, 1931), by a distinguished English Fabian, is one of the best formulations of the ideal of a social democracy. A. D. Lindsay, in *The Essentials of Democracy* (Philadelphia, 1929) and *The Modern Democratic State* (New York, 1944), discusses the basic concepts of democracy in their historical setting. Ralph Barton Perry's *Puritanism and Democracy* (New York, 1944) is a profound study of the meanings and origins of American ideals. J. Allen Smith's *The Spirit of American Government* (New York, 1907), Vernon Louis Parrington's *Main Currents in American Thought* (New York, 1930), R. H. Gabriel's *The Course of American Democratic Thought* (New York, 1940), Merle Curti's *The Growth of American Thought* (New York, 1943), and Max Savelle's *Seeds of Liberty* (New York, 1948) are distinguished studies of the origin and development of the American ideal of democracy. In *What Does America Mean?* (New York, 1935), Alexander Meiklejohn has written a lucid and eloquent plea for the cultivation of wisdom without the sacrifice of equality. Walt Whitman's *Democratic Vistas* (New York, 1919) remains a fresh and vivid statement of the democratic ideal.

Chapter Eleven: The Liberal Ideal

Irwin Edman's *Fountainheads of Freedom* (New York, 1941), Bernard Smith's *The Democratic Spirit* (New York, 1941), and Howard Mumford Jones' *Primer of Intellectual Freedom* (Cambridge, Mass., 1949) contain extensive readings on the historical development of democracy and liberalism. Among English works, John Milton's *Areopagitica,* John Locke's *Second Treatise of Civil Government* and *A Letter Concerning Toleration* (Oxford, 1946), and John Stuart Mill's *On Liberty* are the classic statements. *On Social Freedom,* edited by Dorothy Fosdick (New York, 1941), contains several of Mill's essays which reveal the more socialistic bent of his later thought. *The Federalist,* by Alexander Hamilton, James Madison, and John Jay and the more radical *Rights of Man* by Thomas Paine are brilliant essays in liberal and democratic theory. Carl Becker's *The Declaration of Independence* (New York, 1922) and *The Heavenly City of the Eighteenth-Century Philosophers* (New Haven, 1932) are fascinating interpretations of the social philosophy of the Age of Reason, with particular attention to the ideals inspiring the American Revolution. Harold Laski's *The Rise of European Liberalism* (London, 1936) is a very revealing historical survey of the conflict between traditional liberalism and democracy. Using the dialogue as a literary form, G. Lowes Dickinson in *Justice and Liberty* (London, 1908) superbly dramatizes the conflict between conservatism, liberalism, and radical democratic ideals. L. T. Hobhouse, in his lucid and profound little book, *Liberalism* (New York, 1911), interprets the liberal ideal less individualistically than Mill. A synthesis of liberal and socialist ideals is represented by the influential works of John Dewey; *Freedom and Culture* (New York, 1939), *Individualism, Old and New* (New York, 1930), and (particularly recommended) *Liberalism and Social Action* (New York, 1935). Morton G. White's *Social Thought in America* (New York, 1949) is a critical study of five very influential American liberals: Dewey, Holmes, Veblen, Beard, and Robinson. A. C. Ewing's *The Individual, the State, and World Government* (New York, 1947), Max Lerner's *It Is Later Than You Think* (New York, 1943), Karl Mannheim's *Man and Society in An Age of Reconstruction* (New York, 1940), Bertrand Russell's *Freedom Versus Organization* (New York, 1934), and Arthur M. Schlesinger's *The Vital Center* (Boston, 1949) advocate a social liberalism which seeks to combine freedom and planning. In contrast, Walter Lippmann's *An Inquiry into the Principles of a Good Society* (Boston, 1937), Friedrich von Hayek's *The Road to Serf-*

dom (Chicago, 1944), and Ludwig von Mises' *Human Action* (New Haven, 1949) defend individualistic liberalism ("free enterprise") and criticize socialist trends.

Chapter Twelve: The Fascist Ideal

Authoritative statements of fascist or Nazi theory can be found in Benito Mussolini's "The Political and Social Doctrine of Fascism" in *International Conciliation* (January 1935); Alfredo Rocco's "The Political Doctrine of Fascism" in *International Conciliation* (October 1926); Adolf Hitler's *Mein Kampf* (New York, 1938), especially Chapter 11 in Volume I and Chapters 1, 2, and 4 in Volume II; and Alfred Rosenberg's *Der Mythus des Zwanzigsten Jahrhunderts* (Munich, 1934), which has been conveniently summarized in Albert R. Chandler's *Rosenberg's Nazi Myth* (Ithaca, 1945). Franz Neumann's *Behemoth* (New York, 1942), on nazi Germany, and Robert A. Brady's *Business as a System of Power* (New York, 1943), on authoritarian economic trends in various countries, are heavily documented studies of the class basis and social-economic tendencies of fascism. W. T. Stace's *The Destiny of Western Man* (New York, 1942), Melvin Rader's *No Compromise* (New York, 1939), and William McGovern's *From Luther to Hitler* (Boston, 1941) deal with the theory of fascism and its conflict with democratic principles. McGovern's book is especially valuable in tracing the historical development of authoritarian political theories.

Chapter Thirteen: The Socialist Ideal

Karl Marx's *Selected Works* in two volumes (New York, 1933) and Emile Burns' *A Handbook of Marxism* (New York, 1935) are convenient compilations of the original Marxian literature. H. P. Adams' *Karl Marx in His Earlier Writings* (London, 1940) is an excellent survey, emphasizing the more humanistic and ethical side of Marx's earlier works, some of which are not available in English. Among other useful books on Marxism are G. D. H. Cole's *What Marx Really Meant* (New York, 1934),

Sidney Hook's *Towards the Understanding of Karl Marx* (New York, 1933) and *From Hegel to Marx* (New York, 1936), Harold Laski's *Communism* (New York, 1927), Bertrand Russell's *Proposed Roads to Freedom* (New York, 1919), John Somerville's *Soviet Philosophy* (New York, 1946), John Strachey's *The Theory and Practice of Socialism* (New York, 1936), Vernon Venable's *Human Nature: The Marxian View* (New York, 1945), and Edmund Wilson's *To the Finland Station* (New York, 1940). Volume II of K. R. Popper's *The Open Society and Its Enemies* (London, 1945) contains a provocative attack upon Marx's historical and revolutionary theories. Those who wish to study Russian communist theory should turn directly to V. I. Lenin's *The State and Revolution* (New York, 1932); Joseph Stalin's *Leninism,* two volumes (New York, 1928, 1933) and *Marxism and the National Question* (New York, 1942); and Leon Trotsky's heterodox works, *The History of the Russian Revolution* (New York, 1936) and *The Revolution Betrayed* (New York, 1937). Edward Hallett Carr's *The Soviet Impact on the Western World* (New York, 1947) is a brilliant discussion of the influence of Soviet thought and practice upon the Western democracies. Fabian Socialism is represented by *Fabian Essays in Socialism,* new edition (London, 1920), by G. B. Shaw, Sidney Webb, and others; *Fabian Socialism* (London, 1943) by G. D. H. Cole; and *Fabian Tracts,* published from time to time by the Fabian Society in London. Among the other main sources of liberal socialism are Edouard Bernstein's *Evolutionary Socialism* (New York, 1909); G. D. H. Cole's *Self Government in Industry* (London, 1920), a formulation of the ideal of "Guild Socialism"; Harold Laski's *The State in Theory and Practice* (New York, 1935) and *Reflections on the Revolution of Our Times* (New York, 1943) ; and Sidney and Beatrice Webb's *Industrial Democracy* (London, 1920), *The Collapse of Capitalist Civilization* (New York, 1923), *The History of Trade Unionism* (London, 1920), and *A Constitution for the Socialist Commonwealth of Great Britain* (London, 1920). Opposed to the socialist ideal of state planning and ownership, but sympathetic to the ideal of cooperative collectivism, are the classics of anarchist theory, including Michael Bakunin's *Dieu et L'Etat* (Geneva, 1882), Peter Kropotkin's *Fields, Factories, and Workshops* (London, 1899), Elisee Reclus' *An Anarchist on Anarchy* (London, 1894), and Leo Tolstoy's *What Shall We Do Then* (London, 1885). Bertrand Russell's *Proposed Roads to Freedom* (New York, 1919) is sympathetic to a number of anarchist proposals; and Herbert Read's *The Philosophy of Anarchism* (London, 1941) is an engaging recent statement of anarchist ideals. The ideal of a "welfare state" and of a "mixed economy," involving social planning without doctrinaire socialism, is persuasively advocated in such works as Alvin Hansen's *Fiscal Policy and Business Cycles* (New York, 1941) and John Maynard Keynes' *The General Theory of Employment, Interest, and Money* (New York, 1936). Lawrence R. Klein's *The Keynesian Revolution* (New York, 1947) contrasts this new type of political economy with both socialism and laissez-faire capitalism. An interesting argument for a dual economy, partly socialist and partly capitalist, is to be found in W. P. Montague's essay, "Democracy at the Crossroads," in his *The Ways of Things* (New York, 1940).

Additional References

Many valuable articles on ethical and social philosophy appear in the *Encyclopaedia of the Social Sciences* (New York, 1930) and in the *Encyclopaedia of Religion and Ethics,* edited by James Hastings (Edinburgh, 1908). Likewise innumerable pertinent articles can be found in such periodicals as *Mind,* the *Hibbert Journal,* the *Proceedings of the Aristotelian Society, Philosophy,* the *Journal of Philosophy,* the *Philosophical Review,* the *Journal of Philosophy and Phenomenological Research,* the *Journal of Social Philosophy,* and the *Journal of the History of Ideas.* Bibliographies can be found in Volume III of James Baldwin's *Dictionary of Philosophy* (New York, 1925); the *Bibliographie de la Philosophie* (Paris, annually beginning with 1937); "A Bibliography of Philosophy," for the years 1933 through 1937, published in the August issues of the *Journal of Philosophy,* 1934-1938; *International Index of Periodicals; Cumulative Book Index;* and (under various subject captions) in the *Encyclopaedia Britannica* and the *Encyclopaedia of the Social Sciences.* Most textbooks on ethics and social philosophy contain bibliographies. For other bibliographies, consult the *Bibliographic Index*, a cumulative bibliography of bibliographies (New York, annually beginning with 1944).

INDEX